STUDENT'S
SOLUTIONS MANUAL

ELKA BLOCK   FRANK PURCELL

Twin Prime Editorial

BASIC MATHEMATICS
THROUGH APPLICATIONS
THIRD EDITION

AND

FUNDAMENTAL MATHEMATICS
THROUGH APPLICATIONS
THIRD EDITION

Geoffrey Akst   Sadie Bragg

Borough of Manhattan Community College,
City University of New York

PEARSON
Addison
Wesley

Boston San Francisco New York
London Toronto Sydney Tokyo Singapore Madrid
Mexico City Munich Paris Cape Town Hong Kong Montreal

Reproduced by Pearson Addison-Wesley from electronic files supplied by the author.

Copyright © 2005 Pearson Education, Inc.
Publishing as Pearson Addison-Wesley, 75 Arlington Street, Boston, MA 02116

ISBN   0-321-22890-1

5 6 BRG 08 07 06 05

PEARSON
Addison
Wesley

CONTENTS

CHAPTER 4   BASIC ALGEBRA: SOLVING SIMPLE EQUATIONS

CHAPTER 5   RATIO AND PROPORTION

CHAPTER 6   PERCENTS

CHAPTER 7   SIGNED NUMBERS

Chapter 1

WHOLE NUMBERS

Pretest

1. 205,007; two hundred five thousand, seven

2. 1,235,000

3. Hundred thousands

4. $8,1\textcircled{4}3 \approx 8,100$ since the critical digit is less than 5

5.
$$
\begin{array}{r}
{\scriptstyle 1\,1\,1} \\
38 \\
903 \\
+7,285 \\
\hline
8,226
\end{array}
$$

6.
$$
\begin{array}{r}
{\scriptstyle 9\ \ 9} \\
4\ \cancel{0}\ \cancel{0}\ {}^{1}0 \\
\cancel{5},\cancel{0}\ \cancel{0} \\
-\quad 2\ 8\ 6 \\
\hline
4,7\ 1\ 4
\end{array}
$$

7.
$$
\begin{array}{r}
{\scriptstyle 6\ {}^{1}2} \\
\cancel{7}\ \cancel{3}\ {}^{1}4 \\
-5\ 4\ 9 \\
\hline
1\ 8\ 5
\end{array}
$$

8.
$$
\begin{array}{r}
809 \\
\times\ 36 \\
\hline
4\,854 \\
24\,27\ \\
\hline
29,124
\end{array}
$$

9.
$$
\begin{array}{r}
260 \\
27\overline{)7,020} \\
-54 \\
\hline
1\,62 \\
-1\,62 \\
\hline
0 \\
-0 \\
\hline
\end{array}
$$

10.
$$
\begin{array}{r}
308 \\
44\overline{)13,558} \\
-13\,2 \\
\hline
358 \\
-352 \\
\hline
6
\end{array}
$$

$13,558 \div 44 = 308\,R6$

or $308\frac{6}{44} = 308\frac{3}{22}$

11. $2 \cdot 2 \cdot 2 = 2^3$

12. $6^2 = 6 \cdot 6 = 36$

13. $26 - 7 \cdot 3$
$= 26 - 21$
$= 5$

14. $3 + 2^3 \cdot (8 - 3)$
$= 3 + 2^3 \cdot 5$
$= 3 + 8 \cdot 5$
$= 3 + 40$
$= 43$

15.
$$
\begin{array}{r}
{\scriptstyle 7} \\
1\cancel{8}\ {}^{1}06 \\
-17\ 31 \\
\hline
75
\end{array}
$$

75 years old

16.
$$
\begin{array}{r}
\$75 \\
\times\ 9 \\
\hline
\$675
\end{array}
$$

Nine credits will cost $675.

17. $100,000,000 \times 10 = 1,000,000,000 = 10^9$

18. It takes Fax machine A $12 \times 5 = 60$ seconds to send five pages.
It takes Fax machine B $10 \times 5 = 50$ seconds to send five pages.
It takes machine A $60 - 50 = 10$ seconds longer.

19. The total amount you pay in 12 monthly installments is $\$25 \times 12 = \$300$. You save $\$300 - \$235 = \$65$ by paying cash.

20. Area of Room A: $11\,\text{ft} \times 11\,\text{ft} = 121\,\text{sq ft}$
Area of Room B: $7\,\text{ft} \times 13\,\text{ft} = 91\,\text{sq ft}$
Area of Room C: $21\,\text{ft} \times 6\,\text{ft} = 126\,\text{sq ft}$
Room C has the largest area.

1.1 Introduction to Whole Numbers

Practice

1. a. In 278,056 the digit 8 is in the thousands place.
   b. In 803,746 the digit 8 is in the hundred thousands place.
   c. In 3,080,700,059 the digit 8 is in the ten millions place.

2. 8,000,376,052 is eight billion, three hundred seventy-six thousand, fifty-two.

3. Seven million, three hundred seventy-two thousand, fifty dollars.

4. Ninety-five million, three dollars is written as $95,000,003.

5. $375,000

6. $27,013 = 2$ ten thousands $+7$ thousands $+$ 0 hundreds $+ 1$ ten $+ 3$ ones $=$ $20,000 + 7,000 + 10 + 3$

7. $1,270,093 = 1$ million $+ 2$ hundred thousands $+$ 7 ten thousands $+ 0$ thousands $+ 0$ hundreds $+$ 9 tens $+ 3$ ones $= 1,000,000 + 200,000 + 70,000 +$ $+ 90 + 3$

8. a. $58,760 = 58,\textcircled{7}60 \approx 59,000$
   b. $58,760 = 5\underline{\textcircled{8}},760 \approx 60,000$

9. $\$99,839 = \$99,\underline{\textcircled{8}}39 \approx \$100,000$

Exercises

1. 1,000,000,000; one billion

3. 2,350,000; two million, three hundred fifty thousand

5. 975,135,000; nine hundred seventy-five million, one hundred thirty-five thousand

7. 487,500; four hundred eighty-seven thousand, five hundred

9. 2,000,000,352; two billion, three hundred fifty-two

11. 10,120

13. 150,856

15. 6,000,055

17. 50,600,195

19. 400,072

21. 4,867

23. 316

25. 28,461,013

27. In 691,400, the 6 is in the hundred thousands place.

29. In 7,380 the 7 is in the thousands place.

31. In 8,450,000,000 the 8 is in the billions place.

33. 3 = 3 ones = 3

35. 858 = 8 hundreds + 5 tens + 8 ones = 800 + 50 + 8

37. 2,500,004 = 2 millions + 5 hundred thousands + 4 ones = 2,000,000 + 500,000 + 4

39. 671 = 67①≈ 670

41. 7,103 = 7,1①3 ≈ 7,100

43. 28,241 = 2⑧,241 ≈ 30,000

45. 705,418 = 7①5,418 ≈ 700,000

47. 31,927 = 3①,927 ≈ 30,000

49.

To the nearest	135,800	816,533
Hundred	135,800	816,500
Thousand	136,000	817,000
Ten thousand	140,000	820,000
Hundred thousand	100,000	800,000

51. 700,000 is seven hundred thousand.

53. 300,000,000,000 is three hundred billion.

55. 1,400,085 is one million, four hundred thousand, eighty five.

57. one hundred billion = 100,000,000,000

59. eighty-five million, sixty-one thousand, fifty-eight dollars = $85,061,058

61. one billion, four hundred million = 1,400,000,000

63. 15②ft ≈ 150 ft

65. 2③,452 mi ≈ 20,000 mi

67. 3⑦3 g ≈ 400 g

1.2   Adding and Subtracting Whole Numbers

Practice

1.
$$\begin{array}{r} {}^{1\ 1}\ \\ 198 \\ +\ 37 \\ \hline 235 \end{array}$$

2.
$$\begin{array}{r} {}^{1\ 1}\ \\ 838 \\ 96 \\ +1,002 \\ \hline 1,936 \end{array}$$

3. Compute the perimeter. The missing segment length on the bottom is 2 mi, so the perimeter is 2 + 5 + 3 + 2 + 4 = 16. The fence would need to be 16 mi long.

4.
$$\begin{array}{r} {}^{6}\ \\ \cancel{7}^{1}48 \\ -\ \ 97 \\ \hline 6\ 51 \end{array}$$

5.
$$\begin{array}{r} 8,000\,^{1}0 \\ -3,2\ 5\ 3 \\ \hline 4,7\ 4\ 7 \end{array}$$

6.
$$\begin{array}{rr} \text{Total number of seats} & 750 \\ -\text{ Number of seats occupied} & -372 \\ \hline \text{Number of seats empty} & 378 \end{array}$$
378 seats were empty.

7.
$$\begin{array}{rcr} 196 & \approx & 200 \\ 5,056 & \approx & 5,000 \\ +22,097 & \approx & +20,000 \\ \hline \text{exact } 27,349 & & \text{estimated } 25,200 \end{array}$$
The estimated sum is reasonably close to the exact sum.

8.
$$\begin{array}{rcr} 838 & \approx & 1,000 \\ 962 & \approx & 1,000 \\ +1,002 & \approx & +1,000 \\ \hline \text{exact } 2,802 & & \text{estimated } 3,000 \end{array}$$
2,802 is reasonably close to the estimate, 3000.

9. 17,836 $17,836 \approx 18,000$
       $-15,045$ $-15,045 \approx -15,000$
       ──────   ──────────
       2,791 exact   3,000 estimated

2,791 and 3,000 are fairly close.

Calculator Practice

p. 20. $39,822 + 9,710 = 49,532$

p. 21. $23,801 + 7,116 + 982 = 31,899;$
       $5,280 \text{ ft} - 2,781 \text{ ft} = 2,499 \text{ ft}$

Exercises

1. 100,250   **3.** 9,261
     $+\ 77,528$ $+\ \ \ 412$
     ────────   ──────
      177,778   9,673

5. ¹ ¹   **7.**   ¹¹
      4,663   8,132
     $+\ \ \ 371$ $+6,758$
     ──────   ──────
      5,034   14,710

9. ² ¹   **11.**   ¹ ¹ ¹
      3,750   3,227
      1,725   2,806
     $+4,992$ $+\ 5,481$
     ──────   ──────
      10,467   11,514

13. ² ¹ ¹   **15.**   ¹¹ ¹¹
       7,481   49,002
        702   1,999
      $+5,819$ $+\ 5,187$
      ──────   ──────
       14,002   56,188

17. $1,903 + 5,075 = 6,978$

19. $800 + 20 + 4,000 = 4,820$

21. $31 + 93 + 277 + 12 = 413$

23. 6,482 meters + 9,027 meters = 15,509 meters

25. 35 hours + 47 hours = 82 hours

27. $\$845 + \$39 + \$1,871 = \$2,755$

29. $\$92,258 + \$7,447 + \$5,126 = \$104,831$

31. $281 + 758 + 104 + 533 = 1,676$

33. $5,374 + 4,055 + 20,173 = 29,602$

35. $\$1,863 + \$1,089 + \$9,772 = \$12,724$

37. 8,300 tons + 22,900 tons = 31,200 tons

39.

+	400	200	1,200	300	Total
300	700	500	1,500	600	3,300
800	1,200	1,000	2,000	1,100	5,300
Total	1,900	1,500	3,500	1,700	8,600

41.

+	389	172	1,155	324	Total
255	644	427	1,410	579	3,060
799	1,188	971	1,954	1,123	5,236
Total	1,832	1,398	3,364	1,702	8,296

43. 3,088,281   **45.** 2,008,490
       5,658,137   8,948,227
      $+4,550,239$ $+11,956,174$
      ──────────   ──────────
       13,296,657   22,912,891

47. a. $814 \approx\ \ 1,000$ **b.** $30,812 \approx 31,000$
       $9,106 \approx\ \ 9,000$ $47,045 \approx 47,000$
      $+2,811 \approx +3,000$ $+\ 9,338 \approx +9,000$
      ────── ──────   ──────   ──────
       15,731   13,000   87,195   87,000

   c. $183,066 \approx\ \ 180,000$
        $78,911 \approx\ \ 80,000$
       $+\ 96,527 \approx +100,000$
       ────── ──────────
        358,504   360,000

Part (a) is wrong; the exact sum 15,731 is not
reasonably close to the estimated sum 13,000.

49. a. $\$711,488 \approx \$700,000$
        $102,663 \approx\ \ 100,000$
       $+\ \ \ 95,003 \approx +100,000$
       ────── ──────
        $\$809,154$ $\$900,000$

   b. $\$62,933 \approx\ \ \$60,000$
         $51,858 \approx\ \ \ 50,000$
        $+\ 49,612 \approx +50,000$
        ────── ──────
         $\$164,403$ $\$160,000$

   c. $\$106,729 \approx\ \ \$100,000$
          $99,821 \approx\ \ 100,000$
        $+\ 103,277 \approx +100,000$
        ────── ──────
         $\$309,827$ $\$300,000$

Part (a) is wrong; the exact sum $809,154 is not
reasonably close to the estimated sum $800,000.

51.   371   **53.** 200
        -162 -110
        ────   ────
         217   90

55. ⁴   **57.**   ¹
       $\not{5}^{1}13$ $\not{2}^{1}0,005$
       $-\ \ 92$ $-\ 1\ 3,002$
       ────   ──────
        4 21   7,003

59.   ³ ¹⁰ ¹   **61.**   ⁹ ⁹ ⁹
        $\not{4}\not{0}^{1}1$ ⁶ ¹⁰ ¹⁰ ¹⁰
        $-\ \ \ 39$ $\not{7}\not{0},\not{0}\not{0}^{1}0$
        ──── $-\ \ \ 1,\ 7\ 5\ 9$
         3 6 2   ──────
                                68,2 4 1

63.   ⁹   **65.**   ⁹ ⁹
        ² ¹⁰   ² ¹⁰ ¹⁰
        $\not{3}\not{0}^{1}4$ $\not{3},\not{0}\not{0}^{1}5$
        $-1\ 2\ 9$ $-1,6\ 6\ 6$
        ────   ──────
         1 7 5   1,3 3 9

67.
$$\begin{array}{r} {}^{9\;9} \\ {}^{1}\cancel{10}\cancel{10} \\ \cancel{2},\cancel{0}\cancel{0}{}^{1}1 \\ -\qquad 2 \\ \hline 1,9\;9\;9 \end{array}$$

69.
$$\begin{array}{r} {}^{4}{}^{1}1\,{}^{1}8 \\ \cancel{3}\cancel{2},\cancel{9}{}^{1}47 \\ -2\,7,9\;97 \\ \hline 2\,4,9\;50 \end{array}$$

71.
$$\begin{array}{r} 8,286 \\ -3,100 \\ \hline 5,186 \end{array}$$

73.
$$\begin{array}{r} 5,900 \\ -1,500 \\ \hline 4,400 \end{array}$$

75.
$$\begin{array}{r} 350,840 \\ -230,530 \\ \hline 120,310 \end{array}$$

77.
$$\begin{array}{r} 6,922 \\ -3,002 \\ \hline 3,920 \end{array}$$

79.
$$\begin{array}{r} {}^{4}{}^{1}4 \\ \cancel{5}\cancel{5}{}^{1}0 \\ -1\,8\,2 \\ \hline 3\,6\,8 \end{array}$$

81.
$$\begin{array}{r} {}^{9\;9} \\ 5\,\cancel{10}\cancel{10} \\ \cancel{6},\cancel{0}\cancel{0}{}^{1}0 \\ -1,0\;0\;4 \\ \hline 4,9\;9\;6 \end{array}$$

83.
$$\begin{array}{r} {}^{2}{}^{1}4\,{}^{1}6 \\ \cancel{3},\cancel{5}\cancel{7}{}^{1}0 \\ -2,5\;8\;8 \\ \hline 9\;8\;2 \end{array}$$

85.
$$\begin{array}{r} {}^{9\;9} \\ 4\,\cancel{10}\cancel{10} \\ \cancel{5},\cancel{0}\cancel{0}{}^{1}0\text{ mi} \\ -3,0\;0\;5\text{ mi} \\ \hline 1,9\;9\;5\text{ mi} \end{array}$$

87.
$$\begin{array}{r} {}^{9} \\ 7\,\cancel{10} \\ \$\cancel{8}\cancel{0}{}^{1}0 \\ -\quad1\;3\;1 \\ \hline \$6\;6\;9 \end{array}$$

89.
$$\begin{array}{r} {}^{0} \\ \$4,8\cancel{1}{}^{1}2 \\ -\quad1,2\;0\;3 \\ \hline \$3,6\;0\;9 \end{array}$$

91.
$$\begin{array}{r} {}^{9} \\ 4\,\cancel{10} \\ \cancel{5}\cancel{0}{}^{1}0\text{ books} \\ -2\;2\;7\text{ books} \\ \hline 2\;7\;3\text{ books} \end{array}$$

93.
$$\begin{array}{r} {}^{1} \\ 5\cancel{2}{}^{1}7\text{ m} \\ -3\,1\,8\text{ m} \\ \hline 2\,0\,9\text{ m} \end{array}$$

95.
$$\begin{array}{r} 30,000,000 \\ -27,999,000 \\ \hline 2,001,000 \end{array}$$

97.
$$\begin{array}{r} 3,402,331 \\ -2,588,902 \\ \hline 813,429 \end{array}$$

99. **a.**
$$\begin{array}{rcr} 817,770 & \approx & 800,000 \\ -502,966 & \approx & -500,000 \\ \hline 314,804 & & 300,000 \end{array}$$

  b.
$$\begin{array}{rcr} 11,172,055 & \approx & 11,000,000 \\ -\;7,892,106 & \approx & -8,000,000 \\ \hline 3,279,949 & & 3,000,000 \end{array}$$

  c.
$$\begin{array}{rcr} 120,426,811 & \approx & 120,000,000 \\ -\;98,155,772 & \approx & -100,000,000 \\ \hline 32,271,039 & & 20,000,000 \end{array}$$

Part (c) is wrong.

101. **a.**
$$\begin{array}{rcr} \$381,883 & \approx & \$400,000 \\ -\;173,552 & \approx & -200,000 \\ \hline \$108,330 & & \$200,000 \end{array}$$

  b.
$$\begin{array}{rcr} \$479,116 & \approx & \$500,000 \\ -\;102,663 & \approx & -100,000 \\ \hline \$376,453 & & \$400,000 \end{array}$$

  c.
$$\begin{array}{rcr} \$200,072,639 & \approx & \$200,000,000 \\ -\;150,038,270 & \approx & -150,000,000 \\ \hline \$50,034,369 & & \$50,000,000 \end{array}$$

Part (a) is wrong.

103.
$$\begin{array}{r} 70,000,000 \\ +\;5,000,000 \\ \hline 75,000,000 \end{array}$$

There were 75,000,000 people in 1900.

105.
$$\begin{array}{r} \$800 \\ -\;300 \\ \hline \$500 \end{array}$$

$500 was not reimbursed.

107. **a.** The number of runs the Huskies scored is:
$0+1+1+0+1+1+1+0+3 = 8$ runs.
The number of runs the Ravens scored is:
$1+2+0+0+1+1+2+0+2 = 9$ runs.

  b. The Ravens won the game.

109.
$$\begin{array}{r} {}^{8} \\ 1\cancel{9}{}^{1}37 \\ -18\,94 \\ \hline 43 \end{array}$$

Bessie Smith was 43 years old when she died.

111.
$$\begin{array}{r} {}^{22} \\ 187\text{ lb} \\ 147\text{ lb} \\ 213\text{ lb} \\ 162\text{ lb} \\ 103\text{ lb} \\ 151\text{ lb} \\ \hline 963\text{ lb} \end{array}$$

No, because the total weight of the passengers, 963 lb, doesn't exceed the elevator's maximum capacity of 1,000 lb.

113.
$$\begin{array}{r} {}^{1} \\ \cancel{2}{}^{1}12°\text{F} \\ -\quad32°\text{F} \\ \hline 1\,80°\text{F} \end{array}$$

The difference between the boiling point and the freezing point of water is 180°F.

115. The missing side is 7 m long.
perimeter = 5 m + 5 m + 7 m + 7 m + 7 m = 31 m

117.
$$\begin{array}{r} {}^{9\;9\;9} \\ {}^{1}\cancel{10}\cancel{10}\cancel{10} \\ \$\cancel{2}\cancel{0},\cancel{0}\cancel{0}{}^{1}0 \\ -\;1\,6,9\;9\;8 \\ \hline \$3,0\;0\;2 \end{array}$$

You must make $3,002 more.

119.
$$
\begin{array}{r}
^{1}\\
64,000,000 \text{ sq mi}\\
32,000,000 \text{ sq mi}\\
25,000,000 \text{ sq mi}\\
+\ 5,000,000 \text{ sq mi}\\
\hline
126,000,000 \text{ sq mi}
\end{array}
$$

The total area of the four oceans is 126,000,000 sq mi.

121.
$$
\begin{array}{r}
103,871\\
-\ 92,570\\
\hline
11,301
\end{array}
$$

The number of readers will increase by 11,301. Since this is more than 10,000 readers, you will give the bonus.

123. **a.** addition

b. yes; $83 + $59 + $727 + $183 + $511 = $1,563

c.
$$
\begin{array}{rcr}
\$83 &\approx& \$100\\
\$59 &\approx& 100\\
\$727 &\approx& 700\\
\$183 &\approx& 200\\
\$511 &\approx& 500\\
\hline
&& \$1600
\end{array}
$$

1.3 Multiplying Whole Numbers

Practice

1.
$$
\begin{array}{r}
^{4}\\
76\\
\times\ 8\\
\hline
608
\end{array}
$$

2.
$$
\begin{array}{r}
^{3}\\
705\\
\times\ 6\\
\hline
4,230
\end{array}
$$

3.
$$
\begin{array}{rl}
1,200 & \text{(2 zeros)}\\
\times\ 400 & \text{(2 zeros)}\\
\hline
480,000 & \text{(4 zeros)}
\end{array}
$$

4.
$$
\begin{array}{r}
987\\
\times 208\\
\hline
7896\\
19740\\
\hline
205,296
\end{array}
$$

5. 11 ft × 4 ft = 44 sq ft

9 ft × 7 ft = 63 sq ft

area of room = 44 sq ft + 63 sq ft = 107 sq ft

6.
$$
\begin{array}{rcr}
500 &\approx& 500\\
\times\ 38 &\approx& \times\ 40
\end{array}
$$

Estimate: 500 × 40 = 20,000

No, there isn't enough paper to produce the flyers.

7.
$$
\begin{array}{rcr}
455 &\approx& 500\\
\times 248 &\approx& \times 200\\
\hline
3\,640 && 100,000\\
18\,20 && \text{estimated}\\
91\,0 && \text{product}\\
\hline
112,840 &&\\
\text{exact product} &&
\end{array}
$$

112,840 is close to the estimate, so the answer checks.

Calculator Practice

p. 34. $2,811 × 365 = $1,026,015

p. 35. 2,133 · 18 · 9 = 345,546;

$1,234,567,890 \cdot 987,654,321 = 1.219326311 \times 10^{18}$

Exercises

1. 4 × 100 = 400

3. 71 × 100 = 7,100

5. 85 × 10 = 850

7. 10,000 × 700 = 7,000,000

9.
$$
\begin{array}{rcr}
^{22}\\
398 &\approx& 400\\
\times\ 3 &\approx& \times\ 3\\
\hline
1,194 && 1,200\\
&& \text{estimate}
\end{array}
$$

11.
$$
\begin{array}{rcr}
^{1}\\
964 &\approx& 1,000\\
\times\ 2 &\approx& \times\ 2\\
\hline
1,928 && 2,000\\
&& \text{estimate}
\end{array}
$$

13.
$$
\begin{array}{rcr}
^{1}\\
6,350 &\approx& 6,000\\
\times\ 2 &\approx& \times\ 2\\
\hline
12,700 && 12,000\\
&& \text{estimate}
\end{array}
$$

15.
$$
\begin{array}{rcr}
^{1}\\
209 &\approx& 200\\
\times\ 2 &\approx& \times\ 2\\
\hline
418 && 400\\
&& \text{estimate}
\end{array}
$$

17.
$$
\begin{array}{rcr}
5,420,000 &\approx& 5,000,000\\
\times\ 2 &\approx& \times\ 2\\
\hline
10,840,000 && 10,000,000\\
&& \text{estimate}
\end{array}
$$

19.
$$
\begin{array}{rcr}
812,000 &\approx& 800,000\\
\times\ 4 &\approx& \times\ 4\\
\hline
3,248,000 && 3,200,000\\
&& \text{estimate}
\end{array}
$$

21.
$$
\begin{array}{rcr}
892 &\approx& 900\\
\times\ 35 &\approx& \times\ 40\\
\hline
4\,460 && 36,000\\
26\,76 && \text{estimate}\\
\hline
31,220 &&
\end{array}
$$

23.
$$
\begin{array}{rcr}
992 &\approx& 1,000\\
\times\ 68 &\approx& \times\ 70\\
\hline
7\,936 && 70,000\\
59\,52 && \text{estimate}\\
\hline
67,456 &&
\end{array}
$$

25.
$$
\begin{array}{rcr}
43 &\approx& 40\\
\times 19 &\approx& \times 20\\
\hline
387 && 800\\
43 && \text{estimate}\\
\hline
817 &&
\end{array}
$$

27.
$$
\begin{array}{rcr}
709 &\approx& 700\\
\times\ 48 &\approx& \times\ 50\\
\hline
5\,672 && 35,000\\
28\,36 && \text{estimate}\\
\hline
34,032 &&
\end{array}
$$

29.
$$
\begin{array}{rcr}
273 & \approx & 300 \\
\times\ 11 & \approx & \times\ 10 \\
\hline
273 & & \overline{3{,}000} \\
2\ 73 & & \text{estimate} \\
\hline
3{,}003 & &
\end{array}
$$

31.
$$
\begin{array}{rcr}
301 & \approx & 300 \\
\times\ 12 & \approx & \times\ 10 \\
\hline
602 & & \overline{3{,}000} \\
3\ 01 & & \text{estimate} \\
\hline
3{,}612 & &
\end{array}
$$

33.
$$
\begin{array}{rcr}
3{,}001 & \approx & 3{,}000 \\
\times\ 19 & \approx & \times\ 20 \\
\hline
27\ 009 & & \overline{60{,}000} \\
30\ 01 & & \text{estimate} \\
\hline
57{,}019 & &
\end{array}
$$

35.
$$
\begin{array}{rcr}
5{,}072 & \approx & 5{,}000 \\
\times\ 48 & \approx & \times\ 50 \\
\hline
40\ 576 & & \overline{250{,}000} \\
202\ 88 & & \text{estimate} \\
\hline
243{,}456 & &
\end{array}
$$

37.
$$
\begin{array}{rcr}
8{,}801 & \approx & 9{,}000 \\
\times\ 25 & \approx & \times\ 30 \\
\hline
44\ 005 & & \overline{270{,}000} \\
176\ 02 & & \text{estimate} \\
\hline
220{,}025 & &
\end{array}
$$

39.
$$
\begin{array}{rcr}
2{,}881 & \approx & 3{,}000 \\
\times\ 70 & \approx & \times\ 70 \\
\hline
201{,}670 & & \overline{210{,}000} \\
& & \text{estimate}
\end{array}
$$

41.
$$
\begin{array}{rcr}
302 & \approx & 400 \\
\times 403 & \approx & \times 400 \\
\hline
906 & & 120{,}000 \\
120\ 80 & & \text{estimate} \\
\hline
121{,}706 & &
\end{array}
$$

43.
$$
\begin{array}{rcr}
8{,}500 & \approx & 8{,}500 \\
\times\ 17 & \approx & \times\ 20 \\
\hline
59\ 500 & & 170{,}000 \\
85\ 00 & & \text{estimate} \\
\hline
144{,}500 & &
\end{array}
$$

45.
$$
\begin{array}{rcr}
406 & \approx & 400 \\
\times 305 & \approx & \times 300 \\
\hline
2\ 030 & & 120{,}000 \\
121\ 80 & & \text{estimate} \\
\hline
123{,}830 & &
\end{array}
$$

47.
$$
\begin{array}{rl}
46 & \text{estimate} \\
\times\ 8 & 46 \cdot 8 \cdot 9 \\
\hline
368 & \downarrow\ \downarrow\ \downarrow \\
\times\ 9 & 50 \cdot 10 \cdot 10 = 5{,}000 \\
\hline
3{,}312 &
\end{array}
$$

49.
$$
\begin{array}{rl}
81 & \text{estimate} \\
\times\ 2 & 81 \times 2 \times 13 \\
\hline
162 & \downarrow\ \downarrow\ \downarrow \\
\times\ 13 & 80 \times 2 \times 10 = 1{,}600 \\
\hline
486 & \\
1\ 62 & \\
\hline
2{,}106 &
\end{array}
$$

51. $(10)(10)(400) = 40{,}000$

53.
$$
\begin{array}{rl}
57 & \text{estimate} \\
\times 81 & 57 \times 81 \times 5 \\
\hline
57 & \downarrow\ \downarrow\ \downarrow \\
4\ 56 & 60 \times 80 \times 5 = 24{,}000 \\
\hline
4{,}617 & \\
\times\ 5 & \\
\hline
23{,}085 &
\end{array}
$$

55.
$$
\begin{array}{rcr}
8{,}972 & \approx & 9{,}000 \\
\times\ 365 & \approx & \times\ 400 \\
\hline
44\ 860 & & \overline{3{,}600{,}000} \\
538\ 32 & & \text{estimate} \\
2\ 6916 & & \\
\hline
3{,}274{,}780 & &
\end{array}
$$

57.
$$
\begin{array}{rcr}
18{,}650 & \approx & 19{,}000 \\
\times\ 2{,}949 & \approx & \times\ 3{,}000 \\
\hline
167\ 850 & & \overline{57{,}000{,}000} \\
746\ 00 & & \text{estimate} \\
16\ 785\ 0 & & \\
37\ 300 & & \\
\hline
54{,}998{,}850 & &
\end{array}
$$

59. **a.**
$$
\begin{array}{rcr}
802 & \approx & 800 \\
\times 755 & \approx & \times 800 \\
\hline
605{,}510 & & 640{,}000
\end{array}
$$

b.
$$
\begin{array}{rcr}
4{,}722 & \approx & 4{,}700 \\
\times\ 39 & \approx & \times\ 40 \\
\hline
184{,}158 & & 188{,}000
\end{array}
$$

c.
$$
\begin{array}{rcr}
6{,}005 & \approx & 6{,}000 \\
\times\ 77 & \approx & \times\ 80 \\
\hline
46{,}385 & & 480{,}000
\end{array}
$$

The product in part (c) is incorrect.

61. **a.**
$$
\begin{array}{rcr}
37{,}118 & \approx & 40{,}000 \\
\times\ 9 & \approx & \times\ 10 \\
\hline
334{,}062 & & 400{,}000
\end{array}
$$

b.
$$
\begin{array}{rcr}
961 & \approx & 1{,}000 \\
\times\ 82 & \approx & \times\ 80 \\
\hline
7{,}882 & & 80{,}000
\end{array}
$$

c.
$$
\begin{array}{rcr}
986 & \approx & 1{,}000 \\
\times\ 13 & \approx & \times\ 10 \\
\hline
12{,}818 & & 10{,}000
\end{array}
$$

The product in part (b) is incorrect.

63. $33 \times 100 = 3{,}300$
$$
\begin{array}{cc}
\downarrow & \downarrow
\end{array}
$$
$30 \times 100 = 3{,}000$ estimate
The Egyptian ship sank 3,300 years ago.

65. $100{,}000 \times 30 = 3{,}000{,}000$
There are 3,000,000 contractions in 30 days.

67. $32 \times 18 = 576$
Since you can go 576 miles without refilling, you can drive to a town 520 miles away.

69.
$$
\begin{array}{r}
\$725 \\
\times\ 12 \\
\hline
1\ 450 \\
7\ 25 \\
\hline
\$8{,}700
\end{array}
$$
The rent for the year is $8,700.

71. $250\text{ mi} \times 7 = 1{,}750\text{ mi}$
1,750 mi actually separate towns A and B.

73.
$$
\begin{array}{r}
\$21 \\
\times\,19 \\
\hline
189 \\
21 \\
\hline
\$399 \\
\end{array}
$$
← amount you pay each man

$$
\begin{array}{r}
\$399 \\
\times\quad 7 \\
\hline
\$2,793 \\
\end{array}
$$
← amount you pay 7 men

75. a. Multiplication   **b.** area of Colorado = 106,700 sq mi

c.
$$
\begin{array}{r}
388 \approx \quad 400 \\
\times 275 \approx \quad \times 300 \\
\hline
120,000 \text{ sq mi}
\end{array}
$$

1.4   Dividing Whole Numbers

Practice

1.
$$
\begin{array}{r}
807 \\
9\overline{)7,263} \\
-7\,2 \\
\hline
06 \\
-0 \\
\hline
63 \\
-63 \\
\hline
0
\end{array}
$$

2.
$$
\begin{array}{r}
7,002 \\
8\overline{)56,016} \\
-56 \\
\hline
0 \\
-0 \\
\hline
01 \\
-0 \\
\hline
16 \\
-16 \\
\hline
0
\end{array}
$$

3.
$$
\begin{array}{r}
5,291\ \text{R1} \\
8\overline{)42,329} \\
-40 \\
\hline
2\,3 \\
-1\,6 \\
\hline
72 \\
-72 \\
\hline
09 \\
-8 \\
\hline
1
\end{array}
$$

4.
$$
\begin{array}{r}
79 \\
23\overline{)1,817} \\
-1\,61 \\
\hline
207 \\
-207 \\
\hline
0
\end{array}
$$
Check: $79 \times 23 = 1,817$

5.
$$
\begin{array}{r}
94\ \text{R10} \\
15\overline{)1,420} \\
-1\,35 \\
\hline
70 \\
-60 \\
\hline
10
\end{array}
$$
Check: $(94 \times 15) + 10 = 1,420$

6.
$$
\begin{array}{r}
607\ \text{R3} \\
28\overline{)16,999} \\
-16\,8 \\
\hline
19 \\
-0 \\
\hline
199 \\
-196 \\
\hline
3
\end{array}
$$
Check: $(607 \times 28) + 3 = 16,999$

7.
$$
\begin{array}{r}
200 \\
40\overline{)8,000} \\
-8\,0 \\
\hline
0\,0 \\
-00 \\
\hline
00 \\
-00 \\
\hline
0
\end{array}
$$
Check: $200 \times 40 = 8,000$

8.
$$
\begin{array}{r}
967 \\
104\overline{)100,568} \\
-93\,6 \\
\hline
6\,96 \\
-6\,24 \\
\hline
728 \\
-728 \\
\hline
0
\end{array}
$$
Check:
$$
104\overline{)100,568}
$$
$$
\downarrow \qquad \downarrow
$$
$$
100\overline{)100,000}
$$
1,000 estimated quotient
$$
100\overline{)100,000}
$$

Calculator Practice

p. 47. $\dfrac{47,034}{78} = 603$

A reasonable estimate is $50,000 \div 80 = 625$, which is close to 603.

Exercises

1.
$$
\begin{array}{r}
400 \\
5\overline{)2,000} \\
-2\,0 \\
\hline
00 \\
-0 \\
\hline
00 \\
-0 \\
\hline
0
\end{array}
$$
$400 \times 5 = 2,000$

3.
$$
\begin{array}{r}
3,000,000 \\
3\overline{)9,000,000}
\end{array}
$$
$3,000,000 \times 3 = 9,000,000$

5.
$$
\begin{array}{r}
50 \\
3\overline{)150} \\
-15 \\
\hline
00 \\
-0 \\
\hline
0
\end{array}
$$
$50 \times 3 = 150$

7.
$$
\begin{array}{r}
121 \\
6\overline{)726} \\
-6 \\
\hline
12 \\
-12 \\
\hline
06 \\
-6 \\
\hline
0
\end{array}
$$
$121 \times 6 = 726$

9.
$$
\begin{array}{r}
560 \\
5)\overline{2,800} \\
\underline{-2\,5} \\
30 \\
\underline{-30} \\
00 \\
\underline{-0} \\
0
\end{array}
$$
$560 \times 5 = 2,800$

11.
$$
\begin{array}{r}
301 \\
9)\overline{2,709} \\
\underline{-2\,7} \\
00 \\
\underline{-0} \\
09 \\
\underline{-9} \\
0
\end{array}
$$
$301 \times 9 = 2,709$

33.
$$
\begin{array}{r}
651 \text{ R2} \\
10)\overline{6,512} \\
\underline{-6\,0} \\
51 \\
\underline{-50} \\
12 \\
\underline{-10} \\
2
\end{array}
$$
$(651 \times 10) + 2 = 6,512$

35.
$$
\begin{array}{r}
11 \text{ R7} \\
27)\overline{304} \\
\underline{-27} \\
34 \\
\underline{-27} \\
7
\end{array}
$$
$(11 \times 27) + 7 = 304$

13.
$$
\begin{array}{r}
3,003 \\
7)\overline{21,021} \\
\underline{-21} \\
00 \\
\underline{-0} \\
02 \\
\underline{-0} \\
21 \\
\underline{-21} \\
0
\end{array}
$$
$3,003 \times 7 = 21,021$

15.
$$
\begin{array}{r}
5,490 \\
5)\overline{27,450} \\
\underline{-25} \\
24 \\
\underline{-20} \\
45 \\
\underline{-45} \\
00 \\
\underline{-0} \\
0
\end{array}
$$
$5490 \times 5 = 27,450$

37.
$$
\begin{array}{r}
117 \\
87)\overline{10,179} \\
\underline{-87} \\
147 \\
\underline{-87} \\
609 \\
\underline{-609} \\
0
\end{array}
$$
$177 \times 87 = 10,179$

39.
$$
\begin{array}{r}
808 \\
99)\overline{79,992} \\
\underline{-79\,2} \\
79 \\
\underline{-0} \\
792 \\
\underline{-792} \\
0
\end{array}
$$
$808 \times 99 = 79,992$

17.
$$
\begin{array}{r}
202 \\
3)\overline{606} \\
\underline{-6} \\
00 \\
\underline{-0} \\
06 \\
\underline{-6} \\
0
\end{array}
$$
$202 \times 3 = 606$

19.
$$
\begin{array}{r}
219 \\
9)\overline{1,971} \\
\underline{-18} \\
17 \\
\underline{-9} \\
81 \\
\underline{-81} \\
0
\end{array}
$$
$219 \times 9 = 1,971$

41.
$$
\begin{array}{r}
159 \\
44)\overline{6,996} \\
\underline{-44} \\
2\,59 \\
\underline{-2\,20} \\
396 \\
\underline{-396} \\
0
\end{array}
$$
$159 \times 44 = 6,996$

43.
$$
\begin{array}{r}
5,353 \\
15)\overline{80,295} \\
\underline{-75} \\
5\,2 \\
\underline{-4\,5} \\
79 \\
\underline{-75} \\
45 \\
\underline{-45} \\
0
\end{array}
$$
$5,353 \times 15 = 80,295$

21.
$$
\begin{array}{r}
500 \\
9)\overline{4,500} \\
\underline{-4\,5} \\
00 \\
\underline{-0} \\
00 \\
\underline{-0} \\
0
\end{array}
$$
$500 \times 9 = 4,500$

23.
$$
\begin{array}{r}
841 \\
5)\overline{4,205} \\
\underline{-4\,0} \\
20 \\
\underline{-20} \\
05 \\
\underline{-5} \\
0
\end{array}
$$
$841 \times 5 = 4,205$

45.
$$
\begin{array}{r}
1,002 \\
39)\overline{39,078} \\
\underline{-39} \\
0\,0 \\
\underline{-0} \\
07 \\
\underline{-0} \\
78 \\
\underline{-78} \\
0
\end{array}
$$
$1,002 \times 39 = 39,078$

47.
$$
\begin{array}{r}
6,944 \\
36)\overline{249,984} \\
\underline{-216} \\
33\,9 \\
\underline{-32\,4} \\
1\,58 \\
\underline{-1\,44} \\
144 \\
\underline{-144} \\
0
\end{array}
$$
$6,944 \times 36 = 249,984$

25.
$$
10)\overline{30\cancel{0}} = 1)\overline{\substack{30 \\ 30}}
$$
$30 \times 10 = 300$

27.
$$
5\cancel{0})\overline{70\cancel{0}} = 5)\overline{\substack{14 \\ 70}}
$$
$14 \times 50 = 700$

49.
$$
\begin{array}{r}
723 \text{ R19} \\
47)\overline{34,000} \\
\underline{-32\,9} \\
110 \\
\underline{-94} \\
160 \\
\underline{-141} \\
19
\end{array}
$$
$(723 \times 47) + 19 = 34,000$

29.
$$
5\cancel{0})\overline{8,00\cancel{0}} = 5)\overline{\substack{160 \\ 800}}
$$
$160 \times 50 = 8,000$

31.
$$
4\cancel{0})\overline{2,00\cancel{0}} = 4)\overline{\substack{50 \\ 200}}
$$
$50 \times 40 = 2,000$

51.
$$\begin{array}{r} 428 \text{ R}8 \\ 14\overline{)6,000} \\ \underline{-56} \\ 40 \\ \underline{-28} \\ 120 \\ \underline{-112} \\ 8 \end{array}$$

$(428 \times 14) + 8 = 6,000$

53.
$$\begin{array}{r} 1,001 \\ 52\overline{)52,052} \\ \underline{-52} \\ 0\ 0 \\ \underline{-0} \\ 05 \\ \underline{-0} \\ 52 \\ \underline{-52} \\ 0 \end{array}$$

$1,001 \times 52 = 52,052$

55.
$$\begin{array}{r} 3,050 \\ 12\overline{)36,600} \\ \underline{-36} \\ 0\ 6 \\ \underline{-0} \\ 60 \\ \underline{-60} \\ 00 \\ \underline{-0} \\ 0 \end{array}$$

$3,050 \times 12 = 36,600$

57. $387,177 \div 537 = 721$

59. $98,890 \div 638 = 155$

61. a.
$$\begin{array}{r} 704 \\ 65\overline{)455,260} \end{array}$$
$$\downarrow \quad \downarrow$$
$$70\overline{)500,000} \approx 7,000$$

b.
$$\begin{array}{r} 201 \\ 57\overline{)11,457} \end{array}$$
$$\downarrow \quad \downarrow$$
$$60\overline{)12,000} \approx 200$$

c.
$$\begin{array}{r} 108 \\ 93\overline{)10,044} \end{array}$$
$$\downarrow \quad \downarrow$$
$$100\overline{)10,000} \approx 100$$

The quotient in part (a) is wrong.

63. a.
$$\begin{array}{r} 47 \\ 93\overline{)43,710} \end{array}$$
$$\downarrow \quad \downarrow$$
$$100\overline{)40,000} \approx 400$$

b.
$$\begin{array}{r} 664 \\ 107\overline{)71,048} \end{array}$$
$$\downarrow \quad \downarrow$$
$$100\overline{)70,000} \approx 700$$

c.
$$\begin{array}{r} 371 \\ 31\overline{)11,501} \end{array}$$
$$\downarrow \quad \downarrow$$
$$30\overline{)12,000} \approx 400$$

The quotient in part (a) is wrong.

65.
$$\begin{array}{r} 89 \\ 5\overline{)445} \\ \underline{-40} \\ 45 \\ \underline{-45} \\ 0 \end{array}$$

The family spent $89 per night.

67.
$$\begin{array}{r} 2 \\ 32,000,000\overline{)64,000,000} \\ \underline{-64,000,000} \\ 0 \end{array}$$

The Pacific Ocean is 2 times as large as the Atlantic Ocean.

69.
$$\begin{array}{r} 20 \\ 15\overline{)300} \\ \underline{-30} \\ 00 \\ \underline{-0} \\ 0 \end{array}$$

The car got 20 miles per gallon.

71.
$$\begin{array}{r} 2 \text{ R}10 \\ 120\overline{)250} \\ \underline{-240} \\ 10 \end{array}$$

250 min would need more than 2 120-min tapes. You should buy 3 tapes.

73.
$$\begin{array}{r} 2,496 \\ 12\overline{)29,952} \\ \underline{-24} \\ 59 \\ \underline{-48} \\ 115 \\ \underline{-108} \\ 72 \\ \underline{-72} \\ 0 \end{array}$$

The monthly income is $2,496.

75. a. Division

b. $15,950 \div 275 = 58$ min

c. $300\overline{)15,000} \approx 50$ min (possible estimate)

1.5 Exponents, Order of Operations, and Averages

Practice

1. $5 \cdot 5 \cdot 5 \cdot 5 \cdot 5 = 5^5$

2. $1^8 = 1 \cdot 1 \cdot 1 \cdot 1 \cdot 1 \cdot 1 \cdot 1 \cdot 1 = 1$

3. $11^3 = 11 \cdot 11 \cdot 11 = 1,331$

4. $7^2 \cdot 2^4 = (7 \cdot 7) \cdot (2 \cdot 2 \cdot 2 \cdot 2)$
$$= 49 \cdot 16$$
$$= 784$$

5. $1,000,000,000 = 10^9$

6. $2 \cdot 8 + 4 \cdot 3 = 16 + 12 = 28$

7. $(4+1)^2 \times 6 - 4$

$= 5^2 \times 6 - 4$

$= 25 \times 6 - 4$

$= 150 - 4$

$= 146$

8. $10 + \dfrac{24}{12-8} - 3 \times 4$

$= 10 + \dfrac{24}{4} - 3 \times 4$

$= 10 + 6 - 12$

$= 16 - 12$

$= 4$

9. $\dfrac{\$30 + \$0 + \$90}{3} = \dfrac{\$120}{3} = \$40$

10. $\$84 + \$85 + \$88 + \$92 + \$80 + \$96 +$

$\$150 + \$175 + \$100 + \$95 + \$75 + \$80 = \$1,200$

average monthly bill $=$

$\dfrac{\text{sum of the bills}}{\text{number of months}} = \dfrac{\$1,200}{12} = \$100$

Your average monthly bills were not higher than
your average monthly bill last year.

Calculator Practice

p. 57. $375^2 = 140,625$

p. 58. $135 - 44 \div 11 = 131$

Exercises

1.

n	0	2	4	6	8	10
n^2	0	4	16	36	64	100

n	12	14	16	18	20
n^2	144	196	256	324	400

3.

n	0	2	4	6	8	10
n^3	0	8	64	216	512	1,000

5. $100 = 10^2$

7. $10,000 = 10^4$

9. $1,000,000 = 10^6$

11. $2 \cdot 2 \cdot 3 \cdot 3 = 2^2 \cdot 3^2$

13. $2 \cdot 3 \cdot 3 \cdot 3 = 2^1 \cdot 3^3$

15. $2 \cdot 3 \cdot 2 = 2^2 \cdot 3^1$

17. $8 + 5 \cdot 2$

$= 8 + 10$

$= 18$

19. $8 - 2 \times 3$

$= 8 - 6$

$= 2$

21. $10 + 5^2$

$= 10 + 25$

$= 35$

23. $(9-2)^3$

$= 7^3$

$= 343$

25. 10×5^2

$= 10 \times 25$

$= 250$

27. $(12 \div 2)^2$

$= 6^2$

$= 36$

29. $(24 \div 4) + 2$

$= 6 + 2$

$= 8$

31. $15 \cdot 6 + 2$

$= 90 + 2$

$= 92$

33. $15 \cdot (6 - 2)$

$= 15 \cdot 4$

$= 60$

35. $2^6 - 6^2$

$= 64 - 36$

$= 28$

37. $8 + 5 - 2 \times 2$

$= 8 + 5 - 4$

$= 13 - 4$

$= 9$

39. $\dfrac{8+2}{7-2}$

$= \dfrac{10}{5}$

$= 2$

41. $(10-1)(10+1)$

$= (9)(11)$

$= 99$

43. $10^2 - 1$

$= 100 - 1$

$= 99$

45. $\left(\dfrac{8+1}{5-2}\right)^2$

$= \left(\dfrac{9}{3}\right)^2$

$= 3^2$

$= 9$

47. $32 + 9 \cdot 215 \div 5$

$= 32 + 1,935 \div 5$

$= 32 + 387$

$= 419$

49. $48(48-31)(48-24)(48-41)$

$= 48(17)(24)(7)$

$= (816)(24)(7)$

$= (19,584)(7)$

$137,088$

51. $4 \cdot 3 + 6 \cdot 5 + 8 \cdot 7$

$= 12 + 30 + 56$

$= 98$

53. $(8)(3+4) - 2 \cdot 6$

$= (8)(7) - 12$

$= 56 - 12$

$= 44$

55. $8 + 10 \times 4 - 6 \div 2$

$= 8 + 40 - 3$

$= 48 - 3$

$= 45$

57. $(5+2) \cdot 4^2$

$= 7 \cdot 16$

$= 112$

59. $(5 + 2 \cdot 4)^2$

$= (5+8)^2$

$= 13^2$

$= 169$

61. $(8-4) \div 2^2$

$= 4 \div 4$

$= 1$

63. area $= (11\,\text{cm} \times 18\,\text{cm}) + (11\,\text{cm} \times 4\,\text{cm})$

$= 198\,\text{cm}^2 + 44\,\text{cm}^2$

$= 242\,\text{cm}^2$

65. area $= (135\,\text{in.} \times 93\,\text{in.}) - (111\,\text{in.} \times 85\,\text{in.})$

$= 12,555\,\text{in.}^2 - 9,435\,\text{in.}^2$

$= 3,120\,\text{in.}^2$

67. $21+3\times0=21+0=21$
$21+3\times1=21+3=24$
$21+3\times2=21+6=27$

69. average $=\dfrac{20+30}{2}=\dfrac{50}{2}=25$

71. average $=\dfrac{30+60+30}{3}=\dfrac{120}{3}=40$

73. average $=\dfrac{10+0+3+3}{4}=\dfrac{16}{4}=4$

75. average $=\dfrac{3,527\text{ mi}+1,788\text{ mi}+1,921\text{ mi}}{3}$
$=\dfrac{7,236\text{ mi}}{3}$
$=2,412\text{ mi}$

77. average
$=\dfrac{10+10+10+10+10+10+5+5+5+5}{10}$
$=\dfrac{6\cdot10+4\cdot5}{10}$
$=\dfrac{60+20}{10}$
$=\dfrac{80}{10}$
$=8$

79. $\dfrac{163+185+154+127+156+153+140}{7}$
$=\dfrac{1,078}{7}=154$

Your average bowling score for 7 games is 154.

81. average for the first 2 years $=\dfrac{\$19,400+\$21,400}{2}$
$=\dfrac{\$40,800}{2}=\$20,400$

average for all 3 years $=\dfrac{\$19,400+\$21,400+\$23,70}{3}$
$=\dfrac{\$64,500}{3}=\$21,500$

Your average salary for all 3 years was greater than your average salary for the first two years by $1,100.

83. men's average $=\dfrac{2+4}{2}=\dfrac{6}{2}=3$ hr

women's average $=\dfrac{4+0+2}{3}=\dfrac{6}{3}=2$ hr

On average, the men spent more time watching TV.

85. average space on a floor $=\dfrac{\text{total space}}{\text{number of floors}}$
$=\dfrac{25,000\text{ sq ft}}{40}$
$=625$ sq ft

The average rental space on a floor is 625 sq ft.

87. $5^2+12^2\overset{?}{=}13^2$

$25+144\overset{?}{=}169$

$169\overset{\checkmark}{=}169$

Yes, 5, 12, and 13 are a Pythagorean triple.

89. a. Addition, division, and subtraction.
b.
average circulation for newspaper B
$=\dfrac{85,774+72,503+68,513+74,812+89,002+92,331+102,447}{7}$
$=\dfrac{585,382}{7}$
$=83,626$

Newspaper B average circulation $=$ 83,626
Newspaper A average circulation $=$ $\dfrac{-82,073}{1,553}$

Newspaper B is more popular by 1,553 people.
c. The numbers are too close to estimate which is larger.

1.6   More on Solving Word Problems

Practice

1. Find the total number of employees laid off:
1,150
+2,235
———
3,385
Add this total to the number of employees remaining:
7,285
+3,385
———
10,670
10,670 employees worked for the company before the layoffs.
Check: $1,000,+2,000+7,000=10,000$

2. Teddy Roosevelt's age when he died was $1919-1858=61$ yr. Franklin Roosevelt's age when he died was $1945-1882=63$ yr. Franklin lived 2 yr longer than Teddy.

3. Since each section has 33 students and there are 47 sections in all, we need to multiply to find the total number of students:

$47 \times 33 = 1,551$ students

4. Find the numbers of pounds lost after 15 weeks:

$2 \cdot 15 = 30$ lb

Find your weight remaining after losing 30 lb:

$210 - 30 - 180$ lb

You will weigh 180 lb after 15 weeks.

Exercises

1. The net sales is what remains after the customer returns and allowances are subtracted from the gross sales: $\$2,538 - \$388 = \$2,150$

The store's net sales was $2,150.

3. If you travel east and then travel west, you are moving in opposite directions, so we must subtract to find the distance traveled:

27 mi $+ 31$ mi $- 45$ mi $+ 14$ mi

$= 58$ mi $- 45$ mi $+ 14$ mi

$= 13$ mi $+ 14$ mi

$= 27$ mi

You are 27 mi from your starting point.

5. We need to divide to see how many times 36 disks will fit in 400 disks:

$400 \div 36 = 11$ R4

You will need 12 shelves.

7. To find the increase, we will need to subtract last year's expenses from this year's expenses:

$\$9,055 - \$7,228 = \$1,827$

The increase in expenses is $1,827.

9. Find the difference between the weights:

$93,000,000 - 63,000,000 = 30,000,000$

The Titanic was 30,000,000 lb heavier than the Lusitania.

11. 3 rolls of film for $15 cost $15 \div 3 = \$5$ per roll.
2 rolls of film for $12 cost $12 \div 2 = \$6$ per roll.
Buying 3 rolls of film is $1 less expensive per roll than buying 2 rolls of film.

13. $144 \times 7 = 1,008$
7 gross contains 1,008 pens.
$1,008 - 1,000 = 8$
You ordered 8 extra pens.

15. $442 - 89 = 353$
In the 1952 election Eisenhower received 353 more electoral votes than Stevenson.
$457 - 73 = 384$
In the 1956 election Eisenhower received 384 more electoral votes than Stevenson.

$384 - 353 = 31$
The 1952 election was closer by 31 votes.

17. **a.** Subtraction and division
b. $\$165,00 = \$23,448 = \$141,552$
$\$141,552 \div 144 = \$983$
You will pay $983 in each installment.
c. Possible estimate:
$\$160,00 - \$20,000 = \$140,000$
$\$140,000 \div 140 = \$1,000$
$1,000 is fairly close to $983.

Review Exercises

1. In 23, the 3 is in the ones place.

2. In 30,802, the 3 is in the ten thousands place.

3. In 385,000,000, the 3 is in the hundred millions place.

4. In 30,000,000,000, the 3 is in the ten billions place.

5. 497 is four hundred ninety-seven.

6. 2,050 is two thousand, fifty.

7. 3,000,007 is three million, seven.

8. 85,000,000,000 is eighty-five billion.

9. Two hundred fifty-one is 251.

10. Nine thousand, two is 9,002.

11. Fourteen million, twenty-five is 14,000,025.

12. Three billion, three thousand is 3,000,003,000.

13. $308 = 3$ hundreds $+ 8$ ones $= 300 + 8$

14. $2,500,000 = 2$ millions $+ 5$ hundred thousands $= 2,000,000 + 500,000$

15. $42,770 = 4$ ten thousands $+ 2$ thousands $+ 7$ hundreds $+ 7$ tens $= 40,000 + 2,000 + 700 + 70$

16. $30,000,012 = 3$ ten millions $+ 1$ ten $+ 2$ ones $= 30,000,000 + 10 + 2$

17. $571 \approx 600$ 18. $938 \approx 1,000$

19. $384,056 \approx 380,000$ 20. $68,332 \approx 70,000$

21.
```
    102
  4,251
 +5,133
 ------
  9,486
```
22.
```
      1
 53,569
 10,000
 + 2,123
 ------
 65,692
```

23.
```
 21 12
 48,758
 37,226
+87,559
-------
173,543
```
24.
```
      1
 95,000
 25,895
+30,000
-------
150,895
```

25.
$$\begin{array}{r} \overset{1}{}\overset{1\,1}{} \\ 972,558 \\ +\ 87,055 \\ \hline 1,059,613 \end{array}$$

26.
$$\begin{array}{r} \overset{1\,2\,2\ \,1\,1}{} \\ \$138,865 \\ 729 \\ 8,002 \\ +\ 75,471 \\ \hline \$223,067 \end{array}$$

27.
$$\begin{array}{r} 876 \\ -431 \\ \hline 445 \end{array}$$

28.
$$\begin{array}{r} 500,000 \\ -200,000 \\ \hline 300,000 \end{array}$$

29.
$$\begin{array}{r} \overset{0}{}\overset{1}{}{}^{1}8 \\ 98,1\!\!\!/1\,8 \\ -87,00\ 9 \\ \hline 11,10\ 9 \end{array}$$

30.
$$\begin{array}{r} \overset{6}{}{}^{1} \\ 7\!\!\!/,100 \\ -1,\,500 \\ \hline 5,\,600 \end{array}$$

31. $60,000,000 - 48,957,777 = 11,042,223$

32. $\$5,000,000 - \$2,937,148 = \$2,062,852$

33.
$$\begin{array}{r} 72 \\ \times\ 6 \\ \hline 432 \end{array}$$

34.
$$\begin{array}{r} 400 \\ \times\ \ 3 \\ \hline 1,200 \end{array}$$

35.
$$\begin{array}{r} 2,923 \\ \times\ \ \ 51 \\ \hline 2\ 923 \\ 146\ 15 \\ \hline 149,073 \end{array}$$

36.
$$\begin{array}{r} 6,000 \\ \times 2,000 \\ \hline 12,000,000 \end{array}$$

37. $2,751 \cdot 508 = 1,397,508$

38. $(681)(498)(555) = 188,221,590$

39.
$$\begin{array}{r} 94 \\ 4\overline{)376} \\ -36 \\ \hline 16 \\ -16 \\ \hline 0 \end{array}$$

40.
$$\begin{array}{r} 39 \\ 25\overline{)975} \\ -75 \\ \hline 225 \\ -225 \\ \hline 0 \end{array}$$

41.
$$\begin{array}{r} 37\ R10 \\ 13\overline{)491} \\ -39 \\ \hline 101 \\ -91 \\ \hline 10 \end{array}$$

42.
$$\begin{array}{r} 800 \\ 2\!\!\!/0\overline{)16,00\!\!\!/0} \end{array}$$

43.
$$\begin{array}{r} 25,625 \\ 8\overline{)205,000} \\ -16 \\ \hline 45 \\ -40 \\ \hline 5\ 0 \\ -4\ 8 \\ \hline 20 \\ -16 \\ \hline 40 \\ -40 \\ \hline 0 \end{array}$$

44.
$$\begin{array}{r} 957 \\ 347\overline{)332,079} \\ -312\ 3 \\ \hline 19\ 77 \\ -17\ 35 \\ \hline 2429 \\ -2429 \\ \hline 0 \end{array}$$

45. $7^3 = 7 \cdot 7 \cdot 7 = 343$

46. $1^{10} = 1 \cdot 1 \cdot 1 \cdot 1 \cdot 1 \cdot 1 \cdot 1 \cdot 1 \cdot 1 \cdot 1 = 1$

47. $2^3 \cdot 3^2$
$= \underbrace{2 \cdot 2 \cdot 2}_{8} \cdot \underbrace{3 \cdot 3}_{9}$
$= 72$

48. $5^2 \cdot 5^3$
$= \underbrace{5 \cdot 5}_{25} \cdot \underbrace{5 \cdot 5 \cdot 5}_{125}$
$= 3,125$

49. $20 - 3 \times 5$
$= 20 - 15$
$= 5$

50. $(9 + 4)^2$
$= 13^2$
$= 13 \cdot 13$
$= 169$

51. $10 - \dfrac{6+4}{2}$
$= 10 - \dfrac{10}{2}$
$= 10 - 5$
$= 5$

52. $3 + (5-1)^2$
$= 3 + 4^2$
$= 3 + 16$
$= 19$

53. $98(50-1)(50-2)(50-3)$
$= 98(49)(48)(47)$
$= 10,833,312$

54. $\dfrac{28^3 + 29^3 + 37^3 - 10}{(7-1)^2}$
$= \dfrac{21,952 + 24,389 + 50,653 - 10}{36}$
$= 2,694$

55. $7 \cdot 7 \cdot 5 \cdot 5 = 7^2 \cdot 5^2$

56. $5 \cdot 2 \cdot 5 \cdot 2 \cdot 5$
$= 2 \cdot 2 \cdot 5 \cdot 5 \cdot 5$
$= 2^2 \cdot 5^3$

57. average $= \dfrac{34+44}{2} = \dfrac{78}{2} = 39$

58. average $= \dfrac{20+0+1}{3} = \dfrac{21}{3} = 7$

59. average $= \dfrac{5+8+5}{3} = \dfrac{18}{3} = 6$

60. average $= \dfrac{4+6+3+7}{4} = \dfrac{20}{4} = 5$

61. $2,400,000 =$ two million, four hundred thousand

62. one hundred fifty million $= 150,000,000$

63.
$$\begin{array}{r} \$307 \\ 52\overline{)\$15,964} \\ -15\ 6 \\ \hline 36 \\ -0 \\ \hline 364 \\ -364 \\ \hline 0 \end{array}$$
   You earned \$307 per week.

64.   1682
      + 76
      ‾‾‾‾‾
       1758

The second sighting of Halley's comet was in 1758.

65. 8,223,618 acres ≈ 8,000,000 acres (rounded to the nearest million)

66.   308
      27)8,316
        −81
      ‾‾‾‾
         21
        −0
      ‾‾‾‾
        216
       −216
      ‾‾‾‾
          0

The crew build 308 ft of road per week.

67.   8 R34
      152)1,250
        −1 216
      ‾‾‾‾‾
           34

9 Statues of Liberty would have to be stacked to be taller than the Empire State Building.

68. 68×4 = 272
The millipede has 272 legs.

69. 28×100,000 = 2,800,000 contractions
              for a 28-day month
      30×100,000 = 3,000,000 contractions
              for a 30-day month
      31×100,000 = 3,100,000 contractions
              for a 31-day month

70. 84,601 books ≈ 80,000 books (rounded to the nearest ten thousand)

71. 60,000 + 20,000 + 58,000 + 26,000 + 82,000 = 246,000
The total area of the five Great Lakes is 246,000 sq km.

72.
Net sales	$430,00
− Cost of merchandise sold	− 175,000
Gross margin	$255,000
− Operating expenses	− 135,000
Net profit	$120,000

73. area of rug   area of room   225 sq ft
        12 ft   15 ft   −144 sq ft
       ×12 ft   ×15 ft   ‾‾‾‾‾‾
      ‾‾‾‾   ‾‾‾‾   81 sq ft
        24   75
        12   15
      ‾‾‾‾   ‾‾‾‾
      144 sq ft   225 sq ft

81 sq ft of the floor will be exposed.

74.   78   160
        ×27   ×300
      ‾‾‾‾   ‾‾‾‾‾‾
        546   48,000 sq ft
       1 56
      ‾‾‾‾
      2,106 sq ft

      2,106)48,00
         ↓   ↓
                 20
      2000)40,000

The area of the football field is about 20 times the area of the tennis court.

75. increase in votes from 1960 to 1972:
      47,166,234
     −34,108,546
     ‾‾‾‾‾‾
      13,056,688

increase in votes from 1968 to 1972:
      47,166,234
     −31,785,480
     ‾‾‾‾‾‾
      15,379,754

The increase in votes from 1968 to 1972 was greater.

76.   1,745
       +2,596
      ‾‾‾‾
       4,341 miles
You earned 4,341 points.

77. $55 $175
          27   − 116
       + 34   ‾‾‾‾
      ‾‾‾‾ $59
       $116
You need $59 more to buy the disk player.

78. 24 · 10^13 =
24·10·10·10·10·10·10·10·10·10·10·10·10·10 = 240,000,000,000,000 mi

79.

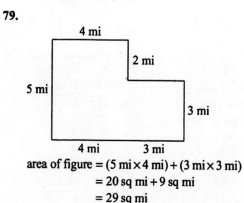

area of figure = (5 mi × 4 mi) + (3 mi × 3 mi)
              = 20 sq mi + 9 sq mi
              = 29 sq mi

80. perimeter of figure =
$35 \text{ cm} + 9 \text{ cm} + 11 \text{ cm} + 8 \text{ cm} + 11 \text{ cm} +$
$7 \text{ cm} + 35 \text{ cm} + 7 \text{ cm} + 11 \text{ cm} + 8 \text{ cm} +$
$11 \text{ cm} + 9 \text{ cm}$
$= 162 \text{ cm}$

Posttest

1. two hundred twenty-five thousand, sixty-seven = 225,067

2. $1,7\underline{6}8,405$

3. $1,205,007 =$ one million, two hundred five thousand, seven

4. $196,593 \approx 200,000$

5.
$$\begin{array}{r} {\scriptstyle 1\ 1} \\ 1,496 \\ +\ 398 \\ \hline 1,894 \end{array}$$

6.
$$\begin{array}{r} {\scriptstyle 9\ 9} \\ 0\ \cancel{10}\ \cancel{10} \\ \cancel{1},\cancel{0}\ \cancel{0}\ {}^{1}5 \\ -\ 3\ 9\ 8 \\ \hline 6\ 0\ 7 \end{array}$$

7.
$$\begin{array}{r} {\scriptstyle 9\ 9} \\ 1\ \cancel{10}\ \cancel{10} \\ \cancel{2},\cancel{0}\ \cancel{0}\ {}^{1}0 \\ -1,8\ 5\ 3 \\ \hline 1\ 4\ 7 \end{array}$$

8.
$$\begin{array}{r} 328 \\ \times 907 \\ \hline 2\ 296 \\ 295\ 2 \\ \hline 297,496 \end{array}$$

9.
$$\begin{array}{r} 70 \\ 3\cancel{00}\overline{)21,0\cancel{00}} \end{array}$$

10.
$$\begin{array}{r} 509 \\ 47\overline{)23,923} \\ \underline{-23\ 5} \\ 42 \\ \underline{-0} \\ 423 \\ \underline{-423} \\ 0 \end{array}$$

11. $5^3 = 5 \cdot 5 \cdot 5 = 25 \cdot 5 = 125$

12. $2 \cdot 2 \cdot 3 \cdot 3 \cdot 3 = 2^2 \cdot 3^3$

13. $4 \cdot 9 + 3 \cdot 4^2$
$= 4 \cdot 9 + 3 \cdot 16$
$= 36 + 48$
$= 84$

14. $29 - 3^3 \cdot (10 - 9)$
$= 29 - 27 \cdot (1)$
$= 29 - 27$
$= 2$

15.
$$\begin{array}{r} {\scriptstyle 6} \\ 1\cancel{7},{}^{1}400 \text{ sq mi} \\ -11,700 \text{ sq mi} \\ \hline 5,700 \text{ sq mi} \end{array}$$
Asia is 5,700 sq mi larger than Africa.

16.
$$\begin{array}{r} \$175 \\ \times\ \ 17 \\ \hline 1\ 225 \\ 1\ 75 \\ \hline \$2,975 \end{array}$$
The club paid $2,975 for the trip.

17. $100,000 \cdot 10 = 1,000,000 = 10^6$

There are 10^6 transactions in 10 days.

18. average score $= \dfrac{82 + 85 + 87 + 92 + 89}{5}$
$= \dfrac{435}{5}$
$= 87$

Your average score was 87.

19.
$$\begin{array}{r} 20 \\ 2\overline{)40} \end{array}$$
You can buy 20 yellow roses for $40.
$$\begin{array}{r} 10 \\ 4\overline{)40} \end{array}$$
You can buy 10 red roses for $40.
$20 - 10 = 10$
You can buy 10 more yellow roses than red roses.

20.
$$\begin{array}{r} 1 \text{ 8 oz cup of yogurt} = 1 \times 2 \text{ mg} = 2 \text{ mg} \\ 1 \text{ cup black coffee} = 1 \times 0 \text{ mg} = 0 \text{ mg} \\ 2 \text{ cups pineapple juice} = 2 \times 23 \text{ mg} = 46 \text{ mg} \\ \hline 48 \text{ mg} \end{array}$$

$60 \text{ mg} - 48 \text{ mg} = 12 \text{ mg}$
You need 12 more mg of Vitamin C.

Chapter 2

FRACTIONS

Pretest

1. $\dfrac{20}{1} = 20 \text{ R0}$ a factor

   $\dfrac{20}{2} = 10 \text{ R0}$ a factor

   $\dfrac{20}{3} = 6 \text{ R2}$ not a factor

   $\dfrac{20}{4} = 5 \text{ R0}$ a factor

   $\dfrac{20}{5} = 4 \text{ R0}$ a factor

   Since the factors are beginning to repeat, we can stop dividing. The factors of 20 are 1, 2, 4, 5, 10, and 20.

2. $72 = 2 \times 36$
   $= 2 \times 2 \times 18$
   $= 2 \times 2 \times 2 \times 9$
   $= 2 \times 2 \times 2 \times 3 \times 3$

3. $\dfrac{2}{5}$

4. $20\dfrac{1}{3} = \dfrac{(20 \times 3) + 1}{3} = \dfrac{61}{3}$

5. $\dfrac{31}{30} = 30\overline{)31}^{\ 1 \text{ R1}}$
   $\quad\quad\quad \underline{-30}$
   $\quad\quad\quad\quad\ 1$

   $\dfrac{31}{30} = 1\dfrac{1}{30}$

6. $\dfrac{9}{12} = \dfrac{3 \times \cancel{3}}{4 \times \cancel{3}} = \dfrac{3}{4}$

7. 20

8. $\dfrac{1}{8}$

9. $\begin{aligned} \dfrac{1}{2} &= \dfrac{5}{10} \\ +\dfrac{7}{10} &= +\dfrac{7}{10} \\ &\ \ \dfrac{12}{10} = 1\dfrac{2}{10} = 1\dfrac{1}{5} \end{aligned}$

10. $\begin{aligned} 7\dfrac{1}{3} &= 7\dfrac{2}{6} \\ +5\dfrac{1}{2} &= +5\dfrac{3}{6} \\ &\ \ 12\dfrac{5}{6} \end{aligned}$

11. $\begin{aligned} 8\dfrac{1}{4} \\ -6\phantom{\dfrac{1}{4}} \\ \hline 2\dfrac{1}{4} \end{aligned}$

12. $\begin{aligned} 12\dfrac{1}{2} &= 12\dfrac{4}{8} = 11\dfrac{12}{8} \\ -7\dfrac{7}{8} &= -7\dfrac{7}{8} = -7\dfrac{7}{8} \\ & 4\dfrac{5}{8} \end{aligned}$

13. $2\dfrac{1}{3} \times 1\dfrac{1}{2} = \dfrac{7}{\cancel{3}} \times \dfrac{\cancel{3}^{1}}{2} = \dfrac{7}{2} = 3\dfrac{1}{2}$

14. $\dfrac{5}{8} \times 96 = \dfrac{5}{\cancel{8}_{1}} \times \dfrac{\cancel{96}^{12}}{1} = \dfrac{60}{1} = 60$

15. $3\dfrac{1}{3} \div 5 = \dfrac{\cancel{10}^{2}}{3} \times \dfrac{1}{\cancel{5}_{1}} = \dfrac{2}{3}$

16. $2\dfrac{2}{5} \div 1\dfrac{1}{6} = \dfrac{12}{5} \times \dfrac{6}{7} = \dfrac{72}{35} = 2\dfrac{2}{35}$

17. $\dfrac{\text{amount reimbursed}}{\text{amount paid}} = \dfrac{\$40}{\$90} = \dfrac{4 \times \cancel{10}^{1}}{9 \times \cancel{10}_{1}} = \dfrac{4}{9}$

18. $\dfrac{3}{4} \times 24 = \dfrac{3}{\cancel{4}_{1}} \times \dfrac{\cancel{24}^{6}}{1} = 18$; 18 students received a passing grade.
    $\begin{aligned} 24 \\ \underline{-18} \\ 6 \end{aligned}$; 6 students received failing grades.

16

19. perimeter $= 8\frac{1}{8}$ ft $+ 6\frac{3}{4}$ ft $+ 6$ ft

$= 8\frac{1}{8}$ ft $+ 6\frac{6}{8}$ ft $+ 6$ ft

$= 20\frac{7}{8}$ ft

20. $13\frac{1}{3} \div 40 = \frac{40}{3} \div 40 = \frac{\cancel{40}^{1}}{3} \times \frac{1}{\cancel{40}_{1}} = \frac{1}{3}$

Each plot will be $\frac{1}{3}$ acre.

2.1   Factors and Prime Numbers

Practice

1. $\frac{7}{1} = 7$ R0 $\frac{7}{2} = 3$ R1 $\frac{7}{3} = 2$ R1 $\frac{7}{4} = 1$ R3

$\frac{7}{5} = 1$ R2 $\frac{7}{6} = 1$ R1 $\frac{7}{7} = 1$ R0

The factors of 7 are 1 and 7.

2. 75 is divisible by

1; $\frac{75}{1} = 75$ so 75 is a factor.

3, because $7 + 5 = 12$, which is divisible by 3;

$\frac{75}{3} = 25$ so 25 is a factor.

5, because the ones digit is 5; $\frac{75}{5} = 15$ so

15 is a factor.

The factors of 75 are 1, 3, 5, 15, 25, and 75.

3. Is 90 divisible by

1?   Yes; $\frac{90}{1} = 90$ so 90 is also a factor.

2?   Yes, because 90 is even; $\frac{90}{2} = 45$ so

45 is also a factor.

3?   Yes, because $9 + 0 = 9$, which is divisible

by 3; $\frac{90}{3} = 30$, so 30 is also a factor.

4?   No, 4 does not divide 90 evenly.

5?   Yes, the ones digit is 0; $\frac{90}{5} = 18$, so

18 is also a factor.

6?   Yes, because 90 is even and is divisible

by 3; $\frac{90}{6} = 15$, so 15 is also a factor.

7?   No, because $90 \div 7$ has a remainder.

8?   No, because $90 \div 8$ has a remainder.

9?   Yes, because $9 + 0 = 9$, which is divisible

by 9; $\frac{90}{9} = 10$, so 10 is also a factor.

10?   Yes, we already know that 10 is a factor.

The factors of 90 are 1, 2, 3, 5, 6, 9, 10, 15, 18, 30, 45, and 90.

4. Yes, because 24 is a multiple of 3: $\frac{24}{3} = 8$ R0

5. a. The only factors of 3 are 1 and 3, so 3 is prime.
   b. $57 = 3 \cdot 19$, so 57 is composite.
   c. The only factors of 29 are 1 and 29, so 29 is prime.
   d. $34 = 2 \cdot 17$, so 34 is composite.
   e. The only factors of 17 are 1 and 17, so 17 is prime.

6.
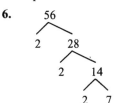

The prime factorization of 56 is

$2 \times 2 \times 2 \times 7 = 2^3 \times 7$

7.

The prime factorization of 45 is

$3 \times 3 \times 5 = 3^2 \times 5$

8. $9 = 3 \times 3$ $6 = 2 \times 3$

LCM $= 2 \times 3^2 = 2 \times 9 = 18$

9. $3 = 3$ $22 = 2 \times 11$

LCM $= 3 \times 2 \times 11 = 66$

10. $2 = 2$ $3 = 3$ $4 = 2 \times 2 = 2^2$

LCM $= 2^2 \times 3 = 4 \times 3 = 12$

11. $2 = 2$ $6 = 2 \times 3$

LCM $= 2 \times 3 = 6$

Both will be up for election in 6 yr.

Exercises

1. $\dfrac{21}{1} = 21$ R0

$\dfrac{21}{3} = 7$ R0

The factors of 21 are 1, 3, 7, and 21.

3. $\dfrac{17}{1} = 17$ R0

The factors of 17 are 1 and 17.

5. $\dfrac{12}{1} = 12$ R0

$\dfrac{12}{2} = 6$ R0

$\dfrac{12}{3} = 4$ R0

The factors of 12 are 1, 2, 3, 4, 6, and 12.

7. $\dfrac{31}{1} = 31$ R0

The factors of 31 are 1 and 31.

9. $36 \div 1 = 36$ R0
$36 \div 2 = 18$ R0
$36 \div 3 = 12$ R0
$36 \div 4 = 9$ R0
$36 \div 6 = 6$ R0
The factors of 36 are 1, 2, 3, 4, 6, 9, 12, 18, and 36.

11. $\dfrac{29}{1} = 29$ R0

The factors of 29 are 1 and 29.

13. $\dfrac{100}{1} = 100$ R0 $\dfrac{100}{2} = 50$ R0 $\dfrac{100}{4} = 25$ R0

$\dfrac{100}{5} = 20$ R0 $\dfrac{100}{10} = 10$ R0

The factors of 100 are 1, 2, 4, 5, 10, 20, 25, 50, and 100.

15. $\dfrac{28}{1} = 28$ R0 $\dfrac{28}{2} = 14$ R0 $\dfrac{28}{4} = 7$ R0

The factors of 28 are 1, 2, 4, 7, 14, and 28.

17. 5 is prime.

19. 16 is composite; 2, 4, and 8 are factors.

21. 49 is composite; 7 is a factor.

23. 11 is prime.

25. 81 is composite; 3, 9 and 27 are factors.

27.

```
        8
       / \
      2   4
         / \
        2   2
```

$8 = 2 \times 2 \times 2 = 2^3$

29.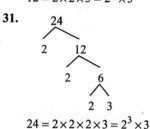

$12 = 2 \times 2 \times 3 = 2^2 \times 3$

31.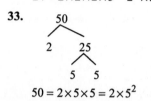

$24 = 2 \times 2 \times 2 \times 3 = 2^3 \times 3$

33.

$50 = 2 \times 5 \times 5 = 2 \times 5^2$

35.

```
      77
     /  \
    7    11
```

$77 = 7 \times 11$

37.

```
      51
     /  \
    3    17
```

$51 = 3 \times 17$

39.

```
      25
     /  \
    5    5
```

$25 = 5 \times 5 = 5^2$

41.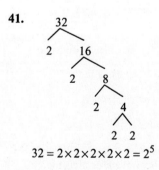

$32 = 2 \times 2 \times 2 \times 2 \times 2 = 2^5$

43.

$$21 = 3 \times 7$$

45.

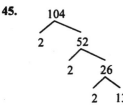

$$104 = 2 \times 2 \times 2 \times 13 = 2^3 \times 13$$

47.

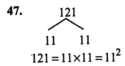

$$121 = 11 \times 11 = 11^2$$

49.

142

2   71

$$142 = 2 \times 71$$

51.

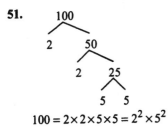

$$100 = 2 \times 2 \times 5 \times 5 = 2^2 \times 5^2$$

53.

125

5   25

    5   5

$$125 = 5 \times 5 \times 5 = 5^3$$

55.

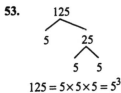

$$135 = 3 \times 3 \times 3 \times 5 = 3^3 \times 5$$

57. $3 = 3 \quad 15 = 3 \times 5$
$LCM = 3 \times 5 = 15$

59. $8 = 2^3 \quad 10 = 2 \times 5$ **61.** $9 = 3^2 \quad 30 = 2 \times 3 \times 5$
$LCM = 2^3 \times 5$ $LCM = 2 \times 3^2 \times 5$
$\quad = 8 \times 5 = 40$ $\quad = 2 \times 9 \times 5 = 90$

63. $10 = 2 \times 5 \quad 11 = 11$
$LCM = 2 \times 5 \times 11 = 110$

65. $18 = 2 \times 3^2 \quad 24 = 2^3 \times 3$
$LCM = 2^3 \times 3^2 = 8 \times 9 = 72$

67. $40 = 2^3 \times 5 \quad 180 = 2^2 \times 3^2 \times 5$
$LCM = 2^3 \times 3^2 \times 5 = 8 \times 9 \times 5 = 360$

69. $12 = 2^2 \times 3 \quad 5 = 5 \quad 50 = 2 \times 5^2$
$LCM = 2^2 \times 3 \times 5^2 = 4 \times 3 \times 25 = 300$

71. $3 = 3 \quad 5 = 5 \quad 6 = 2 \times 3$
$LCM = 2 \times 3 \times 5 = 30$

73. $3 = 3 \quad 5 = 5 \quad 7 = 7$
$LCM = 3 \times 5 \times 7 = 105$

75. $5 = 5 \quad 15 = 3 \times 5 \quad 20 = 2^2 \times 5$
$LCM = 2^2 \times 3 \times 5 = 4 \times 3 \times 5 = 60$

77. There was not a census in 1985 because 1985 is not divisible by 10 (that is, 1985 is not a multiple of 10); there was a census in 1990 because 1990 is a multiple of 10.

79. The length of a side of the smallest square you can make using 6-in. by 8-in. tiles would be the least common multiple of 6 and 8, which is 24. So the smallest square would be $24 \text{ in.} \times 24 \text{ in.}$

2.2   Introduction to Fractions

Practice

1. The whole is divided into 8 equal parts. Five of these parts are shaded. The diagram illustrates the fraction $\dfrac{5}{8}$.

2. The total tuition is \$2,451, so the denominator is \$2,451. The part of the tuition the student paid is \$1,000, so the numerator is \$1,000. The student paid $\dfrac{1,000}{2,451}$ of the tuition.

3. The total number of pages in the book is $125 + 39$, or 164. So you have read $\dfrac{125}{164}$ of the book.

4.

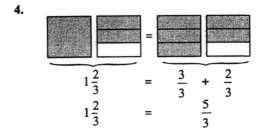

$$1\frac{2}{3} \quad = \quad \frac{3}{3} \quad + \quad \frac{2}{3}$$

$$1\frac{2}{3} \quad = \quad \frac{5}{3}$$

5. a. $5\dfrac{1}{3} = \dfrac{(5 \times 3) + 1}{3} = \dfrac{16}{3}$

b. $20\dfrac{2}{5} = \dfrac{(5 \times 20) + 2}{5} = \dfrac{102}{5}$

6. a. $\dfrac{4}{2} = 2\overline{)4}^{\,2} \qquad \dfrac{4}{2} = 2$

b. $\dfrac{50}{9} = 9\overline{)50}^{\,5\,R5} \qquad \dfrac{50}{9} = 5\dfrac{5}{9}$

c. $\dfrac{8}{3} = 3\overline{)8}^{\,2\,R2} \qquad \dfrac{8}{3} = 2\dfrac{2}{3}$

7. Possible answers are

$\dfrac{2}{5} = \dfrac{2 \cdot 2}{5 \cdot 2} = \dfrac{4}{10}$

$\dfrac{2}{5} = \dfrac{2 \cdot 3}{5 \cdot 3} = \dfrac{6}{15}$

$\dfrac{2}{5} = \dfrac{2 \cdot 4}{5 \cdot 4} = \dfrac{8}{20}$

8. $\dfrac{5}{8} = \dfrac{n}{72}$

$\dfrac{5}{8} = \dfrac{n}{8 \cdot 9}$

$\dfrac{5 \cdot 9}{8 \cdot 9} = \dfrac{n}{8 \cdot 9}$

$\dfrac{5}{8} = \dfrac{45}{72}$

9. $\dfrac{14}{21} = \dfrac{14 \div 7}{21 \div 7} = \dfrac{2}{3}$

10. $\dfrac{45}{18} = \dfrac{\overset{1}{\cancel{3}} \cdot \overset{1}{\cancel{3}} \cdot 5}{2 \cdot \underset{1}{\cancel{3}} \cdot \underset{1}{\cancel{3}}} = \dfrac{5}{2}$

11. The area of the land is the part of the whole (acre):
$50 \text{ yd} \times 30 \text{ yd} = 1{,}500 \text{ sq yd}$

The fraction is $\dfrac{1{,}5\cancel{00}}{4{,}9\cancel{00}} = \dfrac{15}{49}$

So the parcel of land is $\dfrac{15}{49}$ of an acre.

12. One common denominator is the LCM of 24 and 16.

$24 = 2^3 \times 3 \qquad 16 = 2^4$

$\text{LCM} = 2^4 \times 3 = 16 \times 3 = 48$

$\dfrac{13}{24} = \dfrac{13 \cdot 2}{24 \cdot 2} = \dfrac{26}{48}$

$\dfrac{11}{16} = \dfrac{11 \cdot 3}{16 \cdot 3} = \dfrac{33}{48}$

$\dfrac{11}{16} > \dfrac{13}{24}$ because $\dfrac{33}{48} > \dfrac{26}{48}$

13. $10 = 2 \times 5 \quad 30 = 2 \times 3 \times 5 \quad 15 = 3 \times 5$

$\text{LCM} = 2 \times 3 \times 5 = 30$

$\dfrac{9}{10} = \dfrac{9 \cdot 3}{10 \cdot 3} = \dfrac{27}{30}$

$\dfrac{8}{15} = \dfrac{8 \cdot 2}{15 \cdot 2} = \dfrac{16}{30}$

$\dfrac{23}{30} = \dfrac{23}{30}$

$\dfrac{16}{30} < \dfrac{23}{30} < \dfrac{27}{30}$, or $\dfrac{8}{15} < \dfrac{23}{30} < \dfrac{9}{10}$

14. $\dfrac{1}{3} = \dfrac{1 \cdot 8}{3 \cdot 8} = \dfrac{8}{24}$

$\dfrac{7}{24} = \dfrac{7}{24}$

You spend more time working because $\dfrac{1}{3} > \dfrac{7}{24}$.

Exercises

1. There are 3 equal parts of which 1 part is shaded.
The fraction is $\dfrac{1}{3}$.

3. There are 6 equal parts of which 3 parts are shaded.
The fraction is $\dfrac{3}{6}$.

5. The wholes are divided into 4 equal parts. There are 1 whole and $\dfrac{1}{4}$ of a whole shaded. The mixed number is $1\dfrac{1}{4}$.

7. The wholes are divided into 4 equal parts. There are 3 wholes and $\dfrac{2}{4}$ of a whole shaded. The mixed number is $3\dfrac{2}{4}$.

9. $\frac{5}{8}$

11. $\frac{2}{9}$

13. $\frac{6}{6}$

15. $\frac{6}{5}$

17. $2\frac{1}{2}$

19. $1\frac{2}{3}$

21. $\frac{3}{4}$, proper **23.** $\frac{10}{9}$, improper

25. $16\frac{2}{3}$, mixed number **27.** $\frac{5}{5}$, improper

29. $\frac{5}{8}$, proper **31.** $66\frac{2}{3}$, mixed number

33. $2\frac{3}{5} = \frac{(5\times2)+3}{5} = \frac{13}{5}$ **35.** $6\frac{1}{9} = \frac{(9\times6)+1}{9} = \frac{55}{9}$

37. $11\frac{2}{5} = \frac{(5\times11)+2}{5} = \frac{57}{5}$

39. $5 = \frac{5}{1}$ **41.** $7\frac{3}{8} = \frac{(8\times7)+3}{8} = \frac{59}{8}$

43. $9\frac{7}{9} = \frac{(9\times9)+7}{9} = \frac{88}{9}$

45. $12\frac{2}{3} = \frac{(3\times12)+2}{3} = \frac{38}{3}$

47. $19\frac{3}{5} = \frac{(5\times19)+3}{5} = \frac{98}{5}$

49. $14 = \frac{14}{1}$

51. $4\frac{10}{11} = \frac{(11\times4)+10}{11} = \frac{54}{11}$

53. $8\frac{3}{14} = \frac{(14\times8)+3}{14} = \frac{115}{14}$

55. $8\frac{2}{25} = \frac{(25\times8)+2}{25} = \frac{202}{25}$

57. $\frac{4}{3} = 3\overline{)4}^{\,1\ R1}$ $\frac{4}{3} = 1\frac{1}{3}$

59. $\frac{10}{9} = 9\overline{)10}^{\,1\ R1}$ $\frac{10}{9} = 1\frac{1}{9}$

61. $\frac{9}{3} = 3\overline{)9}^{\,3\ R0}$ $\frac{9}{3} = 3$

63. $\frac{15}{15} = 15\overline{)15}^{\,1\ R0}$ $\frac{15}{15} = 1$

65. $\frac{99}{5} = 5\overline{)99}^{\,19\ R4}$ $\frac{99}{5} = 19\frac{4}{5}$

67. $\frac{82}{9} = 9\overline{)82}^{\,9\ R1}$ $\frac{82}{9} = 9\frac{1}{9}$

69. $\frac{45}{45} = 45\overline{)45}^{\,1\ R0}$ $\frac{45}{45} = 1$

71. $\frac{74}{9} = 9\overline{)74}^{\,8\ R2}$ $\frac{74}{9} = 8\frac{2}{9}$

73. $\frac{27}{2} = 2\overline{)27}^{\,13\ R1}$ $\frac{27}{2} = 13\frac{1}{2}$

75. $\frac{100}{9} = 9\overline{)100}^{\,11\ R1}$ $\frac{100}{9} = 11\frac{1}{9}$

77. $\frac{27}{1} = 1\overline{)27}^{\,27\ R0}$ $\frac{27}{1} = 27$

79. $\frac{56}{7} = 7\overline{)56}^{\,8\ R0}$ $\frac{56}{7} = 8$

81. Possible answer: **83.** Possible answer:

$\frac{1}{8} = \frac{1\cdot2}{8\cdot2} = \frac{2}{16}$ $\frac{2}{11} = \frac{2\cdot2}{11\cdot2} = \frac{4}{22}$

$\frac{1}{8} = \frac{1\cdot3}{8\cdot3} = \frac{3}{24}$ $\frac{2}{11} = \frac{2\cdot3}{11\cdot3} = \frac{6}{33}$

85. Possible answer:

$$\frac{3}{4} = \frac{3\cdot 2}{4\cdot 2} = \frac{6}{8}$$

$$\frac{3}{4} = \frac{3\cdot 3}{4\cdot 3} = \frac{9}{12}$$

87. Possible answer:

$$\frac{1}{7} = \frac{1\cdot 2}{7\cdot 2} = \frac{2}{14}$$

$$\frac{1}{7} = \frac{1\cdot 3}{7\cdot 3} = \frac{3}{21}$$

101.

$$\frac{4}{9} = \frac{n}{81}$$

$$\frac{4}{9} = \frac{n}{9\cdot 9}$$

$$\frac{4\cdot 9}{9\cdot 9} = \frac{n}{9\cdot 9}$$

$$n = 36$$

Check: $\quad \dfrac{4}{9} \overset{?}{=} \dfrac{36}{81}$

$$4\cdot 81 \overset{?}{=} 9\cdot 36$$

$$324 \overset{\checkmark}{=} 324$$

103.

$$\frac{6}{7} = \frac{n}{49}$$

$$\frac{6}{7} = \frac{n}{7\cdot 7}$$

$$\frac{6\cdot 7}{7\cdot 7} = \frac{n}{7\cdot 7}$$

$$n = 42$$

Check: $\quad \dfrac{6}{7} \overset{?}{=} \dfrac{42}{49}$

$$6\cdot 49 \overset{?}{=} 7\cdot 42$$

$$294 \overset{\checkmark}{=} 294$$

89.

$$\frac{3}{4} = \frac{n}{12}$$

$$\frac{3}{4} = \frac{n}{4\cdot 3}$$

$$\frac{3\cdot 3}{4\cdot 3} = \frac{n}{4\cdot 3}$$

$$n = 9$$

Check: $\quad \dfrac{3}{4} \overset{?}{=} \dfrac{9}{12}$

$$3\cdot 12 \overset{?}{=} 4\cdot 9$$

$$36 \overset{\checkmark}{=} 36$$

91.

$$\frac{5}{8} = \frac{n}{24}$$

$$\frac{5}{8} = \frac{n}{8\cdot 3}$$

$$\frac{5\cdot 3}{8\cdot 3} = \frac{n}{8\cdot 3}$$

$$n = 15$$

Check: $\quad \dfrac{5}{8} \overset{?}{=} \dfrac{15}{24}$

$$5\cdot 24 \overset{?}{=} 8\cdot 15$$

$$120 \overset{\checkmark}{=} 120$$

105.

$$\frac{2}{17} = \frac{n}{51}$$

$$\frac{2}{17} = \frac{n}{17\cdot 3}$$

$$\frac{2\cdot 3}{17\cdot 3} = \frac{n}{17\cdot 3}$$

$$n = 6$$

Check: $\quad \dfrac{2}{17} \overset{?}{=} \dfrac{6}{51}$

$$2\cdot 51 \overset{?}{=} 17\cdot 6$$

$$102 \overset{\checkmark}{=} 102$$

107.

$$\frac{7}{12} = \frac{n}{84}$$

$$\frac{7}{12} = \frac{n}{12\cdot 7}$$

$$\frac{7\cdot 7}{12\cdot 7} = \frac{n}{12\cdot 7}$$

$$n = 49$$

Check: $\quad \dfrac{7}{12} \overset{?}{=} \dfrac{49}{84}$

$$7\cdot 84 \overset{?}{=} 12\cdot 49$$

$$588 \overset{\checkmark}{=} 588$$

93.

$$4 = \frac{n}{10}$$

$$\frac{4}{1} = \frac{n}{1\cdot 10}$$

$$\frac{4\cdot 10}{1\cdot 10} = \frac{n}{1\cdot 10}$$

$$n = 40$$

Check: $\quad \dfrac{4}{1} \overset{?}{=} \dfrac{40}{10}$

$$4\cdot 10 \overset{?}{=} 1\cdot 40$$

$$40 \overset{\checkmark}{=} 40$$

95.

$$\frac{3}{5} = \frac{n}{60}$$

$$\frac{3}{5} = \frac{n}{5\cdot 12}$$

$$\frac{3\cdot 12}{5\cdot 12} = \frac{n}{5\cdot 12}$$

$$n = 36$$

Check: $\quad \dfrac{3}{5} \overset{?}{=} \dfrac{36}{60}$

$$3\cdot 60 \overset{?}{=} 5\cdot 36$$

$$180 \overset{\checkmark}{=} 180$$

109.

$$\frac{2}{3} = \frac{n}{48}$$

$$\frac{2}{3} = \frac{n}{3\cdot 16}$$

$$\frac{2\cdot 16}{3\cdot 16} = \frac{n}{3\cdot 16}$$

$$n = 32$$

Check: $\quad \dfrac{2}{3} \overset{?}{=} \dfrac{32}{48}$

$$2\cdot 48 \overset{?}{=} 3\cdot 32$$

$$96 \overset{\checkmark}{=} 96$$

111.

$$\frac{3}{10} = \frac{n}{100}$$

$$\frac{3}{10} = \frac{n}{10\cdot 10}$$

$$\frac{3\cdot 10}{10\cdot 10} = \frac{n}{10\cdot 10}$$

$$n = 30$$

Check: $\quad \dfrac{3}{10} \overset{?}{=} \dfrac{30}{100}$

$$3\cdot 100 \overset{?}{=} 10\cdot 30$$

$$300 \overset{\checkmark}{=} 300$$

97.

$$\frac{5}{8} = \frac{n}{64}$$

$$\frac{5}{8} = \frac{n}{8\cdot 8}$$

$$\frac{5\cdot 8}{8\cdot 8} = \frac{n}{8\cdot 8}$$

$$n = 40$$

Check: $\quad \dfrac{5}{8} \overset{?}{=} \dfrac{40}{64}$

$$5\cdot 64 \overset{?}{=} 8\cdot 40$$

$$320 \overset{\checkmark}{=} 320$$

99.

$$3 = \frac{n}{18}$$

$$\frac{3}{1} = \frac{n}{1\cdot 18}$$

$$\frac{3\cdot 18}{1\cdot 18} = \frac{n}{1\cdot 18}$$

$$n = 54$$

Check: $\quad \dfrac{3}{1} \overset{?}{=} \dfrac{54}{18}$

$$3\cdot 18 \overset{?}{=} 1\cdot 54$$

$$54 \overset{\checkmark}{=} 54$$

113. $\quad \dfrac{2}{4} = \dfrac{\cancel{2}^{1}\cdot 1}{\cancel{2}_{1}\cdot 2} = \dfrac{1}{2}$

115. $\quad \dfrac{6}{9} = \dfrac{2\cdot \cancel{3}^{1}}{3\cdot \cancel{3}_{1}} = \dfrac{2}{3}$

117. $\quad \dfrac{10}{10} = \dfrac{\cancel{2}^{1}\cdot \cancel{5}^{1}}{\cancel{2}_{1}\cdot \cancel{5}_{1}} = 1$

119. $\quad \dfrac{5}{15} = \dfrac{1\cdot \cancel{5}^{1}}{3\cdot \cancel{5}_{1}} = \dfrac{1}{3}$

121. $\quad \dfrac{42}{10} = \dfrac{\cancel{2}^{1}\cdot 3\cdot 7}{\cancel{2}_{1}\cdot 5} = \dfrac{21}{5} \text{ or } 4\dfrac{1}{5}$

123. $\dfrac{66}{99} = \dfrac{2 \cdot \cancel{33}}{3 \cdot \cancel{33}} = \dfrac{2}{3}$ **125.** $\dfrac{25}{100} = \dfrac{\cancel{5} \cdot \cancel{5}}{2 \cdot 2 \cdot \cancel{5} \cdot \cancel{5}} = \dfrac{1}{4}$

127. $\dfrac{125}{1,000} = \dfrac{\cancel{5} \cdot \cancel{5} \cdot \cancel{5}}{\cancel{5} \cdot \cancel{5} \cdot \cancel{5} \cdot 8} = \dfrac{1}{8}$

129. $\dfrac{20}{16} = \dfrac{\cancel{4} \cdot 5}{\cancel{4} \cdot 4} = \dfrac{5}{4}$ or $1\dfrac{1}{4}$

131. $\dfrac{66}{32} = \dfrac{\cancel{2} \cdot 33}{\cancel{2} \cdot 16} = \dfrac{33}{16}$ or $2\dfrac{1}{16}$

133. $\dfrac{18}{32} = \dfrac{\cancel{2} \cdot 9}{\cancel{2} \cdot 16} = \dfrac{9}{16}$

135. $\dfrac{50}{1,000} = \dfrac{\cancel{50} \cdot 1}{\cancel{50} \cdot 20} = \dfrac{1}{20}$

137. $\dfrac{36}{28} = \dfrac{\cancel{4} \cdot 9}{\cancel{4} \cdot 7} = \dfrac{9}{7}$ or $1\dfrac{2}{7}$

139. $\dfrac{19}{51} = \dfrac{1 \cdot 19}{3 \cdot 17} = \dfrac{19}{51}$ **141.** $\dfrac{27}{9} = \dfrac{\cancel{9} \cdot 3}{\cancel{9} \cdot 1} = \dfrac{3}{1} = 3$

143. $\dfrac{12}{84} = \dfrac{1 \cdot \cancel{12}}{7 \cdot \cancel{12}} = \dfrac{1}{7}$ **145.** $\dfrac{36}{48} = \dfrac{\cancel{12} \cdot 3}{\cancel{12} \cdot 4} = \dfrac{3}{4}$

147. $\dfrac{375}{1,000} = \dfrac{\cancel{25} \cdot 3 \cdot \cancel{5}}{\cancel{25} \cdot 8 \cdot \cancel{5}} = \dfrac{3}{8}$

149. $4\dfrac{71}{142} = 4\dfrac{1 \cdot \cancel{71}}{2 \cdot \cancel{71}} = 4\dfrac{1}{2}$

151. $5\dfrac{200}{300} = 5\dfrac{2 \cdot \cancel{100}}{3 \cdot \cancel{100}} = 5\dfrac{2}{3}$

153. $7\dfrac{6}{15} = 7\dfrac{2 \cdot \cancel{3}}{5 \cdot \cancel{3}} = 7\dfrac{2}{5}$

155. $2\dfrac{100}{100} = 2 + 1 = 3$

157. $\dfrac{7}{20} < \dfrac{11}{20}$ because $7 < 11$

159. $\dfrac{1}{8} > \dfrac{1}{9}$ because $\dfrac{9}{72} > \dfrac{8}{72}$

161. $\dfrac{2}{3} = \dfrac{6}{9}$ because $2 \cdot 9 = 3 \cdot 6, 18 = 18$

163. $2\dfrac{1}{3} < 2\dfrac{9}{15}$ because $\dfrac{7}{3} < \dfrac{39}{15}$ since $\dfrac{35}{15} < \dfrac{39}{15}$

165. $2 = 2 \quad 3 = 3 \quad 4 = 2^2$

LCM $= 2^2 \cdot 3 = 4 \cdot 3 = 12$

$\dfrac{1}{2} = \dfrac{1 \cdot 6}{2 \cdot 6} = \dfrac{6}{12}$

$\dfrac{1}{3} = \dfrac{1 \cdot 4}{3 \cdot 4} = \dfrac{4}{12}$

$\dfrac{1}{4} = \dfrac{1 \cdot 3}{4 \cdot 3} = \dfrac{3}{12}$

The fraction between $\dfrac{1}{4}$ and $\dfrac{1}{2}$ is $\dfrac{1}{3}$.

167. $3 = 3 \quad 12 = 2^2 \cdot 3 \quad 6 = 2 \cdot 3$

LCM $= 2^2 \cdot 3 = 4 \cdot 3 = 12$

$\dfrac{2}{3} = \dfrac{2 \cdot 4}{3 \cdot 4} = \dfrac{8}{12}$

$\dfrac{7}{12} = \dfrac{7}{12}$

$\dfrac{5}{6} = \dfrac{5 \cdot 2}{6 \cdot 2} = \dfrac{10}{12}$

The fraction between $\dfrac{7}{12}$ and $\dfrac{5}{6}$ is $\dfrac{2}{3}$.

169. $5 = 5 \quad 3 = 3 \quad 9 = 3^2$

LCM $= 3^3 \cdot 5 = 9 \cdot 5 = 45$

$\dfrac{3}{5} = \dfrac{3 \cdot 9}{5 \cdot 9} = \dfrac{27}{45}$

$\dfrac{2}{3} = \dfrac{2 \cdot 15}{3 \cdot 15} = \dfrac{30}{45}$

$\dfrac{8}{9} = \dfrac{8 \cdot 5}{9 \cdot 5} = \dfrac{40}{45}$

The fraction between $\dfrac{3}{5}$ and $\dfrac{8}{9}$ is $\dfrac{2}{3}$.

171. The total number of senators is $98 + 2 = 100$.

    a. $\dfrac{\text{number of female senators}}{\text{number of senators}} = \dfrac{2}{100} = \dfrac{1}{50}$

    $\dfrac{1}{50}$ of the senators were women.

    b. $\dfrac{\text{number of male senators}}{\text{number of senators}} = \dfrac{98}{100} = \dfrac{49}{50}$

    $\dfrac{49}{50}$ of the senators were men.

173. If 30 articles are accepted, then $50 - 30$, or 20 articles are rejected.

    $\dfrac{\text{number of articles rejected}}{\text{total number of articles}} = \dfrac{20}{50} = \dfrac{2}{5}$

    $\dfrac{2}{5}$ of the articles are rejected.

175. $\dfrac{1}{4} = \dfrac{1 \cdot 25}{4 \cdot 25} = \dfrac{25}{100}$

    Since $\dfrac{23}{100} < \dfrac{25}{100}$, the gutter did not overflow.

177. a. The LCM of 8 and 16 is 16.

    $\dfrac{1}{8} = \dfrac{1 \cdot 2}{8 \cdot 2} = \dfrac{2}{16}$ $\dfrac{3}{8} = \dfrac{3 \cdot 2}{8 \cdot 2} = \dfrac{6}{16}$ $\dfrac{3}{16} = \dfrac{3}{16}$

    The $\dfrac{3}{8}$-in. hole is the largest.

    b. $\dfrac{1}{8} = \dfrac{1 \cdot 4}{8 \cdot 4} = \dfrac{4}{32}$ $\dfrac{3}{16} = \dfrac{3 \cdot 2}{16 \cdot 2} = \dfrac{6}{32}$

    $\dfrac{3}{8} = \dfrac{3 \cdot 4}{8 \cdot 4} = \dfrac{12}{32}$

    No, the $\dfrac{5}{32}$-in. bolt will fit through only the $\dfrac{1}{8}$-in. hole.

179. $\text{average rainfall} = \dfrac{2 \text{ in.} + 1 \text{ in.} + 2 \text{ in.} + 0 \text{ in.}}{4}$

    $= \dfrac{5}{4} \text{ in.} = 1\dfrac{1}{4}\text{in.}$

2.3   Adding and Subtracting Fractions

Practice

1. $\dfrac{7}{15} + \dfrac{3}{15} = \dfrac{7 + 3}{15} = \dfrac{10}{15} = \dfrac{2}{3}$

2. $\dfrac{13}{40} + \dfrac{11}{40} + \dfrac{28}{40} = \dfrac{47}{40} = 1\dfrac{7}{40}$

3. $\dfrac{19}{20} - \dfrac{11}{20} = \dfrac{19 - 11}{20} = \dfrac{8}{20} = \dfrac{2}{5}$

4. From college to library via city hall:

    $\dfrac{3}{8} \text{ mi} + \dfrac{5}{8} \text{ mi} = \dfrac{8}{8} \text{ mi} = 1 \text{ mi}$

    From college to library via hospital:

    $\dfrac{1}{8} \text{ mi} + \dfrac{7}{8} \text{ mi} = \dfrac{8}{8} \text{ mi} = 1 \text{ mi}$

    Neither route is shorter since they are both 1 mi.

5. $\dfrac{3}{4} \text{ yd} - \dfrac{1}{4} \text{ yd} = \dfrac{3 - 1}{4} \text{ yd} = \dfrac{2}{4} \text{ yd} = \dfrac{1}{2} \text{ yd}$

    There will be $\dfrac{1}{2}$ yd of material left over.

6. $\begin{aligned} \dfrac{11}{12} &= \dfrac{11}{12} \\ +\dfrac{3}{4} &= +\dfrac{9}{12} \\ \hline \dfrac{20}{12} &= \dfrac{5}{3}, \text{ or } 1\dfrac{2}{3} \end{aligned}$

7. $\begin{aligned} \dfrac{4}{5} &= \dfrac{8}{10} \\ -\dfrac{1}{2} &= -\dfrac{5}{10} \\ \hline &\quad\dfrac{3}{10} \end{aligned}$

8. $\begin{aligned} \dfrac{1}{3} &= \dfrac{3}{9} \\ -\dfrac{2}{9} &= -\dfrac{2}{9} \\ \hline &\quad\dfrac{1}{9} \end{aligned}$ $\begin{aligned} \dfrac{1}{9} &= \dfrac{8}{72} \\ +\dfrac{7}{8} &= +\dfrac{63}{72} \\ \hline &\quad\dfrac{71}{72} \end{aligned}$

9. $\begin{aligned} \dfrac{1}{2} &= \dfrac{5}{10} \\ \dfrac{3}{5} &= \dfrac{6}{10} \\ +\dfrac{9}{10} &= +\dfrac{9}{10} \\ \hline \dfrac{20}{10} &= 2 \end{aligned}$

    The perimeter is 2 mi.

10. $\begin{aligned} 25&\dfrac{3}{10} \\ +9&\dfrac{9}{10} \\ \hline 34&\dfrac{12}{10} = 34 + 1\dfrac{2}{10} = 35\dfrac{1}{5} \end{aligned}$

11.
$$2\frac{5}{16}$$
$$1\frac{3}{16}$$
$$+\ 4$$
$$\overline{7\frac{8}{16}=7\frac{1}{2}}$$

12.
$$9\frac{7}{10}$$
$$-5\frac{3}{10}$$
$$\overline{4\frac{4}{10}=4\frac{2}{5}}$$

13.
$$1\frac{1}{2}$$
$$+2\frac{1}{2}$$
$$\overline{3\frac{2}{2}=3+1=4}$$

The third-place horse lost by 4 lengths.

14.
$$7\frac{3}{16}$$
$$-5\frac{1}{16}$$
$$\overline{2\frac{2}{16}=2\frac{1}{8}}$$

The difference in their heights is $2\frac{1}{8}$ in.

15.
$$3\frac{1}{2}\ =\ 3\frac{4}{8}$$
$$+4\frac{1}{8}\ =\ +4\frac{1}{8}$$
$$\overline{\phantom{+4\frac{1}{8}=+}7\frac{5}{8}}$$

16.
$$8\frac{2}{3}\ =\ 8\frac{6}{4}$$
$$-4\frac{1}{6}\ =\ -4\frac{1}{6}$$
$$\overline{\phantom{-4\frac{1}{6}=}4\frac{3}{6}\text{ or }4\frac{1}{2}}$$

17.
$$5\frac{5}{8}\ =\ 5\frac{15}{24}$$
$$3\frac{1}{6}\ =\ 3\frac{4}{24}$$
$$+2\frac{5}{12}\ =\ +2\frac{10}{24}$$
$$\overline{\phantom{+2\frac{5}{12}=}10\frac{29}{24}=11\frac{5}{24}}$$

18.
$$3\ =\ \ \ 3$$
$$2\frac{3}{4}\ =\ 2\frac{2}{4}$$
$$+8\frac{1}{2}\ =\ +8\frac{2}{4}$$
$$\overline{\phantom{+8\frac{1}{2}=}13\frac{5}{4}=14\frac{1}{4}}$$

$$20\frac{1}{2}\ =\ 20\frac{2}{4}$$
$$-14\frac{1}{4}=-14\frac{1}{4}$$
$$\overline{\phantom{-14\frac{1}{4}=}6\frac{1}{4}}$$

The left side is $6\frac{1}{4}$ mi long.

19.
$$9\ =\ 8\frac{7}{7}$$
$$-7\frac{5}{7}=-7\frac{5}{7}$$
$$\overline{\phantom{-7\frac{5}{7}=}1\frac{2}{7}}$$

20.
$$15\frac{1}{12}=14\frac{13}{12}$$
$$-9\frac{11}{12}=-9\frac{11}{12}$$
$$\overline{\phantom{-9\frac{11}{12}=}5\frac{2}{12}\text{ or }5\frac{1}{6}}$$

21.
$$16\frac{2}{5}=16\frac{16}{40}=15\frac{56}{40}$$
$$-3\frac{7}{8}=-3\frac{35}{40}=-3\frac{35}{40}$$
$$\overline{\phantom{-3\frac{7}{8}=-3\frac{35}{40}=}12\frac{21}{40}}$$

22.
$$30\frac{1}{2}\ =\ 30\frac{4}{8}\ =\ 29\frac{12}{8}$$
$$-26\frac{7}{8}=-26\frac{7}{8}=-26\frac{7}{8}$$
$$\overline{\phantom{-26\frac{7}{8}=-26\frac{7}{8}=}3\frac{5}{8}}$$

No, there will not be enough paper because there will be only $3\frac{5}{8}$ yd left.

23.
$$8\frac{1}{4}\ =\ 8\frac{5}{20}=\ 7\frac{25}{20}\qquad 4\frac{9}{20}=\ 4\frac{9}{20}$$
$$-3\frac{4}{5}=-3\frac{16}{20}=-3\frac{16}{20}\qquad +1\frac{9}{10}=+1\frac{18}{20}$$
$$\overline{\phantom{-3\frac{4}{5}=-3\frac{16}{20}=}4\frac{9}{20}}\qquad\overline{\phantom{+1\frac{9}{10}=}5\frac{27}{20}=6\frac{7}{20}}$$

Check:
$$8\frac{1}{4}-3\frac{4}{5}+1\frac{9}{10}$$
$$\downarrow\quad\ \downarrow\quad\ \downarrow$$
$$8\ -\ 4\ +\ 2=6$$

The estimate is sufficiently close to the answer.

Exercises

1. $\dfrac{2}{3}+\dfrac{2}{3}=\dfrac{4}{3}=1\dfrac{1}{3}$ **3.** $\dfrac{3}{5}+\dfrac{3}{5}=\dfrac{6}{5}=1\dfrac{1}{5}$

5. $\dfrac{5}{8}+\dfrac{5}{8}=\dfrac{10}{8}=1\dfrac{2}{8}\text{ or }1\dfrac{1}{4}$

7. $\dfrac{11}{12}+\dfrac{7}{12}=\dfrac{18}{12}=1\dfrac{6}{12}=1\dfrac{1}{2}$

9. $\dfrac{1}{5}+\dfrac{1}{5}+\dfrac{2}{5}=\dfrac{4}{5}$

11. $\dfrac{3}{20}+\dfrac{1}{20}+\dfrac{8}{20}=\dfrac{12}{20}=\dfrac{3}{5}$

13.
$$\frac{2}{3}\ =\ \frac{4}{6}$$
$$+\frac{1}{2}\ =\ +\frac{3}{6}$$
$$\overline{\phantom{+\frac{1}{2}=+}\frac{7}{6}=1\frac{1}{6}}$$

15.
$$\frac{1}{2}\ =\ \frac{4}{8}$$
$$+\frac{3}{8}\ =\ +\frac{3}{8}$$
$$\overline{\phantom{+\frac{3}{8}=+}\frac{7}{8}}$$

17. $\dfrac{7}{10} = \dfrac{70}{100}$

$+\dfrac{7}{100} = +\dfrac{7}{100}$

$\dfrac{77}{100}$

19. $\dfrac{4}{5} = \dfrac{32}{40}$

$+\dfrac{1}{8} = +\dfrac{5}{40}$

$\dfrac{37}{40}$

21. $\dfrac{2}{9} = \dfrac{16}{72}$

$+\dfrac{5}{8} = +\dfrac{45}{72}$

$\dfrac{61}{72}$

23. $\dfrac{3}{8} = \dfrac{9}{24}$

$+\dfrac{1}{6} = +\dfrac{4}{24}$

$\dfrac{13}{24}$

25. $\dfrac{4}{9} = \dfrac{8}{18}$

$+\dfrac{5}{6} = +\dfrac{15}{18}$

$\dfrac{23}{18} = 1\dfrac{5}{18}$

27. $\dfrac{87}{100} = \dfrac{87}{100}$

$+\dfrac{3}{10} = +\dfrac{30}{100}$

$\dfrac{117}{100} = 1\dfrac{17}{100}$

29. $\dfrac{1}{4}\,\text{hr} = \dfrac{1}{4}\,\text{hr}$

$+\dfrac{1}{2}\,\text{hr} = +\dfrac{2}{4}\,\text{hr}$

$\dfrac{3}{4}\,\text{hr}$

31. $\dfrac{1}{4}\,\text{mi} = \dfrac{3}{12}\,\text{mi}$

$+\dfrac{1}{6}\,\text{mi} = +\dfrac{2}{12}\,\text{mi}$

$\dfrac{5}{12}\,\text{mi}$

33. $\dfrac{1}{2} = \dfrac{6}{12}$

$\dfrac{1}{3} = \dfrac{4}{12}$

$+\dfrac{1}{4} = +\dfrac{3}{12}$

$\dfrac{13}{12} = 1\dfrac{1}{12}$

35. $\dfrac{7}{8} = \dfrac{35}{40}$

$\dfrac{1}{5} = \dfrac{8}{40}$

$+\dfrac{1}{4} = +\dfrac{10}{40}$

$\dfrac{53}{40} = 1\dfrac{13}{40}$

37. $1\dfrac{1}{3}$

$+2\dfrac{1}{3}$

$3\dfrac{2}{3}$

Check: $1\dfrac{1}{2} + 2\dfrac{1}{3}$

$\downarrow \qquad \downarrow$

$1 + 2 = 3$

39. $8\dfrac{1}{10}$

$+7\dfrac{3}{10}$

$15\dfrac{4}{10} = 15\dfrac{2}{5}$

Check: $8\dfrac{1}{10} + 7\dfrac{3}{10}$

$\downarrow \qquad \downarrow$

$8 + 7 = 15$

41. $7\dfrac{3}{10}$

$+6\dfrac{9}{10}$

$13\dfrac{12}{10} = 14\dfrac{2}{10} = 14\dfrac{1}{5}$

Check: $7\dfrac{3}{10} + 6\dfrac{9}{10}$

$\downarrow \qquad \downarrow$

$7 + 7 = 14$

43. $5\dfrac{1}{6}$

$+9\dfrac{5}{6}$

$14\dfrac{6}{6} = 15$

Check: $5\dfrac{1}{6} + 9\dfrac{5}{6}$

$\downarrow \qquad \downarrow$

$5 + 10 = 15$

45. $4\dfrac{1}{4}$

$+3\dfrac{3}{4}$

$7\dfrac{4}{4} = 8$

Check: $4\dfrac{1}{4} + 3\dfrac{3}{4}$

$\downarrow \qquad \downarrow$

$4 + 4 = 8$

47. $2\dfrac{4}{5}$

$+2\dfrac{3}{5}$

$4\dfrac{7}{5} = 5\dfrac{2}{5}$

Check: $2\dfrac{4}{5} + 2\dfrac{3}{5}$

$\downarrow \qquad \downarrow$

$3 + 3 = 6$

49. $37\dfrac{1}{2} = 37\dfrac{3}{6}$

$+5\dfrac{1}{3} = +5\dfrac{2}{6}$

$42\dfrac{5}{6}$

Check: $37\dfrac{1}{2} + 5\dfrac{1}{3}$

$\downarrow \qquad \downarrow$

$38 + 5 = 43$

51. $8\dfrac{1}{12} = 8\dfrac{1}{12}$

$+6\dfrac{5}{6} = +6\dfrac{10}{12}$

$14\dfrac{11}{12}$

Check: $8\dfrac{1}{12} + 6\dfrac{5}{6}$

$\downarrow \qquad \downarrow$

$8 + 7 = 15$

53. $5\dfrac{1}{4} = 5\dfrac{3}{12}$

$+5\dfrac{1}{6} = +5\dfrac{2}{12}$

$10\dfrac{5}{12}$

Check: $5\dfrac{1}{4} + 5\dfrac{1}{6}$

$\downarrow \qquad \downarrow$

$5 + 5 = 10$

55. $3\dfrac{1}{3} = 3\dfrac{5}{15}$

$+\dfrac{2}{5} = +\dfrac{6}{15}$

$3\dfrac{11}{15}$

Check: $3\dfrac{1}{3} + \dfrac{2}{5}$

$\downarrow \qquad \downarrow$

$3 + 0 = 3$

57. $8\frac{1}{5} = 8\frac{3}{15}$

$+5\frac{2}{3} = +5\frac{10}{15}$

$\phantom{+5\frac{2}{3}} = 13\frac{13}{15}$

Check: $8\frac{1}{5} + 5\frac{2}{3}$

$\downarrow \qquad \downarrow$

$8 \; + \; 6 = 14$

59. $\frac{2}{3} = \frac{16}{24}$

$+6\frac{1}{8} = +6\frac{3}{24}$

$\phantom{+6\frac{1}{8}} = 6\frac{19}{24}$

Check: $\frac{2}{3} + 6\frac{1}{8}$

$\downarrow \qquad \downarrow$

$1 \; + \; 6 = 7$

Check: $22\frac{3}{5} + 22\frac{9}{10}$

$\downarrow \qquad \downarrow$

$23 \; + \; 23 = 46$

69. $10\frac{5}{6} \qquad 10\frac{10}{12}$

$+8\frac{1}{4} = +8\frac{3}{12}$

$\phantom{+8\frac{1}{4}=} 18\frac{13}{12} \text{ or } 19\frac{1}{12}$

Check: $10\frac{5}{6} + 8\frac{1}{4}$

$\downarrow \qquad \downarrow$

$11 \; + \; 8 = 19$

61. $9\frac{2}{3} = 9\frac{8}{12}$

$+10\frac{7}{12} = +1\frac{7}{12}$

$\phantom{+10\frac{7}{12}=} 19\frac{15}{12} = 20\frac{3}{12} \text{ or } 20\frac{1}{4}$

Check: $9\frac{2}{3} + 10\frac{7}{12}$

$\downarrow \qquad \downarrow$

$10 \; + \; 11 = 21$

71. $30\frac{21}{100} = 30\frac{21}{100}$

$+5\frac{17}{20} = +5\frac{85}{100}$

$\phantom{+5\frac{17}{20}=} 35\frac{106}{100} = 36\frac{6}{100} \text{ or } 36\frac{3}{50}$

Check: $30\frac{21}{100} + 5\frac{17}{20}$

$\downarrow \qquad \downarrow$

$30 \; + \; 6 = 36$

63. $65\frac{7}{10} = 65\frac{70}{100}$

$+30\frac{57}{100} = +30\frac{57}{100}$

$\phantom{+30\frac{57}{100}=} 95\frac{127}{100} = 96\frac{27}{100}$

Check: $65\frac{7}{10} + 30\frac{57}{100}$

$\downarrow \qquad \downarrow$

$66 \; + \; 31 = 97$

73. $80\frac{1}{3} = 80\frac{4}{12}$

$\frac{3}{4} = \frac{9}{12}$

$+10\frac{1}{2} = +10\frac{6}{12}$

$\phantom{+10\frac{1}{2}=} 90\frac{19}{12} = 91\frac{7}{12}$

Check: $80\frac{1}{3} + \frac{3}{4} + 10\frac{1}{2}$

$\downarrow \quad \downarrow \quad \downarrow$

$80 \; + \; 1 \; + 11 = 92$

65. $6\frac{1}{10} = 6\frac{10}{100}$

$+3\frac{93}{100} = +3\frac{93}{100}$

$\phantom{+3\frac{93}{100}=} 9\frac{103}{100} = 10\frac{3}{100}$

Check: $6\frac{1}{10} + 3\frac{93}{100}$

$\downarrow \qquad \downarrow$

$6 \; + \; 4 = 10$

75. $5\frac{1}{2} \text{ hr} = 5\frac{1}{4} \text{ hr}$

$6\frac{1}{4} \text{ hr} = 6\frac{1}{4} \text{ hr}$

$+3\frac{1}{2} \text{ hr} = +3\frac{2}{4} \text{ hr}$

$\phantom{+3\frac{1}{2} \text{ hr}=} 14\frac{5}{4} \text{ hr} = 15\frac{1}{4} \text{ hr}$

Check: $5\frac{1}{2} + 6\frac{1}{4} + 3\frac{1}{2}$

$\downarrow \quad \downarrow \quad \downarrow$

$6 \; + \; 6 \; + 4 = 16$

67. $22\frac{3}{5} = 22\frac{6}{10}$

$+22\frac{9}{10} = +22\frac{9}{10}$

$\phantom{+22\frac{9}{10}=} 44\frac{15}{10} = 45\frac{5}{10} \text{ or } 45\frac{1}{2}$

77. $2\frac{1}{3}$ ft $= 2\frac{4}{12}$ ft

$2\frac{1}{4}$ ft $= 2\frac{3}{12}$ ft

$\dfrac{+2\frac{1}{6}\text{ ft}}{} = \dfrac{+2\frac{2}{12}\text{ ft}}{}$

$\phantom{+2\frac{1}{6}\text{ ft}} 6\frac{9}{12}$ ft or $6\frac{3}{4}$ ft

Check: $2\frac{1}{3} + 2\frac{1}{4} + 2\frac{1}{6}$

$\downarrow\downarrow\downarrow$

$2 + 2 + 2 = 6$ ft

79. $6\frac{7}{8}$ in. $= 6\frac{35}{40}$ in.

$2\frac{3}{4}$ in. $= 2\frac{30}{40}$ in.

$\dfrac{+1\frac{1}{5}\text{ in.}}{} = \dfrac{+1\frac{8}{40}\text{ in.}}{}$

$\phantom{+1\frac{1}{5}\text{ in.}} 9\frac{73}{40} = 10\frac{33}{40}$ in.

Check: $6\frac{7}{8} + 2\frac{3}{4} + 1\frac{1}{5}$

$\downarrow\downarrow\downarrow$

$7 + 3 + 1 = 11$ in.

81. $\frac{2}{3}$ min $= \frac{16}{24}$ min

$5\frac{1}{2}$ min $= 5\frac{12}{24}$ min

$\dfrac{+4\frac{7}{8}\text{ min}}{} = \dfrac{+4\frac{21}{24}\text{ min}}{}$

$\phantom{+4\frac{7}{8}\text{ min}} 9\frac{49}{24} = 11\frac{1}{24}$ min

Check: $\frac{2}{3} + 5\frac{1}{2} + 4\frac{7}{8}$

$\downarrow\downarrow\downarrow$

$1 + 6 + 5 = 12$ min

83. $\$20\frac{1}{16} = \$20\frac{1}{16}$

$1\frac{1}{8} = 1\frac{2}{16}$

$\dfrac{+\ 1\frac{1}{2}}{} = \dfrac{+1\frac{8}{16}}{}$

$\phantom{+\ 1\frac{1}{2}} \$22\frac{11}{16}$

Check: $20\frac{1}{16} + 1\frac{1}{8} + 1\frac{1}{2}$

$\downarrow\downarrow\downarrow$

$20 + 1 + 2 = \$23$

85. $\frac{4}{5} - \frac{3}{5} = \frac{1}{5}$

87. $\frac{7}{10} - \frac{3}{10} = \frac{4}{10} = \frac{2}{5}$

89. $\frac{23}{100} - \frac{7}{100} = \frac{16}{100} = \frac{4}{25}$

91. $\frac{3}{2} - \frac{1}{2} = \frac{2}{2} = 1$

93. $\frac{3}{4} - \frac{1}{4} = \frac{2}{4} = \frac{1}{2}$

95. $\frac{12}{5} - \frac{2}{5} = \frac{10}{5} = 2$

97. $\frac{2}{3}$ day $- \frac{1}{3}$ day $= \frac{1}{3}$ day

99. $\dfrac{3}{4} = \dfrac{9}{12}$

$\dfrac{-\dfrac{2}{3}}{} = \dfrac{-\dfrac{8}{12}}{}$

$\phantom{-\dfrac{2}{3}} \dfrac{1}{12}$

101. $\dfrac{4}{9} = \dfrac{8}{18}$

$\dfrac{-\dfrac{1}{6}}{} = \dfrac{-\dfrac{3}{18}}{}$

$\phantom{-\dfrac{1}{6}} \dfrac{5}{18}$

103. $\dfrac{9}{10} = \dfrac{90}{100}$

$\dfrac{-\dfrac{3}{100}}{} = \dfrac{-\dfrac{3}{100}}{}$

$\phantom{-\dfrac{3}{100}} \dfrac{87}{100}$

105. $\dfrac{21}{100} = \dfrac{21}{100}$

$\dfrac{-\dfrac{1}{10}}{} = \dfrac{-\dfrac{10}{100}}{}$

$\phantom{-\dfrac{1}{10}} \dfrac{11}{100}$

107. $\dfrac{4}{7} = \dfrac{8}{14}$

$\dfrac{-\dfrac{1}{2}}{} = \dfrac{-\dfrac{7}{14}}{}$

$\phantom{-\dfrac{1}{2}} \dfrac{1}{14}$

109. $\dfrac{2}{5} = \dfrac{18}{45}$

$\dfrac{-\dfrac{2}{9}}{} = \dfrac{-\dfrac{10}{45}}{}$

$\phantom{-\dfrac{2}{9}} \dfrac{8}{45}$

111. $\dfrac{2}{3} = \dfrac{4}{6}$

$\dfrac{-\dfrac{1}{6}}{} = \dfrac{-\dfrac{1}{6}}{}$

$\phantom{-\dfrac{1}{6}} \dfrac{3}{6} = \dfrac{1}{2}$

113. $\dfrac{4}{9} = \dfrac{32}{72}$

$\dfrac{-\dfrac{3}{8}}{} = \dfrac{-\dfrac{27}{72}}{}$

$\phantom{-\dfrac{3}{8}} \dfrac{5}{72}$

115. $\dfrac{3}{4} = \dfrac{15}{20}$

$\dfrac{-\dfrac{3}{5}}{} = \dfrac{-\dfrac{12}{20}}{}$

$\phantom{-\dfrac{3}{5}} \dfrac{3}{20}$

117. $\dfrac{2}{11} = \dfrac{12}{66}$

$\dfrac{-\dfrac{1}{6}}{} = \dfrac{-\dfrac{11}{66}}{}$

$\phantom{-\dfrac{1}{6}} \dfrac{1}{66}$

119. $\dfrac{5}{6} = \dfrac{5}{6}$

$\dfrac{-\dfrac{2}{3}}{} = \dfrac{-\dfrac{4}{6}}{}$

$\phantom{-\dfrac{2}{3}} \dfrac{1}{6}$

121. $5\frac{3}{7}$

$\dfrac{-1\frac{1}{7}}{}$

$\phantom{-1\frac{1}{7}} 4\frac{2}{7}$

123.

$$8\frac{4}{5}$$
$$-1\frac{2}{5}$$
$$\overline{7\frac{2}{5}}$$

125.

$$3\frac{7}{8}$$
$$-2\frac{1}{8}$$
$$\overline{1\frac{6}{8}=1\frac{3}{4}}$$

127.

$$20\frac{1}{2}$$
$$-\frac{1}{2}$$
$$\overline{20}$$

129.

$$8\frac{1}{10}$$
$$-4$$
$$\overline{4\frac{1}{10}}$$

131.

$$14\frac{1}{2}$$
$$-5$$
$$\overline{9\frac{1}{2}}$$

133.

$$2\frac{1}{3}$$
$$-2$$
$$\overline{\frac{1}{3}}$$

135.

$$7\frac{5}{8}$$
$$-3$$
$$\overline{4\frac{5}{8}}$$

137.

$$6=5\frac{3}{3}$$
$$-2\frac{2}{3}=-2\frac{2}{3}$$
$$\overline{3\frac{1}{3}}$$

139.

$$8=7\frac{10}{10}$$
$$-4\frac{7}{10}=-4\frac{7}{10}$$
$$\overline{3\frac{3}{10}}$$

141.

$$10=9\frac{3}{3}$$
$$-3\frac{2}{3}=-3\frac{2}{3}$$
$$\overline{6\frac{1}{3}}$$

143.

$$6=5\frac{2}{2}$$
$$-\frac{1}{2}=-\frac{1}{2}$$
$$\overline{5\frac{1}{2}}$$

145.

$$7\frac{1}{4}=6\frac{5}{4}$$
$$-2\frac{3}{4}=-2\frac{3}{4}$$
$$\overline{4\frac{2}{4}=4\frac{1}{2}}$$

147.

$$6\frac{1}{8}=5\frac{9}{8}$$
$$-2\frac{7}{8}=-2\frac{7}{8}$$
$$\overline{3\frac{2}{8}=3\frac{1}{4}}$$

149.

$$12\frac{2}{5}=11\frac{7}{5}$$
$$-3\frac{3}{5}=-3\frac{3}{5}$$
$$\overline{8\frac{4}{5}}$$

151.

$$8\frac{1}{3}=7\frac{4}{3}$$
$$-1\frac{2}{3}=-1\frac{2}{3}$$
$$\overline{6\frac{2}{3}}$$

153.

$$13\frac{1}{2}=13\frac{3}{6}=12\frac{9}{6}$$
$$-5\frac{2}{3}=-5\frac{4}{6}=-5\frac{4}{6}$$
$$\overline{7\frac{5}{6}}$$

155.

$$9\frac{3}{8}=9\frac{9}{24}=8\frac{33}{24}$$
$$-5\frac{5}{6}=-5\frac{20}{24}=-5\frac{20}{24}$$
$$\overline{3\frac{13}{24}}$$

157.

$$20\frac{2}{9}=20\frac{8}{36}=19\frac{44}{36}$$
$$-4\frac{5}{6}=-4\frac{30}{36}=-4\frac{30}{36}$$
$$\overline{15\frac{14}{36}=15\frac{7}{18}}$$

159.

$$3\frac{4}{5}=3\frac{24}{30}=2\frac{54}{30}$$
$$-\frac{5}{6}=-\frac{25}{30}=-\frac{25}{30}$$
$$\overline{2\frac{29}{30}}$$

161.

$$1\frac{3}{4}\text{ mi}=1\frac{3}{4}\text{ mi}$$
$$-1\frac{1}{2}\text{ mi}=-1\frac{2}{4}\text{ mi}$$
$$\overline{\frac{1}{4}\text{ mi}}$$

163.

$$10\frac{1}{12}\text{ ft}=10\frac{1}{12}\text{ ft}=9\frac{13}{12}\text{ ft}$$
$$-4\frac{2}{3}\text{ ft}=-4\frac{8}{12}\text{ ft}=-4\frac{8}{12}\text{ ft}$$
$$\overline{5\frac{5}{12}\text{ ft}}$$

165.

$$22\frac{7}{8}\text{ acres}=22\frac{35}{40}\text{ acres}=21\frac{75}{40}\text{ acres}$$
$$-8\frac{9}{10}\text{ acres}=-8\frac{36}{40}\text{ acres}=-8\frac{36}{40}\text{ acres}$$
$$\overline{13\frac{39}{40}\text{ acres}}$$

167.

$$2\frac{1}{2}\text{ pints}=2\frac{2}{4}\text{ pints}=1\frac{6}{4}\text{ pints}$$
$$-1\frac{3}{4}\text{ pints}=-1\frac{3}{4}\text{ pints}=-1\frac{3}{4}\text{ pints}$$
$$\overline{\frac{3}{4}\text{ pint}}$$

169. $\dfrac{5}{8} + \dfrac{9}{10} - \dfrac{1}{4} = \dfrac{25}{40} + \dfrac{36}{40} - \dfrac{10}{40}$

$= \dfrac{51}{40}$

$= 1\dfrac{11}{40}$

171.
$$3\dfrac{1}{2} \qquad\qquad 5 = 4\dfrac{2}{2}$$
$$+1\dfrac{1}{2} = \qquad -\dfrac{1}{2} = -\dfrac{1}{2}$$
$$\overline{\qquad\qquad}\qquad\qquad \overline{\qquad\qquad}$$
$$4\dfrac{2}{2} = 5 \qquad\qquad 4\dfrac{1}{2}$$

173.
$$12\dfrac{1}{6} = 12\dfrac{5}{30} \qquad\qquad 18\dfrac{2}{30} = 18\dfrac{2}{30} = 17\dfrac{32}{30}$$
$$+5\dfrac{9}{10} = +5\dfrac{27}{30} \qquad -1\dfrac{3}{10} = -1\dfrac{9}{30} = -1\dfrac{9}{30}$$
$$\overline{\qquad\qquad\qquad}\qquad\qquad\overline{\qquad\qquad\qquad}$$
$$17\dfrac{32}{30} = 18\dfrac{2}{30} \qquad\qquad 16\dfrac{23}{30}$$

175.
$$4\dfrac{1}{10} \qquad\qquad 7 = 6\dfrac{4}{4}$$
$$+2\dfrac{9}{10} = \qquad -3\dfrac{3}{4} = -3\dfrac{3}{4}$$
$$\overline{\qquad\qquad}\qquad\qquad \overline{\qquad\qquad}$$
$$6\dfrac{10}{10} = 7 \qquad\qquad 3\dfrac{1}{4}$$

177.
$$19\dfrac{1}{6} = 19\dfrac{5}{30} = 18\dfrac{35}{30} \qquad 10\dfrac{8}{30} = 10\dfrac{8}{30}$$
$$-8\dfrac{9}{10} = -8\dfrac{27}{30} = -8\dfrac{27}{30} \qquad -\dfrac{1}{5} = -\dfrac{6}{30}$$
$$\overline{\qquad\qquad\qquad}\qquad\qquad\overline{\qquad\qquad}$$
$$10\dfrac{8}{30} \qquad\qquad 10\dfrac{2}{30} = 10\dfrac{1}{15}$$

179. $\dfrac{3}{4}$ in. $+ \dfrac{1}{8}$ in. $= \dfrac{6}{8}$ in. $+ \dfrac{1}{8}$ in. $= \dfrac{7}{8}$ in.

The nail should be $\dfrac{7}{8}$ in. long.

181.
$$2\dfrac{1}{4}\text{ hr} = 2\dfrac{1}{4}\text{ hr}$$
$$\dfrac{1}{4}\text{ hr} = \dfrac{1}{4}\text{ hr}$$
$$+2\dfrac{1}{2}\text{ hr} = +2\dfrac{2}{4}\text{ hr}$$
$$\overline{\qquad\qquad\qquad\qquad}$$
$$4\dfrac{4}{4}\text{ hr} = 5\text{ hr}$$

The doubleheader took 5 hr to play.

183. $7\text{ mi} + 6\dfrac{3}{4}\text{ mi} + 12\dfrac{1}{2}\text{ mi} + 9\dfrac{1}{8}\text{ mi}$

$= 7\text{ mi} + 6\dfrac{6}{8}\text{ mi} + 12\dfrac{4}{8}\text{ mi} + 9\dfrac{1}{8}\text{ mi}$

$= 34\dfrac{11}{8}\text{ mi} = 35\dfrac{3}{8}\text{ mi}$

The perimeter of the figure is $35\dfrac{3}{8}$ mi.

185. $\dfrac{1}{2} + \dfrac{2}{5} = \dfrac{5}{10} + \dfrac{4}{10} = \dfrac{9}{10}$

$1 - \dfrac{9}{10} = \dfrac{10}{10} - \dfrac{9}{10} = \dfrac{1}{10}$

$\dfrac{1}{10}$ of the patients got worse.

187. The total weight of the packages on the left side of the scale is:

$$1\dfrac{1}{2}\text{ lb} = 1\dfrac{2}{4}\text{ lb}$$
$$+2\dfrac{3}{4}\text{ lb} = +2\dfrac{3}{4}\text{ lb}$$
$$\overline{\qquad\qquad\qquad\qquad}$$
$$3\dfrac{5}{4}\text{ lb} = 4\dfrac{1}{4}\text{ lb}$$

The total weight of the packages on the right side of the scale must also be $4\dfrac{1}{4}$ lb.

$$4\dfrac{1}{4}\text{ lb}$$
$$-3\dfrac{1}{4}\text{ lb}$$
$$\overline{\qquad\qquad}$$
$$1\text{ lb}$$

The weight of the small package on the right is 1 lb.

2.4   Multiplying and Dividing Fractions

Practice

1. $\dfrac{3}{4} \cdot \dfrac{5}{7} = \dfrac{3 \cdot 5}{4 \cdot 7} = \dfrac{15}{28}$

2. $\dfrac{2}{3} \times 30 = \dfrac{2}{3} \times \dfrac{30}{1} = \dfrac{2 \times 30}{3 \times 1} = \dfrac{60}{3} = 20$

3. $\dfrac{7}{10} \cdot \dfrac{5}{11} = \dfrac{7}{\overset{}{\underset{2}{\cancel{10}}}} \cdot \dfrac{\overset{1}{\cancel{5}}}{11} = \dfrac{7 \cdot 1}{2 \cdot 11} = \dfrac{7}{22}$

4. $\dfrac{7}{27} \cdot \dfrac{9}{4} \cdot \dfrac{8}{21} = \dfrac{\overset{1}{\cancel{7}}}{\underset{3}{\cancel{27}}} \cdot \dfrac{\overset{1}{\cancel{9}}}{\underset{1}{\cancel{4}}} \cdot \dfrac{\overset{2}{\cancel{8}}}{\underset{3}{\cancel{21}}} = \dfrac{2}{9}$

5. $\dfrac{3}{4} \times 7 = \dfrac{3}{4} \times \dfrac{7}{1} = \dfrac{21}{4} = 5\dfrac{1}{4}$

The trip from Los Angeles to New York took $5\dfrac{1}{4}$ hr.

6. First find $\dfrac{1}{5}$ of $95,000, and multiply this result by 3 since there are 3 children. Then subtract that result from $95,000.

$95,000 - \left(\dfrac{1}{5} \times 95,000 \times 3\right) = 95,000 - (19,000 \times 3)$

$= 95,000 - 57,000$

$= 38,000$

$38,000 went to charity.

7. $3\dfrac{3}{4} \times 2\dfrac{1}{10} = \dfrac{15}{4} \times \dfrac{21}{10} = \dfrac{\cancel{15}^{3} \times 21}{4 \times \cancel{10}_{2}} = \dfrac{63}{8} = 7\dfrac{7}{8}$

8. $\left(1\dfrac{3}{4}\right)\left(5\dfrac{1}{3}\right)(3) = \left(\dfrac{7}{4}\right)\left(\dfrac{16}{3}\right)\left(\dfrac{3}{1}\right) = \left(\dfrac{7}{\cancel{4}_{1}}\right)\left(\dfrac{\cancel{16}^{4}}{\cancel{3}_{1}}\right)\left(\dfrac{\cancel{3}^{1}}{1}\right)$

$= \dfrac{28}{1} = 28$

9. $\dfrac{1}{12} \times 2\dfrac{1}{4} = \dfrac{1}{12} \times \dfrac{9}{4} = \dfrac{1}{\cancel{12}_{4}} \times \dfrac{\cancel{9}^{3}}{4} = \dfrac{3}{16}$

You will need $\dfrac{3}{16}$ lb of butter.

10. $8\dfrac{1}{2} \times 11 = \dfrac{17}{2} \times \dfrac{11}{1} = \dfrac{187}{2}$, or $93\dfrac{1}{2}$

The area of the letter-size paper is $93\dfrac{1}{2}$ sq in.

$8\dfrac{1}{2} \times 14 = \dfrac{17}{2} \times \dfrac{14}{1} = \dfrac{17}{\cancel{2}} \times \dfrac{\cancel{14}^{7}}{1} = \dfrac{119}{1} = 119$

The area of the legal-size paper is 119 sq in.

$119 = 118\dfrac{2}{2}$

$-93\dfrac{1}{2} = -93\dfrac{1}{2}$

$\rule{3cm}{0.4pt}$

$25\dfrac{1}{2}$

The area of the legal-size paper is $25\dfrac{1}{2}$ sq in. more than the letter-size paper.

11. $\dfrac{3}{4} \div \dfrac{1}{8} = \dfrac{3}{\cancel{4}_{1}} \times \dfrac{\cancel{8}^{2}}{1} = \dfrac{3 \times 2}{1 \times 1} = \dfrac{6}{1} = 6$

12. $5 \div \dfrac{5}{8} = \dfrac{\cancel{5}^{1}}{1} \times \dfrac{8}{\cancel{5}_{1}} = \dfrac{1 \times 8}{1 \times 1} = \dfrac{8}{1} = 8$

13. $2 \div \dfrac{3}{4} = \dfrac{2}{1} \times \dfrac{4}{3} = \dfrac{8}{3}$, or $2\dfrac{2}{3}$

It will take the house $2\dfrac{2}{3}$ years to sink 2 in.

14. $6 \div 3\dfrac{3}{4} = \dfrac{6}{1} \div \dfrac{15}{4} = \dfrac{\cancel{6}^{2}}{1} \times \dfrac{4}{\cancel{15}_{5}} = \dfrac{8}{5}$, or $1\dfrac{3}{5}$

15. $5\dfrac{3}{7} \div 2\dfrac{3}{8} = \dfrac{38}{7} \div \dfrac{19}{8} = \dfrac{\cancel{38}^{2}}{7} \times \dfrac{8}{\cancel{19}_{1}} = \dfrac{16}{7}$, or $2\dfrac{2}{7}$

16. $33 \div 5\dfrac{1}{2} = \dfrac{33}{1} \div \dfrac{11}{2} = \dfrac{\cancel{33}^{3}}{1} \times \dfrac{2}{\cancel{11}_{1}} = 6$

The man lost 6 lb per month.

17. $5\dfrac{3}{5} \div 2\dfrac{1}{10} = \dfrac{28}{5} \div \dfrac{21}{10} = \dfrac{\cancel{28}^{4}}{\cancel{5}_{1}} \times \dfrac{\cancel{10}^{2}}{\cancel{21}_{3}} = \dfrac{8}{3}$

$\dfrac{8}{3} \times 2\dfrac{1}{4} = \dfrac{\cancel{8}^{2}}{\cancel{3}_{1}} \times \dfrac{\cancel{9}^{3}}{\cancel{4}_{1}} = 6$

Check:

$5\dfrac{3}{5} \div 2\dfrac{1}{10} \times 2\dfrac{1}{4}$

$\downarrow \quad \downarrow \quad \downarrow$

$6 \div 2 \times 2 = 6$

Exercises

1. $\dfrac{1}{3} \times \dfrac{2}{5} = \dfrac{2}{15}$

3. $\left(\dfrac{5}{8}\right)\left(\dfrac{2}{3}\right) = \left(\dfrac{5}{\cancel{8}_{4}}\right)\left(\dfrac{\cancel{2}^{1}}{3}\right) = \dfrac{5}{12}$

5. $\left(\dfrac{3}{4}\right)^{2} = \left(\dfrac{3}{4}\right)\left(\dfrac{3}{4}\right) = \dfrac{9}{16}$

7. $\dfrac{4}{5} \times \dfrac{2}{5} = \dfrac{8}{25}$

9. $\dfrac{7}{8} \times \dfrac{5}{4} = \dfrac{35}{32} = 1\dfrac{3}{32}$

11. $\dfrac{5}{2} \cdot \dfrac{9}{8} = \dfrac{45}{16} = 2\dfrac{13}{16}$

13. $\left(\dfrac{2}{5}\right)\left(\dfrac{5}{9}\right) = \left(\dfrac{2}{\cancel{5}}\right)\left(\dfrac{\cancel{5}}{9}\right) = \dfrac{2}{9}$

15. $\dfrac{7}{9} \times \dfrac{3}{4} = \dfrac{7}{\cancel{9}} \times \dfrac{\cancel{3}}{4} = \dfrac{7}{12}$

17. $\left(\dfrac{1}{8}\right)\left(\dfrac{6}{10}\right) = \left(\dfrac{1}{\cancel{8}}\right)\left(\dfrac{\cancel{6}}{10}\right) = \dfrac{3}{40}$

19. $\dfrac{10}{9} \times \dfrac{93}{100} = \dfrac{\cancel{10}}{\cancel{9}} \times \dfrac{\cancel{93}}{\cancel{100}} = \dfrac{31}{30} = 1\dfrac{1}{30}$

21. $5 \cdot \dfrac{1}{3} = \dfrac{5}{1} \cdot \dfrac{1}{3} = \dfrac{5}{3} = 1\dfrac{2}{3}$

23. $\dfrac{2}{5} \times 7 = \dfrac{2}{5} \times \dfrac{7}{1} = \dfrac{14}{5} = 2\dfrac{4}{5}$

25. $\dfrac{2}{3} \times 20 = \dfrac{2}{3} \times \dfrac{20}{1} = \dfrac{40}{3} = 13\dfrac{1}{3}$

27. $\left(\dfrac{10}{3}\right)(4) = \left(\dfrac{10}{3}\right)\left(\dfrac{4}{1}\right) = \dfrac{40}{3} = 13\dfrac{1}{3}$

29. $\dfrac{1}{2} \times 8 = \dfrac{1}{\cancel{2}} \times \dfrac{\cancel{8}}{1} = 4$

31. $\dfrac{7}{8} \cdot 10 = \dfrac{7}{\cancel{8}} \cdot \dfrac{\cancel{10}}{1} = \dfrac{35}{4} = 8\dfrac{3}{4}$

33. $18 \cdot \dfrac{2}{9} = \dfrac{\cancel{18}}{1} \cdot \dfrac{2}{\cancel{9}} = 4$

35. $\dfrac{2}{3} \times 6 = \dfrac{2}{\cancel{3}} \times \dfrac{\cancel{6}}{1} = 4$

37. $\dfrac{2}{5} \cdot 1\dfrac{1}{3} = \dfrac{2}{5} \cdot \dfrac{4}{3} = \dfrac{8}{15}$

39. $\dfrac{1}{3} \times 1\dfrac{1}{3} = \dfrac{1}{3} \times \dfrac{4}{3} = \dfrac{4}{9}$

41. $\left(\dfrac{7}{8}\right)\left(1\dfrac{1}{2}\right) = \left(\dfrac{7}{8}\right)\left(\dfrac{3}{2}\right) = \dfrac{21}{16} = 1\dfrac{5}{16}$

43. $\dfrac{1}{4} \times 8\dfrac{1}{2} = \dfrac{1}{4} \times \dfrac{17}{2} = \dfrac{17}{8} = 2\dfrac{1}{8}$

45. $\left(\dfrac{5}{6}\right)\left(1\dfrac{1}{9}\right) = \left(\dfrac{5}{\cancel{6}}\right)\left(\dfrac{\cancel{10}}{9}\right) = \dfrac{25}{27}$

47. $\dfrac{1}{2} \times 5\dfrac{1}{3} = \dfrac{1}{\cancel{2}} \times \dfrac{\cancel{16}}{3} = \dfrac{8}{3} = 2\dfrac{2}{3}$

49. $\dfrac{4}{5} \cdot 1\dfrac{1}{4} = \dfrac{\cancel{4}}{\cancel{5}} \cdot \dfrac{\cancel{5}}{\cancel{4}} = 1$

51. $\left(\dfrac{3}{16}\right)\left(4\dfrac{2}{3}\right) = \left(\dfrac{\cancel{3}}{\cancel{16}}\right)\left(\dfrac{\cancel{14}}{\cancel{3}}\right) = \dfrac{7}{8}$

53. $1\dfrac{1}{7} \times 1\dfrac{1}{5} = \dfrac{8}{7} \times \dfrac{6}{5} = \dfrac{48}{35} = 1\dfrac{13}{35}$

55. $\left(2\dfrac{1}{10}\right)^2 = \left(\dfrac{21}{10}\right)\left(\dfrac{21}{10}\right) = \dfrac{441}{100} = 4\dfrac{41}{100}$

57. $3\dfrac{9}{10} \cdot 2 = \dfrac{39}{\cancel{10}} \cdot \dfrac{\cancel{2}}{1} = \dfrac{39}{5} = 7\dfrac{4}{5}$

59. $100 \times 3\dfrac{3}{4} = \dfrac{\cancel{100}}{1} \times \dfrac{15}{\cancel{4}} = 375$

61. $1\dfrac{1}{2} \times 5\dfrac{1}{3} = \dfrac{\cancel{3}}{\cancel{2}} \times \dfrac{\cancel{16}}{\cancel{3}} = 8$

63. $\left(2\dfrac{1}{2}\right)\left(1\dfrac{1}{5}\right) = \left(\dfrac{\cancel{5}}{\cancel{2}}\right)\left(\dfrac{\cancel{6}}{\cancel{5}}\right) = 3$

65. $12\dfrac{1}{2} \cdot 3\dfrac{1}{3} = \dfrac{25}{\cancel{2}} \cdot \dfrac{\cancel{10}}{3} = \dfrac{125}{3} = 41\dfrac{2}{3}$

67. $66\dfrac{2}{3} \cdot 1\dfrac{7}{10} = \dfrac{\cancel{200}}{3} \cdot \dfrac{17}{\cancel{10}} = \dfrac{340}{3} = 113\dfrac{1}{3}$

69. $1\dfrac{5}{9} \times \dfrac{3}{8} \times 2 = \dfrac{\overset{7}{\cancel{14}}}{\underset{3}{\cancel{9}}} \times \dfrac{\overset{1}{\cancel{3}}}{\underset{2}{\cancel{8}}} \times \dfrac{\overset{1}{\cancel{2}}}{1} = \dfrac{7}{6} = 1\dfrac{1}{6}$

71. $\left(\dfrac{1}{2}\right)^2\left(2\dfrac{1}{3}\right) = \left(\dfrac{1}{2}\right)\left(\dfrac{1}{2}\right)\left(\dfrac{7}{3}\right) = \dfrac{7}{12}$

73. $\dfrac{4}{5} \times \dfrac{7}{8} \times 1\dfrac{1}{10} = \dfrac{\cancel{4}}{5} \times \dfrac{7}{\underset{2}{\cancel{8}}} \times \dfrac{11}{10} = \dfrac{77}{100}$

75. $\left(1\dfrac{1}{2}\right)^3 = \left(\dfrac{3}{2}\right)\left(\dfrac{3}{2}\right)\left(\dfrac{3}{2}\right) = \dfrac{27}{8} = 3\dfrac{3}{8}$

77. $\dfrac{3}{5} \div \dfrac{2}{3} = \dfrac{3}{5} \times \dfrac{3}{2} = \dfrac{9}{10}$

79. $\dfrac{4}{5} \div \dfrac{7}{8} = \dfrac{4}{5} \times \dfrac{8}{7} = \dfrac{32}{35}$

81. $\dfrac{1}{2} \div \dfrac{1}{7} = \dfrac{1}{2} \times \dfrac{7}{1} = \dfrac{7}{2} = 3\dfrac{1}{2}$

83. $\dfrac{5}{9} \div \dfrac{1}{8} = \dfrac{5}{9} \times \dfrac{8}{1} = \dfrac{40}{9} = 4\dfrac{4}{9}$

85. $\dfrac{4}{5} \div \dfrac{8}{15} = \dfrac{\overset{1}{\cancel{4}}}{\underset{1}{\cancel{5}}} \times \dfrac{\overset{3}{\cancel{15}}}{\underset{2}{\cancel{8}}} = \dfrac{3}{2} = 1\dfrac{1}{2}$

87. $\dfrac{7}{8} \div \dfrac{3}{8} = \dfrac{7}{\underset{1}{\cancel{8}}} \times \dfrac{\overset{1}{\cancel{8}}}{3} = \dfrac{7}{3} = 2\dfrac{1}{3}$

89. $\dfrac{9}{10} \div \dfrac{3}{4} = \dfrac{\overset{3}{\cancel{9}}}{\underset{5}{\cancel{10}}} \times \dfrac{\overset{2}{\cancel{4}}}{\underset{1}{\cancel{3}}} = \dfrac{6}{5} = 1\dfrac{1}{5}$

91. $\dfrac{1}{10} \div \dfrac{2}{5} = \dfrac{1}{\underset{2}{\cancel{10}}} \times \dfrac{\overset{1}{\cancel{5}}}{2} = \dfrac{1}{4}$

93. $\dfrac{2}{3} \div 7 = \dfrac{3}{2} \div \dfrac{7}{1} = \dfrac{2}{3} \times \dfrac{1}{7} = \dfrac{2}{21}$

95. $\dfrac{1}{5} \div 6 = \dfrac{1}{5} \div \dfrac{6}{1} = \dfrac{1}{5} \times \dfrac{1}{6} = \dfrac{1}{30}$

97. $\dfrac{3}{5} \div 6 = \dfrac{3}{5} \div \dfrac{6}{1} = \dfrac{\overset{1}{\cancel{3}}}{5} \times \dfrac{1}{\underset{2}{\cancel{6}}} = \dfrac{1}{10}$

99. $\dfrac{2}{3} \div 6 = \dfrac{2}{3} \div \dfrac{6}{1} = \dfrac{\overset{1}{\cancel{2}}}{3} \times \dfrac{1}{\underset{3}{\cancel{6}}} = \dfrac{1}{9}$

101. $8 \div \dfrac{1}{5} = \dfrac{8}{1} \div \dfrac{1}{5} = \dfrac{8}{1} \times \dfrac{5}{1} = 40$

103. $7 \div \dfrac{3}{7} = \dfrac{7}{1} \div \dfrac{3}{7} = \dfrac{7}{1} \times \dfrac{7}{3} = \dfrac{49}{3} = 16\dfrac{1}{3}$

105. $4 \div \dfrac{3}{10} = \dfrac{4}{1} \times \dfrac{10}{3} = \dfrac{40}{3} = 13\dfrac{1}{3}$

107. $1 \div \dfrac{1}{7} = \dfrac{1}{1} \times \dfrac{7}{1} = 7$

109. $2\dfrac{5}{6} \div \dfrac{3}{7} = \dfrac{17}{6} \times \dfrac{7}{3} = \dfrac{119}{18} = 6\dfrac{11}{18}$

111. $1\dfrac{1}{3} \div \dfrac{4}{5} = \dfrac{4}{3} \div \dfrac{4}{5} = \dfrac{\overset{1}{\cancel{4}}}{3} \times \dfrac{5}{\underset{1}{\cancel{4}}} = \dfrac{5}{3} = 1\dfrac{2}{3}$

113. $8\dfrac{5}{6} \div \dfrac{9}{10} = \dfrac{53}{6} \div \dfrac{9}{10} = \dfrac{53}{\underset{3}{\cancel{6}}} \times \dfrac{\overset{5}{\cancel{10}}}{9} = \dfrac{265}{27} = 9\dfrac{22}{27}$

115. $20\dfrac{1}{10} \div \dfrac{1}{5} = \dfrac{201}{10} \div \dfrac{1}{5} = \dfrac{201}{\underset{2}{\cancel{10}}} \times \dfrac{\overset{1}{\cancel{5}}}{1} = \dfrac{201}{2} = 100\dfrac{1}{2}$

117. $\dfrac{1}{6} \div 2\dfrac{1}{7} = \dfrac{1}{6} \div \dfrac{15}{7} = \dfrac{1}{6} \times \dfrac{7}{15} = \dfrac{7}{90}$

119. $\dfrac{1}{2} \div 2\dfrac{3}{5} = \dfrac{1}{2} \div \dfrac{13}{5} = \dfrac{1}{2} \times \dfrac{5}{13} = \dfrac{5}{26}$

121. $4 \div 1\dfrac{1}{4} = \dfrac{4}{1} \div \dfrac{5}{4} = \dfrac{4}{1} \times \dfrac{4}{5} = \dfrac{16}{5} = 3\dfrac{1}{5}$

123. $2\dfrac{1}{10} \div 20 = \dfrac{21}{10} \div \dfrac{20}{1} = \dfrac{21}{10} \times \dfrac{1}{20} = \dfrac{21}{200}$

125. $2\dfrac{1}{2} \div 3\dfrac{1}{7} = \dfrac{5}{2} \div \dfrac{22}{7} = \dfrac{5}{2} \times \dfrac{7}{22} = \dfrac{35}{44}$

127. $8\dfrac{1}{10} \div 5\dfrac{3}{4} = \dfrac{81}{10} \div \dfrac{23}{4} = \dfrac{81}{\underset{5}{\cancel{10}}} \times \dfrac{\overset{2}{\cancel{4}}}{23} = \dfrac{162}{115} = 1\dfrac{47}{115}$

129. $2\dfrac{1}{3} \div 4\dfrac{1}{2} = \dfrac{7}{3} \div \dfrac{9}{2} = \dfrac{7}{3} \times \dfrac{2}{9} = \dfrac{14}{27}$

131. $6\dfrac{3}{8} \div 2\dfrac{5}{6} = \dfrac{51}{8} \div \dfrac{17}{6} = \dfrac{\overset{3}{\cancel{51}}}{\underset{4}{\cancel{8}}} \times \dfrac{\overset{3}{\cancel{6}}}{\underset{1}{\cancel{17}}} = \dfrac{9}{4} = 2\dfrac{1}{4}$

133. $\dfrac{2}{3} \times 1\dfrac{1}{3} + \dfrac{1}{2} = \left(\dfrac{2}{3} \times 1\dfrac{1}{3}\right) + \dfrac{1}{2}$

$\qquad = \dfrac{8}{9} + \dfrac{1}{2}$

$\qquad = \dfrac{16}{18} + \dfrac{9}{18}$

$\qquad = \dfrac{25}{18} = 1\dfrac{7}{18}$

135. $5 - \dfrac{1}{3} \times \dfrac{2}{5} = 5 - \left(\dfrac{1}{3} \times \dfrac{2}{5}\right)$

$\qquad = 5 - \dfrac{2}{15}$

$\qquad = 4\dfrac{15}{15} - \dfrac{2}{15}$

$\qquad = 4\dfrac{13}{15}$

137. $\dfrac{1}{5} + 2\dfrac{3}{4} \times \dfrac{1}{8} = \dfrac{1}{5} + \left(\dfrac{11}{4} \times \dfrac{1}{8}\right)$

$\qquad = \dfrac{1}{5} + \dfrac{11}{32}$

$\qquad = \dfrac{32}{160} + \dfrac{55}{160}$

$\qquad = \dfrac{87}{160}$

139. $4 \times \dfrac{2}{9} \div \dfrac{3}{4} = \left(\dfrac{4}{1} \times \dfrac{2}{9}\right) \div \dfrac{3}{4}$

$\qquad = \dfrac{8}{9} \times \dfrac{4}{3}$

$\qquad = \dfrac{32}{27} = 1\dfrac{5}{27}$

141. $3\dfrac{1}{2} \times 6 \div 5 = \left(\dfrac{7}{\cancel{2}} \times \dfrac{\cancel{6}^{\,3}}{1}\right) \div \dfrac{5}{1}$

$\qquad = \dfrac{21}{1} \times \dfrac{1}{5}$

$\qquad = \dfrac{21}{5} = 4\dfrac{1}{5}$

143. $10 \times \dfrac{1}{8} \times 2\dfrac{1}{2} = \left(\dfrac{\cancel{10}^{\,5}}{1} \times \dfrac{1}{\cancel{8}_{\,4}}\right) \times \dfrac{5}{2}$

$\qquad = \dfrac{5}{4} \times \dfrac{5}{2}$

$\qquad = \dfrac{25}{8} = 3\dfrac{1}{8}$

145. $\dfrac{1}{2} \times \dfrac{3}{4} = \dfrac{3}{8}$

You swam $\dfrac{3}{8}$ mi this morning.

147. $\dfrac{1}{20} \times 160{,}000 = \dfrac{1}{\cancel{20}} \times \dfrac{\cancel{160{,}000}^{\,8{,}000}}{1} = 8{,}000$

You need to put down $8,000 to buy the house.

149. $2\dfrac{1}{2} \times 2\dfrac{1}{2} = \dfrac{5}{2} \times \dfrac{5}{2} = \dfrac{25}{4} = 6\dfrac{1}{4}$

A first-magnitude start is $6\dfrac{1}{4}$ times as bright as a third-magnitude star.

151. $3 \times 8\dfrac{1}{2} = \dfrac{3}{1} \times \dfrac{17}{2} = \dfrac{51}{2} = 25\dfrac{1}{2}$

The area of the hallway is $25\dfrac{1}{2}$ sq ft.

$25\dfrac{1}{2} \times 7\dfrac{1}{2} = \dfrac{51}{2} \times \dfrac{15}{2} = \dfrac{765}{4} = 191\dfrac{1}{4}$

The cost of the carpet is $\$191\dfrac{1}{4}$.

153. $1{,}000 - \left(\dfrac{1}{\cancel{4}} \times \dfrac{\cancel{1{,}000}^{\,250}}{1}\right) = 1{,}000 - 250 = 750$

$1{,}000 - \left(\dfrac{1}{\cancel{8}} \times \dfrac{\cancel{1{,}000}^{\,125}}{1}\right) = 1{,}000 - 125 = 875$

The total value of your stocks is $750, and the total value of your bonds is $875.

155. $3\dfrac{1}{2} \div \dfrac{1}{2} = \dfrac{7}{2} \div \dfrac{1}{2} = \dfrac{7}{\cancel{2}} \times \dfrac{\cancel{2}^{\,1}}{1} = 7$

The plane is 7 times as fast as the boat.

157. $\dfrac{3}{8} \div \dfrac{1}{8} = \dfrac{3}{\cancel{8}} \times \dfrac{\cancel{8}^{\,2}}{1} = 6$

You can develop 6 rolls of film.

Review Exercises

1. $\dfrac{150}{1} = 150 \text{ R0}$ $\dfrac{150}{2} = 75 \text{ R0}$ $\dfrac{150}{3} = 50 \text{ R0}$

   $\dfrac{150}{5} = 30 \text{ R0}$ $\dfrac{150}{6} = 24 \text{ R0}$ $\dfrac{150}{10} = 15 \text{ R0}$

   The factors of 150 are 1, 2, 3, 5, 6, 10, 15, 25, 30, 50, 75, and 150.

2. $\dfrac{180}{1} = 180 \text{ R0}$ $\dfrac{180}{2} = 90 \text{ R0}$ $\dfrac{180}{3} = 60 \text{ R0}$

   $\dfrac{180}{4} = 45 \text{ R0}$ $\dfrac{180}{5} = 36 \text{ R0}$ $\dfrac{180}{6} = 30 \text{ R0}$

   $\dfrac{180}{9} = 20 \text{ R0}$ $\dfrac{180}{10} = 18 \text{ R0}$ $\dfrac{180}{12} = 15 \text{ R0}$

   The factors of 150 are 1, 2, 3, 4, 5, 6, 9, 10, 12, 15, 18, 20, 30, 36, 45, 60, 90, and 180.

3. $\dfrac{57}{1} = 57 \text{ R0}$ $\dfrac{57}{3} = 19 \text{ R0}$

   The factors of 57 are 1, 3, 19, and 57.

4. $\dfrac{72}{1} = 150 \text{ R0}$ $\dfrac{72}{2} = 36 \text{ R0}$ $\dfrac{72}{3} = 24 \text{ R0}$

   $\dfrac{72}{4} = 18 \text{ R0}$ $\dfrac{72}{6} = 12 \text{ R0}$ $\dfrac{72}{8} = 9 \text{ R0}$

   The factors of 72 are 1, 2, 3, 4, 6, 8, 9, 12, 18, 24, 36, and 72.

5. 23 is prime.

6, 33 is composite; 3 and 33 are factors.

7. 87 is composite; 3 and 29 are factors.

8. 67 is prime.

9.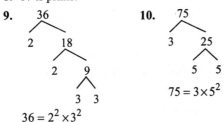

   $36 = 2^2 \times 3^2$

10. $75 = 3 \times 5^2$

11.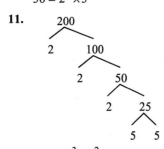

    $200 = 2^3 \times 5^2$

12.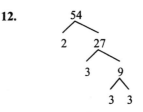

    $54 = 2 \times 3^3$

13. $6 = 2 \times 3$ $8 = 2^3$

    $\text{LCM} = 2^3 \times 3 = 8 \times 3 = 24$

14. $5 = 5$ $10 = 2 \times 5$

    $\text{LCM} = 2 \times 5 = 10$

15. $24 = 2^3 \times 3$ $36 = 2^2 \times 3^2$

    $\text{LCM} = 2^3 \times 3^2 = 8 \times 9 = 72$

16. $15 = 3 \times 5$ $20 = 2^2 \times 5$

    $\text{LCM} = 2^2 \times 3 \times 5 = 4 \times 3 \times 5 = 60$

17. The whole is divided into 3 equal parts. One of these parts is shaded. The diagram illustrates the fraction $\dfrac{1}{3}$.

18. The whole is divided into 4 equal parts. Two of these parts are shaded. The diagram illustrates the fraction $\dfrac{2}{4}$ or $\dfrac{1}{2}$.

19. The whole is divided into 6 equal parts. Three of these parts are shaded. The diagram illustrates the fraction $\dfrac{3}{6}$ or $\dfrac{1}{2}$.

20. The whole is divided into 12 equal parts. Six of these parts are shaded. The diagram illustrates the fraction $\dfrac{6}{12}$ or $\dfrac{1}{2}$.

21. $7\dfrac{2}{3} = \dfrac{(3 \times 7) + 2}{3} = \dfrac{23}{3}$

22. $1\dfrac{4}{5} = \dfrac{(5 \times 1) + 4}{5} = \dfrac{9}{5}$

23. $9\dfrac{1}{10} = \dfrac{(10 \times 9) + 1}{10} = \dfrac{91}{10}$

24. $8\dfrac{3}{7} = \dfrac{(7 \times 8) + 3}{7} = \dfrac{59}{7}$

25. $\dfrac{13}{2} = 2\overline{)13}^{\,6 \text{ R1}}$ $\dfrac{13}{2} = 6\dfrac{1}{2}$

26. $\dfrac{14}{3} = 3\overline{)14}^{\,4 \text{ R2}}$ $\dfrac{14}{3} = 4\dfrac{2}{3}$

27. $\dfrac{11}{4} = 4\overline{)11}\,^{2\ R3}$ $\dfrac{11}{4} = 2\dfrac{3}{4}$

28. $\dfrac{23}{5} = 5\overline{)23}\,^{4\ R3}$ $\dfrac{23}{5} = 4\dfrac{3}{5}$

29.
$$\dfrac{4}{5} = \dfrac{n}{15}$$
$$\dfrac{4}{5} = \dfrac{n}{3\cdot 5}$$
$$\dfrac{4\cdot 3}{5\cdot 3} = \dfrac{n}{3\cdot 5}$$
$$n = 12$$
Check: $\dfrac{4}{5} \overset{?}{=} \dfrac{12}{15}$
$$4\cdot 15 \overset{?}{=} 5\cdot 12$$
$$60 \overset{\checkmark}{=} 60$$

30.
$$\dfrac{2}{7} = \dfrac{n}{14}$$
$$\dfrac{2}{7} = \dfrac{n}{2\cdot 7}$$
$$\dfrac{2\cdot 2}{7\cdot 2} = \dfrac{n}{2\cdot 7}$$
$$n = 4$$
Check: $\dfrac{2}{7} \overset{?}{=} \dfrac{4}{14}$
$$2\cdot 14 \overset{?}{=} 7\cdot 4$$
$$28 \overset{\checkmark}{=} 28$$

31.
$$\dfrac{1}{2} = \dfrac{n}{10}$$
$$\dfrac{1}{2} = \dfrac{n}{2\cdot 5}$$
$$\dfrac{1\cdot 5}{2\cdot 5} = \dfrac{n}{2\cdot 5}$$
$$n = 5$$
Check: $\dfrac{1}{2} \overset{?}{=} \dfrac{5}{10}$
$$1\cdot 10 \overset{?}{=} 2\cdot 5$$
$$10 \overset{\checkmark}{=} 10$$

32.
$$\dfrac{9}{10} = \dfrac{n}{30}$$
$$\dfrac{9}{10} = \dfrac{n}{3\cdot 10}$$
$$\dfrac{9\cdot 3}{10\cdot 3} = \dfrac{n}{3\cdot 10}$$
$$n = 27$$
Check: $\dfrac{9}{10} \overset{?}{=} \dfrac{27}{30}$
$$9\cdot 30 \overset{?}{=} 10\cdot 27$$
$$270 \overset{\checkmark}{=} 270$$

33. $\dfrac{14}{28} = \dfrac{\cancel{2}\cdot\cancel{7}}{2\cdot\cancel{2}\cdot\cancel{7}} = \dfrac{1}{2}$

34. $\dfrac{15}{21} = \dfrac{\cancel{3}\cdot 5}{\cancel{3}\cdot 7} = \dfrac{5}{7}$

35. $\dfrac{30}{45} = \dfrac{2\cdot\cancel{3}\cdot\cancel{5}}{3\cdot\cancel{3}\cdot\cancel{5}} = \dfrac{2}{3}$

36. $\dfrac{54}{72} = \dfrac{\cancel{2}\cdot 3\cdot\cancel{3}\cdot\cancel{3}}{\cancel{2}\cdot 2\cdot 2\cdot\cancel{3}\cdot\cancel{3}} = \dfrac{3}{4}$

37. $5\dfrac{2}{4} = 5\dfrac{\cancel{2}}{\cancel{2}\cdot 2} = 5\dfrac{1}{2}$

38. $8\dfrac{10}{15} = 8\dfrac{2\cdot\cancel{5}}{3\cdot\cancel{5}} = 8\dfrac{2}{3}$

39. $6\dfrac{12}{42} = 6\dfrac{\cancel{2}\cdot 2\cdot\cancel{3}}{\cancel{2}\cdot\cancel{3}\cdot 7} = 6\dfrac{2}{7}$

40. $8\dfrac{45}{63} = 8\dfrac{\cancel{3}\cdot\cancel{3}\cdot 5}{\cancel{3}\cdot\cancel{3}\cdot 7} = 8\dfrac{5}{7}$

41. $\dfrac{5}{8} > \dfrac{3}{8}$ because $5 > 3$

42. $\dfrac{5}{6} > \dfrac{1}{6}$ because $5 > 1$

43. $\dfrac{2}{3} < \dfrac{4}{5}$ because $\dfrac{10}{15} < \dfrac{12}{15}$

44. $\dfrac{9}{10} > \dfrac{7}{8}$ because $\dfrac{36}{40} > \dfrac{35}{40}$

45. $\dfrac{3}{4} > \dfrac{5}{8}$ because $\dfrac{6}{8} > \dfrac{5}{8}$

46. $\dfrac{7}{10} > \dfrac{5}{9}$ because $\dfrac{63}{90} > \dfrac{50}{90}$

47. $3\dfrac{1}{5} > 1\dfrac{9}{10}$ because $\dfrac{32}{10} > \dfrac{19}{10}$

48. $5\dfrac{1}{8} > 5\dfrac{1}{9}$ because $\dfrac{1}{8} > \dfrac{1}{9}$ since $\dfrac{9}{72} > \dfrac{8}{72}$

49. $7 = 7 \qquad 8 = 2^3 \qquad 2 = 2$
LCM $= 2^3 \cdot 7 = 8\cdot 7 = 56$
$$\dfrac{2}{7} = \dfrac{2\cdot 8}{7\cdot 8} = \dfrac{16}{56}$$
$$\dfrac{3}{8} = \dfrac{3\cdot 7}{8\cdot 7} = \dfrac{21}{56}$$
$$\dfrac{1}{2} = \dfrac{1\cdot 28}{2\cdot 28} = \dfrac{28}{56}$$
The fraction between $\dfrac{2}{7}$ and $\dfrac{1}{2}$ is $\dfrac{3}{8}$.

50. $5 = 5 \qquad 3 = 3 \qquad 15 = 3\cdot 5$
LCM $= 3\cdot 5 = 15$
$$\dfrac{1}{5} = \dfrac{1\cdot 3}{5\cdot 3} = \dfrac{3}{15}$$
$$\dfrac{1}{3} = \dfrac{1\cdot 5}{3\cdot 5} = \dfrac{5}{15}$$
$$\dfrac{2}{15} = \dfrac{2}{15}$$
The fraction between $\dfrac{2}{15}$ and $\dfrac{1}{3}$ is $\dfrac{1}{5}$.

51. $5 = 5 \qquad 10 = 2\cdot 5 \qquad 4 = 2^2$
LCM $= 2^2 \cdot 5 = 4\cdot 5 = 20$
$$\dfrac{4}{5} = \dfrac{4\cdot 4}{5\cdot 4} = \dfrac{16}{20}$$
$$\dfrac{9}{10} = \dfrac{9\cdot 2}{10\cdot 2} = \dfrac{18}{20}$$
$$\dfrac{3}{4} = \dfrac{3\cdot 5}{4\cdot 5} = \dfrac{15}{20}$$
The fraction between $\dfrac{3}{4}$ and $\dfrac{9}{10}$ is $\dfrac{4}{5}$.

52. $8 = 2^3 \quad 9 = 3^2 \quad 18 = 2 \cdot 3^2$

$\text{LCM} = 2^3 \cdot 3^2 = 8 \cdot 9 = 72$

$\dfrac{7}{8} = \dfrac{7 \cdot 9}{8 \cdot 9} = \dfrac{63}{72}$

$\dfrac{7}{9} = \dfrac{7 \cdot 8}{9 \cdot 8} = \dfrac{56}{72}$

$\dfrac{13}{18} = \dfrac{13 \cdot 4}{18 \cdot 4} = \dfrac{52}{72}$

The fraction between $\dfrac{13}{18}$ and $\dfrac{7}{8}$ is $\dfrac{7}{9}$.

53. $\dfrac{1}{9} + \dfrac{4}{9} = \dfrac{5}{9}$

54. $\dfrac{7}{8} + \dfrac{3}{8} = \dfrac{10}{8} = \dfrac{5}{4}$ or $1\dfrac{1}{4}$

55. $\dfrac{7}{10} + \dfrac{4}{10} = \dfrac{11}{10}$ or $1\dfrac{1}{10}$

56. $\dfrac{5}{6} + \dfrac{5}{6} = \dfrac{10}{6} = \dfrac{5}{3}$ or $1\dfrac{2}{3}$

57. $\dfrac{2}{5} + \dfrac{4}{5} = \dfrac{6}{5}$ or $1\dfrac{1}{5}$

58. $\dfrac{7}{20} + \dfrac{8}{20} = \dfrac{15}{20} = \dfrac{3}{4}$

59. $\dfrac{5}{8} + \dfrac{7}{8} + \dfrac{3}{8} = \dfrac{15}{8}$ or $1\dfrac{7}{8}$

60. $\dfrac{3}{10} + \dfrac{1}{10} + \dfrac{2}{10} = \dfrac{6}{10} = \dfrac{3}{5}$

61.
$\begin{array}{r} \dfrac{1}{3} = \dfrac{5}{15} \\[6pt] +\dfrac{2}{5} = +\dfrac{6}{15} \\[6pt] \hline \dfrac{11}{15} \end{array}$

62.
$\begin{array}{r} \dfrac{7}{8} = \dfrac{21}{24} \\[6pt] +\dfrac{5}{6} = +\dfrac{20}{24} \\[6pt] \hline \dfrac{41}{24} \text{ or } 1\dfrac{17}{24} \end{array}$

63.
$\begin{array}{r} \dfrac{9}{10} = \dfrac{9}{10} \\[6pt] +\dfrac{1}{2} = +\dfrac{5}{10} \\[6pt] \hline \dfrac{14}{10} = \dfrac{7}{5} \text{ or } 1\dfrac{2}{5} \end{array}$

64.
$\begin{array}{r} \dfrac{3}{8} = \dfrac{15}{40} \\[6pt] +\dfrac{4}{5} = +\dfrac{32}{40} \\[6pt] \hline \dfrac{47}{40} \text{ or } 1\dfrac{7}{40} \end{array}$

65. $2\dfrac{1}{8} + 3\dfrac{7}{8} = 5\dfrac{8}{8} = 6$

66. $6\dfrac{1}{4} + 3\dfrac{1}{4} = 9\dfrac{2}{4} = 9\dfrac{1}{2}$

67. $8\dfrac{7}{10} + 1\dfrac{9}{10} = 9\dfrac{16}{10} = 10\dfrac{6}{10} = 10\dfrac{3}{5}$

68. $5\dfrac{5}{6} + 2\dfrac{1}{6} = 7\dfrac{6}{6} = 8$

69. $2\dfrac{1}{3} + 4\dfrac{1}{3} + 5\dfrac{2}{3} = 11\dfrac{4}{3} = 12\dfrac{1}{3}$

70. $1\dfrac{3}{10} + \dfrac{9}{10} + 2\dfrac{1}{10} = 3\dfrac{13}{10} = 4\dfrac{3}{10}$

71.
$\begin{array}{r} 5\dfrac{2}{5} = 5\dfrac{4}{10} \\[6pt] +1\dfrac{3}{10} = +1\dfrac{3}{10} \\[6pt] \hline 6\dfrac{7}{10} \end{array}$

72.
$\begin{array}{r} 9\dfrac{1}{6} = 9\dfrac{4}{24} \\[6pt] +8\dfrac{3}{8} = +8\dfrac{9}{24} \\[6pt] \hline 17\dfrac{13}{24} \end{array}$

73.
$\begin{array}{r} 10\dfrac{2}{3} = 10\dfrac{8}{12} \\[6pt] +12\dfrac{3}{4} = +12\dfrac{9}{12} \\[6pt] \hline 22\dfrac{17}{12} = 23\dfrac{5}{12} \end{array}$

74.
$\begin{array}{r} 20\dfrac{1}{2} = 20\dfrac{4}{8} \\[6pt] +25\dfrac{7}{8} = +25\dfrac{7}{8} \\[6pt] \hline 45\dfrac{11}{8} = 46\dfrac{3}{8} \end{array}$

75.
$\begin{array}{r} 10\dfrac{3}{5} = 10\dfrac{12}{20} \\[6pt] 7\dfrac{9}{10} = 7\dfrac{18}{20} \\[6pt] +2\dfrac{1}{4} = +2\dfrac{5}{20} \\[6pt] \hline 19\dfrac{35}{20} = 20\dfrac{15}{20} = 20\dfrac{3}{4} \end{array}$

76.
$\begin{array}{r} 20\dfrac{7}{8} = 20\dfrac{21}{24} \\[6pt] 30\dfrac{5}{6} = 30\dfrac{20}{24} \\[6pt] +4\dfrac{1}{3} = +4\dfrac{8}{24} \\[6pt] \hline 54\dfrac{49}{24} = 56\dfrac{1}{24} \end{array}$

77. $\dfrac{3}{8} - \dfrac{1}{8} = \dfrac{2}{8} = \dfrac{1}{4}$

78. $\dfrac{7}{9} - \dfrac{1}{9} = \dfrac{6}{9} = \dfrac{2}{3}$

79. $\dfrac{5}{3} - \dfrac{2}{3} = \dfrac{3}{3} = 1$

80. $\dfrac{4}{6} - \dfrac{4}{6} = 0$

81.
$\begin{array}{r} \dfrac{3}{10} = \dfrac{6}{20} \\[6pt] -\dfrac{1}{20} = -\dfrac{1}{20} \\[6pt] \hline \dfrac{5}{20} = \dfrac{1}{4} \end{array}$

82.
$\begin{array}{r} \dfrac{1}{2} = \dfrac{4}{8} \\[6pt] -\dfrac{1}{8} = -\dfrac{1}{8} \\[6pt] \hline \dfrac{3}{8} \end{array}$

83.
$$\frac{3}{5} = \frac{12}{20}$$
$$-\frac{1}{4} = -\frac{5}{20}$$
$$\frac{7}{20}$$

84.
$$\frac{1}{3} = \frac{10}{30}$$
$$-\frac{1}{10} = -\frac{3}{30}$$
$$\frac{7}{30}$$

85.
$$12\frac{1}{2}$$
$$-5$$
$$7\frac{1}{2}$$

86.
$$4\frac{3}{10}$$
$$-2$$
$$2\frac{3}{10}$$

87.
$$8\frac{7}{8}$$
$$-5\frac{1}{8}$$
$$3\frac{6}{8} = 3\frac{3}{4}$$

88.
$$20\frac{3}{4}$$
$$-2\frac{1}{4}$$
$$18\frac{2}{4} = 18\frac{1}{2}$$

89.
$$12 = 11\frac{2}{2}$$
$$-5\frac{1}{2} = -5\frac{1}{2}$$
$$6\frac{1}{2}$$

90.
$$4 = 3\frac{10}{10}$$
$$-2\frac{3}{10} = -2\frac{3}{10}$$
$$1\frac{7}{10}$$

91.
$$7 = 6\frac{3}{3}$$
$$-4\frac{1}{3} = -4\frac{1}{3}$$
$$2\frac{2}{3}$$

92.
$$1 = \frac{5}{5}$$
$$-\frac{4}{5} = -\frac{4}{5}$$
$$\frac{1}{5}$$

93.
$$6\frac{1}{10} = 5\frac{11}{10}$$
$$-4\frac{3}{10} = -4\frac{3}{10}$$
$$1\frac{8}{10} = 1\frac{4}{5}$$

94.
$$2\frac{5}{8} = 1\frac{13}{8}$$
$$-1\frac{7}{8} = -1\frac{7}{8}$$
$$\frac{6}{8} = \frac{3}{4}$$

95.
$$5\frac{1}{4} = 4\frac{5}{4}$$
$$-2\frac{3}{4} = -2\frac{3}{4}$$
$$2\frac{2}{4} = 2\frac{1}{2}$$

96.
$$7\frac{1}{6} = 6\frac{7}{6}$$
$$-3\frac{5}{6} = -3\frac{5}{6}$$
$$3\frac{2}{6} = 3\frac{1}{3}$$

97.
$$3\frac{1}{10} = 2\frac{11}{10}$$
$$-2\frac{4}{5} = -2\frac{8}{10}$$
$$\frac{3}{10}$$

98.
$$7\frac{1}{2} = 6\frac{12}{8}$$
$$-4\frac{5}{8} = -4\frac{5}{8}$$
$$2\frac{7}{8}$$

99.
$$5\frac{1}{12} = 4\frac{13}{12}$$
$$-4\frac{1}{2} = -4\frac{6}{12}$$
$$\frac{7}{12}$$

100.
$$6\frac{2}{9} = 5\frac{11}{9}$$
$$-2\frac{1}{3} = -2\frac{3}{9}$$
$$3\frac{8}{9}$$

101. $\dfrac{1}{3} \times \dfrac{2}{5} = \dfrac{2}{15}$

102. $\dfrac{1}{2} \times \dfrac{7}{8} = \dfrac{7}{16}$

103. $\left(\dfrac{5}{6}\right)\left(\dfrac{3}{4}\right) = \left(\dfrac{5}{\cancel{6}_{2}}\right)\left(\dfrac{\cancel{3}^{1}}{4}\right) = \dfrac{5}{8}$

104. $\left(\dfrac{2}{3}\right)\left(\dfrac{1}{4}\right) = \left(\dfrac{\cancel{2}^{1}}{3}\right)\left(\dfrac{1}{\cancel{4}_{2}}\right) = \dfrac{1}{6}$

105. $\dfrac{3}{4} \times 100 = \dfrac{3}{\cancel{4}_{1}} \times \dfrac{\cancel{100}^{25}}{1} = 75$

106. $\dfrac{4}{5} \times 200 = \dfrac{4}{\cancel{5}_{1}} \times \dfrac{\cancel{200}^{40}}{1} = 160$

107. $\dfrac{2}{3} \times 8 = \dfrac{2}{3} \times \dfrac{8}{1} = \dfrac{16}{3} = 5\dfrac{1}{3}$

108. $\dfrac{1}{10} \times 7 = \dfrac{1}{10} \times \dfrac{7}{1} = \dfrac{7}{10}$

109. $\left(\dfrac{1}{5}\right)^3 = \left(\dfrac{1}{5}\right)\left(\dfrac{1}{5}\right)\left(\dfrac{1}{5}\right) = \dfrac{1}{125}$

110. $\left(\dfrac{2}{3}\right)^3 = \left(\dfrac{2}{3}\right)\left(\dfrac{2}{3}\right)\left(\dfrac{2}{3}\right) = \dfrac{8}{27}$

111. $\dfrac{1}{2} \times \dfrac{2}{3} \times \dfrac{3}{4} = \dfrac{1}{\cancel{2}_{1}} \times \dfrac{\cancel{2}^{1}}{\cancel{3}_{1}} \times \dfrac{\cancel{3}}{4} = \dfrac{1}{4}$

112. $\dfrac{7}{\cancel{8}_{4}} \times \dfrac{\cancel{2}^{1}}{5} \times \dfrac{1}{6} = \dfrac{7}{120}$

113. $\dfrac{4}{5} \times 1\dfrac{1}{5} = \dfrac{4}{5} \times \dfrac{6}{5} = \dfrac{24}{25}$

114. $\dfrac{2}{3} \times 2\dfrac{1}{3} = \dfrac{2}{3} \times \dfrac{7}{3} = \dfrac{14}{9} = 1\dfrac{5}{9}$

115. $5\dfrac{1}{3} \cdot \dfrac{1}{2} = \dfrac{\overset{8}{\cancel{16}}}{3} \cdot \dfrac{1}{\underset{1}{\cancel{2}}} = \dfrac{8}{3} = 2\dfrac{2}{3}$

116. $\dfrac{1}{10} \cdot 6\dfrac{2}{3} = \dfrac{1}{\underset{1}{\cancel{10}}} \cdot \dfrac{\overset{2}{\cancel{20}}}{3} = \dfrac{2}{3}$

117. $1\dfrac{1}{3} \cdot 4\dfrac{1}{2} = \dfrac{\overset{2}{\cancel{4}}}{\underset{1}{\cancel{3}}} \cdot \dfrac{\overset{3}{\cancel{9}}}{\underset{1}{\cancel{2}}} = 6$

118. $3\dfrac{1}{4} \cdot 5\dfrac{2}{3} = \dfrac{13}{4} \cdot \dfrac{17}{3} = \dfrac{221}{12} = 18\dfrac{5}{12}$

119. $6\dfrac{3}{4} \times 1\dfrac{1}{4} = \dfrac{27}{4} \times \dfrac{5}{4} = \dfrac{135}{16} = 8\dfrac{7}{16}$

120. $8\dfrac{1}{2} \times 2\dfrac{1}{2} = \dfrac{17}{2} \times \dfrac{5}{2} = \dfrac{85}{4} = 21\dfrac{1}{4}$

121. $\dfrac{7}{8} \times 1\dfrac{1}{5} \times \dfrac{3}{7} = \dfrac{\overset{1}{\cancel{7}}}{\underset{4}{\cancel{8}}} \times \dfrac{\overset{3}{\cancel{6}}}{5} \times \dfrac{3}{\underset{1}{\cancel{7}}} = \dfrac{9}{20}$

122. $1\dfrac{3}{8} \times \dfrac{10}{11} \times 1\dfrac{1}{4} = \dfrac{\overset{1}{\cancel{11}}}{8} \times \dfrac{\overset{5}{\cancel{10}}}{\underset{1}{\cancel{11}}} \times \dfrac{5}{\underset{2}{\cancel{4}}} = \dfrac{25}{16} = 1\dfrac{9}{16}$

123. $\left(3\dfrac{1}{3}\right)^3 = \left(\dfrac{10}{3}\right)\left(\dfrac{10}{3}\right)\left(\dfrac{10}{3}\right) = \dfrac{1,000}{27} = 37\dfrac{1}{27}$

124. $\left(1\dfrac{1}{2}\right)^3 = \left(\dfrac{3}{2}\right)\left(\dfrac{3}{2}\right)\left(\dfrac{3}{2}\right) = \dfrac{27}{8} = 3\dfrac{3}{8}$

125. The reciprocal of $\dfrac{2}{3}$ is $\dfrac{3}{2}$.

126. The reciprocal of $1\dfrac{1}{2}$ is the reciprocal of $\dfrac{3}{2}$ which is $\dfrac{2}{3}$.

127. The reciprocal of 8 is the reciprocal of $\dfrac{8}{1}$ which is $\dfrac{1}{8}$.

128. The reciprocal of $\dfrac{1}{4}$ is $\dfrac{4}{1}$ or 4.

129. $\dfrac{7}{8} \div 5 = \dfrac{7}{8} \div \dfrac{5}{1} = \dfrac{7}{8} \times \dfrac{1}{5} = \dfrac{7}{40}$

130. $\dfrac{5}{9} \div 9 = \dfrac{5}{9} \div \dfrac{9}{1} = \dfrac{5}{9} \times \dfrac{1}{9} = \dfrac{5}{81}$

131. $\dfrac{2}{3} \div 5 = \dfrac{2}{3} \div \dfrac{5}{1} = \dfrac{2}{3} \times \dfrac{1}{5} = \dfrac{2}{15}$

132. $\dfrac{1}{100} \div 2 = \dfrac{1}{100} \div \dfrac{2}{1} = \dfrac{1}{100} \times \dfrac{1}{2} = \dfrac{1}{200}$

133. $\dfrac{1}{2} \div \dfrac{2}{3} = \dfrac{1}{2} \times \dfrac{3}{2} = \dfrac{3}{4}$

134. $\dfrac{2}{3} \div \dfrac{1}{2} = \dfrac{2}{3} \times \dfrac{2}{1} = \dfrac{4}{3} = 1\dfrac{1}{3}$

135. $6 \div \dfrac{1}{5} = \dfrac{6}{1} \div \dfrac{1}{5} = \dfrac{6}{1} \times \dfrac{5}{1} = 30$

136. $7 \div \dfrac{4}{5} = \dfrac{7}{1} \div \dfrac{4}{5} = \dfrac{7}{1} \times \dfrac{5}{4} = \dfrac{35}{4} = 8\dfrac{3}{4}$

137. $\dfrac{7}{8} \div \dfrac{3}{4} = \dfrac{7}{\underset{2}{\cancel{8}}} \times \dfrac{\overset{1}{\cancel{4}}}{3} = \dfrac{7}{6} = 1\dfrac{1}{6}$

138. $\dfrac{9}{10} \div \dfrac{1}{2} = \dfrac{9}{\underset{5}{\cancel{10}}} \times \dfrac{\overset{1}{\cancel{2}}}{1} = \dfrac{9}{5} = 1\dfrac{4}{5}$

139. $\dfrac{3}{5} \div \dfrac{3}{10} = \dfrac{\overset{1}{\cancel{3}}}{\underset{1}{\cancel{5}}} \times \dfrac{\overset{2}{\cancel{10}}}{\underset{1}{\cancel{3}}} = 2$

140. $\dfrac{2}{3} \div \dfrac{1}{6} = \dfrac{2}{\underset{1}{\cancel{3}}} \times \dfrac{\overset{2}{\cancel{6}}}{1} = 4$

141. $3\dfrac{1}{2} \div 2 = \dfrac{7}{2} \div \dfrac{2}{1} = \dfrac{7}{2} \times \dfrac{1}{2} = \dfrac{7}{4} = 1\dfrac{3}{4}$

142. $2 \div 3\dfrac{1}{2} = \dfrac{2}{1} \div \dfrac{7}{2} = \dfrac{2}{1} \times \dfrac{2}{7} = \dfrac{4}{7}$

143. $6\dfrac{1}{3} \div 4 = \dfrac{19}{3} \div \dfrac{4}{1} = \dfrac{19}{3} \times \dfrac{1}{4} = \dfrac{19}{12} = 1\dfrac{7}{12}$

144. $4 \div 6\dfrac{1}{3} = \dfrac{4}{1} \div \dfrac{19}{3} = \dfrac{4}{1} \times \dfrac{3}{19} = \dfrac{12}{19}$

145. $8\dfrac{1}{4} \div 1\dfrac{1}{2} = \dfrac{33}{4} \div \dfrac{3}{2} = \dfrac{\overset{11}{\cancel{33}}}{\underset{2}{\cancel{4}}} \times \dfrac{\overset{1}{\cancel{2}}}{\underset{1}{\cancel{3}}} = \dfrac{11}{2} = 5\dfrac{1}{2}$

146. $3\frac{2}{5} \div 1\frac{1}{3} = \frac{17}{5} \div \frac{4}{3} = \frac{17}{5} \times \frac{3}{4} = \frac{51}{20} = 2\frac{11}{20}$

147. $4\frac{1}{2} \div 2\frac{1}{4} = \frac{9}{2} \div \frac{9}{4} = \frac{\overset{1}{\cancel{9}}}{\underset{1}{\cancel{2}}} \times \frac{\overset{2}{\cancel{4}}}{\underset{1}{\cancel{9}}} = 2$

148. $7\frac{1}{5} \div 2\frac{2}{5} = \frac{36}{5} \div \frac{12}{5} = \frac{\overset{3}{\cancel{36}}}{\underset{1}{\cancel{5}}} \times \frac{\overset{1}{\cancel{5}}}{\underset{1}{\cancel{12}}} = 3$

149. $\begin{array}{r} 497 \text{ R2} \\ 4\overline{)1990} \end{array}$ Since the division leaves a remainder of 2, the Olympic Games were not held in 1990.

150. $25 = 5^2 \qquad 10 = 2 \cdot 5$

$\text{LCM} = 2 \cdot 5^2 = 2 \cdot 25 = 50$

The smallest amount is 50¢.

151. $\frac{8}{32} = \frac{\overset{1}{\cancel{8}}}{4 \cdot \underset{1}{\cancel{8}}} = \frac{1}{4}$

$\frac{1}{4}$ of human teeth are incisors.

152. The number of planets is $1 + 2 + 6 = 9$. Two of these are closer to Earth than to the sun, so $\frac{2}{9}$ of the planets in the solar system are closer than Earth to the sun.

153. $\frac{10,000}{70,000} = \frac{1 \cdot \overset{1}{\cancel{10,000}}}{7 \cdot \underset{1}{\cancel{10,000}}} = \frac{1}{7}$

$\frac{1}{7}$ of the marchers finished.

154. $200,000 \times \frac{9}{10} = \frac{200,000}{1} \times \frac{9}{10} = 180,000$

Since $\frac{9}{10}$ of the President's salary is \$180,000, the Vice President makes more than $\frac{9}{10}$ of the President's salary.

155. $\frac{1}{8,000} < \frac{1}{6,000}$ since $8,000 > 6,000$.

The Filmworks camera has the faster shutter speed.

156. $\frac{1}{10} < \frac{1}{2}$ because $10 > 2$. Less than half the population is left-handed.

157. You got back more than $\frac{1}{3}$ because $\frac{275}{700} = \frac{33}{84}$ which is greater than $\frac{1}{3} = \frac{28}{84}$.

158. Yes, it should, because $\frac{23}{32}$ is greater than $\frac{2}{3}$:

$\frac{23}{32} = \frac{69}{96}$ and $\frac{2}{3} = \frac{64}{96}$

159. a. $\frac{12 \text{ jurors}}{23 \text{ jurors}} = \frac{12}{23}$ $\frac{12}{23}$ of the full jury is needed to indict.

b. $\frac{12 \text{ jurors}}{16 \text{ jurors}} = \frac{12}{16} = \frac{3 \cdot \overset{1}{\cancel{4}}}{4 \cdot \underset{1}{\cancel{4}}} = \frac{3}{4}$ $\frac{3}{4}$ of the jurors present are needed to indict.

160. a. Alisa went to the net 12 times and Monica went to the net 6 times, so Alisa Gregory went to the net more often.

b. $\frac{4}{6} > \frac{7}{12}$ because $\frac{8}{12} > \frac{7}{12}$, so Monica Yates had a better rate of winning points at the net.

161.

Employee	Saturday	Sunday	Total
L. Chavis	$7\frac{1}{2}$	$4\frac{1}{4}$	$11\frac{3}{4}$
M. Young	$5\frac{3}{4}$	$6\frac{1}{2}$	$12\frac{1}{4}$
Total	$13\frac{1}{4}$	$10\frac{3}{4}$	24

162.

Worker	Hours per Day	Days Worked	Total Hours	Wage per Hour	Gross Pay
Scott	5	3	15	\$7	\$105.00
Janis	$7\frac{1}{4}$	4	29	\$10	\$290.00
Erwin	$4\frac{1}{2}$	$5\frac{1}{2}$	$24\frac{3}{4}$	\$9	\$222.75

163. $5\frac{15}{16} - 4\frac{7}{8} = 5\frac{15}{16} - 4\frac{14}{16} = 1\frac{1}{16}$

The value dropped by $\$1\frac{1}{16}$.

164. $15 - 3\frac{1}{4} = 14\frac{4}{4} - 3\frac{1}{4} = 11\frac{3}{4}$

The town is $11\frac{3}{4}$ mi away.

165. $\frac{1}{5} \times 35 = \frac{1}{\cancel{5}} \times \frac{\cancel{35}^{7}}{1} = 7$

A 35-lb otter will eat 7 lb a day.

166. $27 \times \frac{1}{3} = \frac{\cancel{27}^{9}}{1} \times \frac{1}{\cancel{3}} = 9$ and $27 - 9 = 18$

You will pay $18 for the roses.

167. $1,000 \times 1\frac{1}{2} = \frac{\cancel{1,000}^{500}}{1} \times \frac{3}{\cancel{2}} = 1,500$

The plane is flying at 1,500 fps.

168. $200 \times 10\frac{1}{2} = \frac{\cancel{200}^{100}}{1} \times \frac{21}{\cancel{2}} = 2,100$

The report contains 2,100 words.

169. $3 \times 2\frac{1}{2} = \frac{3}{1} \times \frac{5}{2} = \frac{15}{2} = 7\frac{1}{2}$

You should plan the bulb $7\frac{1}{2}$ in. deep.

170. $200 \times 2\frac{1}{2} = \frac{\cancel{200}^{100}}{1} \times \frac{5}{\cancel{2}} = 500$

The pressure on your hip joint is 500 lb/sq in.

171. $\frac{8}{100} \div \frac{40}{1,000} = \frac{\cancel{8}^{1}}{\cancel{100}^{1}} \times \frac{\cancel{1,000}^{2}}{\cancel{40}} = 2$

The unemployment rate is 2 times greater in Georgetown.

172. $10 \div \frac{1}{2} = \frac{10}{1} \times \frac{2}{1} = 20$

With 20 goldfish the total length would be equal to the tank capacity in gallons, so to make the total length less than the capacity, you should buy 19 fish.

173. $60 \div 5\frac{1}{2} = \frac{60}{1} \div \frac{11}{2} = \frac{60}{1} \times \frac{2}{11} = \frac{120}{11} = 10\frac{10}{11}$

He lost $10\frac{10}{11}$ lb per month.

174. $\frac{1}{4} + \frac{2}{3} = \frac{3}{12} + \frac{8}{12} = \frac{11}{12}$

The alloy's total weight is $\frac{11}{12}$ oz.

Posttest

1. $\frac{75}{1} = 5\,R0 \qquad \frac{75}{3} = 25\,R0 \qquad \frac{75}{5} = 15\,R0$

The factors of 75 are 1, 3, 5, 15, 25, and 75.

2.

```
        60
       /  \
      2    30
          /  \
         2    15
             /  \
            3    5
```

$60 = 2^2 \times 3 \times 5$

3. The whole is divided into 9 equal parts. Four of these parts are shaded. The diagram illustrates the fraction $\frac{4}{9}$.

4. $12 = \frac{12}{1}$

5. $\frac{41}{4} = 4\overline{)41}\,^{10\ R1} \qquad\qquad \frac{41}{4} = 10\frac{1}{4}$

6. $\frac{875}{1,000} = \frac{\cancel{5}^1 \times \cancel{5}^1 \times \cancel{5}^1 \times 7}{2 \times 2 \times 2 \times \cancel{5}_1 \times \cancel{5}_1 \times \cancel{5}_1} = \frac{7}{8}$

7. $\frac{5}{10} < \frac{2}{3}$ because $\frac{15}{30} < \frac{20}{30}$

8. $8 = 2^3 \qquad 12 = 2^2 \cdot 3$

LCM of 8 and 12 is $2^3 \cdot 3 = 24$
The LCD for the fractions is 24.

9. $\frac{2}{3} = \frac{16}{24}$

$\frac{1}{8} = \frac{3}{24}$

$+\frac{3}{4} = +\frac{18}{24}$

$\frac{37}{24} = 1\frac{13}{24}$

10. $6\frac{7}{8} = 6\frac{35}{40}$

$1\frac{3}{10} = +1\frac{12}{40}$

$7\frac{47}{40} = 8\frac{7}{40}$

11. $6 = 5\frac{7}{7}$

$-1\frac{5}{7} = -1\frac{5}{7}$

$4\frac{2}{7}$

12. $10\frac{1}{6} = 9\frac{35}{30}$

$-4\frac{2}{5} = -4\frac{12}{30}$

$5\frac{23}{30}$

13. $\left(\frac{1}{9}\right)^2 = \frac{1}{9}\times\frac{1}{9} = \frac{1}{81}$

14. $2\frac{2}{3}\times4\frac{1}{2} = \frac{\overset{4}{\cancel{8}}}{\cancel{3}}\times\frac{\overset{3}{\cancel{9}}}{\cancel{2}} = 12$

15. $2\frac{1}{3}\div3 = \frac{7}{3}\div\frac{3}{1} = \frac{7}{3}\times\frac{1}{3} = \frac{7}{9}$

16. $3\frac{3}{8}\div2\frac{1}{4} = \frac{27}{8}\div\frac{9}{4} = \frac{\overset{3}{\cancel{27}}}{\underset{2}{\cancel{8}}}\times\frac{\overset{1}{\cancel{4}}}{\underset{1}{\cancel{9}}} = \frac{3}{2} = 1\frac{1}{2}$

17. The total number of students is $12+24=36$.

$\dfrac{\text{number of men}}{\text{number of students}} = \frac{12}{36} = \frac{1}{3}$

$\frac{1}{3}$ of the students in the class are men.

18. $\frac{2}{3}\div4 = \frac{2}{3}\div\frac{4}{1} = \frac{\cancel{2}}{3}\times\frac{1}{\underset{2}{\cancel{4}}} = \frac{1}{6}$

Each will get $\frac{1}{6}$ of the pie.

19. $10\frac{2}{3}\times8\frac{1}{2} = \frac{\overset{16}{\cancel{32}}}{3}\times\frac{17}{\underset{1}{\cancel{2}}} = \frac{272}{3} = 90\frac{2}{3}$

The area of the floor is $90\frac{2}{3}$ sq ft.

20. $6\frac{1}{3}-1\frac{1}{2}-1\frac{1}{2} = \left(5\frac{8}{6}-1\frac{3}{6}\right)-1\frac{3}{6}$

$= 4\frac{5}{6}-1\frac{3}{6} = 3\frac{2}{6} = 3\frac{1}{3}$

The missing dimension is $3\frac{1}{3}$ in.

Cumulative Review Exercises

1. 5,000,315 is five million, three hundred, fifteen.

2. $\begin{array}{r} 5,814 \text{ (no zeros)} \\ \times\ 100 \text{ (2 zeros)} \\ \hline 581,400 \text{ (2 zeros)} \end{array}$

3. $\begin{array}{r} 908 \\ 89\overline{)80,812} \\ -80\ 1 \\ \hline 71 \\ -0 \\ \hline 712 \\ -712 \\ \hline 0 \end{array}$

4. $\frac{75}{100} = \frac{3\times\cancel{5}\times\cancel{5}}{2\times2\times\cancel{5}\times\cancel{5}} = \frac{3}{4}$

5. $8 = 7\frac{5}{5}$

$-1\frac{3}{5} = -1\frac{3}{5}$

$6\frac{2}{5}$

6. $1\frac{1}{2} = 1\frac{3}{6}$

$+4\frac{2}{3} = +4\frac{4}{6}$

$5\frac{7}{6} = 6\frac{1}{6}$

7. $\frac{3}{8} > \frac{1}{4}$ because $\frac{3}{8} > \frac{2}{8}$

8. $\frac{\$5,000,000,000}{\$5,000} = \frac{1,000,000\times\overset{1}{\cancel{5,000}}}{\underset{1}{\cancel{5,000}}} = 1,000,000$

The amount the company paid is 1 million times the amount the captain paid.

9. $\begin{array}{r} 3\overset{9}{\cancel{10}}\overset{9}{\cancel{0}}\,^1 8 \\ -23,4\ 5\ 9 \\ \hline 5\ 4\ 9 \end{array}$

10. The 8-in. scented candle burns $\frac{1}{2}$ in. every hour:

$8\div\frac{1}{2} = \frac{8}{1}\times\frac{2}{1} = \frac{16}{1} = 16$ hr

The 10-in. unscented candle burns $\frac{1}{3}$ in. every hour:

$10\div\frac{1}{3} = \frac{10}{1}\times\frac{3}{1} = \frac{30}{1} = 30$ hr

Since the scented candle will last 16 hours and the unscented candle will last 30 hours, the unscented candle will last longer.

Chapter 3

DECIMALS

Pretest

1. In 27.081, 8 is in the hundredths place.

2. 4.012 is four and twelve thousandths.

3. $3.\underline{0}79 \approx 3.1$ since the critical digit is greater than 5.

4. 0.00212
   0.0029
   0.000888

   Line up the decimal points and look at the thousandths place. The first two numbers are larger than the third, because $2 > 0$. To compare the first two numbers, look at the ten thousandths place. Since $9 > 2$, 0.0029 is largest.

5. $\begin{array}{r} 7.02 \\ 3.5 \\ +11 \\ \hline 21.52 \end{array}$

6. $\begin{array}{r} 2.37 \\ +5.0038 \\ \hline 7.3738 \end{array}$

7. $\begin{array}{r} 13.79 \\ -2.1 \\ \hline 11.69 \end{array}$

8. $\begin{array}{r} 9 \\ -2.7 \\ \hline 6.3 \end{array}$ $\begin{array}{r} 6.3 \\ +3.51 \\ \hline 9.81 \end{array}$

   The answer is 9.81.

9. Move the decimal point three places to the right:
   $8.3 \times 1,000 = 8,300$

10. $\begin{array}{r} 8.01 \\ \times 2.3 \\ \hline 2\,403 \\ 16\,02 \\ \hline 18.423 \end{array}$

11. $(0.12)^2 = 0.12$
    $\begin{array}{r} \times 0.12 \\ \hline 24 \\ 12 \\ \hline 0.0144 \end{array}$

12. $5 + (3 \times 0.7) = 5 + 2.1 = 7.1$

13. Move the decimal point three places to the left:
    $\begin{array}{r} 0.00605 \\ 1,000\overline{)6.05000} \end{array}$

14. $9.81 \div 0.3 = \begin{array}{r} 32.7 \\ 3\overline{)98.1} \\ \underline{9} \\ 08 \\ \underline{6} \\ 21 \\ \underline{21} \\ 0 \end{array}$

15. $\begin{array}{r} 0.875 \\ 8\overline{)7.000} \\ \underline{64} \\ 60 \\ \underline{56} \\ 40 \\ \underline{40} \\ 0 \end{array}$

16. $2\frac{5}{6} = \frac{17}{6} = \begin{array}{r} 2.833 \\ 6\overline{)17.000} \\ \underline{12} \\ 50 \\ \underline{48} \\ 20 \\ \underline{18} \\ 20 \\ \underline{18} \\ 2 \end{array}$

    $2.8\underline{3}3 \approx 2.83$

17. $2.95 < 3.7$, so the acid with pH 2.95 is stronger than the acid with pH 3.7.

18. $\begin{array}{r} 3.7 \\ 1.8 \\ 2 \\ +0.5 \\ \hline 8.0 \end{array}$ The total profit for the year was $8 million.

19. $11.9 \div 3.6 = \begin{array}{r} 3.3 \\ 36\overline{)119.0} \\ \underline{108} \\ 11\,0 \\ \underline{10\,8} \\ 2 \end{array}$ $3.3 \approx 3$

    Romaine is about 3 times as rich in Vitamin C as iceberg lettuce.

20. For a 20-minute call, there are 17 additional minutes after the first three minutes, so the cost is
    $0.85 + 17 \times 0.17 = 0.85 + 2.89 = 3.74$

    The phone call costs $3.74.

3.1 Introduction to Decimals

Practice

1. **a.** $0.3\underline{6}$ **b.** $0.4\underline{7}2$

   c. $0.0\underline{2}51$ **d.** $897.4\underline{3}$

   e. $1,912.6\underline{4}3$

2. The decimal 2.03 has two decimal places, so the denominator of the fractional part is 100.

   $2.03 = 2\frac{3}{100}$ or $\frac{203}{100}$

3. $0.875 = \dfrac{875}{1000} = \dfrac{7 \cdot \cancel{25}^{1}}{8 \cdot \cancel{25}_{1}} = \dfrac{7}{8}$

4.   **a.** $5.6 = 5\dfrac{6}{10}$, or $5\dfrac{3}{5}$ **b.** $5.6000 = 5\dfrac{6,000}{10,000} = 5\dfrac{3}{5}$

5. $7.006 = 7\dfrac{6}{1000} = 7\dfrac{3}{500}$ **b.** $7.6 = 7\dfrac{6}{10} = 7\dfrac{3}{5}$

6.   **a.** 0.61 is sixty-one hundredths.
     b. 4.923 is four and nine hundred twenty-three thousandths.
     c. 7.05 is seven and five hundredths.

7.   **a.** This is a number of thousandths so the decimal will have three decimal places: 0.043
     b. This is a number of hundredths so the decimal will have two decimal places; the whole number part comes before "and": 10.26

8.   Three and fourteen hundredths is written 3.14.

9. $\downarrow$
     0.83
     0.8297
     $\uparrow$

     Align the decimal points. The digits in the ones place and the tenths place are the same, but in the hundredths place, 3 > 2, so 0.83 is larger.

10. $\downarrow$
     0.9
     0.92
     $\uparrow$

     Align the decimal points. The digits in the ones place and the tenths place are the same, but in the hundredths place, 2 is larger than the 0 that is understood in 0.9, so 0.92 is larger and Uranus has the stronger gravity.

11. $\downarrow$
     3.5
     2.9
     3.8
     $\uparrow$

     In the ones place, 3 > 2, so 2.9 is the smallest decimal. To compare the other two, look at the tenths place, where 8 > 5. So in decreasing order the decimals are 3.8, 3.5, and 2.9.

12. $\downarrow$
     8.2
     9
     8.1
     $\uparrow$

     Since 8 < 9, the units rated 8.2 and 8.1 are less efficient than the 9 unit. Now look at the tenths

place; since 1 < 2, the unit rated 8.1 is the least efficient.

13. **a.** Underline the tenths digit: 748.<u>0</u>772

     The critical digit, 7, is more than 5, so add one to the underlined digit and drop the remaining digits: 748.1

     b. Underline the hundredths digit: 748.0<u>7</u>72

     The critical digit, 7, is more than 5, so add one to the underlined digit and drop the remaining digits: 748.08

     c. Underline the digit in the third place: 748.07<u>7</u>2

     The critical digit, 2, is less than 5, so drop the digits to the right of the underlined digit: 748.077

     d. Underline the units digit: 74<u>8</u>.0772

     The critical digit, 0, is less than 5, drop the digits to the right of the underlined digit: 748

     e. Underline the hundreds digit: 7<u>4</u>8.0772

     The critical digit, 8, is more than 5, so add one to the underlined digit, put a 0 in the ones place, and drop the digits to the right of the decimal point: 700

14. Underline the digit in the hundredths place: 7.2<u>9</u>62

     The critical digit 6 is greater than 5, so we add 1 to the 9, write down a 0 and carry 1 to the 2 getting 3. Drop the last two digits, giving 7.30.

15. $162.\underline{9}62 \approx 163.0$

     To the nearest tenth of a mile per hour, the speed is 163.0 mph.

Exercises

1.   0.61 is sixty-one hundredths.

3.   0.305 is three hundred five thousandths.

5.   0.6 is six tenths.

7.   5.72 five and seventy-two hundredths.

9.   24.002 is twenty-four and two thousandths.

11. $0.6 = \dfrac{6}{10} = \dfrac{3}{5}$ 13. $0.39 = \dfrac{39}{100}$

15. $1.5 = 1\dfrac{5}{10} = 1\dfrac{1}{2}$ 17. $8.000 = 8\dfrac{0}{1,000} = 8$

19. $5.012 = 5\dfrac{12}{1,000} = 5\dfrac{3}{250}$

21. This is a number of tenths, so the decimal will have one decimal place: 0.8

23. The whole number part, 1, comes before "and"; the decimal part is a number of thousandths, so the decimal will have three decimal places: 1.041

25. The whole number part, 60, comes before "and"; the decimal part is a number of hundredths, so the decimal will have two decimal places: 60.01

27. The whole number part, 4, comes before "and"; the decimal part is a number of thousandths, so the decimal will have three decimal places: 4.107

29. The whole number part, 3, comes before "and"; the decimal part is a number of tenths, so the decimal will have one decimal place: 3.2 m

31. 1.467 is one and four hundred sixty-seven thousandths.

33. 18.7 to 18.8 is eighteen and seven tenths to eighteen and eight tenths.

35. 301.3 is three hundred one and three tenths.
55.9 is fifty-five and nine tenths.
268.2 is two hundred sixty-eight and two tenths.
46.6 is forty-six and six tenths.
43.6 is forty-three and six tenths.

37. 0.00001 is one hundred thousandth; 0.00008 is eight hundred thousandths.

39. One and two-tenths acres is 1.2 acres.

41. Seventy-four and fifty-nine hundredths mph is 74.59 mph.

43. Fourteen and seven-tenths lb is 14.7 lb.

45. Five-thousandths of a dollar is $0.005.

47. Three hundred fifty-two and one-tenth kilowatt hours is 352.1 kWh.

49. 2.78

51. 0.03

53. 358.02

55. 0.772

57. Tenths

59. Hundredths

61. Thousandths

63. Ones

65. In the ones place, 3 > 2, so 3.21 > 2.5.

67. In the tenths place, 7 < 8, so 0.71 < 0.8.

69. In the hundredths place, 2 > 1, so 9.123 > 9.11.

71. 4 = 4.000

73. In the tenths place, 1 < 2, so 8.125 ft < 8.2 ft.

75. ↓
7.1
7
7.07
↑

In the tenths place, 1 > 0, so 7.1 is the largest number. To compare the other two, look at the hundredths place, where 7 > 0. So in increasing order the decimals are 7, 7.07, 7.1.

77. ↓
5.001
4.9
5.2
↑

In the ones place, 5 > 4, so 4.9 is the smallest decimal. To compare the other two, look at the tenths place, where 2 > 0. So in increasing order the decimals are 4.9, 5.001, 5.2.

79. ↓
9.6 mi
9.1 mi
9.38 mi
↑

Since the ones digits are all 9, the order is determined by the tenths place. In increasing order the distances are 9.1 mi, 9.38 mi, 9.6 mi.

81. ↓
1.85
2.1
↑

Align the decimal points. The numbers differ in the ones place and 1 < 2, so 1.85 < 2.1. The award was less than $2.1 million.

83. ↓
8.75
8.5
↑

Align the decimal points. In the tenths place, 7 > 5, so 8.75 > 8.5. The average daily heating bill was larger last winter.

85. ↓
0.0004
0.003
↑

Align the decimal points. The numbers differ in the thousandths place, where 3 > 0. So 0.003 in. is greater than 0.0004 in., and a person with reasonably good vision can see the mite.

87. ↓
1.1
2.3
0.95
↑

The ones digit of 0.95 is less than the ones digit of 1.1. Your score is less than the lower end of the range, so it is not in the normal range.

89. 17.36 ≈ 17.4

91. 3.5905 ≈ 3.591

93. $37.\underline{0}8 \approx 37.1$

95. $0.3\underline{9}6 \approx 0.40$
Round the 9 up to 10
and carry the one to
the tenths place.

97. $7.0\underline{5}71 \approx 7.06$

99. $\underline{8}.7 \text{ mi} \approx 9 \text{ mi}$

101.

To the nearest	8.0714	0.9916
Tenth	8.1	1.0
Hundredth	8.07	0.99
Ten	10	0

103. $\$57.0\underline{2}85 \approx \$57.03$ The bank pays $57.03 in interest.

105. $0.00\underline{0}8 \approx 0.001$ Rounded to the nearest thousandth, the probability of winning is 0.001.

107. $1.\underline{7}7 \approx 1.8$ The cost of medical care is about 1.8 times what is was a decade ago.

3.2   Adding and Subtracting Decimals

Practice

1.
```
  5.12
  4.967
+0.3
------
 10.387
```

2.
```
 $7.31
  8.
+23.99
------
$39.30
```

3.
```
 99.4
+2.7
-----
102.1
```
His temperature was 102.1° F.

4.
```
 71.38
-25.17
------
 46.21
```

5.
```
 $735.00
-249.57
-------
$485.43
```

6.
```
 28.5
-15.0
-----
 13.5
```
You have 13.5 mi further to go.

7.
```
 4.3      8.0
+3.7     -5.9
----     ----
 8.0      2.1
```
Going directly is 2.1 mi shorter.

8.
```
  0.093  ≈   0.100
  0.008  ≈   0.010
+0.762  ≈ +0.760
exact 0.863   0.872 estimated
sum                 sum
```

9.
```
 2.3   ≈    2
+1.75  ≈  +2
            4
```
The estimated selling price is $4 million.

10.
```
       0.17   ≈   0.2
      -0.091  ≈  -0.1
exact  0.079      0.1 estimated
difference            difference
```

11.
```
  76.35  ≈   80    Possible answer: $480
 312.95  ≈  310
  42.30  ≈   40
+49.    ≈  +50
          $480
```

Calculator Practice

p. 183.   79.23; 0.00002

Exercises

1.
```
      3.89  ≈    4
     +5.44  ≈  +5
exact 9.33      9 estimated
sum               sum
```

3.
```
      0.6  ≈   1
     +0.3  ≈ +0
exact 0.9      1 estimated
sum              sum
```

5.
```
      6.03  ≈   6
     +2.1  ≈  +2
exact 8.13      8 estimated
sum               sum
```

7.
```
      13.05  ≈  13
     +8.4   ≈ +8
exact 21.45     21 estimated
sum                sum
```

9.
```
      2.67  ≈   3
     +5    = +5
exact 7.67      8 estimated
sum               sum
```

11.
```
       $74.00  ≈ $74
      +3.21   ≈  +3
exact $77.21     $77 estimated
sum                  sum
```

13.
```
       8.01  ≈    8
       6.7   ≈    7
      +9.45  ≈  +9
exact 24.16     24 estimated
sum                sum
```

15.
$$
\begin{aligned}
34.7 &\approx 35\\
5.84 &\approx 6\\
3 &= 3\\
+0.882 &\approx +1\\
\hline
\end{aligned}
$$
exact 44.422   45 estimated
sum   sum

17.
$$
\begin{aligned}
7 \text{ mm} &= 7 \text{ mm}\\
3.5 \text{ mm} &\approx 4 \text{ mm}\\
+9.82 \text{ mm} &\approx +10 \text{ mm}\\
\hline
\end{aligned}
$$
exact 20.32 mm   21 mm estimated
sum   sum

19.
$$
\begin{aligned}
4.7 \text{ kg} &\approx 5 \text{ kg}\\
2.98 \text{ kg} &\approx 3 \text{ kg}\\
+9.002 \text{ kg} &\approx +9 \text{ kg}\\
\hline
\end{aligned}
$$
exact 16.682 kg   17 kg estimated
sum   sum

21. 23.30595

23.
$$
\begin{aligned}
0.8 &\approx 1\\
-0.1 &\approx -0\\
\hline
\end{aligned}
$$
exact 0.7   1 estimated
difference   difference

25.
$$
\begin{aligned}
20.72 &\approx 21\\
-3.92 &\approx -4\\
\hline
\end{aligned}
$$
exact 16.80   17 estimated
difference   difference

The difference is 16.8.

27.
$$
\begin{aligned}
23.81 &\approx 24\\
-5.4 &\approx -5\\
\hline
\end{aligned}
$$
exact 18.41   19 estimated
difference   difference

29.
$$
\begin{aligned}
80.2 &\approx 80\\
-4.57 &\approx -5\\
\hline
\end{aligned}
$$
exact 75.63   75 estimated
difference   difference

31.
$$
\begin{aligned}
25.99 &\approx 26\\
-3.666 &\approx -4\\
\hline
\end{aligned}
$$
exact 22.324   22 estimated
difference   difference

33.
$$
\begin{aligned}
0.27 &\approx 0.3\\
-0.1 &\approx -0.1\\
\hline
\end{aligned}
$$
exact 0.17   0.2 estimated
difference   difference

35.
$$
\begin{aligned}
13.2 &\approx 13\\
-7 &= -7\\
\hline
\end{aligned}
$$
exact 6.2   6 estimated
difference   difference

37.
$$
\begin{aligned}
20 &= 20\\
-4.63 &\approx -5\\
\hline
\end{aligned}
$$
exact 15.37   15 estimated
difference   difference

39.
$$
\begin{aligned}
10 &= 10\\
-4.1 &\approx -4\\
\hline
\end{aligned}
$$
exact 5.9   6 estimated
difference   difference

41.
$$
\begin{aligned}
8 &= 8\\
-1.79 &\approx -2\\
\hline
\end{aligned}
$$
exact 6.21   6 estimated
difference   difference

43.
$$
\begin{aligned}
3.2 \text{ lb} &\approx 3 \text{ lb}\\
-1.35 \text{ lb} &\approx -1 \text{ lb}\\
\hline
\end{aligned}
$$
exact 1.85 lb   2 lb estimated
difference   difference

45.
$$
\begin{aligned}
103.7^\circ F &\approx 104^\circ F\\
-98.8^\circ F &\approx -99^\circ F\\
\hline
\end{aligned}
$$
exact 4.9° F   5° F estimated
difference   difference

47. 41.40896

49. a.
$$
\begin{aligned}
0.059 &\approx 0.06\\
0.00234 &\approx 0.000\\
+0.036 &\approx +0.04\\
\hline
0.09734 & \quad 0.10
\end{aligned}
$$
b.
$$
\begin{aligned}
0.1903 &\approx 0.2\\
0.074 &\approx 0.1\\
+0.2051 &\approx +0.2\\
\hline
0.4694 & \quad 0.5
\end{aligned}
$$
c.
$$
\begin{aligned}
0.00441 &\approx 0.00\\
0.06882 &\approx 0.07\\
+0.0103 &\approx +0.01\\
\hline
0.8353 & \quad 0.08
\end{aligned}
$$
The calculation in part (c) is wrong.

51. a.
$$
\begin{aligned}
0.35 &\approx 0.35\\
-0.1007 &\approx -0.10\\
\hline
0.2493 & \quad 0.25
\end{aligned}
$$
b.
$$
\begin{aligned}
0.072 &\approx 0.07\\
-0.0056 &\approx -0.01\\
\hline
0.664 & \quad 0.06
\end{aligned}
$$
c.
$$
\begin{aligned}
0.03 &\approx 0.03\\
-0.008 &\approx -0.01\\
\hline
0.022 & \quad 0.02
\end{aligned}
$$
The calculation in part (b) is wrong.

53. $13.00   The discount is $1.03.
$$
\begin{aligned}
&\$13.00\\
-&\$11.97\\
\hline
&\$1.03
\end{aligned}
$$

55. 0.8 centuries is $0.8 \times 100 = 80$ years. 56 centuries is $56 \times 100 = 5,600$ years. The greatest possible age of the skeleton is $5,600 + 80 = 5,680$ years.

57. $4 million   Your profit was $1.7 million.
$$
\begin{aligned}
&\$4 \text{ million}\\
-&2.3 \text{ million}\\
\hline
&\$1.7 \text{ million}
\end{aligned}
$$

59. $8.5 - 2 \times 0.83 = 8.5 - 1.66 = 6.84$
Each typed line is 6.84 in. long.

61. Yes: $2.8 + 2.9 + 2.6 + 1.6 = 9.9$

63. $104.3°F$ $101.6°F$
         $\underline{-2.7°F}$ $\underline{+0.9°F}$
         $101.6°F$ $102.5°F$

At 1 P.M. the patient's temperature was $102.5°F$.

65. a. Addition, subtraction
   b. The total is 13.2 mg of iron.
      $18\text{ mg} - 13.2\text{ mg} = 4.8\text{ mg}$
      You need 4.8 mg more.
   c. Possible estimate:
      $1+2+0+2+1+1+1+1+1+2+1+0 = 13$

3.3   Multiplying Decimals

Practice

1. 2.81
      $\underline{\times 3.5}$
      1405
      843
      $\overline{9.835}$

2. The total number of places in the numbers being multiplied is two, so the number of decimal places in the product will be two:
   0.28
   $\underline{\times 5}$
   $\overline{1.40} = 1.4$

3. 0.44
      $\underline{\times 0.03}$
      132
      000
      $\overline{0.0132} \approx 0.01$

4. $(0.2)(0.3)(0.4) =$

   $(0.06)(0.4) = 0.024$

5. $10 - (0.3)^2 = 10 - 0.09 = 9.91$

6. The second factor ends in three zeros. The product will have three decimal places, but they will be zero so they are dropped.
   0.325
   $\underline{\times 1,000}$
   $325.000 = 325$

7. 10,000 has four zeros, so move the decimal point four places to the right, inserting 0s as placeholders.
   $32.7 \times 10,000 = 327000. = 327,000$

8. a. 1.008 **b.** $18.01 \approx 18$
         1.008
         $\underline{+15.994}$
         18.01

9. 0.0037 $\approx$ 0.004
             $\underline{\times\ 0.092}$ $\approx$ $\underline{\times\ 0.09}$
   exact 0.0003404 0.00036 estimated
   product   product

10. $18.6 \approx 19$ Possible answer: 1,140 mi
      $\underline{\times 60} \approx \underline{\times 60}$
                  $1,140$

Calculator Practice

p. 193.   815.6; 9.261

Exercises

1. $2.356 \times 1.27 = 2.99212$
      3 places   2 places   5 places
      Estimate: $2 \times 1 = 2$

3. $0.0019 \times 0.051 = 0.0000969$
      4 places   3 places   7 places
      Estimate: $.002 \times 0.05 = 0.0001$

5. $3,144 \times 0.065 = 204.360 = 204.36$
      0 places   3 places   3 places
      Estimate: $3,000 \times 0.06 = 180$

7. $71.2 \times 35 = 2,492.0 = 2,492$
      1 place   0 places   1 place
      Estimate: $70 \times 35 = 2,450$

9. $2.87 \times 1,000 = 2,870.00 = 2,870$
      2 places   0 places   2 places
      Estimate: $3 \times 1,000 = 3,000$

11. $\$4.25 \times 0.173 = \$0.73525$
       2 places   3 places   5 places
       Estimate: $\$4 \times 0.2 = \$0.8$

13. 0.6
        $\underline{\times 0.3}$
        0.18

The numbers are already rounded so the check will give the same result.

15. 0.5
        $\underline{\times 0.8}$
        0.40

The numbers are already rounded so the check will give the same result.

17. 0.1
        $\underline{\times 0.2}$
        0.02

The numbers are already rounded so the check will give the same result.

19. 0.04
        $\underline{\times 0.02}$
        0.0008

The numbers are already rounded so the check will give the same result.

21.
```
  2.55    Check:      3
 ×0.3               ×0.3
 0.765               0.9
```

23.
```
 0.96    Check:   1
×2.1             ×2
  96              2
1 92
2.016
```

25.
```
38.01    Check:    40
×0.2              ×0.2
7.602               8
```

27.
```
   125    Check:    100
×0.004           × 0.004
   0.5               0.4
```

29.
```
  3.8    Check:    4
×1.5             ×1.5
190                6
 38
 5.7
```

31.
```
12.45    Check:   12
×0.3             ×0.3
3.735             3.6
```

33.
```
 13.74    Check:   14
  ×11             ×10
 13 74            140
137 4
151.14
```

35.
```
 0.21    Check:   0.2
×0.4             ×0.4
0.084            0.08
```

37. 100 has two zeros, so move the decimal point two places to the right.
$83.127 \times 100 = 83\,127. = 8,312.7$

39. 10,000 has four zeros, so move the decimal point four places to the right.
$0.0023 \times 10,000 = .0023. = 23$

41. The exponent on 10^2 is 2, so move the decimal point two places to the right, inserting a 0 placeholder.
$0.7 \times 10^2 = 70$

43. $(0.3)^2 = (0.3)(0.3) = 0.09$

45. $(1.5)(0.6)(0.1)$
$= (0.9)(0.1) = 0.09$

47. In each of the three factors, the 1 is in the thousandths place, so the result will have 9 decimal places:
$(0.001)^3 = (0.001)(0.001)(0.001)$
$= (0.000001)(0.001) = 0.000000001$

49. $30 - 2.5 \times 1.7 = 30 - 4.25 = 25.75$
Estimate: $30 - 2.5 \times 2 = 30 - 5 = 25$

51.
```
 17 ft
×2.5
  85
  34
42.5 ft
```
Check:
$20\,\text{ft} \times 2.5 = 50\,\text{ft}$

53.
```
 3.5 mi
×0.4
1.4 mi
```
Check:
$4\,\text{mi} \times 0.4 = 1.6\,\text{mi}$

55. 3.29025

57. 272,593.75

59.

Input	Output
1	$3.8 \times 1 - 0.2 = 3.6$
2	$3.8 \times 2 - 0.2 = 7.4$
3	$3.8 \times 3 - 0.2 = 11.2$
4	$3.8 \times 4 - 0.2 = 15$

61. a. $51.6 \times 0.813 = 419.51$
$50 \times 1 = 50$
b. $2.93 \times 7.283 = 21.34$
$3 \times 7 = 21$
c. $(5.004)^2 = 25.04$
$5 \times 5 = 25$
The answer in part (a) is wrong.

63. a. $4.913 \times 2.18 = 10.71$
$5 \times 2 = 10$
b. $0.023 \times 0.71 = 0.16$
$0.02 \times 0.7 = 0.014$
c. $(8.92)(1.0027) = 8.94$
$(9)(1) = 9$
The answer in part (b) is wrong.

65. $2.9 \times 1,000 = 2,900$
A speed of Mach 2.9 is 2,900 fps.

67. $2.6 billion is $2,600,000,000.00.

69.
```
   6.25
  ×3.14
  25 00
  62 5
18 75
19.6 2 50 ≈ 19.6
```
The area is approximately 19.6 sq ft.

71. $10 \times 0.125 = 1.25$ mg of Digoxin was administered.

73. a.

Purchase	Quantity	Unit Price	Price
Belt	1	$11.99	$11.99
Shirt	3	$16.95	$50.85
Total Price			$62.84

  b. $(\$20 \times 4) - \$62.84 = \$80 - \$62.84 = \$17.16$
    You should get $17.16 in change.

75. a. Multiplication, addition
  b. $(1.9 \times 29.9) + 32.0 = 88.81$ in. (exact ans.).
  c. $(2 \times 30) + 30 = 90$; a reasonable estimate is 90 in.

3.4 Dividing Decimals

Practice

1.
$$8\overline{)3.000} = 0.375 \qquad \frac{3}{8} = 0.375$$
$$\begin{array}{r} 0.375 \\ 8\overline{)3.000} \\ \underline{2\,4} \\ 60 \\ \underline{56} \\ 40 \\ \underline{40} \\ 0 \end{array}$$

2. First convert the mixed number to an improper fraction.
$$7\frac{5}{8} = \frac{61}{8} \quad \begin{array}{r} 7.625 \\ 8\overline{)61.000} \\ \underline{56} \\ 5\,0 \\ \underline{4\,8} \\ 20 \\ \underline{16} \\ 40 \\ \underline{40} \\ 0 \end{array} \quad 7\frac{5}{8} = 7.625$$

3. First convert the mixed number to an improper fraction. To round to the nearest tenth, divide through the hundredths place.
$$83\frac{1}{3} = \frac{250}{3} \quad \begin{array}{r} 83.33 \\ 3\overline{)250.00} \\ \underline{24} \\ 10 \\ \underline{9} \\ 10 \\ \underline{9} \\ 10 \\ \underline{9} \\ 1 \end{array} \quad 83.3\underline{3} \approx 83.3$$

4.
$$\begin{array}{r} 0.77 \\ 50\overline{)39.00} \\ \underline{35\,0} \\ 400 \\ \underline{3\,50} \\ 50 \end{array} \qquad 0.\underline{7}7 \approx 0.8$$

5. $0.15\overline{)2.706}$ Move the decimal point to the right, making the divisor a whole number:
$$\begin{array}{r} 18.04 \\ 15\overline{)270.60} \\ \underline{15} \\ 120 \\ \underline{120} \\ 06 \\ \underline{0} \\ 60 \\ \underline{60} \\ 0 \end{array} \qquad \begin{array}{r} \text{Check: } 18.04 \\ \times 0.15 \\ \hline 2.706 \end{array}$$

6. $0.004\overline{)8.2}$ Move the decimal point three places to the right.
$$\begin{array}{r} 2,050 \\ 4\overline{)8,200} \\ \underline{8} \\ 00 \\ \underline{0} \\ 20 \\ \underline{20} \\ 00 \\ \underline{0} \\ 0 \end{array} \qquad \begin{array}{r} \text{Check: } 2,050 \\ \times 0.004 \\ \hline 8.200 = 8.2 \end{array}$$

7.
$$\begin{array}{r} 73.36 \\ 11\overline{)807.00} \\ \underline{77} \\ 37 \\ \underline{33} \\ 4\,0 \\ \underline{3\,3} \\ 70 \\ \underline{66} \\ 4 \end{array}$$
$$73.3\underline{6} \approx 73.4$$

8.
$$\begin{array}{r} 0.0341 \\ 100\overline{)3.4100} \\ \underline{3\,00} \\ 410 \\ \underline{400} \\ 100 \\ \underline{100} \\ 0 \end{array}$$
Check:
$$100 \times 0.0341 = 3.410$$

9. Since 1,000 has three zeros, to divide by 1,000, move the decimal point three places to the left:
$0.86 \div 1,000 = 0.00086$

10. $0.6 \div .15 = \begin{array}{r} 4 \\ 15\overline{)60} \\ \underline{60} \\ 0 \end{array}$

You should administer 4 tablets.

11. $\dfrac{6.2+6.7+6.3+6.5+6.5}{5} = \dfrac{32.0}{5} = 6.4$

12. $8.229 \div 0.39 = 39\overline{)822.9}$
$$
\begin{array}{r}
21.1 \\
39\overline{)822.9} \\
\underline{78} \\
42 \\
\underline{39} \\
39 \\
\underline{39} \\
0
\end{array}
$$

To check, round 8.229 to 8 and .39 to .4. The division becomes

$$8 \div .4 = 4\overline{)80}$$
$$
\begin{array}{r}
20 \\
4\overline{)80} \\
\underline{8} \\
00 \\
\underline{0} \\
0
\end{array}
$$

The estimate of 20 is reasonably close to the exact answer, 21.1.

Calculator Practice

p. 205.   4.29; $1.6 \div 8.6 = 0.\underline{1}860... \approx 0.2$

Exercises

1. $2\overline{)11.0}$
$$
\begin{array}{r}
5.5 \\
2\overline{)11.0} \\
\underline{10} \\
1\,0 \\
\underline{1\,0} \\
0
\end{array}
$$
Check: $5.5 = 5\dfrac{5}{10} = 5\dfrac{\cancel{5}\cdot 1}{\cancel{5}\cdot 2} = 5\dfrac{1}{2} = \dfrac{11}{2}$

3. $4\overline{)21.00}$
$$
\begin{array}{r}
5.25 \\
4\overline{)21.00} \\
\underline{20} \\
1\,0 \\
\underline{8} \\
20 \\
\underline{20} \\
0
\end{array}
$$
Check: $5.25 = 5\dfrac{25}{100} = 5\dfrac{\cancel{25}\cdot 1}{\cancel{25}\cdot 4} = 5\dfrac{1}{4} = \dfrac{21}{4}$

5. The divisor has one zero, so move the decimal point one place to the left:

$37 \div 10 = 3.7$ Check: $3.7 = 3\dfrac{7}{10} = \dfrac{37}{10}$

7. $1\dfrac{5}{8} = \dfrac{13}{8} = 8\overline{)13.000}$
$$
\begin{array}{r}
1.625 \\
8\overline{)13.000} \\
\underline{8} \\
5\,0 \\
\underline{4\,8} \\
20 \\
\underline{16} \\
40 \\
\underline{40} \\
0
\end{array}
$$

Check: $1.625 = 1\dfrac{625}{1,000} = 1\dfrac{\cancel{125}\cdot 5}{\cancel{125}\cdot 8} = 1\dfrac{5}{8}$

9. $2\dfrac{7}{8} = \dfrac{23}{8} = 8\overline{)23.000}$
$$
\begin{array}{r}
2.875 \\
8\overline{)23.000} \\
\underline{16} \\
5\,0 \\
\underline{4\,8} \\
20 \\
\underline{16} \\
40 \\
\underline{40} \\
0
\end{array}
$$

Check: $2.875 = 2\dfrac{875}{1,000} = 2\dfrac{\cancel{125}\cdot 7}{\cancel{125}\cdot 8} = 2\dfrac{7}{8}$

11. The fractional part of $21\dfrac{3}{100}$ is $\dfrac{3}{100}$. Since the denominator is a power of 10 with two zeros, move the decimal point two places to the left: $\dfrac{3}{100} = 0.03$ Now add this decimal to the whole number 21. The result is 21.03.

Check: $21.03 = 21\dfrac{3}{100}$

13. $4\overline{)17.00}$
$$
\begin{array}{r}
4.25 \\
4\overline{)17.00} \\
\underline{16} \\
1\,0 \\
\underline{8} \\
20 \\
\underline{20} \\
0
\end{array}
$$

15. $5\overline{)21.0}$
$$
\begin{array}{r}
4.2 \\
5\overline{)21.0} \\
\underline{20} \\
1\,0 \\
\underline{1\,0} \\
0
\end{array}
$$

17.
$$
\begin{array}{r}
1.375 \\
8{\overline{\smash{\big)}\,11.000}} \\
\underline{8} \\
3\,0 \\
\underline{2\,4} \\
60 \\
\underline{56} \\
40 \\
\underline{40} \\
0
\end{array}
$$

19.
$$
\begin{array}{r}
8.5 \\
18{\overline{\smash{\big)}\,153.0}} \\
\underline{144} \\
9\,0 \\
\underline{9\,0} \\
0
\end{array}
$$

33.
$$
\begin{array}{r}
303.66 \\
3{\overline{\smash{\big)}\,911.00}} \\
\underline{9} \\
01 \\
\underline{0} \\
11 \\
\underline{9} \\
2\,0 \\
\underline{18} \\
20 \\
\underline{18} \\
2
\end{array}
$$
$303.\underline{6}6 \approx 303.7$

35.
$$
\begin{array}{r}
6.57 \\
7{\overline{\smash{\big)}\,46.00}} \\
\underline{42} \\
40 \\
\underline{35} \\
50 \\
\underline{49} \\
1
\end{array}
$$
$6.\underline{5}7 \approx 6.6$

21.
$$
\begin{array}{r}
0.666 \\
3{\overline{\smash{\big)}\,2.000}} \\
\underline{1\,8} \\
2 \\
\underline{18} \\
20 \\
\underline{18} \\
2
\end{array}
$$
$0.6\underline{6}6 \approx 0.67$

23.
$$
\begin{array}{r}
0.777 \\
9{\overline{\smash{\big)}\,7.000}} \\
\underline{63} \\
70 \\
\underline{63} \\
70 \\
\underline{63} \\
7
\end{array}
$$
$0.7\underline{7}7 \approx 0.78$

37.
$$
\begin{array}{r}
58.82 \\
0.7{\overline{\smash{\big)}\,41.174}}
\end{array}
$$

39.
$$
\begin{array}{r}
6.9 \\
3.9{\overline{\smash{\big)}\,26.91}}
\end{array}
$$

25. $3\dfrac{1}{9} = \dfrac{28}{9} = 9{\overline{\smash{\big)}\,28.000}}$
$$
\begin{array}{r}
3.111 \\
9{\overline{\smash{\big)}\,28.000}} \\
\underline{27} \\
10 \\
\underline{9} \\
10 \\
\underline{9} \\
10 \\
\underline{9} \\
1
\end{array}
$$
$3.1\underline{1}1 \approx 3.11$

41.
$$
\begin{array}{r}
0.93 \\
4{\overline{\smash{\big)}\,3.72}} \\
\underline{3\,6} \\
12 \\
\underline{12} \\
0
\end{array}
$$

43.
$$
\begin{array}{r}
2.8875 \\
8{\overline{\smash{\big)}\,23.1000}} \\
\underline{16} \\
7\,1 \\
\underline{6\,4} \\
70 \\
\underline{64} \\
60 \\
\underline{56} \\
40 \\
\underline{40} \\
0
\end{array}
$$

27. $5\dfrac{1}{16} = \dfrac{81}{16} = 16{\overline{\smash{\big)}\,81.000}}$
$$
\begin{array}{r}
5.062 \\
16{\overline{\smash{\big)}\,81.000}} \\
\underline{80} \\
1\,0 \\
\underline{0} \\
1\,00 \\
\underline{96} \\
40 \\
\underline{32} \\
8
\end{array}
$$
$5.0\underline{6}2 \approx 5.06$

45.
$$
\begin{array}{r}
27.17 \\
3{\overline{\smash{\big)}\,81.51}} \\
\underline{6} \\
21 \\
\underline{21} \\
0\,5 \\
\underline{3} \\
21 \\
\underline{21} \\
0
\end{array}
$$

47.
$$
\begin{array}{r}
0.286 \\
7{\overline{\smash{\big)}\,2.002}} \\
\underline{1\,4} \\
60 \\
\underline{56} \\
42 \\
\underline{42} \\
0
\end{array}
$$

29.
$$
\begin{array}{r}
3.28 \\
7{\overline{\smash{\big)}\,23.00}} \\
\underline{21} \\
2\,0 \\
\underline{14} \\
60 \\
\underline{56} \\
4
\end{array}
$$
$3.\underline{2}8 \approx 3.3$

31.
$$
\begin{array}{r}
0.27 \\
11{\overline{\smash{\big)}\,3.00}} \\
\underline{2\,2} \\
80 \\
\underline{77} \\
3
\end{array}
$$
$0.\underline{2}7 \approx 0.3$

49.
$$
\begin{array}{r}
4.3 \\
4{\overline{\smash{\big)}\,17.2}} \\
\underline{16} \\
1\,2 \\
\underline{1\,2} \\
0
\end{array}
$$

51.
$$
\begin{array}{r}
0.0015 \\
2{\overline{\smash{\big)}\,0.0030}} \\
\underline{2} \\
10 \\
\underline{10} \\
0
\end{array}
$$

53. $8.65 \div 5 = 5\overline{)8.65}$ with quotient 1.73

$$
\begin{array}{r}
1.73 \\
5\overline{)8.65} \\
\underline{5} \\
3\,6 \\
\underline{3\,5} \\
1\,5 \\
\underline{1\,5} \\
0
\end{array}
$$

55. $11.5 \div 4 = 4\overline{)11.500}$ with quotient 2.875

$$
\begin{array}{r}
2.875 \\
4\overline{)11.500} \\
\underline{8} \\
3\,5 \\
\underline{3\,2} \\
3\,0 \\
\underline{2\,8} \\
2\,0 \\
\underline{2\,0} \\
0
\end{array}
$$

57.

$$
\begin{array}{r}
0.4 \\
2\overline{)0.8} \\
\underline{8} \\
0
\end{array}
$$

59.

$$
\begin{array}{r}
0.704 \\
5\overline{)3.520} \\
\underline{3\,5} \\
0\,2 \\
\underline{0} \\
2\,0 \\
\underline{2\,0} \\
0
\end{array}
$$

61. $4.7 \div 0.5 = 5\overline{)47.0}$ with quotient 9.4

$$
\begin{array}{r}
9.4 \\
5\overline{)47.0} \\
\underline{45} \\
2\,0 \\
\underline{2\,0} \\
0
\end{array}
$$

63. $5 \div 0.4 = 4\overline{)50.0}$ with quotient 12.5

$$
\begin{array}{r}
12.5 \\
4\overline{)50.0} \\
\underline{4} \\
10 \\
\underline{8} \\
2\,0 \\
\underline{2\,0} \\
0
\end{array}
$$

65. Move the decimal point one place to the right:
$0.03 \div 0.1 = 0.3$

67. $0.38 \div 1.9 = 19\overline{)3.8}$ with quotient 0.2

$$
\begin{array}{r}
0.2 \\
19\overline{)3.8} \\
\underline{3\,8} \\
0
\end{array}
$$

69. Move the decimal point two places to the left:
$95.2 \div 100 = 0.952$

71. Move the decimal point one place to the left:
$81.6 \div 10 = 8.16$

73. Move the decimal point three places to the left:
$2.7 \div 1,000 = 0.0027$

75. Move the decimal point one place to the left:
$4.95 \div 10 = 0.495$

77. $0.8\overline{)307.2} = 8\overline{)3,072.0}$ with quotient 384.0

$$
\begin{array}{r}
384.0 \\
8\overline{)3,072.0} \\
\underline{2\,4} \\
67 \\
\underline{64} \\
32 \\
\underline{32} \\
0\,0 \\
\underline{0} \\
0
\end{array}
$$

79. $0.05\overline{)9} = 5\overline{)900.0}$ with quotient 180.0

$$
\begin{array}{r}
180.0 \\
5\overline{)900.0} \\
\underline{5} \\
40 \\
\underline{40} \\
00 \\
\underline{0} \\
0\,0 \\
\underline{0} \\
0
\end{array}
$$

81. $0.9\overline{)0.0057} = 9\overline{)0.057}$ with quotient 0.006 $0.\underline{0}06 \approx 0.0$

$$
\begin{array}{r}
0.006 \\
9\overline{)0.057} \\
\underline{54} \\
3
\end{array}
$$

83. Move the decimal point two places to the right, and put a zero after the decimal point for the tenths place:
$0.01\overline{)98.02} = 9,802.0$

85. $\dfrac{0.057}{0.2} = 2\overline{)0.57}$ with quotient 0.28 $0.\underline{2}8 \approx 0.3$

$$
\begin{array}{r}
0.28 \\
2\overline{)0.57} \\
\underline{4} \\
17 \\
\underline{16} \\
1
\end{array}
$$

87. $\dfrac{4}{0.07} = 7\overline{)400.00}$ with quotient 57.14 $57.\underline{1}4 \approx 57.1$

$$
\begin{array}{r}
57.14 \\
7\overline{)400.00} \\
\underline{35} \\
50 \\
\underline{49} \\
10 \\
\underline{7} \\
30 \\
\underline{28} \\
2
\end{array}
$$

89.

$\dfrac{87}{0.009} = 9\overline{)87,000.00}$ with quotient $9,666.66$ $9,666.\underline{6}6 \approx 9,666.7$

$$
\begin{array}{r}
9,666.66 \\
9\overline{)87,000.00} \\
\underline{81} \\
60 \\
\underline{54} \\
60 \\
\underline{54} \\
60 \\
\underline{54} \\
60 \\
\underline{54} \\
60 \\
\underline{54} \\
0
\end{array}
$$

91. $\dfrac{8.312}{0.7} = 7\overline{)83.12}$

$$\begin{array}{r} 11.87 \\ 7\overline{)83.12} \\ \underline{7} \\ 13 \\ \underline{7} \\ 61 \\ \underline{56} \\ 52 \\ \underline{49} \\ 3 \end{array}$$

$11.\underline{8}7 \approx 11.9$

93. $6.45 \div 1.2 = 12\overline{)64.50}$

$$\begin{array}{r} 5.37 \\ 12\overline{)64.50} \\ \underline{60} \\ 4\,5 \\ \underline{3\,6} \\ 90 \\ \underline{84} \\ 6 \end{array}$$

$5.\underline{3}7 \approx 5.4$

95. $0.8 \div 3.5 = 35\overline{)8.00}$

$$\begin{array}{r} 0.22 \\ 35\overline{)8.00} \\ \underline{7\,0} \\ 1\,00 \\ \underline{70} \\ 30 \end{array}$$

$0.\underline{2}2 \approx 0.2$

97. $35.77 \div 0.11 = 11\overline{)3,577.00}$

$$\begin{array}{r} 325.18 \\ 11\overline{)3,577.00} \\ \underline{33} \\ 27 \\ \underline{22} \\ 57 \\ \underline{55} \\ 2\,0 \\ \underline{1\,1} \\ 90 \\ \underline{88} \\ 2 \end{array}$$

$325.\underline{1}8 \approx 325.2$

99. $961.2 \div 2.1 = 21\overline{)9,612.00}$

$$\begin{array}{r} 457.71 \\ 21\overline{)9,612.00} \\ \underline{8\,4} \\ 1\,21 \\ \underline{1\,05} \\ 162 \\ \underline{147} \\ 15\,0 \\ \underline{14\,7} \\ 30 \\ \underline{21} \\ 9 \end{array}$$

$457.71 \approx 457.7$

101. $8 + \dfrac{3.05}{5} = 8 + 0.61 = 8.\underline{6}1 \approx 8.6$

103. $\dfrac{8.1 \times 0.2}{0.4} = \dfrac{1.62}{0.4} = 4.\underline{0}5 \approx 4.1$

105. $67.\underline{4}052... \approx 67.4$

107. $41.\underline{6}088... \approx 41.6$

109.

Input	Output
1	$15 \div \mathbf{1} - 0.2 = 14.8$
2	$15 \div \mathbf{2} - 0.2 = 7.3$
3	$15 \div \mathbf{3} - 0.2 = 4.8$
4	$15 \div \mathbf{4} - 0.2 = 3.55$

111. a. $5.7 \div 89 \approx 0.06$ **b.** $0.77 \div 0.0019 \approx 405.26$
$6 \div 90 \approx 0.07$ $0.8 \div 0.002 = 400$
   c. $31.5 \div 0.61 \approx 516.39$
$30 \div 0.6 = 50$
The answer for part (c) is wrong.

113. a. $61.27 \div 0.057 \approx 1,074.91$ **b.** $0.614 \div 2.883 \approx 2.13$
$60 \div 0.06 = 1,000$ $0.6 \div 3 = 0.2$
   c. $0.0035 \div 0.00481 \approx 0.73$
$0.004 \div 0.005 = 0.8$
The answer for part (b) is wrong.

115. $3.7 \div 1.000 = 0.0037$
The stalactite grew 0.0037 in. per year.

117. a. The women's team played a total of $21 + 14 = 35$
games. The fraction it won is $\dfrac{21}{35}$ or 0.6.
   b. The men's team played a total of $22 + 18 = 40$
games. The fraction it won is $\dfrac{22}{40}$ or 0.55.
   c. The women's team had the better record since
$0.60 > 0.55$.

119. a. Car A: $\dfrac{18.6 \text{ miles}}{1.6 \text{ gallons}} = 11.625$ miles per gallon

Car B: $\dfrac{7.8 \text{ miles}}{0.6 \text{ gallons}} = 13$ miles per gallon

Car C: $\dfrac{23.4 \text{ miles}}{1.2 \text{ gallons}} = 19.5$ miles per gallon

   b. Comparing the tens places of the three mileages
shows that Car C gives the best mileage.

121. $\dfrac{\$3,000}{\$1.5 \text{ per share}} = 2,000$ shares
You can buy 2,000 shares.

123. $\dfrac{0.0005 \text{ mm}}{0.0000005 \text{ mm}} = 1,000$
The electron microscope is 1,000 times more
powerful.

125. $\dfrac{8.2+8+8.9}{3}=8.37$ $8.37-7.9=0.53\approx0.5$

Her average lap was approximately 0.5 sec longer than the fastest time.

127. a. Division

b. $\dfrac{4,191}{11,429}=.367$ Cobb's average was .367

c. $\dfrac{4,000}{10,000}=0.4$

Review Exercises

1. Hundredths

2. Tenths

3. Tenths

4. Ten thousandths

5. $0.35=\dfrac{35}{100}=\dfrac{7\cdot\cancel{5}}{20\cdot\cancel{5}}=\dfrac{7}{20}$

6. $8.2=8\dfrac{2}{10}=8\dfrac{1\cdot\cancel{2}}{5\cdot\cancel{2}}=8\dfrac{1}{5}$

7. $4.007=4\dfrac{7}{1,000}$

8. $10.000=10\dfrac{0}{1,000}=10$

9. 0.72 is seventy-two hundredths.

10. 5.6 is five and six tenths.

11. 3.0009 is three and nine ten thousandths.

12. 510.036 is five hundred ten and thirty-six thousandths.

13. This is a number of thousandths, so the decimal will have three decimal places: 0.007

14. This is a number of tenths, so the decimal will have one decimal place: 2.1

15. This is a number of hundredths, so the decimal will have two decimal places: 0.03

16. This is a number of thousandths, so the decimal will have three decimal places: 7.041

17. Since $4>3$ in the hundredths place, 0.04 is larger.

18. Since $1>0$ in the thousandths place, 2.031 is larger.

19. Since $5>4$ in the ones place, 5.12 is larger.

20. Since $2>1$ in the ones place, 2 is larger.

21. Since $0<1$ in the ones place, 1.002 is the largest; in the tenths place, $7<8$, so 0.72 is the smallest.

22. In the thousandths place, $0<3$ and $0<4$, so 0.00057 is the smallest.

23. $7.\underline{3}1\approx7.3$

24. $0.03\underline{8}7\approx0.039$

25. $4.3\underline{8}68\approx4.39$

26. $\$899.\underline{0}9\approx\$899$

27.
$$\begin{array}{r}8.2\\+3.91\\\hline12.11\end{array}$$

28.
$$\begin{array}{r}50\\2.7\\+0.05\\\hline52.75\end{array}$$

29.
$$\begin{array}{r}\$8\\\$3.25\\+\$12.88\\\hline\$24.13\end{array}$$

30.
$$\begin{array}{r}8.4\text{ m}\\+3.6\text{ m}\\\hline12\ \ \text{m}\end{array}$$

31.
$$\begin{array}{r}0.5\\-0.2\\\hline0.3\end{array}$$

32.
$$\begin{array}{r}30.7\\-1.92\\\hline28.78\end{array}$$

33.
$$\begin{array}{r}93\\-5.248\\\hline87.752\end{array}$$

34.
$$\begin{array}{r}2.5\\+0.72\\\hline3.22\end{array}\qquad\begin{array}{r}3.22\\-1.6\\\hline1.62\end{array}$$

The answer is 1.62.

35. 98.2033

36. $90,948.80

37.
$$\begin{array}{r}7.28\\\times\ 0.4\\\hline2.912\end{array}$$

38. $(288)(3.5)=$
$$\begin{array}{r}288\\\times3.5\\\hline144\ 0\\864\ \ \ \\\hline1,008.0\end{array}=1,008$$

39.
$$\begin{array}{r}0.005\\\times0.002\\\hline0.00001\end{array}$$

40. $(3.7)^2=$
$$\begin{array}{r}3.7\\\times3.7\\\hline2\ 59\\11\ 1\ \ \\\hline13.69\end{array}$$

41. Move the decimal point three places to the right and insert a 0 placeholder:
$2.71\cdot1,000=2,710$

42. Move the decimal point one place to the right:
$0.0034\times10=0.034$

43. $8-(1.5)^2=8-2.25=5.75$

44. $3(2.4)+7(0.9)=7.2+6.3=13.5$

45. 1,569.36846

46. 5,398.835596

47. $\dfrac{1}{6}=6\overline{)\begin{array}{l}\ \ 0.166\\1.000\end{array}}$
$$\begin{array}{r}\underline{6}\\40\\\underline{36}\\40\\\underline{36}\\4\end{array}$$
$0.1\underline{6}6\approx0.17$

48. $\dfrac{5}{8}=8\overline{)\begin{array}{l}\ \ 0.625\\5.000\end{array}}$
$$\begin{array}{r}\underline{48}\\20\\\underline{16}\\40\\\underline{40}\\0\end{array}$$
$0.6\underline{2}5\approx0.63$

49. $\dfrac{2}{7} = 7\overline{)2.000}$

$$\begin{array}{r} 0.285 \\ 7\overline{)2.000} \\ \underline{1\ 4} \\ 60 \\ \underline{56} \\ 40 \\ \underline{35} \\ 5 \end{array}$$

$0.2\underline{8}5 \approx 0.29$

50. $\dfrac{2}{9} = 9\overline{)2.000}$

$$\begin{array}{r} 0.222 \\ 9\overline{)2.000} \\ \underline{1\ 8} \\ 20 \\ \underline{18} \\ 20 \\ \underline{18} \\ 2 \end{array}$$

$0.2\underline{2}2 \approx 0.22$

51. $4\dfrac{1}{16} = \dfrac{65}{16} = 16\overline{)65.000}$

$$\begin{array}{r} 4.062 \\ 16\overline{)65.000} \\ \underline{64} \\ 1\ 0 \\ \underline{0} \\ 1\ \overline{0}0 \\ \underline{96} \\ 40 \\ \underline{32} \\ 8 \end{array}$$

$4.0\underline{6}2 \approx 4.06$

52. $90\dfrac{1}{8} = \dfrac{721}{8} = 8\overline{)721.000}$

$$\begin{array}{r} 90.125 \\ 8\overline{)721.000} \\ \underline{72} \\ 01 \\ \underline{0} \\ 1\ 0 \\ \underline{8} \\ 20 \\ \underline{16} \\ 40 \\ \underline{40} \\ 0 \end{array}$$

$90.1\underline{2}5 \approx 90.13$

53. $8\dfrac{1}{3} = \dfrac{25}{3} = 3\overline{)25.000}$

$$\begin{array}{r} 8.333 \\ 3\overline{)25.000} \\ \underline{24} \\ 1\ 0 \\ \underline{9} \\ 10 \\ \underline{9} \\ 10 \\ \underline{9} \\ 1 \end{array}$$

$8.3\underline{3}3 \approx 8.33$

54. $11\dfrac{5}{6} = \dfrac{71}{6} = 6\overline{)71.000}$

$$\begin{array}{r} 11.833 \\ 6\overline{)71.000} \\ \underline{6} \\ 11 \\ \underline{6} \\ 5\ 0 \\ \underline{48} \\ 20 \\ \underline{18} \\ 20 \\ \underline{18} \\ 2 \end{array}$$

$11.8\underline{3}3 = 11.83$

55. $5\overline{)38.00}$

$$\begin{array}{r} 7.60 \\ 5\overline{)38.00} \\ \underline{35} \\ 3\ 0 \\ \underline{3\ 0} \\ 0 \\ \underline{00} \\ 0 \end{array}$$

$7.6\underline{0} \approx 7.6$

56. $2\overline{)1.30}$

$$\begin{array}{r} 0.65 \\ 2\overline{)1.30} \\ \underline{1\ 2} \\ 10 \\ \underline{10} \\ 0 \end{array}$$

$0.\underline{6}5 \approx 0.7$

57. $\dfrac{4.8}{3} = 3\overline{)4.80}$

$$\begin{array}{r} 1.60 \\ 3\overline{)4.80} \\ \underline{4\ 8} \\ 00 \\ \underline{0} \\ 0 \end{array}$$

$1.\underline{6}0 \approx 1.6$

58. $0.7 \div 4 = 4\overline{)0.70}$

$$\begin{array}{r} 0.17 \\ 4\overline{)0.70} \\ \underline{4} \\ 30 \\ \underline{28} \\ 2 \end{array}$$

$0.\underline{1}7 \approx 0.2$

59. Move the decimal point one place to the left:
$10\overline{)2.75} = 0.2\underline{7}5 \approx 0.3$

60. Move the decimal point two places to the left:
$100\overline{)1.8} = 0.\underline{0}18 \approx 0.0$

61. Move the decimal point one place to the left:
$\dfrac{2.77}{10} = 0.\underline{2}77 \approx 0.3$

62. Move the decimal point three places to the left:
$1.9 \div 1,000 = 0.\underline{0}019 \approx 0.0$

63. $12 \div 2.4 = 24\overline{)120.00}$

$$\begin{array}{r} 5.00 \\ 24\overline{)120.00} \\ \underline{120} \\ 0 \\ 0\ 0 \\ \underline{0} \\ 00 \\ \underline{0} \\ 0 \end{array}$$

$5.\underline{0}0 \approx 5.0$

64. $3.75 \div 0.005 = 5\overline{)3,750.00}$

$$\begin{array}{r} 750.00 \\ 5\overline{)3,750.00} \\ \underline{3\ 5} \\ 25 \\ \underline{25} \\ 0 \\ 0 \\ \underline{0} \\ 00 \\ \underline{0} \\ 00 \\ \underline{0} \\ 00 \end{array}$$

$750.\underline{0}0 \approx 750.0$

65. $\dfrac{7.11}{0.3} = 3\overline{)71.10}$ $\quad 23.\underline{7}0 \approx 23.7$

$$\begin{array}{r} 23.70 \\ 3\overline{)71.10} \\ \underline{6} \\ 11 \\ 9 \\ \underline{} \\ 2\,1 \\ 2\,1 \\ \underline{} \\ 00 \\ 0 \\ \hline 0 \end{array}$$

66.

$0.06\overline{)981.5} = 6\overline{)98,150.00}$ $\quad 16,358.\underline{3}3 \approx 16,358.3$

$$\begin{array}{r} 16,358.33 \\ 6\overline{)98,150.00} \\ \underline{6} \\ 38 \\ \underline{36} \\ 2\,1 \\ 1\,8 \\ \underline{} \\ 35 \\ \underline{30} \\ 5\,0 \\ 4\,8 \\ \underline{} \\ 20 \\ \underline{18} \\ 20 \\ \underline{18} \\ 0 \end{array}$$

67. $81.37\overline{)247.062} = 3.\underline{0}36278... \approx 3.0$

68. $247.062\overline{)81.37} = 0.\underline{3}29350... \approx 0.3$

69. 0.0000004 is four ten millionths.

70.
$$\begin{array}{r} 2,895.74 \\ -2,799.82 \\ \hline 95.92 \end{array}$$
The stock market average dropped 95.92 points.

71.
$$\begin{array}{r} 25.2 \text{ sec} \\ +29.29 \text{ sec} \\ \hline 54.49 \text{ sec} \end{array}$$
It took her 54.49 sec to swim the 100 m.

72. 6 in. $-$ (2.376 in. $+$ 1.977 in.) $=$ 6 in. $-$ 4.353 in.
$\phantom{6 \text{ in.} - (2.376 \text{ in.} + 1.977 \text{ in.})} = 1.647$ in.

The missing length is 1.647 in.

73. In the hundredths place 333.75 has a five and the other two call numbers have a 0, so 333.75 is the largest. In the thousandths place 333.7095 has a nine and 333.7 has a 0, so 333.7 is the smallest. The books are not in order since the correct order is 333.7 < 333.7095 < 333.75.

74. $66 \div 0.075 = 880$ $\quad 880 \times \$0.05 = \$44.00$
The value of the stack is \$44.00.

75. $1.17 \times \dfrac{1}{2} = 0.585$

It would have traveled 0.585 mi, which is less than 0.75 mi, so it would not reach the wall.

76. $435 \div 100 = 4.35$
There are 4.35 times as many representatives.

77. $\dfrac{\$5.20}{4 \text{ lb}} = \$1.30$ per lb $\qquad \dfrac{\$6.20}{5 \text{ lb}} = \$1.24$ per lb

$\$1.30 - \$1.24 = \$0.06$

The difference between the two prices is 6 cents.

78. 30×0.4 in. $+ 3 \times 1$ in. $= 12$ in. $+ 3$ in. $= 15$ in.
The boxes will need about 15 in. of shelf space.

79. $\dfrac{7.15 \text{ g} + 7.18 \text{ g} + 7.23 \text{ g}}{3} = \dfrac{21.56 \text{ g}}{3} \approx 7.19 \text{ g}$

The average of the weights is 7.19 g.

80. $300 \times 160 = 48,000$ $\qquad 92 \times 50 = 4,600$

$\dfrac{48,000}{4,600} = 10.\underline{4}3478... \approx 10.4$

The football field is 10.4 times as large as the basketball court.

81.
$$\begin{array}{r} 28,774.71 \\ 232.55 \\ 349.77 \\ 511.74 \\ 5,052.71 \\ +1,240.97 \\ \hline 36,162.45 \end{array}$$
The total income is \$36,162.45

82.
$$\begin{array}{llll} \text{Company A:} & 1.357 & \text{Company B:} & 0.829 \\ & 1.074 & & 0.534 \\ & 0.273 & & 0.271 \\ & +2.381 & & +3.425 \\ \hline & 5.085 & & 5.059 \end{array}$$
Since 5.085 > 5.059, Company A had greater earnings for the year.

Posttest

1. In 0.79023, the digit in the thousandths place is 0.

2. 5.102 is five and one hundred-two thousandths.

3. $320.1\underline{5}48 \approx 320.15$

4. Comparing hundredths places shows that 0.04 is the largest number; comparing the ten thousandths places shows that 0.00028 is the smallest number.

5. $3\dfrac{1}{25} = 3\dfrac{4}{100} = 3\dfrac{1 \cdot \cancel{4}^{1}}{25 \cdot \cancel{4}_{1}} = 3\dfrac{1}{25}$

6. Four thousandths has three decimal places: 0.004

7.
```
   2.3
   0.704
 +1.35
 ─────
  4.354
```

8. $(\$5.27 + \$9) - \$8.61 = \$14.27 - \$8.61 = \$5.66$

9. Move the decimal point one place to the right:
$2.09 \times 10 = 20.9$

10.
```
   5.2
  ×1.1
  ────
   5 2
  5 2
  ─────
  5.72
```

11. $(0.1)^3 = (0.1)(0.1)(0.1) = (0.01)(0.1) = 0.001$

12. $\dfrac{3.52}{2} + \dfrac{4.8}{3} = 1.76 + 1.6 = 3.36$

13. Move the decimal point three places to the left.
$2.9 \div 1,000 = 0.0029$

14. $\dfrac{9.81}{0.3} = 3\overline{)98.1}$
```
        32.7
      3)98.1
        9
        ──
        08
         6
        ──
        21
        21
        ──
         0
```

15. $\dfrac{3}{8} = 8\overline{)3.000}$
```
       0.375
      8)3.000
        2 4
        ───
         60
         56
        ───
         40
         40
        ───
          0
```

16. $4\dfrac{1}{6} = \dfrac{25}{6} = 6\overline{)25.000}$ $4.1\underline{6}6 \approx 4.17$
```
        4.166
      6)25.000
        24
        ──
        1 0
          6
        ──
         40
         36
        ──
         40
         36
        ──
          4
```

17. $0.00\underline{5}611 \, \text{lb} \approx 0.01 \, \text{lb}$

18. $5,280 \, \text{ft} \div 2,000 = 2.64 \, \text{ft} \approx 2.6 \, \text{ft}$
A Roman's step was 2.6 ft.

19. Look at the tenths place to put the distances in order:
The largest digit in the tenths place is the 5 in 1.5, so
the Belmont Stakes is the longest of the three races.

20. $0.02733 \times \$100,000 = \$2,733$

Cumulative Review Exercises

1. $591,622 \approx 1,000,000$ (The critical digit is the 5 in
the hundred thousands place, so the 0 in the millions
place gets rounded up to 1.)

2. $7\dfrac{9}{10} \times 4\dfrac{1}{13} \approx 8 \times 4 = 32$

3. Look at the thousandths place. Since $5 > 4$,
$0.035 > 0.03499$.

4. The underlined digit is in the hundredths place.

5. $2.\underline{0}673 \approx 2.1$

6. $(0.3)^2 = (0.3)(0.3) = 0.09$

7.
```
   4.1  lb
 −3.52 lb
 ────────
  0.58 lb
```

8. $6,500 \div 20 = 325$
The rate is 325 marriages per year.

9.
```
   11  in.
  −9.4 in.
 ─────────
  1.6 in.
```
The difference in length is 1.6 in.

10. $33,013.7 \, \text{mi} + 2.5 \, \text{mi} = 33,016.2 \, \text{mi}$
The odometer will read 33,016.2 mi.

Chapter 4

BASIC ALGEBRA:
SOLVING SIMPLE EQUATIONS

Pretest

1. Possible answer: six less than y

2. Possible answer: the quotient of x and 2

3. $m + 8$ **4.** $2n$

5. $\dfrac{16}{4} = 4$ **6.** $5 - 3\frac{1}{2} = 1\frac{1}{2}$

7. $x + 3 = 5$ **8.** $4y = 12$

9.
$$x + 4 = 10$$
$$x + 4 - 4 = 10 - 4$$
$$x = 6$$
Check:
$$x + 4 = 10$$
$$6 + 4 \stackrel{?}{=} 10$$
$$10 \stackrel{\checkmark}{=} 10$$

10.
$$y - 3 = 7$$
$$y - 3 + 3 = 7 + 3$$
$$y = 10$$
Check:
$$y - 3 = 7$$
$$10 - 3 \stackrel{?}{=} 7$$
$$7 \stackrel{\checkmark}{=} 7$$

11.
$$2n = 26$$
$$\frac{2n}{2} = \frac{26}{2}$$
$$n = 13$$
Check:
$$2n = 26$$
$$2(13) \stackrel{?}{=} 26$$
$$26 \stackrel{\checkmark}{=} 26$$

12.
$$\frac{a}{4} = 3$$
$$\frac{a}{4} \cdot 4 = 3 \cdot 4$$
$$\frac{a}{4} \cdot \frac{4}{1} = 12$$
$$a = 12$$
Check:
$$\frac{a}{4} = 3$$
$$\frac{12}{4} \stackrel{?}{=} 3$$
$$3 \stackrel{\checkmark}{=} 3$$

13.
$$m + 1.9 = 8$$
$$m + 1.9 - 1.9 = 8 - 1.9$$
$$m = 6.1$$
Check:
$$m + 1.9 = 8$$
$$6.1 + 1.9 \stackrel{?}{=} 8$$
$$8 \stackrel{\checkmark}{=} 8$$

14.
$$0.5n = 15$$
$$(0.5n) \div 0.5 = 15 \div 0.5$$
$$n = 30$$
Check:
$$0.5n = 15$$
$$0.5(30) \stackrel{?}{=} 15$$
$$15 \stackrel{\checkmark}{=} 15$$

15.
$$100m = 48$$
$$\frac{100m}{100} = \frac{48}{100}$$
$$m = 0.48$$
Check:
$$100m = 48$$
$$100(0.48) \stackrel{?}{=} 48$$
$$48 \stackrel{\checkmark}{=} 48$$

16.
$$\frac{n}{10} = 1.5$$
$$\frac{n}{10} \cdot 10 = 1.5 \cdot 10$$
$$\frac{n}{10} \cdot \frac{10}{1} = 15$$
$$n = 15$$
Check:
$$\frac{n}{10} = 1.5$$
$$\frac{15}{10} \stackrel{?}{=} 1.5$$
$$1.5 \stackrel{\checkmark}{=} 1.5$$

17.
$$b + 77.50 = 403.25$$
$$b + 77.50 - 77.50 = 403.25 - 77.50$$
$$b = 325.75$$
The previous balance was \$325.75.
Check:
$$b + 77.50 = 403.25$$
$$325.75 + 77.50 \stackrel{?}{=} 403.25$$
$$403.25 \stackrel{\checkmark}{=} 403.25$$

18.
$$d - 1\frac{3}{4} = 10\frac{1}{3}$$
$$d - 1\frac{3}{4} + 1\frac{3}{4} = 10\frac{1}{3} + 1\frac{3}{4}$$
$$d = 11 + \frac{4}{12} + \frac{9}{12} = 11\frac{13}{12} = 12\frac{1}{2}$$
The depth before the dry spell was $12\frac{1}{12}$ ft.
Check:
$$d - 1\frac{3}{4} = 10\frac{1}{3}$$
$$12\frac{1}{12} - 1\frac{3}{4} \stackrel{?}{=} 10\frac{1}{3}$$
$$11\frac{13}{12} - 1\frac{9}{12} \stackrel{?}{=} 10\frac{1}{3}$$
$$10\frac{1}{3} \stackrel{\checkmark}{=} 10\frac{1}{3}$$

19. $\dfrac{1}{8}A = 9,000$ Check:

$\left(\dfrac{8}{1}\right)\left(\dfrac{1}{8}A\right) = \dfrac{8}{1} \cdot 9,000$ $\dfrac{1}{8}A = 9,000$

$A = 72,000$ $\dfrac{1}{8} \cdot 72,000 \overset{?}{=} 9,000$

$9,000 \overset{\checkmark}{=} 9,000$

The area of the New England States is 72,000 sq mi.

20. $2c = 5.35$ Check:

$\dfrac{2c}{2} = \dfrac{5.35}{2}$ $2c = 5.35$

$c = 2.675 \approx 2.68$ $2(2.675) \overset{?}{=} 5.35$

$5.35 \overset{\checkmark}{=} 5.35$

Each call cost $2.68.

4.1   Introduction to Basic Algebra

Practice

1.

Algebraic Expression	Translation
a. $\dfrac{1}{2}p$	One-half of p
b. $5 - x$	x less than 5
c. $y \div 4$	y divided by 4
d. $n + 3$	3 more than n
e. $\dfrac{3}{5}b$	$\dfrac{3}{5}$ of b

2.

Word Phrase	Translation
a. x plus 9	$x + 9$
b. Ten times y	$10y$
c. The difference between n and 7	$n - 7$
d. A number divided by 5	Possible answer: $n \div 5$
e. Two-fifths of a number	Possible answer: $\dfrac{2}{5}n$

3. You will have $\dfrac{h}{4}$ hr.

4.

Algebraic Expression	Solution
a. $\dfrac{s}{4}$, if $s = 100$	$\dfrac{100}{4} = 25$
b. $0.2y$, if $y = 1.9$	$(0.2)(1.9) = 0.38$
c. $x - 4.2$, if $x = 9$	$9 - 4.2 = 4.8$
d. $25 + z$, if $z = 1.6$	$25 + 1.6 = 26.6$

5. $55m$ words in m minutes; $55(30) = 1,650$ words in 30 minutes.

6. You pay $(15.45 + t)$ dollars; if $t = \$3$, you pay $\$15.45 + \$3$, or $\$18.45$.

Exercises

1. 3 more than t; t plus 3

3. c minus 4; 4 subtracted from c

5. c divided by 3; the quotient of c and 3

7. 10 times s; the product of 10 and s

9. y minus 10; 10 less than y

11. 7 times a; the product of 7 and a

13. x divided by 4; the quotient of x and 4

15. x minus $\dfrac{1}{2}$; $\dfrac{1}{2}$ less than x

17. $\dfrac{1}{2}$ times w; $\dfrac{1}{2}$ of w

19. x minus 2; the difference between x and 2

21. 1 increased by x; x added to 1

23. 3 times p; the product of 3 and p

25. n decreased by 1.1; n minus 1.1

27. y divided by 0.9; the quotient of y and 0.9

29. $x + 10$ **31.** $n - 5$

33. $y + 5$ **35.** $t \div 6$ or $\dfrac{t}{6}$

37. $10y$ **39.** $w - 5$

41. $n + 100$ **43.** $z \div 3$ or $\dfrac{z}{3}$

45. $\dfrac{2}{5}x$ **47.** $k - 6$

49. $n + 5$ **51.** $n - 5\dfrac{1}{2}$

53. $19 + 7 = 26$

55. $7 - 4.5 = 2.5$

57. $\frac{3}{4} \cdot 20 = 15$

59. $2\frac{1}{3} \div 2 = 1\frac{1}{6}$

61. $9 - 7.9 = 1.1$

63. $\frac{1}{6} + \frac{5}{6} = 1$

65.

x	$x + 8$
1	9
2	10
3	11
4	12

67.

n	$n - 0.2$
1	0.8
2	1.8
3	2.8
4	3.8

69.

x	$\frac{3}{4}x$
4	3
8	6
12	9
16	12

71.

z	$\frac{z}{2}$
2	1
4	2
6	3
8	4

73. Your friend has $c + 2$ classes.

75. The sum of the measures of the three angles is $30° + 90° + d°$ or $120° + d°$.

77. distance $= r \cdot t$ mi; distance $= 50 \cdot 3$ mi $= 150$ mi.

79. **a.** Your earnings are $2s$ dollars.
b. If your sell 14 subscriptions, your earnings are $2 \cdot 14$ dollars $= \$28$.

4.2   Solving Addition and Subtraction Equations

Practice

1.

Sentence	Equation
a. n decreased by 5.1 is 9.	$n - 5.1 = 9$
b. y plus 5 is equal to 12.	$y + 5 = 12$
c. The difference between a number and 4 is the same as 12.	$n - 4 = 12$
d. Five more than a number is $7\frac{3}{4}$.	$n + 5 = 7\frac{3}{4}$

2. $p - 6 = 49.95$, where p is the regular price.

3.
$$x + 5 = 14$$
$$x + 5 - 5 = 14 - 5$$
$$x + 0 = 9$$
$$x = 9$$

Check:
$$x + 5 = 14$$
$$9 + 5 \overset{?}{=} 14$$
$$9 + 5 \overset{\checkmark}{=} 14$$

4.
$$t - 0.9 = 1.8$$
$$t - 0.9 + 0.9 = 1.8 + 0.9$$
$$t - 0 = 2.7$$
$$t = 2.7$$

Check:
$$t - 0.9 = 1.8$$
$$2.7 - 0.9 \overset{?}{=} 1.8$$
$$1.8 \overset{\checkmark}{=} 1.8$$

5.
$$m + \frac{1}{4} = 5\frac{1}{2}$$
$$m + \frac{1}{4} - \frac{1}{4} = 5\frac{1}{2} - \frac{1}{4}$$
$$m + 0 = 5\frac{1}{4} - \frac{1}{4}$$
$$m = 5\frac{1}{4}$$

Check:
$$m + \frac{1}{4} = 5\frac{1}{2}$$
$$5\frac{1}{4} + \frac{1}{4} \overset{?}{=} 5\frac{1}{2}$$
$$5\frac{2}{4} \overset{?}{=} 5\frac{1}{2}$$
$$5\frac{1}{2} \overset{\checkmark}{=} 5\frac{1}{2}$$

6. a.
$$11 = m - 4$$
$$11 + 4 = m - 4 + 4$$
$$15 = m$$

Check:
$$11 = m - 4$$
$$11 \overset{?}{=} 15 - 4$$
$$11 \overset{\checkmark}{=} 11$$

b.
$$12 + n = 21$$
$$12 - 12 + n = 21 - 12$$
$$n = 9$$

Check:
$$12 + n = 21$$
$$12 + 9 \overset{?}{=} 21$$
$$21 \overset{\checkmark}{=} 21$$

7.
$$809.46 = 144.95 + x$$
$$809.46 - 144.95 = 144.95 - 144.95 + x$$
$$664.51 = x$$

The amount you had yesterday is $664.51.

Check:
$$809.46 = 144.95 + x$$
$$809.46 \overset{?}{=} 144.95 + 664.51$$
$$809.46 \overset{\checkmark}{=} 809.46$$

8.
$$26\frac{1}{4} = x - 1\frac{5}{8}$$
$$26\frac{1}{4} + 1\frac{5}{8} = x - 1\frac{5}{8} + 1\frac{5}{8}$$
$$27\frac{7}{8} = x$$

The stock opened at $27\frac{7}{8}$.

Check:
$$26\frac{1}{4} = x - 1\frac{5}{8}$$
$$26\frac{1}{4} \overset{?}{=} 27\frac{7}{8} - 1\frac{5}{8}$$
$$26\frac{1}{4} \overset{\checkmark}{=} 26\frac{1}{4}$$

Exercises

1. $z - 9 = 25$

3. $7 + x = 25$

5. $t - 3.1 = 4$

7. $\frac{3}{2} + y = \frac{9}{2}$

9. $n - 3\frac{1}{2} = 7$

11.

Equation	Value of x	Solution?
a. $x + 1 = 9$	8	Yes
b. $x - 3 = 4$	5	No
c. $x + 0.2 = 5$	4.8	Yes
d. $x - \frac{1}{2} = 1$	$\frac{1}{2}$	No

13. Subtract 4

15. Add 11

17. Add 7

19. Subtract 2

21.
$$a - 7 = 24$$
$$a - 7 + 7 = 24 + 7$$
$$a = 31$$

Check:
$$a - 7 = 24$$
$$31 - 7 \overset{?}{=} 24$$
$$24 \overset{\checkmark}{=} 24$$

23.
$$y + 19 = 21$$
$$y + 19 - 19 = 21 - 19$$
$$y = 2$$

Check:
$$y + 19 = 21$$
$$2 + 19 \overset{?}{=} 21$$
$$21 \overset{\checkmark}{=} 21$$

25.
$$x - 2 = 10$$
$$x - 2 + 2 = 10 + 2$$
$$x = 12$$

Check:
$$x - 2 = 10$$
$$12 - 2 \overset{?}{=} 10$$
$$10 \overset{\checkmark}{=} 10$$

27.
$$n + 9 = 13$$
$$n + 9 - 9 = 13 - 9$$
$$n = 4$$

Check:
$$n + 9 = 13$$
$$4 + 9 \overset{?}{=} 13$$
$$13 \overset{\checkmark}{=} 13$$

29.
$$c - 14 = 33$$
$$c - 14 + 14 = 33 + 14$$
$$c = 47$$

Check:
$$c - 14 = 33$$
$$47 - 14 \overset{?}{=} 33$$
$$33 \overset{\checkmark}{=} 33$$

31.
$$x - 3.4 = 9.6$$
$$x - 3.4 + 3.4 = 9.6 + 3.4$$
$$x = 13$$

Check:
$$x - 3.4 = 9.6$$
$$13 - 3.4 \overset{?}{=} 9.6$$
$$9.6 \overset{\checkmark}{=} 9.6$$

33.
$$z + 2.4 = 5.3$$
$$z + 2.4 - 2.4 = 5.3 - 2.4$$
$$z = 2.9$$

Check:
$$z + 2.4 = 5.3$$
$$2.9 + 2.4 \overset{?}{=} 5.3$$
$$5.3 \overset{\checkmark}{=} 5.3$$

35.
$$n - 8 = 0.9$$
$$n - 8 + 8 = 0.9 + 8$$
$$n = 8.9$$

Check:
$$n - 8 = 0.9$$
$$8.9 - 8 \overset{?}{=} 0.9$$
$$0.9 \overset{\checkmark}{=} 0.9$$

37.
$$y + 8.1 = 9$$
$$y + 8.1 - 8.1 = 9 - 8.1$$
$$y = 0.9$$

Check:
$$y + 8.1 = 9$$
$$0.9 + 8.1 \overset{?}{=} 9$$
$$9 \overset{\checkmark}{=} 9$$

39.
$$x + 2\tfrac{1}{3} = 9$$
$$x + 2\tfrac{1}{3} - 2\tfrac{1}{3} = 9 - 2\tfrac{1}{3}$$
$$x = 8\tfrac{3}{3} - 2\tfrac{1}{3}$$
$$x = 6\tfrac{2}{3}$$

Check:
$$x + 2\tfrac{1}{3} = 9$$
$$6\tfrac{2}{3} + 2\tfrac{1}{3} \overset{?}{=} 9$$
$$8\tfrac{3}{3} \overset{?}{=} 9$$
$$9 \overset{\checkmark}{=} 9$$

41.
$$m - 1\tfrac{1}{3} = 4$$
$$m - 1\tfrac{1}{3} + 1\tfrac{1}{3} = 4 + 1\tfrac{1}{3}$$
$$m = 5\tfrac{1}{3}$$

Check:
$$m - 1\tfrac{1}{3} = 4$$
$$5\tfrac{1}{3} - 1\tfrac{1}{3} \overset{?}{=} 4$$
$$4 \overset{\checkmark}{=} 4$$

43.
$$x + 3\tfrac{1}{4} = 7$$
$$x + 3\tfrac{1}{4} - 3\tfrac{1}{4} = 7 - 3\tfrac{1}{4}$$
$$x = 6\tfrac{4}{4} - 3\tfrac{1}{4}$$
$$x = 3\tfrac{3}{4}$$

Check:
$$x + 3\tfrac{1}{4} = 7$$
$$3\tfrac{3}{4} + 3\tfrac{1}{4} \overset{?}{=} 7$$
$$7 \overset{\checkmark}{=} 7$$

45.
$$5 + m = 7$$
$$5 - 5 + m = 7 - 5$$
$$m = 2$$

Check:
$$5 + m = 7$$
$$5 + 2 \overset{?}{=} 7$$
$$7 \overset{\checkmark}{=} 7$$

47.
$$39 = y - 51$$
$$39 + 51 = y - 51 + 51$$
$$90 = y$$

Check:
$$39 = y - 51$$
$$39 \overset{?}{=} 90 - 51$$
$$39 \overset{\checkmark}{=} 39$$

49.
$$5 = y - 1\tfrac{1}{4}$$
$$5 + 1\tfrac{1}{4} = y - 1\tfrac{1}{4} + 1\tfrac{1}{4}$$
$$6\tfrac{1}{4} = y$$

Check:
$$5 = y - 1\tfrac{1}{4}$$
$$5 \overset{?}{=} 6\tfrac{1}{4} - 1\tfrac{1}{4}$$
$$5 \overset{\checkmark}{=} 5$$

51.
$$4 = n + 3\tfrac{1}{2}$$
$$4 - 3\tfrac{1}{2} = n + 3\tfrac{1}{2} - 3\tfrac{1}{2}$$
$$\tfrac{1}{2} = n$$

Check:
$$4 = n + 3\tfrac{1}{2}$$
$$4 \overset{?}{=} \tfrac{1}{2} + 3\tfrac{1}{2}$$
$$4 \overset{\checkmark}{=} 4$$

53.
$$2.3 = x - 5.9$$
$$2.3 + 5.9 = x - 5.9 + 5.9$$
$$8.2 = x$$

Check:
$$2.3 = x - 5.9$$
$$2.3 \overset{\checkmark}{=} 8.2 - 5.9$$
$$2.3 \overset{\checkmark}{=} 2.3$$

55.
$$y - 7.01 = 12.9$$
$$y - 7.01 + 7.01 = 12.9 + 7.01$$
$$y = 19.91$$

Check:
$$y - 7.01 = 12.9$$
$$19.91 - 7.01 \overset{?}{=} 12.9$$
$$12.9 \overset{\checkmark}{=} 12.9$$

57.
$$x + 3.443 = 8$$
$$x + 3.443 - 3.443 = 8 - 3.443$$
$$x = 4.557$$

Check:
$$x + 3.443 = 8$$
$$4.557 + 3.443 \overset{?}{=} 8$$
$$8 \overset{\checkmark}{=} 8$$

59.
$$2.986 = y - 7.265$$
$$2.986 + 7.256 = y - 7.256 + 7.256$$
$$10.251 = y$$
Check:
$$2.986 = y - 7.265$$
$$2.986 \overset{?}{=} 10.251 - 7.265$$
$$2.986 \overset{\checkmark}{=} 2.986$$

61.
$$n + 3 = 11$$
$$n + 3 - 3 = 11 - 3$$
$$n = 8$$

Check:
$$n + 3 = 11$$
$$n + 8 \overset{?}{=} 11$$
$$11 \overset{\checkmark}{=} 11$$

63.
$$y - 6 = 7$$
$$y - 6 + 6 = 7 + 6$$
$$y = 13$$

Check:
$$y - 6 = 7$$
$$13 - 6 \overset{?}{=} 7$$
$$7 \overset{\checkmark}{=} 7$$

65.
$$n + 10 = 19$$
$$n + 10 - 10 = 19 - 10$$
$$n = 9$$

Check:
$$n + 10 = 19$$
$$9 + 10 \overset{?}{=} 19$$
$$19 \overset{\checkmark}{=} 19$$

67.
$$x + 3.6 = 9$$
$$x + 3.6 - 3.6 = 9 - 3.6$$
$$x = 5.4$$

Check:
$$x + 3.6 = 9$$
$$5.4 + 3.6 \overset{?}{=} 9$$
$$9 \overset{\checkmark}{=} 9$$

69. $n - 4\frac{1}{3} = 2\frac{2}{3}$ Check:

$n = 4\frac{1}{3} + 4\frac{1}{3} = 2\frac{2}{3} + 4\frac{1}{3}$ $n - 4\frac{1}{3} = 2\frac{2}{3}$

$n = 6\frac{3}{3}$ $7 - 4\frac{1}{3} \overset{?}{=} 2\frac{2}{3}$

$n = 7$ $6\frac{3}{3} - 4\frac{1}{3} \overset{\checkmark}{=} 2\frac{2}{3}$

71. Equation c: $w - 8\frac{1}{2} = 135$

73. Equation d: $x + 8.7 = 200$

75. $621,000 = x - 13,000$

$621,000 + 13,000 = x - 13,000 + 13,000$

$634,000 = x$

The show took in $634,000 last week.

Check:

$621,000 = x - 13,000$

$621,000 \overset{?}{=} 634,000 - 13,000$

$621,000 \overset{\checkmark}{=} 621,000$

77. $40° + \angle B = 90°$

$40° - 40° + \angle B = 90° - 40°$

$\angle B = 50°$

The number of degrees in $\angle B$ is $50°$.

Check:

$40° + \angle B = 90°$

$40° + 50° \overset{?}{=} 90°$

$90° \overset{\checkmark}{=} 90°$

4.3   Solving Multiplication and Division Equations

Practice

1.

Sentence	Equation
a. Twice x is the same as 14.	$2x = 14$
b. The quotient of a and 6 is 1.5.	$\dfrac{a}{6} = 1.5$
c. Some number divided by 0.3 is equal to ..	$\dfrac{n}{0.3} = 1$
d. Ten is equal to one half of some number.	$10 = \dfrac{1}{2}n$

2. $15 = 3w.$

3. $6x = 30$ Check:

$\dfrac{6x}{6} = \dfrac{30}{6}$ $6x = 30$

$x = 5$ $6(5) \overset{?}{=} 30$

$30 \overset{\checkmark}{=} 30$

4. $1 = \dfrac{a}{6}$ Check:

$6 \cdot 1 = 6 \cdot \dfrac{a}{6}$ $1 = \dfrac{a}{6}$

$6 = a$ $1 \overset{?}{=} \dfrac{6}{6}$

$1 \overset{\checkmark}{=} 1$

5. $1.5x = 6$ Check:

$\dfrac{1.5x}{1.5} = \dfrac{6}{1.5}$ $1.5x = 6$

$x = 4$ $1.5(4) \overset{?}{=} 6$

$6 \overset{\checkmark}{=} 6$

6. $\dfrac{a}{2.4} = 1.2$ Check:

$(2.4)\dfrac{a}{2.4} = (2.4)(12)$ $\dfrac{a}{2.4} = 1.2$

$a = 2.88$ $\dfrac{2.88}{2.4} \overset{?}{=} 1.2$

$1.2 \overset{\checkmark}{=} 1.2$

7. $\dfrac{3}{4}x = 12$ Check:

$\dfrac{3}{4}x \div \dfrac{3}{4} = 12 \div \dfrac{3}{4}$ $\dfrac{3}{4}x = 12$

$\left(\dfrac{3}{4}x\right)\left(\dfrac{4}{3}\right) = 12\left(\dfrac{4}{3}\right)$ $\dfrac{3}{4}(16) \overset{?}{=} 12$

$x = 16$ $\left(\dfrac{3}{4}\right)\left(\dfrac{16}{1}\right) \overset{?}{=} 12$

$12 \overset{\checkmark}{=} 12$

8. a. $12 = \dfrac{z}{6}$ Check:

$(6)12 = (6)\dfrac{z}{6}$ $12 = \dfrac{z}{6}$

$72 = z$ $12 \overset{?}{=} \dfrac{72}{6}$

$12 \overset{\checkmark}{=} 12$

b. $16 = 2x$ Check:

$\dfrac{16}{2} = \dfrac{2x}{2}$ $16 = 2x$

$8 = x$ $16 \overset{?}{=} 2(8)$

$16 \overset{\checkmark}{=} 16$

9. $1.6 = 5x$

$\dfrac{1.6}{5} = \dfrac{5x}{5}$

$0.32 = x$

The length of each side of the Pentagon is 0.32 km.

Check:

$1.6 = 5x$

$1.6 \overset{?}{=} 5(0.32)$

$1.6 \overset{\checkmark}{=} 1.6$

10. $\dfrac{1}{5}x = 725$

$5 \cdot \dfrac{1}{5}x = 5 \cdot 725$

$x = 3,625$

The original price was $3,625

Check:

$\dfrac{1}{5}x = 725$

$\dfrac{1}{5}(3,625) \overset{?}{=} 725$

$725 \overset{\checkmark}{=} 725$

Exercises

1. $\dfrac{3}{4}y = 12$

3. $\dfrac{x}{7} = \dfrac{7}{2}$

5. $\dfrac{1}{3}x = 2$

7. $\dfrac{x}{3} = \dfrac{1}{3}$

9. $9z = 27$

11. Divide by 3

13. Multiply by 2

15. Divide by $\dfrac{3}{4}$ or

multiply by $\dfrac{4}{3}$

17. Divide by 1.5

19.

Equation	Value of x	Solution?
a. $5x = 20$	4	$5 \cdot 4 = 20$; Yes
b. $3x = 12$	36	$3 \cdot 36 = 108$; No
c. $\dfrac{x}{4} = 8$	2	$\dfrac{2}{4} = \dfrac{1}{2}$; No
d. $\dfrac{x}{0.2} = 4$	8	$\dfrac{8}{0.2} = 40$; No

21. $5x = 30$

$\dfrac{5x}{5} = \dfrac{30}{5}$

$x = 6$

Check:

$5x = 30$

$5(6) \overset{?}{=} 30$

$30 \overset{\checkmark}{=} 30$

23. $\dfrac{x}{2} = 9$

$\dfrac{x}{2} \cdot 2 = 9 \cdot 2$

$x = 18$

Check:

$\dfrac{x}{2} = 9$

$\dfrac{18}{2} \overset{?}{=} 9$

$9 \overset{\checkmark}{=} 9$

25. $36 = 9n$

$\dfrac{36}{9} = \dfrac{9n}{9}$

$4 = n$

Check:

$36 = 9n$

$36 \overset{?}{=} 9(4)$

$36 \overset{\checkmark}{=} 36$

27. $\dfrac{x}{7} = 13$

$\dfrac{x}{7} \cdot 7 = 13 \cdot 7$

$x = 91$

Check:

$\dfrac{x}{7} = 13$

$\dfrac{91}{7} \overset{?}{=} 13$

$13 \overset{\checkmark}{=} 13$

29. $1.7y = 6.8$

$\dfrac{1.7y}{1.7} = \dfrac{6.8}{1.7}$

$y = 4$

Check:

$1.7y = 6.8$

$1.7(4) \overset{?}{=} 6.8$

$6.8 \overset{\checkmark}{=} 6.8$

31. $2.1b = 42$

$\dfrac{2.1b}{2.1} = \dfrac{42}{2.1}$

$b = 20$

Check:

$2.1b = 42$

$2.1(20) \overset{?}{=} 42$

$42 \overset{\checkmark}{=} 42$

33. $\dfrac{m}{15} = 10.5$

$\left(\dfrac{m}{15}\right)(15) = (10.5)(15)$

$m = 157.5$

Check:

$\dfrac{m}{15} = 10.5$

$\dfrac{157.5}{15} \overset{?}{=} 10.5$

$10.5 \overset{\checkmark}{=} 10.5$

35. $\dfrac{t}{0.4} = 1$

$\left(\dfrac{t}{0.4}\right)(0.4) = (1)(0.4)$

$t = 0.4$

Check:

$\dfrac{t}{0.4} = 1$

$\dfrac{0.4}{0.4} \overset{?}{=} 1$

$1 \overset{\checkmark}{=} 1$

37. $\dfrac{2}{3}x = 1$ Check:

$\dfrac{3}{2} \cdot \dfrac{2}{3}x = \dfrac{3}{2} \cdot 1$ $\qquad \dfrac{2}{3}x = 1$

$x = \dfrac{3}{2}$, or $1\dfrac{1}{2}$ $\qquad \dfrac{2}{3}\left(\dfrac{3}{2}\right) \overset{?}{=} 1$

$\qquad\qquad\qquad\qquad 1 \overset{\checkmark}{=} 1$

39. $\dfrac{1}{4}x = 9$ Check:

$4 \cdot \dfrac{1}{4}x = 4 \cdot 9$ $\qquad \dfrac{1}{4}x = 9$

$x = 36$ $\qquad \dfrac{1}{4} \cdot 36 \overset{?}{=} 9$

$\qquad\qquad\qquad\qquad 9 \overset{\checkmark}{=} 9$

41. $17t = 51$ Check:

$\dfrac{17t}{17} = \dfrac{51}{17}$ $\qquad 17t = 51$

$t = 3$ $\qquad 17(3) \overset{?}{=} 51$

$\qquad\qquad\qquad 51 \overset{\checkmark}{=} 51$

43. $10y = 4$ Check:

$\dfrac{10y}{10} = \dfrac{4}{10}$ $\qquad 10y = 4$

$y = \dfrac{4}{10}$ $\qquad 10 \cdot \dfrac{2}{5} \overset{?}{=} 4$

$y = \dfrac{2}{5}$ $\qquad \dfrac{20}{5} \overset{?}{=} 4$

$\qquad\qquad\qquad 4 \overset{\checkmark}{=} 4$

45. $7 = \dfrac{n}{100}$ Check:

$7 \cdot 100 = \dfrac{n}{100} \cdot 100$ $\qquad 7 = \dfrac{n}{100}$

$700 = n$ $\qquad 7 \overset{?}{=} \dfrac{700}{100}$

$\qquad\qquad\qquad 7 \overset{\checkmark}{=} 7$

47. $2.5 = \dfrac{x}{5}$ Check:

$2.5(5) = \left(\dfrac{x}{5}\right)(5)$ $\qquad 2.5 = \dfrac{x}{5}$

$12.5 = x$ $\qquad 2.5 \overset{?}{=} \dfrac{12.5}{5}$

$\qquad\qquad\qquad 2.5 \overset{\checkmark}{=} 2.5$

49. $2 = 4x$ Check:

$\dfrac{2}{4} = \dfrac{4x}{4}$ $\qquad 2 = 4x$

$\dfrac{1}{2} = x$ $\qquad 2 \overset{?}{=} 4 \cdot \dfrac{1}{2}$

$\qquad\qquad\qquad 2 \overset{\checkmark}{=} 2$

51. $\dfrac{14}{3} = \dfrac{7}{9}m$ Check:

$\dfrac{9}{7} \cdot \dfrac{14}{3} = \dfrac{9}{7} \cdot \dfrac{7}{9}m$ $\qquad \dfrac{14}{3} = \dfrac{7}{9}m$

$\dfrac{3 \cdot \overset{1}{\cancel{3}}}{\cancel{7}} \cdot \dfrac{2 \cdot \overset{1}{\cancel{7}}}{\underset{1}{\cancel{3}}} = m$ $\qquad \dfrac{14}{3} \overset{?}{=} \dfrac{7}{9} \cdot 6$

$6 = m$ $\qquad \dfrac{14}{3} \overset{?}{=} \dfrac{7}{3 \cdot \cancel{3}} \cdot \dfrac{2 \cdot \overset{1}{\cancel{3}}}{1}$

$\qquad\qquad\qquad \dfrac{14}{3} \overset{\checkmark}{=} \dfrac{14}{3}$

53. $3.14x = 21.3834$

$(3.14x) \div 3.14 = 21.3834 \div 3.14$

$x = 6.81$

Check:

$3.14x = 21.3834$

$3.14(6.81) \overset{?}{=} 21.3834$

$21.3834 \overset{\checkmark}{=} 21.3834$

55. $\dfrac{x}{1.414} = 3.5$ Check:

$\left(\dfrac{x}{1.414}\right)(1.414) = (3.5)(1.414)$ $\qquad \dfrac{x}{1.414} = 3.5$

$x = 4.949$ $\qquad \dfrac{4.949}{1.414} \overset{?}{=} 3.5$

$\qquad\qquad\qquad 3.5 \overset{\checkmark}{=} 3.5$

57. $8n = 56$ Check:

$\dfrac{8n}{8} = \dfrac{56}{8}$ $\qquad 8n = 56$

$n = 7$ $\qquad 8(7) \overset{?}{=} 56$

$\qquad\qquad\qquad 56 \overset{\checkmark}{=} 56$

59. $\dfrac{3}{4}y = 18$ Check:

$\dfrac{4}{3} \cdot \dfrac{3}{4}y = \dfrac{4}{3} \cdot 18$ $\qquad \dfrac{3}{4}y = 18$

$y = \dfrac{4}{\cancel{3}} \cdot \dfrac{\overset{1}{\cancel{3}} \cdot 6}{1}$ $\qquad \dfrac{3}{4} \cdot 24 \overset{?}{=} 18$

$y = 24$ $\qquad \dfrac{3}{\cancel{4}} \cdot \dfrac{\cancel{4} \cdot 6}{1} \overset{?}{=} 18$

$\qquad\qquad\qquad 18 \overset{\checkmark}{=} 18$

61. $\dfrac{x}{5} = 11$ Check:

$\dfrac{x}{5} \cdot 5 = 11 \cdot 5$ $\qquad \dfrac{x}{5} = 11$

$x = 55$ $\qquad \dfrac{55}{5} \overset{?}{=} 11$

$\qquad\qquad\qquad 11 \overset{\checkmark}{=} 11$

63. $2x = 36$ Check:
$$\frac{2x}{2} = \frac{36}{2}$$ $2x = 36$
$$x = 18$$ $2(18) \overset{?}{=} 36$
$$36 \overset{\checkmark}{=} 36$$

65. $\frac{1}{3}x = 4$ Check:
$$3 \cdot \frac{1}{3}x = 3 \cdot 4$$ $\frac{1}{3}x = 4$
$$x = 12$$ $\frac{1}{3} \cdot 12 \overset{?}{=} 4$
$$\frac{1}{\underset{1}{3}} \cdot \frac{\overset{1}{3} \cdot 4}{1} \overset{?}{=} 4$$
$$4 \overset{\checkmark}{=} 4$$

67. $\frac{n}{5} = 1\frac{3}{5}$ Check:
$$\frac{n}{5} = \frac{8}{5}$$ $\frac{n}{5} = 1\frac{3}{5}$
$$\frac{n}{5} \cdot 5 = \frac{8}{5} \cdot 5$$ $\frac{8}{5} \overset{?}{=} 1\frac{3}{5}$
$$n = 8$$ $1\frac{3}{5} = 1\frac{3}{5}$

69. $\frac{y}{2.5} = 10$ Check:
$$\left(\frac{y}{2.5}\right)(2.5) = (10)(2.5)$$ $\frac{y}{2.5} = 10$
$$y = 25$$ $\frac{25}{2.5} \overset{?}{=} 10$
$$10 \overset{\checkmark}{=} 10$$

71. Equation d: $\frac{1}{4}m = 20$

73. Equation a: $8c = 340$

75. $4s = 60$
$$\frac{4s}{4} = \frac{60}{4}$$
$$s = 15$$
Each side of the square is 15 units long.
Check:
$$4s = 60$$
$$4(15) \overset{?}{=} 60$$
$$60 \overset{\checkmark}{=} 60$$

77. $\frac{1}{6}x = 750$
$$6 \cdot \frac{1}{6}x = 6 \cdot 750$$
$$x = 4,500$$
Before the drop, the airplane was at 4,500 ft.
Check:
$$\frac{1}{6}x = 750$$
$$\frac{1}{6} \cdot 4,500 \overset{?}{=} 750$$
$$\frac{1}{\underset{1}{6}} \cdot \frac{\overset{1}{6} \cdot 750}{1} \overset{?}{=} 750$$
$$750 \overset{\checkmark}{=} 750$$

79. a. The equation is $\frac{x}{34} = 0.67$

b. $\frac{x}{34} = 0.67$
$$\left(\frac{x}{34}\right)(34) = (0.67)(34)$$
$$x = 22.78 \approx 23$$
To the nearest million, the personnel cost is $23 million.

c. Possible estimate: $\frac{2}{3} \cdot 33 = 22$ or $22 million.

Review Exercises

1. x plus 1
2. 4 more than y
3. w minus 1
4. 3 less than s
5. c over 7
6. The quotient of a and 10
7. 2 times x
8. The product of 6 and y
9. y divided by 0.1
10. The quotient of n and 1.5
11. $\frac{1}{3}$ of x
12. $\frac{1}{10}$ of w
13. $m + 16$
14. $b + \frac{1}{2}$
15. $y - 1.4$
16. $z - 8$
17. $\frac{6}{z}$
18. $n \div 2.5$
19. $3n$
20. $12n$
21. $4 + 8 = 12$
22. $7 + 12 = 19$
23. $5 - 5 = 0$
24. $15 - 9 = 6$

25. $1.5(0.2) = 0.3$

26. $1.3(5) = 6.5$

27. $\frac{1}{2}(3) = \frac{3}{2}$ or $1\frac{1}{2}$

28. $\left(\frac{1}{6}\right)\left(2\frac{1}{2}\right) = \frac{1}{6} \cdot \frac{5}{2} = \frac{5}{12}$

29. $10 - 9.6 = 0.4$

30. $8 - 3\frac{1}{2} = 7\frac{2}{2} - 3\frac{1}{2} = 4\frac{1}{2}$

31. $\dfrac{2.5}{1.5} = \dfrac{(5)(\cancel{0.5})}{(3)(\cancel{0.5})} = \dfrac{5}{3}$ or $1\frac{2}{3}$

32. $\dfrac{1.8}{0.2} = 9$

33.
$$x + 11 = 20$$
$$x + 11 - 11 = 20 - 11$$
$$x = 9$$
Check:
$$x + 11 = 20$$
$$9 + 11 \overset{?}{=} 20$$
$$20 \overset{\checkmark}{=} 20$$

34.
$$y + 15 = 24$$
$$y + 15 - 15 = 24 - 15$$
$$y = 9$$
Check:
$$y + 15 = 24$$
$$9 + 15 \overset{?}{=} 24$$
$$24 \overset{\checkmark}{=} 24$$

35.
$$n - 19 = 7$$
$$n - 19 + 19 = 7 + 19$$
$$n = 26$$
Check:
$$n - 19 = 7$$
$$26 - 19 \overset{?}{=} 7$$
$$7 \overset{\checkmark}{=} 7$$

36.
$$b - 12 = 8$$
$$b - 12 + 12 = 8 + 12$$
$$b = 20$$
Check:
$$b - 12 = 8$$
$$20 - 12 \overset{?}{=} 8$$
$$8 \overset{\checkmark}{=} 8$$

37.
$$a + 2.5 = 6$$
$$a + 2.5 - 2.5 = 6 - 2.5$$
$$a = 3.5$$
Check:
$$a + 2.5 = 6$$
$$3.5 + 2.5 \overset{?}{=} 6$$
$$6 \overset{\checkmark}{=} 6$$

38.
$$c + 1.6 = 9.1$$
$$c + 1.6 - 1.6 = 9.1 - 1.6$$
$$c = 7.5$$
Check:
$$c + 1.6 = 9.1$$
$$7.5 + 9.6 \overset{?}{=} 9.1$$
$$9.1 \overset{\checkmark}{=} 9.1$$

39.
$$x - 1.8 = 9.2$$
$$x - 1.8 + 1.8 = 9.2 + 1.8$$
$$x = 11$$
Check:
$$x - 1.8 = 9.2$$
$$11 - 1.8 = 9.2$$
$$9.2 = 9.2$$

40.
$$y - 1.4 = 0.6$$
$$y - 1.4 + 1.4 = 0.6 + 1.4$$
$$y = 2$$
Check:
$$y - 1.4 = 0.6$$
$$2 - 1.4 \overset{?}{=} 0.6$$
$$0.6 \overset{\checkmark}{=} 0.6$$

41.
$$w + 1\frac{1}{2} = 3$$
$$w + 1\frac{1}{2} - 1\frac{1}{2} = 3 - 1\frac{1}{2}$$
$$w = 2\frac{2}{2} - 1\frac{1}{2} = 1\frac{1}{2}$$
Check:
$$w + 1\frac{1}{2} = 3$$
$$1\frac{1}{2} + 1\frac{1}{2} \overset{?}{=} 3$$
$$2\frac{2}{2} \overset{?}{=} 3$$
$$3 \overset{\checkmark}{=} 3$$

42.
$$s + \frac{2}{3} = 1$$
$$s + \frac{2}{3} - \frac{2}{3} = 1 - \frac{2}{3}$$
$$s = \frac{3}{3} - \frac{2}{3}$$
$$s = \frac{1}{3}$$
Check:
$$s + \frac{2}{3} = 1$$
$$\frac{1}{3} + \frac{2}{3} \overset{?}{=} 1$$
$$\frac{3}{3} \overset{?}{=} 1$$
$$1 \overset{\checkmark}{=} 1$$

43.
$$c - 1\frac{1}{4} = 5$$
$$c - 1\frac{1}{4} + 1\frac{1}{4} = 5 + 1\frac{1}{4}$$
$$c = 6\frac{1}{4}$$
Check:
$$c - 1\frac{1}{4} = 5$$
$$6\frac{1}{4} - 1\frac{1}{4} \overset{?}{=} 5$$
$$5 \overset{\checkmark}{=} 5$$

44.
$$p - 6 = 5\frac{2}{3}$$
$$p - 6 + 6 = 5\frac{2}{3} + 6$$
$$p = 11\frac{2}{3}$$
Check:
$$p - 6 = 5\frac{2}{3}$$
$$11\frac{2}{3} - 6 \overset{?}{=} 5\frac{2}{3}$$
$$5\frac{2}{3} \overset{\checkmark}{=} 5\frac{2}{3}$$

45.
$$7 = m + 2$$
$$7 - 2 = m + 2 - 2$$
$$5 = m$$
Check:
$$7 = m + 2$$
$$7 \overset{?}{=} 5 + 2$$
$$7 \overset{\checkmark}{=} 7$$

46.
$$10 = n + 10$$
$$10 - 10 = n + 10 - 10$$
$$0 = n$$
Check:
$$10 = n + 10$$
$$10 \overset{?}{=} 0 + 10$$
$$10 \overset{\checkmark}{=} 10$$

47. $39 = c - 39$ Check:
$39 + 39 = c - 39 + 39$ $39 = c - 39$
$78 = c$ $39 \overset{?}{=} 78 - 39$
                          $39 \overset{\checkmark}{=} 39$

48. $72 = y - 18$ Check:
$72 + 18 = y - 18 + 18$ $72 = y - 18$
$90 = y$ $72 \overset{?}{=} 90 - 18$
                          $72 \overset{\checkmark}{=} 72$

49. $38 + n = 49$ Check:
$38 - 38 + n = 49 - 38$ $38 + n = 49$
$n = 11$ $38 + 11 \overset{?}{=} 49$
                          $49 \overset{\checkmark}{=} 49$

50. $37 + x = 62$ Check:
$37 - 37 + x = 62 - 37$ $37 + x = 62$
$x = 25$ $37 + 25 \overset{?}{=} 62$
                          $62 \overset{\checkmark}{=} 62$

51. $4.0875 + x = 35.136$
$4.0875 - 4.0875 + x = 35.136 - 4.0875$
$x = 31.0485$
Check:
$4.0875 + x = 35.136$
$4.0875 + 31.0485 \overset{?}{=} 35.136$
$35.136 \overset{\checkmark}{=} 35.136$

52. $24.625 = m - 1.9975$
$24.625 + 1.9975 = m - 1.9975 + 1.9975$
$26.6225 = m$
Check:
$24.625 = m - 1.9975$
$24.625 \overset{?}{=} 26.6225 - 1.9975$
$24.625 \overset{\checkmark}{=} 24.625$

53. $n - 19 = 35$ **54.** $t - 37 = 234$

55. $9 + x = 5\frac{1}{2}$ **56.** $s + 26 = 30\frac{1}{3}$

57. $2y = 16$ **58.** $25t = 175$

59. $\frac{n}{19} = 34$ **60.** $\frac{z}{13} = 17$

61. $\frac{1}{3}n = 27$ **62.** $\frac{2}{5}n = 4$

63.

Equation	Value of x	Solution?
a. $0.3x = 6$	1	No
b. $x - \frac{1}{2} = 1\frac{2}{3}$	$1\frac{1}{6}$	No
c. $\frac{x}{0.5} = 7$	35	No
d. $x + 0.1 = 3$	3.1	No

64.

Equation	Value of x	Solution?
a. $0.2x = 6$	30	Yes
b. $x + \frac{1}{2} = 1\frac{2}{3}$	$\frac{5}{6}$	No
c. $\frac{x}{0.2} = 4.1$	8.2	No
d. $x + 0.5 = 7.4$	2.4	No

65. $2x = 10$ Check:
$\dfrac{2x}{2} = \dfrac{10}{2}$ $2x = 10$
$x = 5$ $2(5) \overset{?}{=} 10$
                    $10 \overset{\checkmark}{=} 10$

66. $8t = 16$ Check:
$\dfrac{8t}{8} = \dfrac{16}{8}$ $8t = 16$
$t = 2$ $8(2) \overset{?}{=} 16$
                    $16 \overset{\checkmark}{=} 16$

67. $\dfrac{a}{7} = 15$ Check:
$\dfrac{a}{7} \cdot 7 = 15 \cdot 7$ $\dfrac{a}{7} = 15$
$a = 105$ $\dfrac{105}{7} \overset{?}{=} 15$
                    $15 \overset{\checkmark}{=} 15$

68. $\dfrac{n}{6} = 9$ Check:
$\dfrac{n}{6} \cdot 6 = 9 \cdot 6$ $\dfrac{n}{6} = 9$
$n = 54$ $\dfrac{54}{6} \overset{?}{=} 9$
                    $9 \overset{\checkmark}{=} 9$

69. $9y = 81$ Check:
$\dfrac{9y}{9} = \dfrac{81}{9}$ $9y = 81$
$y = 9$ $9(9) \overset{?}{=} 81$
                    $81 \overset{\checkmark}{=} 81$

70. $10r = 100$ Check:
$$\frac{10r}{10} = \frac{100}{10}$$ $10r = 100$
$$r = 10$$ $10(10) \overset{?}{=} 100$
                $100 \overset{\checkmark}{=} 100$

71. $\frac{w}{10} = 9$ Check:
$$\frac{w}{10} \cdot 10 = 9 \cdot 10$$ $\frac{w}{10} = 9$
    $w = 90$ $\frac{90}{10} \overset{?}{=} 9$
                $9 = 9$

72. $\frac{x}{100} = 1$ Check:
$$\frac{x}{100} \cdot 100 = 1 \cdot 100$$ $\frac{x}{100} = 1$
    $x = 100$ $\frac{100}{100} \overset{?}{=} 1$
                $1 \overset{\checkmark}{=} 1$

73. $1.5y = 30$ Check:
$$\frac{1.5y}{1.5} = \frac{30}{1.5}$$ $1.5y = 30$
    $y = 20$ $(1.5)(20) \overset{?}{=} 30$
                $30 \overset{\checkmark}{=} 30$

74. $1.2a = 144$ Check:
$$\frac{1.2a}{1.2} = \frac{144}{1.2}$$ $1.2a = 144$
    $a = 120$ $(1.2)(120) \overset{?}{=} 144$
                $144 \overset{\checkmark}{=} 144$

75. $\frac{1}{8}n = 4$ Check:
$$8 \cdot \frac{1}{8}n = 8 \cdot 4$$ $\frac{1}{8}n = 4$
    $n = 32$ $\frac{1}{8} \cdot (32) \overset{?}{=} 4$
                $4 \overset{\checkmark}{=} 4$

76. $\frac{1}{2}b = 16$ Check:
$$2 \cdot \frac{1}{2}b = 2 \cdot 16$$ $\frac{1}{2}b = 16$
    $b = 32$ $\frac{1}{2}(32) \overset{?}{=} 16$
                $16 \overset{\checkmark}{=} 16$

77. $\frac{m}{1.5} = 2.1$ Check:
$$\left(\frac{m}{1.5}\right)(1.5) = (2.1)(1.5)$$ $\frac{m}{1.5} = 2.1$
    $m = 3.15$ $\frac{3.15}{1.5} \overset{?}{=} 2.1$
                $2.1 \overset{\checkmark}{=} 2.1$

78. $\frac{z}{0.3} = 1.9$ Check:
$$\left(\frac{z}{0.3}\right)(0.3) = (1.9)(0.3)$$ $\frac{z}{0.3} = 1.9$
    $z = 0.57$ $\frac{0.57}{0.3} \overset{?}{=} 1.9$
                $1.9 \overset{\checkmark}{=} 1.9$

79. $100x = 40$ Check:
$$\frac{100x}{100} = \frac{40}{100}$$ $100x = 40$
                $100 \cdot \frac{2}{5} \overset{?}{=} 40$
$$x = \frac{2 \cdot \cancel{20}^{1}}{5 \cdot \cancel{20}_{1}}$$ $\frac{\cancel{20} \cdot 5}{1} \cdot \frac{2}{\cancel{5}} \overset{?}{=} 40$
$$x = \frac{2}{5}$$ $40 \overset{\checkmark}{=} 40$

80. $10y = 5$ Check:
$$\frac{10y}{10} = \frac{5}{10}$$ $10y = 5$
    $y = \frac{1}{2}$ $10\left(\frac{1}{2}\right) \overset{?}{=} 5$
                $5 \overset{\checkmark}{=} 5$

81. $0.3 = \frac{m}{4}$ Check:
$$(0.3)(4) = \left(\frac{m}{4}\right)(4)$$ $0.3 = \frac{m}{3}$
    $1.2 = m$ $0.3 \overset{?}{=} \frac{1.2}{4}$
                $0.3 \overset{\checkmark}{=} 0.3$

82. $1.4 = \frac{b}{7}$ Check:
$$(1.4)(7) = \left(\frac{b}{7}\right)(7)$$ $1.4 = \frac{b}{7}$
    $9.8 = b$ $1.4 \overset{?}{=} \frac{9.8}{7}$
                $1.4 \overset{\checkmark}{=} 1.4$

83. $0.866x = 10.825$
$$(0.866x) \div 0.866 = 10.825 \div 0.866$$
    $x = 12.5$
Check:
    $0.866x = 10.825$
    $(0.866)(12.5) \overset{?}{=} 10.825$
    $10.825 \overset{\checkmark}{=} 10.825$

84.
$$\frac{x}{0.707} = 2.1$$

$$\left(\frac{x}{0.707}\right)(0.707) = (2.1)(0.707)$$

$$x = 1.4847$$

Check:

$$\frac{x}{0.707} = 2.1$$

$$\frac{1.4847}{0.707} \overset{?}{=} 2.1$$

$$2.1 \overset{\checkmark}{=} 2.1$$

85. x DVDs will cost $12.99x$ dollars.
8 DVDs will cost $12.99(8) = 103.92$ dollars
or $103.92.

86. Your hourly wage is $\dfrac{d}{40}$ dollars/hr .

If you earn $382 per week, your hourly wage is

$\dfrac{382}{40}$ dollars/hr $= 9.55$ dollars/hr or $9.55/hr .

87. p pounds of fruit will cost $89p$ cents.
3 lb will cost $(89)(3)$ cents or $2.67.

88. If d is the finance charge, you will pay the bank
$3,000 + d$ dollars. If the finance charge is $225, you
will pay $3,000 + 225$ dollars or $3,225.

89.
$$9.59 + x = 19.14$$
$$9.59 - 9.59 + x = 19.14 - 9.59$$
$$x = 9.55$$
His score in the other event was 9.55.
Check:
$$9.59 + x = 19.14$$
$$9.59 + 9.55 \overset{?}{=} 19.14$$
$$19.14 \overset{\checkmark}{=} 19.14$$

90.
$$\frac{1}{4}x = 500,000$$
$$\left(\frac{1}{4}x\right)(4) = (500,000)(4)$$
$$x = 2,000,000$$
Approximately 2 million people lived in Jamaica.
Check:
$$\frac{1}{4}x = 500,000$$
$$\frac{1}{4} \cdot 2,000,000 \overset{?}{=} 500,000$$
$$500,000 \overset{\checkmark}{=} 500,000$$

91.
$$10,000t = 1,000$$
$$\frac{10,000t}{10,000} = \frac{1,000}{10,000}$$
$$t = 0.1$$
A one-dollar bill is 0.1 mm thick.
Check:
$$10,000t = 1,000$$
$$(10,000)(0.1) \overset{?}{=} 1,000$$
$$1,000 \overset{\checkmark}{=} 1,000$$

92.
$$225 = x + 50$$
$$225 - 50 = x + 50 - 50$$
$$175 = x$$
Her scratch score was 175.
Check:
$$225 = x + 50$$
$$225 \overset{?}{=} 175 + 50$$
$$225 \overset{\checkmark}{=} 225$$

93.
$$2\frac{3}{5}w = 286$$
$$\frac{13}{5}w = 286$$
$$\frac{5}{13} \cdot \frac{13}{5}w = 286 \cdot \frac{5}{13}$$
$$w = \frac{22 \cdot \cancel{13}}{1} \cdot \frac{5}{\cancel{13}}$$
$$w = 110$$
On Earth you weigh 110 lb.
Check:
$$2\frac{3}{5}w = 286$$
$$\frac{13}{5} \cdot 110 \overset{?}{=} 286$$
$$\frac{13}{\cancel{5}} \cdot \frac{\cancel{5} \cdot 22}{1} \overset{?}{=} 286$$
$$286 \overset{\checkmark}{=} 286$$

94.
$$1.8x = 6,696$$
$$\frac{1.8x}{1.8} = \frac{6,696}{1.8}$$
$$x = 3,720$$
The Missouri is approximately 3,720 km long.
Check:
$$1.8x = 6,696$$
$$(1.8)(3,720) \overset{?}{=} 6,696$$
$$6,696 \overset{\checkmark}{=} 6,696$$

95. $98.6 + x = 101$

$98.6 - 98.6 + x = 101 - 98.6$

$x = 2.4$

Your temperature was $2.4°F$ above normal.

Check:

$98.6 + x = 101$

$98.6 + 2.4 \overset{?}{=} 101$

$101 \overset{\checkmark}{=} 101$

96. $y - 8 = 42$

$y - 8 + 8 = 42 + 8$

$y = 50$

The price in Maxine's is $50.

Check:

$y - 8 = 42$

$50 - 8 \overset{?}{=} 42$

$42 \overset{\checkmark}{=} 42$

Posttest

1. Possible answer: x plus $\dfrac{1}{2}$

2. Possible answer: the quotient of a and 3

3. $n + 8$

4. $\dfrac{1}{8}p$

5. $1.5 - 1.5 = 0$

6. $\dfrac{2\frac{1}{4}}{9} = \dfrac{\overset{1}{\cancel{9}}}{4} \cdot \dfrac{1}{\underset{1}{\cancel{9}}} = \dfrac{1}{4}$

7. $x - 6 = 4\dfrac{1}{2}$

8. $\dfrac{y}{8} = 3.2$

9. $x + 10 = 10$ Check:

$x + 10 - 10 = 10 - 10$ $x + 10 = 10$

$x = 0$ $0 + 10 \overset{?}{=} 10$

$10 \overset{\checkmark}{=} 10$

10. $y - 6 = 6$ Check:

$y - 6 + 6 = 6 + 6$ $y - 6 = 6$

$y = 12$ $12 - 6 \overset{?}{=} 6$

$6 \overset{\checkmark}{=} 6$

11. $3n = 81$ Check:

$\dfrac{3n}{3} = \dfrac{81}{3}$ $3n = 81$

$n = 27$ $3(27) \overset{?}{=} 81$

$81 \overset{\checkmark}{=} 81$

12. $\dfrac{a}{9} = 82$ Check:

$\dfrac{a}{9} \cdot 9 = 82 \cdot 9$ $\dfrac{a}{9} = 82$

$a = 738$ $\dfrac{738}{9} \overset{?}{=} 82$

$82 \overset{\checkmark}{=} 82$

13. $m - 1.8 = 6$ Check:

$m - 1.8 + 1.8 = 6 + 1.8$ $m - 1.8 = 6$

$m = 7.8$ $7.8 - 1.8 = 6$

$6 = 6$

14. $1.5n = 75$ Check:

$\dfrac{1.5n}{1.5} = \dfrac{75}{1.5}$ $1.5n = 75$

$n = 50$ $1.5(50) \overset{?}{=} 75$

$75 \overset{\checkmark}{=} 75$

15. $10x = 54$ Check:

$\dfrac{10x}{10} = \dfrac{54}{10}$ $10x = 54$

$x = 5.4$ or $\dfrac{27}{5}$ or $5\dfrac{2}{5}$ $10(5.4) \overset{?}{=} 54$

$54 = 54$

16. $\dfrac{n}{100} = 7.6$ Check:

$\left(\dfrac{n}{100}\right)(100) = (7.6)(100)$ $\dfrac{n}{100} = 7.6$

$n = 760$ $\dfrac{760}{100} \overset{?}{=} 7.6$

$7.6 \overset{\checkmark}{=} 7.6$

17. $1\dfrac{3}{4} + x = 2\dfrac{1}{4}$

$1\dfrac{3}{4} - 1\dfrac{3}{4} + x = 2\dfrac{1}{4} - 1\dfrac{3}{4}$

$x = 1\dfrac{5}{4} - 1\dfrac{3}{4} = \dfrac{2}{4}$

$x = \dfrac{1}{2}$

You should by $\dfrac{1}{2}$ lb of codfish.

Check:

$1\dfrac{3}{4} + x = 2\dfrac{1}{4}$

$1\dfrac{3}{4} + \dfrac{1}{2} \overset{?}{=} 2\dfrac{1}{4}$

$1\dfrac{3}{4} + \dfrac{2}{4} \overset{?}{=} 2\dfrac{1}{4}$

$1\dfrac{5}{4} \overset{?}{=} 2\dfrac{1}{4}$

$2\dfrac{1}{4} \overset{\checkmark}{=} 2\dfrac{1}{4}$

18. $\dfrac{1}{3}x = 30{,}000$

$3 \cdot \dfrac{1}{3}x = 3 \cdot 30{,}000$

$x = 90{,}000$

There were 90,000 elephants at the beginning of the year.

Check:

$$\dfrac{1}{3}x = 30{,}000$$

$$\dfrac{1}{3} \cdot 90{,}000 \overset{?}{=} 30{,}000$$

$$30{,}000 \overset{\checkmark}{=} 30{,}000$$

19. $7.25x = 145$

$\dfrac{7.25x}{7.25} = \dfrac{145}{7.25}$

$x = 20$

The aide worked 20 hr.

Check:

$$7.25x = 145$$

$$(7.25)(20) \overset{?}{=} 145$$

$$145 \overset{\checkmark}{=} 145$$

20. $x - 14\dfrac{1}{2} = 156\dfrac{1}{2}$

$x - 14\dfrac{1}{2} + 14\dfrac{1}{2} = 156\dfrac{1}{2} + 14\dfrac{1}{2}$

$x = 170\dfrac{2}{2}$

$x = 171$

You weighed 171 lb.

Check:

$$x - 14\dfrac{1}{2} = 156\dfrac{1}{2}$$

$$171 - 14\dfrac{1}{2} \overset{?}{=} 156\dfrac{1}{2}$$

$$170\dfrac{2}{2} = 14\dfrac{1}{2} \overset{?}{=} 156\dfrac{1}{2}$$

$$156\dfrac{1}{2} \overset{\checkmark}{=} 156\dfrac{1}{2}$$

Cumulative Review Exercises

1. $8\dfrac{1}{4} - 2\dfrac{7}{8} = 8\dfrac{2}{8} - 2\dfrac{7}{8}$

$= 7\dfrac{10}{8} - 2\dfrac{7}{8}$

$= 5\dfrac{3}{8}$

2. The divisor 1,000 has three zeros, so move the decimal point three places to the left:
$7.5 \div 1{,}000 = 0.0075$

3. $2 + 3 = 5$, so 2 is a solution.

4. $9y = 27$ Check:

$\dfrac{9y}{9} = \dfrac{27}{9}$ $9y = 27$

$y = 3$ $9(3) \overset{?}{=} 27$

$27 \overset{\checkmark}{=} 27$

5. $w + 2\dfrac{1}{3} = 4$ Check:

$w + 2\dfrac{1}{3} - 2\dfrac{1}{3} = 4 - 2\dfrac{1}{3}$ $w + 2\dfrac{1}{3} = 4$

$w = 3\dfrac{3}{3} - 2\dfrac{1}{3}$ $1\dfrac{2}{3} + 2\dfrac{1}{3} \overset{?}{=} 4$

$w = 1\dfrac{2}{3}$ $3\dfrac{3}{3} \overset{?}{=} 4$

$4 \overset{\checkmark}{=} 4$

6. $n - 3.8 = 4$ Check:

$n - 3.8 + 3.8 = 4 + 3.8$ $n - 3.8 = 4$

$n = 7.8$ $7.8 - 3.8 \overset{?}{=} 4$

$4 \overset{\checkmark}{=} 4$

7. $\dfrac{x}{2} = 16$ Check:

$\dfrac{x}{2} \cdot 2 = 16 \cdot 2$ $\dfrac{x}{2} = 16$

$x = 32$ $\dfrac{32}{2} \overset{?}{=} 16$

$16 \overset{\checkmark}{=} 16$

8. $5 \text{ min} = 5 \cdot 60 \text{ sec} = 300 \text{ sec}$

$24 \cdot 300 = 7{,}200$

The artists had to draw 7,200 cartoons.

9. $\dfrac{\$200}{\$700} = \dfrac{2}{7}$; you received $\dfrac{2}{7}$ of your money.

$\dfrac{2}{7} = \dfrac{6}{21} \quad \dfrac{1}{3} = \dfrac{7}{21}$

$\dfrac{2}{7} < \dfrac{1}{3}$ because $\dfrac{6}{21} < \dfrac{7}{21}$

You got back less than $\dfrac{1}{3}$ of your money.

10. $150 \times 0.167 = 25.05$

He weighs 25.05 lb on the moon.

Chapter 5

RATIO AND PROPORTION

Pretest

1. $\dfrac{6}{8} = \dfrac{\cancel{2} \cdot 3}{\cancel{2} \cdot 4} = \dfrac{3}{4}$ in simplest form

2. $\dfrac{21}{27} = \dfrac{\cancel{3} \cdot 7}{\cancel{3} \cdot 9} = \dfrac{7}{9}$ in simplest form

3. $\dfrac{\$30}{\$18} = \dfrac{30}{18} = \dfrac{\cancel{6} \cdot 5}{\cancel{6} \cdot 3} = \dfrac{5}{3}$ in simplest form

4. $\dfrac{19\,\text{ft}}{51\,\text{ft}} = \dfrac{19}{51}$ in simplest form

5. $\dfrac{12 \text{ dental assistants}}{6 \text{ dentists}} = \dfrac{2 \text{ dental assistants}}{1 \text{ dentist}}$

6. $\dfrac{48 \text{ gal}}{15 \text{ min}} = \dfrac{16 \text{ gal}}{5 \text{ min}}$ or $\dfrac{3.2 \text{ gal}}{1 \text{ min}}$

7. $\dfrac{60 \text{ baskets}}{180 \text{ attempts}} = \dfrac{1 \text{ basket}}{3 \text{ attempts}}$

8. $\dfrac{10 \text{ mg}}{6 \text{ hr}} = \dfrac{5 \text{ mg}}{3 \text{ hr}}$ or $\dfrac{1\frac{2}{3} \text{ mg}}{1 \text{ hr}}$

9. $\dfrac{\$690}{3 \text{ boxes}} = \$230/\text{box}$

10. $\dfrac{15 \text{ pages}}{75 \text{ min}} = \dfrac{1 \text{ page}}{5 \text{ min}}$ or 0.2 page/min

11. $\dfrac{2}{3} \overset{?}{=} \dfrac{16}{24}$

$3 \cdot 16 \overset{?}{=} 2 \cdot 24$

$48 \overset{\checkmark}{=} 48$

a true proportion

12. $\dfrac{32}{20} \overset{?}{=} \dfrac{8}{3}$

$20 \cdot 8 \overset{?}{=} 32 \cdot 3$

$160 \neq 96$

a false proportion

13. $\dfrac{6}{8} = \dfrac{x}{12}$

$8x = 6 \cdot 12$

$8x = 72$

$x = 9$

Check:

$\dfrac{6}{8} = \dfrac{x}{12}$

$\dfrac{6}{8} \overset{?}{=} \dfrac{9}{12}$

$8 \cdot 9 \overset{?}{=} 6 \cdot 12$

$72 \overset{\checkmark}{=} 72$

14. $\dfrac{21}{x} = \dfrac{2}{3}$

$2x = 21 \cdot 3$

$2x = 63$

$x = 31\frac{1}{2}$

Check:

$\dfrac{21}{x} = \dfrac{2}{3}$

$\dfrac{21}{31\frac{1}{2}} \overset{?}{=} \dfrac{2}{3}$

$\left(31\frac{1}{2}\right)(2) \overset{?}{=} 21 \cdot 3$

$\left(\dfrac{63}{2}\right)(2) \overset{?}{=} 63$

$63 \overset{\checkmark}{=} 63$

15. $\dfrac{\frac{1}{2}}{4} = \dfrac{2}{x}$

$4 \cdot 2 = \dfrac{1}{2}x$

$8 \cdot 2 = x$

$16 = x$

Check:

$\dfrac{\frac{1}{2}}{4} = \dfrac{2}{x}$

$\dfrac{\frac{1}{2}}{4} \overset{?}{=} \dfrac{2}{16}$

$\dfrac{1}{2} \cdot 16 \overset{?}{=} 4 \cdot 2$

$8 \overset{\checkmark}{=} 8$

16. $\dfrac{x}{6} = \dfrac{8}{0.3}$

$6 \cdot 8 = 0.3x$

$48 = 0.3x$

$\dfrac{48}{0.3} = x$

$160 = x$

Check:

$\dfrac{x}{6} = \dfrac{8}{0.3}$

$\dfrac{160}{6} \overset{?}{=} \dfrac{8}{0.3}$

$6 \cdot 8 \overset{?}{=} (160)(0.3)$

$48 \overset{\checkmark}{=} 48$

17. $\dfrac{\text{weight of sand}}{\text{weight of gravel}} = \dfrac{80\,\text{lb}}{100\,\text{lb}} = \dfrac{80}{100} = \dfrac{4}{5}$

The ratio of sand to gravel is $\dfrac{4}{5}$.

18. $\dfrac{\$54}{27\,\text{lb}} = \dfrac{\$2}{1\,\text{lb}}$ You pay \$2 per pound.

19. $\dfrac{35}{2} = \dfrac{3,570}{x}$ ← students ← faculty

$35x = 2 \cdot 3,570$

$35x = 7,140$

$x = 204$

The college should have 204 faculty members.

20. $\dfrac{3\,\text{in.}}{31\,\text{mi}} = \dfrac{8.4\,\text{in.}}{d\,\text{mi}}$ ← distance on map ← actual distance

$3d = 31 \cdot 8.4$

$3d = 260.4$

$d = 86.8 \approx 87$

The actual distance is 87 mi.

5.1   Introduction to Ratios

Practice

1. $\dfrac{8}{12} = \dfrac{\cancel{4} \cdot 2}{\cancel{4} \cdot 3} = \dfrac{2}{3}$ 2. $\dfrac{9\,\text{ft}}{5\,\text{ft}} = \dfrac{9}{5}$

The ratio $\dfrac{8}{12}$ in simplest form is $\dfrac{2}{3}$.

3. The increase in value is $\$12.00 - \$9.50 = \$2.50$.

$\dfrac{\text{increase}}{\text{original value}} = \dfrac{\$2.50}{\$9.50} = \dfrac{\cancel{50} \cdot 5}{\cancel{50} \cdot 19} = \dfrac{5}{19}$

4. a. 12 nurses for 40 patients =
   $\dfrac{12\,\text{nurses}}{40\,\text{patients}} = \dfrac{3\,\text{nurses}}{10\,\text{patients}}$

   b. 15 lab stations for every 60 students =
   $\dfrac{15\,\text{lab stations}}{60\,\text{students}} = \dfrac{1\,\text{lab station}}{4\,\text{students}}$

5. a. $\dfrac{192\,\text{ft}}{4\,\text{sec}} = \dfrac{192 \div 4\,\text{ft}}{4 \div 4\,\text{sec}} = \dfrac{48\,\text{ft}}{1\,\text{sec}}$, or 48 fps

   b. $\dfrac{15\,\text{hits}}{40\,\text{times at bat}} = \dfrac{15 \div 40\,\text{hits}}{40 \div 40\,\text{times at bat}} = \dfrac{0.375\,\text{hit}}{1\,\text{time at bat}}$, or 0.375 hit per time at bat

6. $\dfrac{375\,\text{words}}{5\,\text{min}} = \dfrac{75\,\text{words}}{1\,\text{min}} = 75\,\text{wpm}$

7. a. $\dfrac{\$696}{4\,\text{flights}} = \$174/\text{flight}$

   b. $\dfrac{\$4,475}{5\,\text{fax machines}} = \$895/\text{fax machine}$

8. 15-oz can: $\dfrac{45\cent}{15\,\text{oz}} = 3\cent/\text{oz}$

   32-oz can: $\dfrac{92\cent}{32\,\text{oz}} = 2.875\cent/\text{oz}$

   The 32-oz can has the lower unit price.

Exercises

1. $\dfrac{6}{9} = \dfrac{3 \cdot 2}{3 \cdot 3} = \dfrac{2}{3}$ 3. $\dfrac{10}{15} = \dfrac{5 \cdot 2}{5 \cdot 3} = \dfrac{2}{3}$

5. $\dfrac{55}{35} = \dfrac{5 \cdot 11}{5 \cdot 7} = \dfrac{11}{7}$ 7. $\dfrac{12}{8} = \dfrac{4 \cdot 3}{4 \cdot 2} = \dfrac{3}{2}$

9. $\dfrac{2.5}{10} = \dfrac{(2.5)(1)}{(2.5)(4)} = \dfrac{1}{4}$

11. $\dfrac{60\,\text{min}}{45\,\text{min}} = \dfrac{60}{45} = \dfrac{15 \cdot 4}{15 \cdot 3} = \dfrac{4}{3}$

13. $\dfrac{10\,\text{ft}}{10\,\text{ft}} = \dfrac{10}{10} = \dfrac{1}{1}$ 15. $\dfrac{30\cent}{18\cent} = \dfrac{30}{18} = \dfrac{6 \cdot 5}{6 \cdot 3} = \dfrac{5}{3}$

17. $\dfrac{7\,\text{mph}}{24\,\text{mph}} = \dfrac{7}{24}$

19. $\dfrac{1,000\,\text{acres}}{50\,\text{acres}} = \dfrac{1,000}{50} = \dfrac{50 \cdot 20}{50 \cdot 1} = \dfrac{20}{1}$

21. $\dfrac{8\,\text{g}}{7\,\text{g}} = \dfrac{8}{7}$

23. $\dfrac{24\,\text{sec}}{30\,\text{sec}} = \dfrac{24}{30} = \dfrac{6 \cdot 4}{6 \cdot 5} = \dfrac{4}{5}$

25. $\dfrac{25\,\text{telephone calls}}{10\,\text{days}} = \dfrac{5\,\text{calls}}{2\,\text{days}}$

27. $\dfrac{20\,\text{children}}{6\,\text{families}} = \dfrac{10\,\text{children}}{3\,\text{families}}$

29. $\dfrac{3,000\,\text{students}}{160\,\text{faculty}} = \dfrac{75\,\text{students}}{4\,\text{faculty}}$

31. $\dfrac{68\,\text{baskets}}{120\,\text{attempts}} = \dfrac{17\,\text{baskets}}{30\,\text{attempts}}$

33. $\dfrac{10\,\text{cars}}{10\,\text{people}} = \dfrac{1\,\text{car}}{1\,\text{person}}$ 35. $\dfrac{400\,\text{mi}}{18\,\text{gal}} = \dfrac{200\,\text{mi}}{9\,\text{gal}}$

37. $\dfrac{48 \text{ males}}{9 \text{ females}} = \dfrac{16 \text{ males}}{3 \text{ females}}$

39. $\dfrac{40 \text{ Democrats}}{35 \text{ Republicans}} = \dfrac{8 \text{ Democrats}}{7 \text{ Republicans}}$

41. $\dfrac{2 \text{ lb}}{16 \text{ servings}} = \dfrac{1 \text{ lb}}{8 \text{ servings}}$

43. $\dfrac{100 \text{ pages}}{120 \text{ min}} = \dfrac{5 \text{ pages}}{6 \text{ min}}$ **45.** $\dfrac{3 \text{ lb}}{600 \text{ ft}^2} = \dfrac{1 \text{ lb}}{200 \text{ ft}^2}$

47. $\dfrac{110 \text{ mi}}{2 \text{ hr}} = \dfrac{110 \text{ mi} \div 2}{2 \text{ hr} \div 2} = \dfrac{55 \text{ mi}}{1 \text{ hr}}$ or 55 mph

49. $\dfrac{120 \text{ gal}}{15 \text{ days}} = \dfrac{120 \text{ gal} \div 15}{15 \text{ days} \div 15} = \dfrac{8 \text{ gal}}{1 \text{ day}}$ or 8 gal/day

51. $\dfrac{3 \text{ tanks}}{10 \text{ acres}} = \dfrac{3 \text{ tanks} \div 10}{10 \text{ acres} \div 10} = \dfrac{0.3 \text{ tank}}{1 \text{ acre}}$
or 0.3 tank/acre

53. $\dfrac{8 \text{ yd}}{5 \text{ dresses}} = \dfrac{8 \text{ yd} \div 5}{5 \text{ dresses} \div 5} = \dfrac{1.6 \text{ yd}}{1 \text{ dress}}$ or 1.6 yd/dress

55. $\dfrac{20 \text{ hr}}{10 \text{ days}} = \dfrac{20 \text{ hr} \div 10}{10 \text{ days} \div 10} = \dfrac{2 \text{ hr}}{1 \text{ day}}$ or 2 hr/day

57. $\dfrac{5 \text{ km}}{20 \text{ min}} = \dfrac{5 \text{ km} \div 20}{20 \text{ min} \div 20} = \dfrac{0.25 \text{ km}}{1 \text{ min}}$ or 0.25 km/min

59. $\dfrac{396 \text{ mi}}{22 \text{ gal}} = \dfrac{396 \text{ mi} \div 22}{22 \text{ gal} \div 22} = \dfrac{18 \text{ mi}}{1 \text{ gal}}$ or 18 mpg

61. $\dfrac{\$5.40}{12 \text{ bars}} = \$0.45/\text{bar}$ **63.** $\dfrac{\$17.70}{6 \text{ rolls}} = \$2.95/\text{roll}$

65. $\dfrac{\$200}{3 \text{ plants}} = \$66.67/\text{plant}$

67. $\dfrac{\$495}{5 \text{ nights}} = \$99/\text{night}$

69. a. $\dfrac{\$11.96}{4 \text{ cassettes}} = \$2.99/\text{cassette}$

   b. $\dfrac{\$16.25}{5 \text{ cassettes}} = \$3.25/\text{cassette}$
   Choice a is the better buy.

71. a. $\dfrac{\$5.75}{100 \text{ copies}} = \$0.0575/\text{copy}$

   b. $\dfrac{\$6.60}{120 \text{ copies}} = \$0.055/\text{copy}$
   Choice b is the better buy.

73. a. $\dfrac{\$6.60}{3 \text{ notebooks}} = \$2.20/\text{notebook}$

   b. $\dfrac{\$7.50}{4 \text{ notebooks}} = \$1.875/\text{notebook}$
   Choice b is the better buy.

75. $\dfrac{\text{votes against the bill}}{\text{votes in favor of the bill}} = \dfrac{228}{182} = \dfrac{114}{91}$
The ratio of members who voted against the bill to members who voted for it was $\dfrac{114}{91}$.

77. x is the distance from 0 to 4, which is 4.
y is the distance from 2 to 8, which is $8 - 2$ or 6.
$\dfrac{x}{y} = \dfrac{4}{6} = \dfrac{2}{3}$

79. $\dfrac{1{,}700 \text{ Cal}}{10 \text{ oz}} = \dfrac{170 \text{ Cal}}{1 \text{ oz}}$
There are 170 Calories per ounce.

81. $\dfrac{100 \text{ blinks}}{4 \text{ min}} = \dfrac{25 \text{ blinks}}{1 \text{ min}}$
A person blinks 25 times/min.

83. $\dfrac{400 \text{ cm}^3}{7 \text{ g}} = \dfrac{400 \text{ cm}^3 \div 7}{7 \text{ g} \div 7} =$
$\dfrac{57.142... \text{ cm}^3}{\text{g}} \approx \dfrac{57.1 \text{ cm}^3}{\text{g}}$
The unit rate is $57.1 \text{ cm}^3/\text{g}$.

85. Total votes $= 1{,}000 + 900 + 100 = 2{,}000$
$\dfrac{\text{Alvin's votes}}{\text{Total votes}} = \dfrac{1{,}000}{2{,}000} = \dfrac{1}{2}$
The ratio of Alvin's votes to the total was $\dfrac{1}{2}$.

87. a. Division
   b. $\dfrac{\text{Losses paid}}{\text{Premiums collected}} = \dfrac{\$6{,}400{,}000}{\$12{,}472{,}000}$
   $= 0.5131... \approx 0.51$
   c. Loss ratio $\approx \dfrac{\$6{,}000{,}000}{\$12{,}000{,}000} = \dfrac{1}{2}$

5.2   Solving Proportions

Practice

1. First write the ratios in fractional form: $\dfrac{10}{4} = \dfrac{15}{6}$

   Cross multiply.

   $4 \cdot 15 \overset{?}{=} 10 \cdot 6$

   $60 \overset{\checkmark}{=} 60$

   The ratios 10 to 4 and 15 to 6 are in proportion.

2. $\dfrac{15}{6} = \dfrac{8}{3}$

   $6 \cdot 8 \overset{?}{=} 15 \cdot 3$

   $48 \neq 45$

   This is not a true proportion.

3. Compare the two rates:

   $\dfrac{300 \text{ words}}{5 \text{ min}} \overset{?}{=} \dfrac{350 \text{ words}}{6 \text{ min}}$

   $5 \cdot 350 \overset{?}{=} 300 \cdot 6$

   $1{,}750 \neq 1{,}800$

   The two candidates have different typing rates.

4. $\dfrac{x}{6} = \dfrac{12}{9}$

   $6 \cdot 12 = x \cdot 9$ Cross multiply.

   $72 = 9x$ Divide each side by 9.

   $8 = x$

   Check:

   $\dfrac{x}{6} = \dfrac{12}{9}$

   $\dfrac{8}{6} \overset{?}{=} \dfrac{12}{9}$

   $6 \cdot 12 \overset{?}{=} 8 \cdot 9$

   $72 \overset{\checkmark}{=} 72$

5. $\dfrac{\frac{1}{2}}{2} = \dfrac{3}{x}$

   $\dfrac{1}{2} \cdot x = 2 \cdot 3$ Cross multiply.

   $x = 2 \cdot 2 \cdot 3$ Multiply each side by 2.

   $x = 12$

   Check:

   $\dfrac{\frac{1}{2}}{2} = \dfrac{3}{x}$

   $\dfrac{1}{2} \cdot \dfrac{1}{2} \overset{?}{=} \dfrac{3}{12}$

   $\dfrac{1}{4} \overset{\checkmark}{=} \dfrac{1}{4}$

6. $\dfrac{2}{8{,}000} = \dfrac{16}{f}$ $\leftarrow$ ounces of saffron
   $\leftarrow$ number of flowers

   $8{,}000 \cdot 16 = 2f$ Cross multiply.

   $128{,}000 = 2f$

   $64{,}000 = f$ Divide each side by 2.

   Check: $\dfrac{2}{8{,}000} = \dfrac{16}{f}$

   $\dfrac{2}{8{,}000} \overset{?}{=} \dfrac{16}{64{,}000}$

   $8{,}000 \cdot 16 \overset{?}{=} 2 \cdot 64{,}000$

   $128{,}000 \overset{\checkmark}{=} 128{,}000$

7. $\dfrac{10 \text{ gal}}{60 \text{ mi}} = \dfrac{g \text{ gal}}{90 \text{ mi}}$

   $\dfrac{10}{60} = \dfrac{g}{90}$

   $60g = 10 \cdot 90$ Cross multiply.

   $60g = 900$ Divide each side by 60.

   $g = 15$

   Check:

   $\dfrac{10}{60} = \dfrac{g}{90}$

   $\dfrac{10}{60} \overset{?}{=} \dfrac{15}{90}$

   $60 \cdot 15 \overset{?}{=} 10 \cdot 90$

   $900 \overset{\checkmark}{=} 900$

   The truck will need 15 gal of gas to go 90 mi.

8. $\dfrac{h \text{ ft}}{10 \text{ ft}} = \dfrac{3 \text{ ft}}{20 \text{ ft}}$ $\leftarrow$ height
   $\leftarrow$ base

   $\dfrac{h}{10} = \dfrac{3}{20}$

   $10 \cdot 3 = 20 \cdot h$

   $\dfrac{30}{20} = \dfrac{20h}{20}$

   $1.5 = h$

   Check:

   $\dfrac{h}{10} = \dfrac{3}{20}$

   $\dfrac{1.5}{10} \overset{?}{=} \dfrac{3}{20}$

   $10 \cdot 3 \overset{?}{=} 1.5 \cdot 20$

   $30 \overset{?}{=} 30$

   The height of the smaller triangle is 1.5 ft.

Exercises

1. True, since $9 \cdot 40 = 30 \cdot 12$.

3. False, since $3 \cdot 7 \neq 2 \cdot 16$.

5. True, since $(0.3)(44) = (1.1)(12)$.

7. False, since $6 \cdot 2 \neq 3 \cdot 5$.

9. True, since $28 \cdot 18 = 12 \cdot 42$.

11. True, since $1 \cdot 3 = 6 \cdot \dfrac{1}{2}$.

For Exercises 13 through 49, check by substituting the solution for x in the original proportion and cross multiplying.

13. $\dfrac{4}{8} = \dfrac{10}{x}$

$8 \cdot 10 = 4 \cdot x$

$80 = 4x$

$20 = x$

15. $\dfrac{x}{19} = \dfrac{10}{5}$

$19 \cdot 10 = 5 \cdot x$

$190 = 5x$

$38 = x$

17. $\dfrac{5}{x} = \dfrac{15}{12}$

$15 \cdot x = 5 \cdot 12$

$15x = 60$

$x = 4$

19. $\dfrac{4}{1} = \dfrac{52}{x}$

$1 \cdot 52 = 4 \cdot x$

$52 = 4x$

$13 = x$

21. $\dfrac{7}{4} = \dfrac{14}{x}$

$4 \cdot 14 = 7 \cdot x$

$56 = 7x$

$8 = x$

23. $\dfrac{x}{8} = \dfrac{3}{6}$

$8 \cdot 3 = 6 \cdot x$

$24 = 6x$

$x = 4$

25. $\dfrac{6}{21} = \dfrac{x}{70}$

$21 \cdot x = 6 \cdot 70$

$21x = 420$

$x = 20$

27. $\dfrac{x}{12} = \dfrac{25}{20}$

$12 \cdot 25 = 20 \cdot x$

$300 = 20x$

$15 = x$

29. $\dfrac{28}{x} = \dfrac{36}{27}$

$36 \cdot x = 28 \cdot 27$

$36x = 756$

$x = 21$

31. $\dfrac{x}{10} = \dfrac{4}{3}$

$10 \cdot 4 = 3 \cdot x$

$40 = 3x$

$\dfrac{40}{3} = x$

$13\dfrac{1}{3} = x$

33. $\dfrac{15}{2} = \dfrac{x}{2\frac{2}{3}}$

$2 \cdot x = 15 \cdot 2\dfrac{2}{3}$

$2x = 15 \cdot \dfrac{8}{3}$

$2x = 40$

$x = 20$

35. $\dfrac{x}{27} = \dfrac{1.6}{24}$

$27 \cdot 1.6 = 24 \cdot x$

$43.2 = 24x$

$1.8 = x$

37. $\dfrac{10.5}{x} = \dfrac{5}{10}$

$5 \cdot x = (10.5)(10)$

$5x = 105$

$x = 21$

39. $\dfrac{7}{0.9} = \dfrac{x}{36}$

$(0.9)(x) = 7 \cdot 36$

$0.9x = 252$

$x = 280$

41. $\dfrac{600}{x} = \dfrac{3}{\frac{1}{2}}$

$3 \cdot x = 600 \cdot \dfrac{1}{2}$

$3x = 300$

$x = 100$

43. $\dfrac{4}{x} = \dfrac{\frac{1}{5}}{10}$

$\dfrac{2}{5} \cdot x = 4 \cdot 10$

$x = 40 \cdot \dfrac{5}{2}$

$x = 100$

45. $\dfrac{32}{x} = \dfrac{5.6}{49}$

$(5.6)(x) = 32 \cdot 49$

$5.6x = 1568$

$x = 280$

47. $\dfrac{9}{6\frac{1}{2}} = \dfrac{4}{x}$

$\left(6\dfrac{1}{2}\right)(4) = 9 \cdot x$

$26 = 9x$

$\dfrac{26}{9} = x$

$2\dfrac{8}{9} = x$

49. $\dfrac{x}{0.16} = \dfrac{0.15}{4.8}$

$(0.16)(0.15) = (4.8)(x)$

$0.024 = 4.8x$

$0.005 = x$

51. $\dfrac{8}{6} \overset{?}{=} \dfrac{7}{3}$

$6 \cdot 7 \overset{?}{=} 8 \cdot 3$

$42 \neq 24$

The two rates are not the same.

53. One day is 24 hours.

$\dfrac{15}{24} = \dfrac{x}{3}$

$24 \cdot x = 15 \cdot 3$

$24x = 45$

$x = \dfrac{15 \cdot 3}{8 \cdot 3} = \dfrac{15}{8}$

$x = 1\dfrac{7}{8}$

About $1\dfrac{7}{8}$ gal are wasted in 3 hr.

55. $\dfrac{0.8}{2.2} = \dfrac{x}{150}$

$(2.2)(x) = (0.8)(150)$

$2.2x = 120$

$x = 54.5454...$

$x \approx 54.5$

You should consume about 54.5 g of protein.

57. $\dfrac{\frac{1}{2}}{4} = \dfrac{x}{9}$

$4 \cdot x = \dfrac{1}{2} \cdot 9$

$4x = \dfrac{9}{2}$

$x = \dfrac{9}{8}$

$1\dfrac{1}{8}$ lb of zucchini are

needed.

59. $\dfrac{3}{5} = \dfrac{25}{x}$

$5 \cdot 25 = 3 \cdot x$

$125 = 3x$

$\dfrac{125}{3} = x$

$41\dfrac{2}{3} = x$

The length should be

$41\dfrac{2}{3}$ in.

61. If the ratio of the substances is 9 to 5, then since $9 + 5 = 14$, the first substance is 9 parts out 14 and the second substance is 5 parts out of 14.

$\dfrac{9}{14} = \dfrac{x}{140}$

$14 \cdot x = 9 \cdot 140$

$x = \dfrac{9 \cdot 140}{14}$

$x = 90$

There will be 90 mg of the first substance. Since the total is 140 mg, there will be $140 - 90 = 50$ mg of the other substance.

63. $\dfrac{1}{160} = \dfrac{x}{40}$

$160 \cdot x = 1 \cdot 40$

$160x = 40$

$x = \dfrac{40}{160}$

$x = \dfrac{1}{4}$

The model boxcar will be $\dfrac{1}{4}$ ft or 3 in. long.

65. $\dfrac{10}{3} = \dfrac{2,000}{x}$

$10 \cdot x = 3 \cdot 2,000$

$10x = 6,000$

$x = 600$

Your state tax is $600.

67. $\dfrac{6}{480} = \dfrac{150}{x}$

$480 \cdot 150 = 6 \cdot x$

$72,000 = 6x$

$12,000 = x$

There are about 12,000 fish in the lake.

69. $\dfrac{9}{14} = \dfrac{180}{x}$

$14 \cdot 180 = 9 \cdot x$

$2,520 = 9x$

$280 = x$

The rear wheel turns 280 times.

71. a. Multiplication, division

b. $\dfrac{640}{660,000} = \dfrac{810}{x}$

$660,000 \cdot 810 = 640 \cdot x$

$534,600,000 = 640x$

$x = 835,312.5$

835,312.5 gal of nuclear waste are produced.

c. The ratio 640 to 660,000 is approximately 660 to 660,000 or 1,000 to 1. So a reasonable estimate is $1,000 \times 810$ or 810,000.

Review Exercises

1. $\dfrac{10}{15} = \dfrac{\cancel{5} \cdot 2}{\cancel{5} \cdot 3} = \dfrac{2}{3}$

2. $\dfrac{28}{56} = \dfrac{\cancel{28} \cdot 1}{\cancel{28} \cdot 2} = \dfrac{1}{2}$

3. $\dfrac{3}{4} = \dfrac{3}{4}$ in simplest form

4. $\dfrac{50}{16} = \dfrac{\cancel{2} \cdot 25}{\cancel{2} \cdot 8} = \dfrac{25}{8}$

5. $\dfrac{10,400 \text{ votes}}{6,500 \text{ votes}} = \dfrac{10,400}{6,500} = \dfrac{\cancel{1,300} \cdot 8}{\cancel{1,300} \cdot 5} = \dfrac{8}{5}$

6. $\dfrac{9 \text{ cups}}{12 \text{ cups}} = \dfrac{9}{12} = \dfrac{\cancel{3} \cdot 3}{\cancel{3} \cdot 4} = \dfrac{3}{4}$

7. $\dfrac{88 \text{ ft}}{10 \text{ sec}} = \dfrac{44 \text{ ft}}{5 \text{ sec}}$

8. $\dfrac{16 \text{ applicants}}{45 \text{ positions}}$

9. $\dfrac{4 \text{ lb}}{1,600 \text{ ft}^2} = \dfrac{4 \text{ lb} \div 1,600}{1,600 \text{ ft}^2 \div 1,600} = \dfrac{0.0025 \text{ lb}}{1 \text{ ft}^2}$

or $0.0025 \text{ lb}/\text{ft}^2$

10. $\dfrac{75 \text{ billion calls}}{150 \text{ days}} = \dfrac{75,000,000,000 \text{ calls} \div 150}{150 \text{ days} \div 150} =$

$\dfrac{500,000,000 \text{ calls}}{1 \text{ day}}$ or 500 million calls/day

11. $\dfrac{600 \text{ mi}}{3 \text{ hr}} = \dfrac{600 \text{ mi} \div 3}{3 \text{ hr} \div 3} = \dfrac{200 \text{ mi}}{1 \text{ hr}}$

or 200 mph

12. $\dfrac{750 \text{ VCRs}}{500 \text{ households}} = \dfrac{750 \text{ VCRs} \div 500}{500 \text{ households} \div 500} =$

$\dfrac{1.5 \text{ VCRs}}{1 \text{ household}}$ or 1.5 VCRs/household

13. $\dfrac{21,000,000 \text{ vehicles}}{2 \text{ yr}} = \dfrac{21,000,000 \text{ vehicles} \div 2}{2 \text{ yr} \div 2} =$

$\dfrac{10,500,000 \text{ vehicles}}{1 \text{ yr}}$ or 10,500,000 vehicles/yr

14. $\dfrac{532,000 \text{ commuters}}{7 \text{ days}} = \dfrac{532,000 \text{ commuters} \div 7}{7 \text{ days} \div 7} =$

$\dfrac{76,000 \text{ commuters}}{1 \text{ day}}$ or 76,000 commuters/day

15. $\dfrac{\$475}{4 \text{ nights}} = \dfrac{\$475 \div 4}{4 \text{ nights} \div 4} = \dfrac{\$118.75}{1 \text{ night}}$
or $118.75/night

16. $\dfrac{\$1,785}{105 \text{ tickets}} = \dfrac{\$1,785 \div 105}{105 \text{ tickets} \div 105} = \dfrac{\$17}{1 \text{ ticket}}$
or $17/ticket

17. $\dfrac{\$80,000}{32 \text{ stations}} = \dfrac{\$80,000 \div 32}{32 \text{ stations} \div 32} = \dfrac{\$2,500}{1 \text{ station}}$
or $2,500/station

18. $\dfrac{\$9,364}{100 \text{ shares}} = \dfrac{\$9,364 \div 100}{100 \text{ shares} \div 100} = \dfrac{\$93.64}{1 \text{ share}}$
or $93.64/share

19. a. $\dfrac{\$35}{12 \text{ issues}} \approx \$2.92/\text{issue}$

b. $\dfrac{\$107.50}{36 \text{ issues}} \approx \$2.99/\text{issue}$

Choice a is the better buy.

20. a. $\dfrac{\$1,400,000}{2,000,000 \text{ posters}} = \$0.70/\text{poster}$

b. $\dfrac{\$1,000,000}{1,500,000 \text{ posters}} \approx \$0.67/\text{poster}$

Choice b is the better buy.

21. a. $\dfrac{\$55}{10 \text{ visits}} = \$5.50/\text{visit}$

b. $\dfrac{\$100}{20 \text{ visits}} = \$5.00/\text{visit}$

Choice b is the better buy.

22. a. $\dfrac{\$84.00}{12 \text{ tickets}} = \$7.00/\text{ticket}$

b. $\dfrac{\$112.50}{15 \text{ tickets}} = \$7.50/\text{ticket}$

Choice a is the better buy.

23. $\dfrac{15}{25} = \dfrac{3}{5}$

$25 \cdot 3 \overset{?}{=} 15 \cdot 5$

$75 \overset{\checkmark}{=} 75$

a true proportion

24. $\dfrac{3}{1} = \dfrac{1}{3}$

$1 \cdot 1 \overset{?}{=} 3 \cdot 3$

$1 \neq 9$

a false proportion

25. $\dfrac{50}{45} = \dfrac{10}{8}$

$45 \cdot 10 \overset{?}{=} 50 \cdot 8$

$450 \neq 400$

a false proportion

26. $\dfrac{15}{6} = \dfrac{5}{2}$

$6 \cdot 5 \overset{?}{=} 15 \cdot 2$

$30 \overset{\checkmark}{=} 20$

a true proportion

For Exercises 27 through 38, check by substituting the solution for x in the original proportion and cross multiplying.

27. $\dfrac{1}{2} = \dfrac{x}{12}$

$2 \cdot x = 1 \cdot 12$

$2x = 12$

$x = 6$

28. $\dfrac{9}{12} = \dfrac{x}{4}$

$12 \cdot x = 9 \cdot 4$

$12x = 36$

$x = 3$

29. $\dfrac{12}{x} = \dfrac{3}{8}$

$3 \cdot x = 12 \cdot 8$

$3x = 96$

$x = 32$

30. $\dfrac{x}{72} = \dfrac{5}{12}$

$72 \cdot 5 = 12 \cdot x$

$360 = 12x$

$x = 30$

31. $\dfrac{1.6}{7.2} = \dfrac{x}{9}$

$(7.2)(x) = (1.6)(9)$

$7.2x = 14.4$

$x = 2$

32. $\dfrac{x}{12} = \dfrac{1.2}{1.8}$

$(1.8)(x) = (12)(1.2)$

$1.8x = 14.4$

$x = 8$

33. $\dfrac{5}{37} = \dfrac{7}{x}$

$37 \cdot 7 = 5 \cdot x$

$259 = 5x$

$\dfrac{259}{5} = x$

$51\dfrac{4}{5} = x$

34. $\dfrac{3}{5} = \dfrac{x}{2}$

$5 \cdot x = 3 \cdot 2$

$5x = 6$

$x = \dfrac{6}{5}$

$x = 1\dfrac{1}{5}$

35. $\dfrac{2\frac{1}{4}}{x} = \dfrac{1}{30}$

$1 \cdot x = \dfrac{9}{4} \cdot 30$

$x = \dfrac{135}{2}$

$x = 67\frac{1}{2}$

36. $\dfrac{3}{1\frac{3}{5}} = \dfrac{x}{24}$

$\dfrac{8}{5} \cdot x = 3 \cdot 24$

$x = 72 \cdot \dfrac{5}{8}$

$x = 45$

37. $\dfrac{0.36}{4.2} = \dfrac{2.4}{x}$

$(0.36)(x) = (4.2)(2.4)$

$0.36x = 10.08$

$x = 28$

38. $\dfrac{x}{0.21} = \dfrac{0.12}{0.18}$

$(0.18)(x) = (0.21)(0.12)$

$0.18x = 0.0252$

$x = 0.14$

39. $\dfrac{12 \text{ first-class seats}}{180 \text{ coach seats}} = \dfrac{12}{180} = \dfrac{1}{15}$

The ratio of first-class to coach seats is $\dfrac{1}{15}$.

40. $\dfrac{\$23,000 \text{ worth of Dills}}{\$45,000 \text{ worth of Oranges}} = \dfrac{23,000}{45,000} = \dfrac{23}{45}$

The Dill to Orange sales ratio is $\dfrac{23}{45}$.

41. $\dfrac{\$450}{6 \text{ days}} = \dfrac{\$90}{1 \text{ day}}$

You earn $\$90/\text{day}$.

42. $\dfrac{2 \text{ in.}}{16 \text{ mo}} = \dfrac{1 \text{ in.}}{8 \text{ mo}} = \dfrac{0.125 \text{ in.}}{1 \text{ mo}}$

The glacier moves $0.125 \text{ in.}/\text{mo}$.

43. The total estate is the sum of $40,000 and $100,000 which is $140,000.

$\dfrac{\$40,000}{\$140,000} = \dfrac{40,000}{140,000} = \dfrac{2}{7}$

The ratio of the older child's share to the total estate is $\dfrac{2}{7}$.

44. $\dfrac{\$9.50 \text{ in expenses}}{1 \text{ book}} = \dfrac{\$475,000 \text{ in expenses}}{x \text{ books}}$

$(9.50)(x) = 475,000$

$x = 50,000$

The total circulation is 50,000 books.

45. $\dfrac{2 \text{ staff}}{5 \text{ children}} = 0.4 \text{ staff/child}$

$\dfrac{12 \text{ staff}}{60 \text{ children}} = 0.2 \text{ staff/child}$

Since 0.2 is less than 0.4, the center is not in compliance.

46. $\dfrac{8}{1} = \dfrac{440 \text{ cc}}{x \text{ cc}}$

$8x = 440$

$x = 55$

The compressed fuel occupies 55 cc.

47. $\dfrac{42 \text{ reels}}{9 \text{ reels}} = \dfrac{9 \text{ hr}}{x \text{ hr}}$

$42x = 81$

$x = \dfrac{81}{42} \approx 2$

The edited version was about 2 hr long.

48. $\dfrac{25 \text{ ft}}{2 \text{ in.}} = \dfrac{62.5 \text{ ft}}{x \text{ in.}}$

$25x = 125$

$x = 5$

The distance in the drawing is 5 in.

49. $\dfrac{216.21 \text{ g}}{317.45 \text{ cc}} = \dfrac{0.6810... \text{ g}}{1 \text{ cc}} \approx \dfrac{0.68 \text{ g}}{1 \text{ cc}}$

The density of gasoline is about 0.68 g/cc.

50. $\dfrac{176.56 \text{ mi}}{5.25 \text{ gal}} = \dfrac{254 \text{ mi}}{x \text{ gal}}$

$(176.56)(x) = (5.25)(254)$

$x = 7.5526...$

$x \approx 7.55$

The trip will take 7.55 gal.

Posttest

1. $\dfrac{8}{12} = \dfrac{4 \cdot 2}{4 \cdot 3} = \dfrac{2}{3}$

2. $\dfrac{15}{42} = \dfrac{3 \cdot 5}{3 \cdot 14} = \dfrac{5}{14}$

3. $\dfrac{55 \text{ oz}}{31 \text{ oz}} = \dfrac{55}{31}$

4. $\dfrac{180 \text{ mi}}{15 \text{ mi}} = \dfrac{180}{15} = \dfrac{15 \cdot 12}{15 \cdot 1} = \dfrac{12}{1}$

5. $\dfrac{65 \text{ revolutions}}{60 \text{ sec}} = \dfrac{5 \cdot 13 \text{ revolutions}}{5 \cdot 12 \text{ sec}} = \dfrac{13 \text{ revolutions}}{12 \text{ sec}}$

6. $\dfrac{3 \text{ cm}}{75 \text{ km}} = \dfrac{3 \cdot 1 \text{ cm}}{3 \cdot 25 \text{ km}} = \dfrac{1 \text{ cm}}{25 \text{ km}}$

7. $\dfrac{340 \text{ mi}}{5 \text{ hr}} = \dfrac{340 \text{ mi} \div 5}{5 \text{ hr} \div 5} = 68 \text{ mph}$

8. $\dfrac{\$4,080}{30 \text{ days}} = \dfrac{\$4,080 \div 30}{30 \text{ days} \div 30} = \$136/\text{day}$

9. $\dfrac{200 \text{ m}}{30 \text{ sec}} = \dfrac{200 \text{ m} \div 30}{30 \text{ sec} \div 30} = \dfrac{\frac{200}{30} \text{ m}}{1 \text{ sec}} = 6\dfrac{2}{3} \text{ m/sec}$

10. $\dfrac{302 \text{ mi}}{17 \text{ gal}} = \dfrac{302 \text{ mi} \div 17}{17 \text{ gal} \div 17} = \dfrac{\frac{302}{17} \text{ mi}}{1 \text{ gal}} = 17\dfrac{13}{17} \text{ mpg}$

11. $\dfrac{8}{21} = \dfrac{16}{40}$

$21 \cdot 16 \overset{?}{=} 8 \cdot 40$

$336 \neq 320$

a false proportion

12. $\dfrac{7}{3} = \dfrac{63}{27}$

$3 \cdot 63 \overset{?}{=} 7 \cdot 27$

$189 \overset{\checkmark}{=} 189$

a true proportion

For Questions 13 through 16, check by substituting the solution for x in the original proportion and cross multiplying.

13. $\dfrac{15}{x} = \dfrac{6}{10}$

$6 \cdot x = 15 \cdot 10$

$6x = 150$

$x = 25$

14. $\dfrac{102}{17} = \dfrac{36}{x}$

$17 \cdot 36 = 102 \cdot x$

$612 = 102x$

$6 = x$

15. $\dfrac{0.9}{36} = \dfrac{0.7}{x}$

$(36)(0.7) = (0.9)(x)$

$25.2 = 0.9x$

$28 = x$

16. $\dfrac{\frac{1}{3}}{4} = \dfrac{x}{12}$

$4 \cdot x = \dfrac{1}{3} \cdot 12$

$4x = 4$

$x = 1$

17. $\dfrac{3,000,000 \text{ addresses}}{\$400} = 7,500 \text{ addresses/dollar}$

$\dfrac{5,000,000 \text{ addresses}}{\$600} \approx 8,333 \text{ addresses/dollar}$

You get more addresses per dollar with the \$600 option.

18. The increase was $\$110,000 - \$95,000$ or \$15,000.

$\dfrac{\$15,000}{\$95,000} = \dfrac{\$5,000 \cdot 3}{\$5,000 \cdot 19} = \dfrac{3}{19}$

The ratio of the increase to original value is $\dfrac{3}{19}$

19. $\dfrac{6\frac{1}{4}}{5} = \dfrac{x}{20}$

$5 \cdot x = \left(6\dfrac{1}{4}\right)(20)$

$5x = 125$

$x = 25$

The tree is 25 ft tall.

20. $1 \text{ min} = 60 \text{ sec}$

$\dfrac{12}{15} = \dfrac{x}{60}$

$15 \cdot x = 12 \cdot 60$

$15x = 720$

$x = 48$

Her pulse is 48 beats/minute .

Cumulative Review Exercises

1. $3\dfrac{1}{10} - 2\dfrac{7}{10} = 2\dfrac{11}{10} - 2\dfrac{7}{10} = \dfrac{4}{10} = \dfrac{2}{5}$

2. To multiply by 1,000, shift the decimal point 3 places to the right, adding zero placeholders:
$8.2 \times 1,000 = 8,200$

3. $\dfrac{2}{9} = \dfrac{x}{45}$

$9 \cdot x = 2 \cdot 45$

$9x = 90$

$x = 10$

4. $\dfrac{2.5}{10} = \dfrac{2.5 \times 2}{10 \times 2} = \dfrac{5}{20} = \dfrac{1}{4}$

5. $\dfrac{\$12}{3 \text{ yd}} = \dfrac{\$12 \div 3}{3 \text{ yd} \div 3} = \dfrac{\$4}{1 \text{ yd}}$ or \$4/yd

6. $12\dfrac{1}{7} \div 3\dfrac{9}{10} \approx 12 \div 4 = 3$

A possible estimate is 3.

7. Price per pound $\times$ number of pounds $=$
$\$D \times \dfrac{11}{16} = \$\dfrac{11}{16}D$

8. $54.44 + 0.10 = 54.54$.
The second place swimmer's time was 54.54 sec.

9. $\dfrac{\text{depth}}{\text{width}} = \dfrac{3}{1} = \dfrac{x}{2.5}$

$1 \cdot x = (3)(2.5)$

$x = 7.5$

You should plant the bulb 7.5 in. deep.

10. $\dfrac{\$120}{10 \text{ hr}} = \dfrac{x}{15 \text{ hr}}$

$10 \cdot x = 120 \cdot 15$

$10x = 1,800$

$x = 180$

An employee makes \$180 for a 15-hr week.

PERCENTS

Pretest

1. $5\% = \dfrac{5}{100} = \dfrac{1}{20}$

2. $37\dfrac{1}{2}\% = \dfrac{37\frac{1}{2}}{100} = \dfrac{\overset{3}{\cancel{75}}}{2} \cdot \dfrac{1}{\underset{4}{\cancel{100}}} = \dfrac{3}{8}$

3. $250\% = \dfrac{250}{100} = 2.5$

4. $3\% = \underset{\smile}{03}.\% = .03$ or 0.03

5. $0.\underset{\smile}{007} = 0.7\%$

6. $8 = 8.\underset{\smile}{00} = 800.\% = 800\%$

7. $\dfrac{2}{3} = \dfrac{2}{3} \times 100\% = \dfrac{2}{3} \times \dfrac{100}{1}\% = \dfrac{200}{3}\% = 66\dfrac{2}{3}\%$

   $66\dfrac{2}{3}\% \approx 67\%$

8. First convert the fractional part, $\dfrac{1}{10}$, to a percent:

   $\dfrac{1}{10} = .\underset{\smile}{10} = 10.\%$ or 10%

   The whole number part, 1, is equal to 100%.
   Adding 100% and 10% gives the answer, 110%.

9. What is 75% of 50 ft?
   $$\downarrow \quad \downarrow \quad \downarrow \quad \downarrow \quad \downarrow$$
   $$x \;\; = 0.75 \;\; \cdot \quad 50$$
   $x = (0.75)(50) = 37.5$
   75% of 50 ft is 37.5 ft.

10. What is 110% of 50?
    $$\downarrow \quad \downarrow \quad \downarrow \quad \downarrow \quad \downarrow$$
    $$x \;\; = 1.10 \;\; \cdot \quad 50$$
    $x = (1.1)(50) = 55$
    110% of 50 is 55.

11. A possible estimate is 80% of $60, which is $(0.8)(\$60)$ or $48.

12. 2% of what number is 5?
    $$\downarrow \quad \downarrow \qquad \downarrow \qquad \downarrow \; \downarrow$$
    $$0.02 \quad \cdot \qquad x \qquad = 5$$
    $0.02x = 5$
    $$x = \dfrac{5}{0.02} = 250$$
    2% of 250 is 5.

13. What percent of 10 is 4?
    $$\downarrow \qquad \downarrow \downarrow \downarrow \downarrow$$
    $$x \qquad \cdot \; 10 = 4$$
    $10x = 4$
    $$x = \dfrac{4}{10} = 0.40 = \underset{\smile}{40}.\%$$ or 40%

14. What percent of 4 is 10?
    $$\downarrow \qquad \downarrow \downarrow \downarrow \downarrow$$
    $$x \qquad \cdot \; 4 = 10$$
    $4x = 10$
    $$x = \dfrac{10}{4} = 2.50 = \underset{\smile}{250}.\%$$ or 250%

15. What is 4% of $350?
    $$\downarrow \quad \downarrow \quad \downarrow \quad \downarrow \quad \downarrow$$
    $$x \;\; = 0.04 \; \cdot \quad 350$$
    $x = (0.04)(350) = 14$
    You earn $14 in interest.

16. The change is $8 - 6$ or 2.
    What percent of 6 is 2?
    $$\downarrow \qquad \downarrow \downarrow \downarrow$$
    $$x \qquad \cdot \; 6 = 2$$
    $6x = 2$
    $$x = \dfrac{2}{6} = \dfrac{1}{3} \times 100\% = \dfrac{100}{3}\% = 33\dfrac{1}{3}\%$$

17. $24\% = \dfrac{24}{100} = \dfrac{6}{25}$

18. The total volume of the solution was $10\text{ ml} + 30\text{ ml}$
    or 40 ml. The fraction of acid was $\dfrac{10\text{ ml}}{40\text{ ml}}$ or $\dfrac{1}{4}$.

    $\dfrac{1}{4} = 0.\underset{\smile}{25} = 25.\%$ or 25%

    25% of the solution was acid.

19. What is 10% of $25,000?

$$\downarrow \quad \downarrow \downarrow \quad \downarrow \qquad \downarrow$$
$$x \ = 0.1 \quad \cdot \quad 25,000$$

$x = (0.1)(25,000)$

$x = 2,500$

Your bonus is $2,500.

20. If your insurance paid 80%, you paid the remaining 20%.

20% of what amount is $2,000?

$$\downarrow \quad \downarrow \qquad \downarrow \qquad \downarrow \ \downarrow$$
$$0.2 \quad \cdot \qquad x \qquad = 2,000$$

$0.2x = 2,000$

$$x = \frac{2,000}{0.2} = 10,000$$

The total cost of the operation was $10,000.

6.1 Introduction to Percents

Practice

1. Drop the percent sign and write the number over 100:

$$21\% = \frac{21}{100}$$

2. Drop the percent sign, write the number over 100, and simplify:

$$200\% = \frac{200}{100} = \frac{2}{1} \text{ or } 2$$

3. Drop the percent sign, write the number over 100, and simplify:

$$12\frac{1}{2}\% = \frac{12\frac{1}{2}}{100} = \frac{25}{2} \div \frac{100}{1} = \frac{\overset{1}{\cancel{25}}}{2} \times \frac{1}{\underset{4}{\cancel{100}}} = \frac{1}{8}$$

4. $90\% = \dfrac{90}{100} = \dfrac{9}{10}$

5. Move the decimal point two places to the left and drop the percent sign:
$300\% = 3\underline{00}.\% = 3.00, \text{ or } 3$

6. Move the decimal point two places to the left and drop the percent sign:
$5\% = \underline{05}.\% = .05, \text{ or } 0.05$

7. Move the decimal point two places to the left and drop the percent sign:
$4\underline{8}.2\% = .482, \text{ or } 0.482$

8. First convert the fraction in the mixed number to its decimal equivalent:

$$\frac{1}{4} = 4\overline{)1.00}^{\;0.25}$$

Now replace the fraction by its decimal equivalent:

$$62\frac{1}{4}\% = \underline{62}.25\% = .6225, \text{ or } 0.6225$$

9. $\underline{1}\,\underline{1}\% = .11, \text{ or } 0.11$

10. Move the decimal point two places to the right and add the percent sign:
$0.\underline{025} = 02.5\%, \text{ or } 2.5\%$

11. $0.\underline{01} = 01.\%, \text{ or } 1\%$

12. To move the decimal point two places to the right, we need to insert a 0 placeholder:
$0.7 = 0.\underline{70} = 70.\%, \text{ or } 70\%$

13. Insert two 0 placeholders:
$3 = 3.\underline{00} = 300.\%, \text{ or } 300\%$

14. First find the exact percent equivalent:
$0.\underline{7}18 = 71.8\%$

Now round up since the critical digit in the tenths place is more than 5:
$7\underline{1}.8\% \approx 72\%$

15. Change 0.78 to a percent and then compare:
$0.\underline{78} = 78.\% \text{ or } 78\%$

$78\% > 0.93\%$ since $78 > 0.93$

There is more nitrogen than argon in air.

16. Convert the fraction to a decimal, then convert the decimal to a percent:

$$\frac{4}{25} = 25\overline{)4.00}^{\;0.16} \qquad 0.\underline{16} = 16.\% \text{ or } 16\%$$

17. First express $\dfrac{2}{3}$ as a percent, rounded to the nearest whole percent. Then compare the two percents.

$$\frac{2}{3} = 0.\underline{666}... = 66.6...\% \approx 67\%$$

$67\% > 60\%$, so $\dfrac{2}{3} > 60\%$

18. $\dfrac{95}{435} = 0.\underline{2}18... = 21.8...\% \approx 22\%$

Exercises

1. $5\% = \dfrac{5}{100} = \dfrac{1}{20}$ **3.** $250\% = \dfrac{250}{100} = \dfrac{5}{2} = 2\dfrac{1}{2}$

5. $33\% = \dfrac{33}{100}$ **7.** $18\% = \dfrac{18}{100} = \dfrac{9}{50}$

9. $14\% = \dfrac{14}{100} = \dfrac{7}{50}$ **11.** $65\% = \dfrac{65}{100} = \dfrac{13}{20}$

13. $\dfrac{3}{4}\% = \dfrac{\frac{3}{4}}{100} = \dfrac{3}{4} \cdot \dfrac{1}{100} = \dfrac{3}{400}$

15. $\dfrac{3}{10}\% = \dfrac{\frac{3}{10}}{100} = \dfrac{3}{10} \cdot \dfrac{1}{100} = \dfrac{3}{1,000}$

17. $12\dfrac{1}{2}\% = \dfrac{12\frac{1}{2}}{100} = \dfrac{\overset{25}{\cancel{25}}}{2} \cdot \dfrac{1}{\underset{4}{\cancel{100}}} = \dfrac{1}{8}$

19. $33\dfrac{1}{3}\% = \dfrac{33\frac{1}{3}}{100} = \dfrac{\overset{1}{\cancel{100}}}{3} \cdot \dfrac{1}{\underset{1}{\cancel{100}}} = \dfrac{1}{3}$

21. $6\% = \underset{\smile}{06}.\% = .06$, or 0.06

23. $72\% = 72.\% = .72$, or 0.72

25. $0.1\% = \underset{\smile}{00}.1\% = .001$, or 0.001

27. $102\% = 102.\% = 1.02$

29. $87.5\% = 87.5\% = .875$, or 0.875

31. $18.2\% = 18.2\% = .182$, or 0.182

33. First convert the fractional part of the percent to a decimal:

$\dfrac{9}{10} = 10\overline{)9.0}^{\,0.9}$

Replace the fraction by its decimal equivalent in the original percent, and convert the percent to a decimal:

$6\dfrac{9}{10}\% = 6.9\% = 06.9\% = .069$, or 0.069

35. First convert the fractional part of the percent to a decimal:

$\dfrac{1}{2} = 2\overline{)1.0}^{\,0.5}$

Replace the fraction by its decimal equivalent in the original percent, and convert the percent to a decimal:

$3\dfrac{1}{2}\% = 3.5\% = 03.5\% = .035$, or 0.035

37. First convert the fractional part of the percent to a decimal:

$\dfrac{9}{10} = 10\overline{)9.0}^{\,0.9}$

Replace the fraction by its decimal equivalent in the original percent, and convert the percent to a decimal:

$\dfrac{9}{10}\% = 0.9\% = 00.9\% = .009$, or 0.009

39. First convert the fractional part of the percent to a decimal:

$\dfrac{3}{4} = 4\overline{)3.00}^{\,0.75}$

Replace the fraction by its decimal equivalent in the original percent, and convert the percent to a decimal:

$\dfrac{3}{4}\% = 0.75\% = 00.75\% = .0075$, or 0.0075

41. $0.31 = 31.\%$ or 31% **43.** $0.875 = 87.5\%$

45. $0.3 = 0.30 = 30.\%$ or 30%

47. $0.04 = 4.\%$, or 4% **49.** $0.18 = 18.\%$, or 18%

51. $1.29 = 129.\%$, or 129%

53. $2.9 = 2.90 = 290.\%$, or 290%

55. $2.87 = 287.\%$, or 287%

57. $1.016 = 101.6\%$

59. $5 = 5.00 = 500.\%$, or 500%

61. $\dfrac{3}{4} = 4\overline{)3.00}^{\,0.75}$ $0.75 = 75\%$

63. $\dfrac{1}{10} = 0.1 = 0.10 = 10\%$

65. $3 = 3.00 = 300\%$

67. $\dfrac{4}{5} = 5\overline{)4.0}^{\,0.8}$ $0.8 = 0.80 = 80\%$

69. $\dfrac{9}{10} = 0.9 = 0.90 = 90\%$

71. $\dfrac{1}{8} = 8\overline{)1.000}^{\,0.125}$ $0.125 = 12.5\%$

73. $\dfrac{5}{9} = \dfrac{5}{9} \times 100\% = \dfrac{5}{9} \times \dfrac{100}{1}\% = \dfrac{500}{9}\% = 55\dfrac{5}{9}\%$

75. $\dfrac{2}{3} = \dfrac{2}{3} \times 100\% = \dfrac{2}{3} \times \dfrac{100}{1}\% = \dfrac{200}{3}\% = 66\dfrac{2}{3}\%$

77. Find the decimal equivalent of $\dfrac{5}{8}$ and add this to 1.

$\dfrac{5}{8} = 8\overline{)5.000}^{\,0.625}$ $1\dfrac{5}{8} = 1.625 = 162.5\%$

79. $2\frac{1}{6} = \frac{13}{6} \times 100\% = \frac{13}{\cancel{6}} \times \frac{\overset{50}{\cancel{100}}}{1}\% = \frac{650}{3}\% = 216\frac{2}{3}\%$

81.

Fraction	Decimal	Percent
$\frac{1}{2}$	0.5	50%
$\frac{1}{4}$	0.25	25%
$\frac{3}{4}$	0.75	75%
$\frac{1}{5}$	0.2	20%
$\frac{2}{5}$	0.4	40%
$\frac{3}{5}$	0.6	60%
$\frac{4}{5}$	0.8	80%

83. $0.1 = 0.\underline{1}0 = 10\%$

85. $24\% = \frac{24}{100} = \frac{\cancel{4} \cdot 6}{\cancel{4} \cdot 25} = \frac{6}{25}$

87. $9.7 = 9.\underline{70} = 970\%$

89. $135\% = \frac{135}{100} = \frac{\cancel{5} \cdot 27}{\cancel{5} \cdot 20} = \frac{27}{20} = 1\frac{7}{20}$

91. $80\% = \underline{80}.\% = .80,$ or 0.8

93. $\frac{1}{3} = \frac{1}{3} \times 100\% = \frac{1}{3} \times \frac{100}{1}\% = \frac{100}{3}\% = 33\frac{1}{3}\%$

$40\% > 33\frac{1}{3}\%$

The condition is more common among men.

95. a. Subtraction, division, multiplication
   b. $1,753 - 12 = 1,741$, so the senator voted 1,723 times.
   $$\frac{1,741}{1,753} = 0.99315... \approx 99.32\%$$
   The senator was correct.
   c. Since 12 is very small compared to 1,753, 100% is a reasonable estimate.

6.2   Solving Percent Problems

Practice

1. a. What percent of 40 is 20?
   $x \quad \cdot \quad 40 = 20$

   b. 50% of what number is 10?
   $0.5 \quad \cdot \quad x \quad = 10$

   c. What is 70% of 80?
   $x \quad = 0.7 \quad \cdot \quad 80$

2. What is 20% of 40?
   $x \quad = 0.2 \quad \cdot \quad 40$
   $x = (0.2)(40)$
   $x = 8$

3. 150% of 8 is what number?
   $1.50 \quad \cdot \; 8 = \quad x$
   $(1.5)(8) = x$
   $12 = x$

4. What is $8\frac{1}{2}\%$ of 600?
   $x \quad = 0.085 \quad \cdot \quad 600$
   $x = (0.085)(600)$
   $x = 51$
   51 workers are in the union.

5. Round 49.3% to 50% and round 401.6 to 400. What is 50% of 400?
   $x \quad = \; 0.5 \quad \cdot \quad 400$
   $x = (0.5)(400)$
   $x = 200$

6. What is 15% of 380?
   $x \quad = \; 0.15 \quad \cdot \quad 380$
   $x = (0.15)(380)$
   $x = 57$
   57 students made the Dean's List.
   A reasonable estimate is 15% of 400, or $(0.15)(400)$ which is equal to 60.

7. 6 is 12% of what number?

$$\downarrow \downarrow \downarrow \quad \downarrow \qquad \downarrow$$
$$6 = 0.12 \quad \cdot \qquad x$$
$$6 = 0.12x$$
$$\frac{6}{0.12} = \frac{0.12}{0.12}x$$
$$50 = x$$

8. 16% of what number is 400,000?

$$\downarrow \qquad \downarrow \qquad \downarrow \qquad \downarrow \quad \downarrow$$
$$0.16 \cdot \qquad x \qquad = 400,000$$
$$0.16x = 400,000$$
$$\frac{0.16}{0.16}x = \frac{400,000}{0.16}$$
$$x = 2,500,000$$

Your city has 2,500,000 sq ft of office space.

9. 15 is 20% of what number?

$$\downarrow \downarrow \downarrow \quad \downarrow \qquad \downarrow$$
$$15 = 0.2 \quad \cdot \qquad x$$
$$15 = 0.2x$$
$$\frac{15}{0.2} = \frac{0.2}{0.2}x$$
$$75 = x$$

If the quarterback completed 15 out of 75 passes, he did *not* complete 60 passes.

10. What percent of 6 is 5?

$$\qquad \downarrow \qquad \quad \downarrow \downarrow \downarrow$$
$$\qquad x \qquad \cdot \; 6 = 5$$
$$6x = 5$$
$$\frac{6}{6}x = \frac{5}{6}$$
$$x = \frac{5}{6}$$

To change $\frac{5}{6}$ to a percent, multiply it by 1 expressed in the form 100%:

$$\frac{5}{6} = \frac{5}{6} \cdot 100\% = \frac{500}{6}\% = 83\frac{2}{6}\% = 83\frac{1}{3}\%$$

11. What percent of 5 is 6?

$$\qquad \downarrow \qquad \quad \downarrow \downarrow \downarrow$$
$$\qquad x \qquad \cdot \; 5 = 6$$
$$5x = 6$$
$$\frac{5}{5}x = \frac{6}{5} \qquad x = \frac{6}{5} = 1.20$$
$$x = 1.20 = 120.\% = 120\%$$

12. What percent of 105 is 45?

$$\qquad \downarrow \qquad \quad \downarrow \quad \downarrow \downarrow$$
$$\qquad x \qquad \cdot 105 = 45$$
$$105x = 45$$
$$\frac{105}{105}x = \frac{45}{105}$$
$$x = \frac{45}{105} = 0.428...$$
$$x = 0.428... = 42.8...\% \approx 43\%$$

About 43% of the members voted for the resolution.

13. $\dfrac{\text{Amount}}{\text{Base}} = \dfrac{\text{Percent}}{100}$

$$\frac{x}{250} = \frac{108}{100}$$
$$100x = 27,000 \qquad \text{Cross multiply.}$$
$$\frac{100}{100}x = \frac{27,000}{100} \qquad \text{Divide both sides by 100.}$$
$$x = 270$$

14. $\dfrac{\text{Amount}}{\text{Base}} = \dfrac{\text{Percent}}{100}$

$$\frac{21.6}{x} = \frac{2}{100}$$
$$2x = 2,160 \qquad \text{Cross multiply.}$$
$$\frac{2}{2}x = \frac{2,160}{2} \qquad \text{Divide both sides by 2.}$$
$$x = 1,080$$

15. $\dfrac{\text{Amount}}{\text{Base}} = \dfrac{\text{Percent}}{100}$

$$\frac{105}{45} = \frac{x}{100}$$
$$45x = 10,500 \qquad \text{Cross multiply.}$$
$$\frac{45}{45}x = \frac{10,500}{45} \qquad \text{Divide both sides by 100.}$$
$$x = \frac{3 \cdot 3 \cdot 700}{3 \cdot 3 \cdot 3} = \frac{700}{3} = 233\frac{1}{3}$$

$233\frac{1}{3}\%$ of 45 is 105.

16. $\dfrac{x}{373,000} = \dfrac{3}{100}$

$$100x = 1,119,000$$
$$\frac{100}{100}x = \frac{1,119,000}{100}$$
$$x = 11,190$$

11,900 employees were let go.

17. $\dfrac{\$129,200}{x} = \dfrac{38}{100}$

$\quad\quad 38x = \$12,920,000$

$\quad\quad \dfrac{\cancel{38}}{\cancel{38}}x = \dfrac{\$12,920,000}{38}$

$\quad\quad\quad x = \$340,000$

His Nobel prize was worth $340,000.

18. $\dfrac{17.4}{20} = \dfrac{x}{100}$

$\quad\quad 20x = 1,740$

$\quad\quad \dfrac{\cancel{20}}{\cancel{20}}x = \dfrac{1,740}{20}$

$\quad\quad\quad x = 87$

You have used 87% of the storage capacity.

Calculator Practice

p. 311. $72.37 \boxed{\times} 8.25 \boxed{\%} = 5.970... \approx 5.97$

$\quad\quad\quad$ 8.25% of $72.37 is $5.97.

p. 312. $299.95 \boxed{-} 15 \boxed{\%} = 254.9575$

$\quad\quad\quad\quad$ $299.95 reduced by 15% is $254.96

$\quad\quad\quad\quad 49.88 \boxed{\div} 103 \boxed{\%} = 48.427... \approx 48.43$

$\quad\quad\quad\quad\quad$ 49.88 is 103% of 48.43.

$\quad\quad\quad\quad\quad 7.99 \boxed{\div} 35.66 \boxed{=} 0.224...$

$\quad\quad\quad\quad\quad\quad 0.\underline{2}24... = 22.4...\% \approx 22\%$

$\quad\quad\quad\quad\quad\quad$ $7.99 is 22% of $35.66

Exercises

1. What is 75% of 8?
$\quad \downarrow \; \downarrow \; \downarrow \quad \downarrow \; \downarrow$
$\quad\quad x \;=\; 0.75 \;\cdot\; 8$

$x = (0.75)(8) = 6$

Estimate: Think of 75% as $\dfrac{3}{4}$; $\dfrac{3}{4} \times \dfrac{8}{1} = 6$.

3. What is 100% of 23?
$\quad \downarrow \; \downarrow \; \downarrow \quad \downarrow \; \downarrow$
$\quad\quad x \;=\; 1.00 \quad\cdot\quad 23$

$x = (1.00)(23) = 23$

Estimate: Think of 100% as one whole; one whole of 23 is 23.

5. What is 41% of 7?
$\quad \downarrow \; \downarrow \; \downarrow \quad \downarrow\downarrow$
$\quad\quad x \;=\; 0.41 \;\cdot\; 7$

$x = (0.41)(7) = 2.87$

Estimate: 40% of 7 would be (0.4)(7) or 2.8.

7. What is 35% of $400?
$\quad \downarrow \; \downarrow \; \downarrow \; \downarrow \; \downarrow$
$\quad\quad x \;=\; 0.35 \;\cdot\; 400$

$x = (0.35)(400) = 140$

35% of $400 is $140.
Estimate: 35% of 100 is 35, so the answer will be $4 \times \$35$ or $140.

9. What is 13% of 5 L?
$\quad \downarrow \; \downarrow \; \downarrow \quad \downarrow \; \downarrow$
$\quad\quad x \;=\; 0.13 \;\cdot\; 5$

$x = (0.13)(5) = 0.65$

13% of 5 L is 0.65 L.
Estimate: 0.13×5 is an easy multiplication, so check by repeating the calculation.

11. What is 3.1% of 20?
$\quad \downarrow \; \downarrow \; \downarrow \quad \downarrow \; \downarrow$
$\quad\quad x \;=\; 0.031 \;\cdot\; 20$

$x = (0.031)(20) = 0.62$

Estimate: 30% of 20 is 0.3×20 or 0.6.

13. What is $\dfrac{1}{2}$% of 20?
$\quad \downarrow \; \downarrow \; \downarrow \quad \downarrow \; \downarrow$
$\quad\quad x \;=\; 0.05 \;\cdot\; 20$

$x = (0.05)(20) = 0.1$

Estimate: 1% of 20 would be 0.2, so the answer will be half of this, or 0.1.

15. What is 8% of $500?
$\quad \downarrow \; \downarrow \; \downarrow \; \downarrow \quad \downarrow$
$\quad\quad x \;=\; 0.08 \;\cdot\; 500$

$x = (0.08)(500) = 40$

8% of $500 is $40.
Estimate: 10% of $500 would be $50.

17. What is $12\dfrac{1}{2}$% of 32?
$\quad \downarrow \; \downarrow \; \downarrow \quad \downarrow \; \downarrow$
$\quad\quad x \;=\; 0.125 \;\cdot\; 32$

$x = (0.125)(32) = 4$

Estimate: $12\dfrac{1}{2}\% = \dfrac{1}{8}$, and $\dfrac{1}{8}$ of 32 is 4.

19. What is $7\dfrac{1}{8}$% of $257.13?
$\quad \downarrow \; \downarrow \; \downarrow \quad \downarrow \quad \downarrow$
$\quad\quad x \;=\; 0.07125 \;\cdot\; 257.13$

$x = (0.07125)(257.13) = 18.3205... \approx 18.32$

$7\dfrac{1}{8}$% of $257.13 is $18.32 to the nearest cent.
Estimate: 7% of $250 is $17.50.

21. What is 25% of $24,000?

$\quad \downarrow \quad \downarrow \quad \downarrow \quad \downarrow \quad \downarrow$

$\quad x \ = \ 0.25 \ \cdot \ 24,000$

$x = (0.25)(24,000) = 6,000$

You can spend up to $6,000.

23. What is 70% of 35 hr?

$\quad \downarrow \quad \downarrow \quad \downarrow \quad \downarrow \quad \downarrow$

$\quad x \ = \ 0.70 \ \cdot \ 35$

$x = (0.7)(35) = 24.5$

You enter data for 24.5 hr a week.

25. What is 60% of 90?

$\quad \downarrow \quad \downarrow \quad \downarrow \quad \downarrow \quad \downarrow$

$\quad x \ = \ 0.60 \ \cdot \ 90$

$x = (0.6)(90) = 54$

There are 54 tables in the no-smoking section.

27. First find out how many of the 160 employees are women:

What is 55% of 160?

$\quad \downarrow \quad \downarrow \quad \downarrow \quad \downarrow \quad \downarrow$

$\quad x \ = \ 0.55 \ \cdot \ 160$

$x = (0.55)(160) = 88$

Since there are 88 women, the number of men is $160 - 88$, or 72. There are $88 - 72$, or 16, more women than men.

29. 25% of what number is 8?

$\downarrow \quad \downarrow \quad \quad \downarrow \quad \quad \downarrow \downarrow$

$0.25 \ \cdot \quad x \quad = 8$

$0.25x = 8$

$x = \dfrac{8}{0.25}$

$x = 32$

31. $12 is 10% of how much money?

$\downarrow \quad \downarrow \quad \downarrow \quad \downarrow \quad \quad \downarrow$

$12 \ = \ 0.1 \ \cdot \quad x$

$12 = 0.1x$

$\dfrac{12}{0.1} = x$

$120 = x$

$12 is 10% of $120.

33. 30 is 40% of what number?

$\downarrow \downarrow \quad \downarrow \quad \downarrow \quad \quad \downarrow$

$30 = 0.4 \ \cdot \quad x$

$30 = 0.4x$

$\dfrac{30}{0.4} = x$

$75 = x$

35. 7% of what weight is 14 lb?

$\downarrow \quad \downarrow \quad \quad \downarrow \quad \quad \downarrow \downarrow$

$0.07 \ \cdot \quad \quad x \quad = 14$

$0.07x = 14$

$x = \dfrac{14}{0.07}$

$x = 200$

7% of 200 lb is 14 lb.

37. 5 is 200% of what number?

$\downarrow \downarrow \downarrow \quad \downarrow \quad \quad \downarrow$

$5 \ = \ 2.00 \ \cdot \quad x$

$5 = 2x$

$\dfrac{5}{2} = x$

$2.5 = x$

39. $20 is 10% of how much money?

$\downarrow \quad \downarrow \quad \downarrow \quad \downarrow \quad \quad \downarrow$

$20 \ = \ 0.1 \ \cdot \quad x$

$20 = 0.1x$

$\dfrac{20}{0.1} = x$

$200 = x$

$20 is 10% of $200.

41. 2% of what amount is $5?

$\downarrow \quad \downarrow \quad \quad \downarrow \quad \quad \downarrow \downarrow$

$0.02 \ \cdot \quad x \quad = 5$

$0.02x = 5$

$x = \dfrac{5}{0.02}$

$x = 250$

2% of $250 is $5.

43. 3.5 is 200% of what number?

$\downarrow \downarrow \downarrow \quad \downarrow \quad \quad \downarrow$

$3.5 \ = \ 2.00 \ \cdot \quad x$

$3.5 = 2x$

$\dfrac{3.5}{2} = x$

$1.75 = x$

45. 0.5% of what number is 23?

$\downarrow \quad \downarrow \quad \quad \downarrow \quad \quad \downarrow \downarrow$

$0.005 \ \cdot \quad x \quad = 23$

$0.005x = 23$

$x = \dfrac{23}{0.005}$

$x = 4,600$

Chapter 6   Percents

47. $3\frac{1}{2}\%$ of what is 98?

$$\downarrow \quad \downarrow \quad \downarrow \quad \downarrow\downarrow$$
$$0.035 \cdot x = 98$$
$$0.035x = 98$$
$$x = \frac{98}{0.035}$$
$$x = 2{,}800$$

49. 8 is 25% of what number?

$$\downarrow\downarrow\downarrow \quad \downarrow \quad \downarrow$$
$$8 = 0.25 \cdot x$$
$$8 = 0.25x$$
$$\frac{8}{0.25} = x$$
$$32 = x$$

There are 32 employees.

51. 1.5 million is 8% of what number?

$$\downarrow \quad \downarrow\downarrow \quad \downarrow \quad \downarrow$$
$$1{,}500{,}000 = 0.08 \cdot x$$
$$1{,}500{,}000 = 0.08x$$
$$\frac{1{,}500{,}000}{0.08} = x$$
$$18{,}750{,}000 = x$$

The workforce was 18,750,000 people.

53. 300 is 20% of what number?

$$\downarrow\downarrow\downarrow \quad \downarrow \quad \downarrow$$
$$300 = 0.20 \cdot x$$
$$300 = 0.2x$$
$$\frac{300}{0.2} = x$$
$$1{,}500 = x$$

Last year's output was 1,500 tons.

55. 50 is what percent of 100?

$$\downarrow\downarrow \quad \downarrow \quad \downarrow\downarrow$$
$$50 = x \cdot 100$$
$$50 = 100x$$
$$\frac{50}{100} = x$$
$$x = 0.50 = 50\%$$

50 is 50% of 100.

57. What percent of 8 is 6?

$$\downarrow \quad \downarrow\downarrow\downarrow$$
$$x \cdot 8 = 6$$
$$8x = 6$$
$$x = \frac{6}{8} = \frac{3}{4} = 0.75 = 75\%$$

59. What percent of 12 is 10?

$$\downarrow \quad \downarrow\downarrow\downarrow$$
$$x \cdot 12 = 10$$
$$12x = 10$$
$$x = \frac{10}{12} = \frac{5}{6}$$
$$x = \frac{5}{6} \times 100\% = \frac{5}{6} \times \frac{100}{1}\% = \frac{250}{3}\% = 83\frac{1}{3}\%$$

61. What percent of 50 is 20?

$$\downarrow \quad \downarrow\downarrow\downarrow$$
$$x \cdot 50 = 20$$
$$50x = 20$$
$$x = \frac{20}{50} = \frac{2}{5} = 0.40 = 40\%$$

63. 2 mi is what percent of 8 mi?

$$\downarrow \quad \downarrow \quad \downarrow \quad \downarrow\downarrow$$
$$2 = x \cdot 8$$
$$2 = 8x$$
$$\frac{2}{8} = x$$
$$x = \frac{2}{8} = \frac{1}{4} = 0.25 = 25\%$$

2 mi is 25% of 8 mi.

65. $30 is what percent of $20?

$$\downarrow\downarrow \quad \downarrow \quad \downarrow\downarrow$$
$$30 = x \cdot 20$$
$$30 = 20x$$
$$\frac{30}{20} = x$$
$$x = \frac{30}{20} = \frac{3}{2} = 1.50 = 150\%$$

$30 is 150% of $20.

67. 2.5 is what percent of 4?

$$\downarrow\downarrow \quad \downarrow \quad \downarrow\downarrow$$
$$2.5 = x \cdot 4$$
$$2.5 = 4x$$
$$\frac{2.5}{4} = x$$
$$x = 0.625 = 62.5\%$$

2.5 is 62.5% of 4.

69. $8 is what percent of $240?

$$\begin{array}{ccccc}\downarrow\downarrow & & \downarrow & & \downarrow\;\downarrow\\ 8\;= & & x & \cdot & 240\end{array}$$

$$8 = 240x$$

$$\frac{8}{240} = x$$

$$x = \frac{8}{240} = \frac{1}{30}\times 100\% = \frac{1}{\cancel{30}}\times\frac{\overset{10}{\cancel{100}}}{1}\% = \frac{10}{3}\% = 3\frac{1}{3}\%$$

$8 is $3\frac{1}{3}\%$ of $240.

71. What percent of 5 is $\frac{1}{2}$?

$$\begin{array}{ccccc}\downarrow & & \downarrow\downarrow\downarrow\\ x & \cdot & 5\; = \frac{1}{2}\end{array}$$

$$5x = \frac{1}{2}$$

$$x = \frac{1}{2}\cdot\frac{1}{5} = \frac{1}{10} = 0.10 = 10\%$$

73. 300 Cal is what percent of 2,000 Cal?

$$\begin{array}{ccccc}\downarrow & & \downarrow & & \downarrow\;\downarrow\\ 300 & = & x & \cdot & 2,000\end{array}$$

$$300 = 2,000x$$

$$\frac{300}{2,000} = x$$

$$x = \frac{300}{2,000} = \frac{3}{20} = 0.15 = 15\%$$

You reach 15% of your goal.

75. 9 mo is what percent of 36 mo?

$$\begin{array}{ccccc}\downarrow & & \downarrow & & \downarrow\;\downarrow\\ 9 & = & x & \cdot & 36\end{array}$$

$$9 = 36x$$

$$\frac{9}{36} = x$$

$$x = \frac{9}{36} = \frac{1}{4} = 0.25 = 25\%$$

25% of your enlistment has passed.

77. $30,000 is what percent of $150,000?

$$\begin{array}{ccccc}\downarrow\downarrow & & \downarrow & & \downarrow\\ 30,000\;= & & x & \cdot & 150,000\end{array}$$

$$30,000 = 150,000x$$

$$\frac{30,000}{150,000} = x$$

$$x = \frac{30,000}{150,000} = \frac{1}{5} = 0.20 = 20\%$$

The down payment is 20% of the purchase price.

79. If the player got hits in 12 out of 20 at-bats, 30 − 12 or 18 at-bats were not hits.

18 is what percent of 30?

$$\begin{array}{ccccc}\downarrow\downarrow & & \downarrow & & \downarrow\;\downarrow\\ 18\;= & & x & \cdot & 30\end{array}$$

$$18 = 30x$$

$$\frac{18}{30} = x$$

$$x = \frac{18}{30} = \frac{3}{5} = 0.60 = 60\%$$

60% of the at-bats were not hits.

6.3   More on Percents

Practice

1. The increase is 100 − 25 or 75.

What percent of 25 is 75?

$$\begin{array}{ccccc}\downarrow & & \downarrow\downarrow\downarrow\downarrow\\ x & \cdot & 25\; = 75\end{array}$$

$$25x = 75$$

$$\frac{\cancel{25}}{\cancel{25}}x = \frac{75}{25}$$

$$x = 3,\text{ or }300\%$$

The percent increase in beds is 300%.

2. Find the percent drop in the index for each crash.

$$300 - 230 = 70$$

What percent of 300 is 70?

$$\begin{array}{ccccc}\downarrow & & \downarrow\downarrow\downarrow\downarrow\\ x & \cdot & 300\; = 70\end{array}$$

$$300x = 70$$

$$x = \frac{70}{300} = 0.2333\ldots\text{ or about }23.3\%$$

$$2,250 - 1,750 = 500$$

What percent of 2,250 is 500?

$$\begin{array}{ccccc}\downarrow & & \downarrow\downarrow\downarrow\downarrow\\ x & \cdot & 2,250\; = 500\end{array}$$

$$2,250x = 500$$

$$x = \frac{500}{2,250} = 0.2222\ldots\text{ or about }22.2\%$$

Since 23.3% is greater than 22.2%, the drop in 1929 was greater as a percent.

3. What is 7% of $53.50?

$x = 0.07 \cdot \$53.50$

$x = (0.07)(53.50)$

$x = \$3.745 \approx 3.75$

$53.50 + 3.75 = 57.25$

The total cost is $57.25 to the nearest cent.

4. If the shop's total sales are $4,500, the sales in excess of $2,000 are $4,500 - \$2,000$ or $2,500.

What is $7\frac{1}{2}\%$ of $2,500?

$x = 0.075 \cdot 2,500$

$x = (0.075)(2,500) = 412.50$

Your earnings for the week are $412.50.

5. Since the sale price is 20% off, the buyer pays 80% of the regular price.

What is 80% of $87.00?

$x = 0.8 \cdot 87.00$

$x = (0.8)(87.00) = 69.60$

The sale price is $69.60.

6. The store pays $\dfrac{\$480}{12}$ or $40 per pair. Since the trousers sell for $80, the markup is $80 - \$40$ or $40.

What percent of 80 is 40?

$x \cdot 80 = 40$

$80x = 40$

$x = \dfrac{40}{80} = \dfrac{2}{4} = 0.5$ or 50%

Based on the selling price, the markup is 50%.

7. What is $8\frac{1}{2}\%$ of $1,600?

$x = 0.085 \cdot 1,600$

$x = (0.085)(1,600) = 136$

Since the interest is $136, the balance after one year is $1,600 + \$136$ or $1,736.

8.

| | Rate of | Number |
| Principal | Interest | of Years |

Interest $= 20,000 \times 0.06 \times 3$

Interest $= 3,600$

The interest over 3 years is $3,600.

9.

| Principal | First Year | Second Year | Third Year | Fourth Year |

$2,000 \times 1.06 \times 1.06 \times 1.06 \times 1.06$

Interest $= 2,524.95392$

At the end of four years the balance is $2,524.95.

Exercises

1.

Original Value	New Value	Percent Increase or Decrease
10	12	The change is an increase of 2. $\dfrac{2}{10} = 0.20 = 20\%$ increase
10	8	The change is a decrease of 2. $\dfrac{2}{10} = 0.20 = 20\%$ decrease
6	18	The change is an increase of 12. $\dfrac{12}{6} = 2.00 = 200\%$ increase
35	70	The change is an increase of 35. $\dfrac{35}{35} = 1.00 = 100\%$ increase
14	21	The change is an increase of 7. $\dfrac{7}{14} = \dfrac{1}{2} = 0.50 = 50\%$ increase
10	1	The change is a decrease of 9. $\dfrac{90}{10} = 0.90 = 90\%$ decrease
$8	$6.50	The change is a decrease of $1.50. $\dfrac{1.50}{8} = 0.1875 = 18.75\%$ decrease or $18\frac{3}{4}\%$ decrease
$6	$5.25	The change is a decrease of $0.75. $\dfrac{0.75}{6} = 0.125 = 12.5\%$ decrease or $12\frac{1}{2}\%$ decrease

3.

Selling Price	Rate of Sales Tax	Sales Tax
$30.00	5%	$(0.05)(\$30) = \$1.50$
$24.88	3%	$(0.03)(\$24.88) = \$0.7464$ $\approx \$0.75$
$51.00	$7\frac{1}{2}\%$	$(0.075)(\$51.00) = \$3.825$ $\approx \$3.83$
$196.23	4.5%	$(0.045)(\$196.23) = \$8.83035$ $\approx \$8.83$

5.

Sales	Rate of Commission	Sales Tax
$700	10%	$(0.10)(\$700) = \$70.00$
$450	2%	$(0.02)(\$450) = \$9.00$
$870	$4\frac{1}{2}\%$	$(0.045)(\$870) = \$39.15$
$922	7.5%	$(0.075)(\$922) = \$69.15$

7.

Original Price	Rate of Discount	Discount and Sale Price
$700.00	25%	Discount: $(0.25)(\$700.00) = \$175.00$ Sale Price: $\$700.00 - \$175.00 = \$525.00$
$18.00	10%	Discount: $(0.10)(\$18.00) = \$1.80$ Sale Price: $\$18.00 - \$1.80 = \$16.20$
$43.50	20%	Discount: $(0.20)(\$43.50) = \$8.70$ Sale Price: $\$43.50 - \$8.70 = \$34.80$
$16.99	5%	Discount: $(0.05)(\$16.99) = \$0.8495$ $\approx \$0.85$ Sale Price: $\$19.99 - \$0.85 = \$16.14$

9.

Selling Price	Rate of Markup	Markup and Original Price
$10.00	50%	Markup: $(0.50)(\$10.00) = \$5.00$ Original Price: $\$10.00 - \$5.00 = \$5.00$
$23.00	70%	Markup: $(0.70)(\$23.00) = \$16.10$ Original Price: $\$23.00 - \$16.10 = \$6.90$
$18.40	10%	Markup: $(0.10)(\$18.40) = \$1.84$ Original Price: $\$18.40 - \$1.84 = \$16.56$
$13.55	60%	Markup: $(0.60)(\$13.55) = \$8.13$ Original Price: $\$13.55 - \$8.13 = \$5.42$

11.

Principal	Interest Rate and Time	Interest and Final Balance
$300	4% 2 years	$\$300 \times 0.04 \times 2 = \$24.00$ $\$300 + \$24.00 = \$324.00$
$600	4% 2 years	$\$600 \times 0.04 \times 2 = \$48.00$ $\$600 + \$48.00 = \$648.00$
$300	8% 2 years	$\$300 \times 0.08 \times 2 = \$48.00$ $\$300 + \$48.00 = \$348.00$
$300	4% 4 years	$\$300 \times 0.04 \times 4 = \$48.00$ $\$300 + \$48.00 = \$348.00$
$375	10% 3 years	$\$375 \times 0.10 \times 3 = \$112.50$ $\$375 + \$112.50 = \$487.50$
$70,000	6% 30 years	$\$70,000 \times 0.06 \times 30 = \$126,000.00$ $\$70,000 + \$126,000.00 = \$196,000.00$

13.

Principal	Interest Rate and Time	Final Balance
$500	4% 2 years	$(1.04)^2 \times \$500 = \$540.80$
$6,200	3% 5 years	$(1.03)^5 \times \$6,200 = \$7,187.499... \approx \$7,187.50$
$300	5% 8 years	$(1.05)^8 \times \$300 = \$443.236... \approx \$443.24$
$20,000	4% 2 years	$(1.04)^2 \times \$20,000 = \$21,632.00$
$145	3.8% 3 years	$(1.038)^3 \times \$145 = \$162.166... \approx \$162.17$
$810	2.9% 10 years	$(1.029)^{10} \times \$810 = \$1,078.049... \approx \$1,078.05$

15. The decrease in value was $150,000 - 90,000$ or $60,000.

What percent of $150,000 is $60,000?

$$\downarrow \quad\quad \downarrow \quad\quad \downarrow \quad \downarrow \quad \downarrow$$
$$x \quad\quad \cdot \quad 150,000 = 60,000$$

$$150,000x = 60,000$$

$$x = \frac{60,000}{150,000}$$

$$x = \frac{2}{5} = 0.40 = 40\%$$

The value dropped by 40%.

17. The increase was $1,300,000 - 200,000$ or 1.1 million.

What percent of 200,000 is 1,100,000?

$$\downarrow \quad\quad \downarrow \quad \downarrow \quad \downarrow \quad\quad \downarrow$$
$$x \quad\quad \cdot 200,000 = 1,100,000$$

$$200,000x = 1,100,000$$

$$x = \frac{1,100,000}{200,000}$$

$$x = \frac{11}{2} = 5.50 = 550\%$$

The number of residents increased by 550%.

19. The increase was $200,000 - 50,000$ or 150,000.

What percent of 50,000 is 150,000?

$$\downarrow \quad\quad \downarrow \quad \downarrow \quad \downarrow \quad\quad \downarrow$$
$$x \quad\quad \cdot 50,000 = 150,000$$

$$50,000x = 150,000$$

$$x = \frac{150,000}{50,000} = 3.00 = 300\%$$

The number of phones increased by 300%.

21. What is 8% of $80?

$$\downarrow \quad \downarrow \downarrow \quad \downarrow \quad \downarrow$$
$$x \quad = 0.08 \cdot \quad 80$$

$$x = (0.08)(80) = 6.40$$

The sales tax will be $6.40.

23. What percent of $700 is $53?

$$\downarrow \quad\quad \downarrow \quad \downarrow \downarrow \quad \downarrow$$
$$x \quad\quad \cdot \quad 700 = 53$$

$$700x = 53$$

$$x = \frac{53}{700} = 0.0757... \approx 7.6\%$$

The sales tax is 7.6% to the nearest tenth of a percent.

25. What is $2\frac{1}{2}\%$ of $20,000?

$$\downarrow \quad \downarrow \quad \downarrow \quad\quad \downarrow \quad\quad \downarrow$$
$$x \quad = 0.025 \quad \cdot \quad 20,000$$

$$x = (0.025)(20,000) = 500$$

Your commission is $500.

27. $1.35 is 15% of what amount?

$$\downarrow \quad \downarrow \quad \downarrow \quad \downarrow \quad\quad \downarrow$$
$$1.35 = 0.15 \quad \cdot \quad\quad x$$

$$1.35 = 0.15x$$

$$\frac{1.35}{0.15} = x$$

$$9 = x$$

The bill before tip was $9.

29. The markup is $25 - 20$ or $5.

What percent of $25 is $5?

$$\downarrow \quad\quad \downarrow \quad \downarrow \downarrow$$
$$x \quad\quad \cdot \quad 25 = 5$$

$$25x = 5$$

$$x = \frac{5}{25} = \frac{1}{5} = 0.2 \text{ or } 20\%$$

Based on the selling price, the markup is 20%.

31. What percent of $15 is $8?

$$\downarrow \quad\quad \downarrow \quad \downarrow \downarrow$$
$$x \quad\quad \cdot \quad 15 = 8$$

$$15x = 8$$

$$x = \frac{8}{\cancel{15}_{3}} \times \frac{\overset{20}{\cancel{100}}}{1}\% = \frac{160}{3}\% = 53\frac{1}{3}\%$$

The markup is $53\frac{1}{3}\%$.

33. If the discount rate is 35%, the television sells for 65% of its list price.

What is 65% of $399?

$$\downarrow \quad \downarrow \downarrow \quad \downarrow \quad\quad \downarrow$$
$$x \quad = 0.65 \quad \cdot \quad 399$$

$$x = (0.65)(399) = 259.35$$

The sale price is $259.35.

35. $3,000 \times 0.05 \times 1 = \$150$

You paid $150 in interest.

37. $5,000 \times 0.05 \times 1 = \$250$

You will have earned $250.

39. $3,000 \times (1.06)^2 = \$3,370.80$

The account will contain $3,370.80.

41. $4,000 \times (1.10)^4 = 5,856.4$

The city's population was about 5,856.

Review Exercises

1.

Fraction	Decimal	Percent
$\dfrac{1}{4}$	0.25	25%
$\dfrac{7}{10}$	0.7	70%
$\dfrac{3}{400}$	0.0075	$\dfrac{3}{4}$%
$\dfrac{5}{8}$	0.625	62.5%
$1\dfrac{1}{5}$	1.2	120%
$1\dfrac{1}{100}$	1.01	101%
$2\dfrac{3}{5}$	2.6	260%
$3\dfrac{3}{10}$	3.3	330%
$\dfrac{3}{25}$	0.12	12%
$\dfrac{7}{8}$	0.875	$87\dfrac{1}{2}$%
$\dfrac{1}{6}$	$0.16\dfrac{2}{3}$	$16\dfrac{2}{3}$%

2.

Fraction	Decimal	Percent
$\dfrac{3}{8}$	0.375	37.5%
$\dfrac{2}{5}$	0.4	40%
$\dfrac{1}{1,000}$	0.001	$\dfrac{1}{10}$%
$1\dfrac{1}{2}$	1.5	150%
$\dfrac{7}{8}$	0.875	87.5%
$\dfrac{5}{6}$	$0.83\dfrac{1}{3}$	$83\dfrac{1}{3}$%
$2\dfrac{3}{4}$	2.75	275%
$1\dfrac{1}{5}$	1.2	120%
$\dfrac{3}{4}$	0.75	75%
$\dfrac{1}{10}$	0.1	10%
$\dfrac{1}{3}$	$0.33\dfrac{1}{3}$	$33\dfrac{1}{3}$%

3. $\dfrac{113}{758} = 0.149... \approx 0.1\underline{5} = 15\%$

4. $\dfrac{1}{32} = 0.0\underline{3}125 = 3.125\%$

5. What is 40% of 30?
$$\downarrow \quad \downarrow \downarrow \quad \downarrow \quad \downarrow$$
$$x \ = \ 0.40 \ \cdot \ 30$$
$$x = (0.4)(30) = 12$$

6. What percent of 5 is 6?
$$\downarrow \qquad \downarrow \downarrow \downarrow \downarrow$$
$$x \qquad \cdot \ 5 = 6$$
$$5x = 6$$
$$x = \dfrac{6}{5} = 1.\underline{20} = 120\%$$

7. 2 ft is what percent of 4 ft?
$$\downarrow \quad \downarrow \quad \downarrow \quad \downarrow \downarrow$$
$$2 \ = \quad x \quad \cdot \ 4$$
$$2 = 4x$$
$$x = \dfrac{2}{4} = \dfrac{1}{2} = 0.5\underline{0} = 50\%$$

8. 30% of what number is 6?
$$\downarrow \quad \downarrow \qquad \downarrow \qquad \downarrow \downarrow$$
$$0.30 \ \cdot \qquad x \qquad = \ 6$$
$$0.3x = 6$$
$$x = \dfrac{6}{0.3} = 20$$
30% of 20 is 6.

9. What percent of 8 is 3.5?
$$\downarrow \qquad \downarrow \downarrow \downarrow \ \downarrow$$
$$x \qquad \cdot \ 8 = 3.5$$
$$8x = 3.5$$
$$x = \dfrac{3.5}{8} = 0.4\underline{3}75 = 43.75\%$$

10. What is 55% of 10?

$$\downarrow \quad \downarrow \downarrow \quad \downarrow \downarrow$$

$$x \;=\; 0.55 \;\cdot\; 10$$

$$x = (0.55)(10) = 5.5$$

11. $12 is 200% of what amount?

$$\downarrow \quad \downarrow \downarrow \quad \downarrow \quad \downarrow$$

$$12 \;=\; 2.00 \;\cdot\; x$$

$$12 = 2x$$

$$\frac{12}{2} = x$$

$$6 = x$$

$12 is 200% of $6.

12. 2 is what percent of 10?

$$\downarrow\downarrow \qquad \downarrow \qquad \downarrow \downarrow$$

$$2 \;=\; x \;\cdot\; 10$$

$$2 = 10x$$

$$x = \frac{2}{10} = \frac{1}{5} = 0.2\underline{0} = 20\%$$

13. What is 1.2% of 25?

$$\downarrow \quad \downarrow \downarrow \quad \downarrow \downarrow$$

$$x \;=\; 0.012 \;\cdot\; 25$$

$$x = (0.012)(25) = 0.3$$

14. A reasonable estimate is 100% of 16, or 16.

15. 35% of $200 is what?

$$\downarrow \quad \downarrow \quad \downarrow \downarrow \quad \downarrow$$

$$0.35 \;\cdot\; 200 \;=\; x$$

$$x = (0.035)(200) = 70$$

35% of $200 is $70.

16. $\frac{1}{2}$% of what number is 5?

$$\downarrow \qquad \downarrow \qquad \downarrow \qquad \downarrow\downarrow$$

$$0.005 \;\cdot\; x \;=\; 5$$

$$0.005x = 5$$

$$x = \frac{5}{0.005} = 1{,}000$$

$\frac{1}{2}$% of 1,000 is 5.

17. 15 is what percent of 0.75?

$$\downarrow\downarrow \qquad \downarrow \qquad \downarrow \downarrow$$

$$15 \;=\; x \;\cdot\; 0.75$$

$$15 = 0.75x$$

$$\frac{15}{0.75} = x$$

$$x = \frac{15}{0.75} = 20.\underline{00} = 2{,}000\%$$

15 is 2,000% of 0.75.

18. 4.5 is what percent of 18?

$$\downarrow\downarrow \qquad \downarrow \qquad \downarrow \downarrow$$

$$4.5 = \quad x \quad \cdot \quad 18$$

$$4.5 = 18x$$

$$\frac{4.5}{18} = x$$

$$x = \frac{4.5}{18} = \frac{1}{4} = 0.2\underline{5} = 25\%$$

4.5 is 25% of 18.

19. What is $33\frac{1}{3}$% of $600?

$$\downarrow \quad \downarrow \downarrow \quad \downarrow \quad \downarrow$$

$$x \;=\; 0.33\frac{1}{3} \;\cdot\; 600$$

$$x = (0.33\tfrac{1}{3})(600) = \frac{1}{3} \times 600 = 200$$

$33\frac{1}{3}$% of $600 is $200.

20. What percent of $9 is $4?

$$\downarrow \qquad \downarrow \downarrow \quad \downarrow \downarrow$$

$$x \;\cdot\; 9 \;=\; 4$$

$$9x = 4$$

$$x = \frac{4}{9} = \frac{4}{9} \times \frac{100}{1}\% = \frac{400}{9}\% = 44\frac{4}{9}\%$$

$4 is $44\frac{4}{9}$% of $9.

21. A reasonable estimate is 60% of $20, or $12.

22. 2.5% of how much money is $40?

$$\downarrow \quad \downarrow \qquad \downarrow \qquad \downarrow \downarrow$$

$$0.025 \;\cdot\; x \;=\; 40$$

$$0.025x = 40$$

$$x = \frac{40}{0.025}$$

$$x = 1{,}600$$

2.5% of $1,600 is $40.

23. What percent of $7.99 is $1.35?

$$\downarrow \qquad \downarrow \downarrow \quad \downarrow \downarrow$$

$$x \;\cdot\; 7.99 \;=\; 1.35$$

$$7.99x = 1.35$$

$$x = \frac{1.35}{7.99} = 0.168\ldots \approx 0.1\underline{7} = 17\%$$

24. 3.5 is $8\frac{1}{4}\%$ of what number?

$\downarrow\downarrow\;\downarrow\quad\downarrow\quad\;\downarrow$

$3.5 = 0.0825\;\cdot\;x$

$3.5 = 0.0825x$

$x = \dfrac{3.5}{0.0825} = 42.424... \approx 42.42$

3.5 is $8\frac{1}{4}\%$ of 42.42.

25.

Original Value	New Value	Percent Decrease
24	16	$33\frac{1}{3}\%$

26.

Selling Price	Rate of Sales Tax	Sales Tax
$50	6%	$3.00

27.

Sales	Rate of Commission	Commission
$600	4%	$24

28.

Original Price	Rate of Discount	Discount and Sale Price
$200	15%	Discount: $30 Sale Price: $170

29.

Selling Price	Rate of Markup	Markup and Original Price
$51	50%	Markup: $25.50 Original Price: $25.50

30.

Principal	Interest Rate and Time	Simple Interest and Final Balance
$200	4% 2 years	Interest: $16 Final Balance: $216

31. $85\% = \dfrac{85}{100} = \dfrac{17}{20}$

32. The drop in polio cases between 1955 and 1956 was $29,000 - 15,000$ or 14,000 cases.

14,000 is what percent of 29,000?

$\downarrow\;\downarrow\quad\downarrow\qquad\quad\downarrow\;\downarrow$

$14,000 = \quad x\quad\cdot\;29,000$

$14,000 = 29,000x$

$x = \dfrac{24,000}{29,000} = 0.482... \approx 0.48 = 48\%$

There was a 48% drop in cases.

33. One month's rent is $\frac{1}{12}$ of a year's rent, and

$\dfrac{1}{12} = 0.0833 \approx 0.083 = 8.3\%$. So the agent who charges 11% charges more.

34. $\dfrac{3}{5} = 0.60 = 60\%$

60% of respondents regularly recycle.

35. $100\% - 49\% - 31\% = 100\% - 80\% = 20\%$

20% of the respondents neither approved nor disapproved.

36. $\dfrac{1}{4} = 0.25 = 25\%$. Since 25% is greater than 18.8%, the XYZ network did better.

37. $75\% = \dfrac{75}{100} = \dfrac{3}{4}$

$\frac{3}{4}$ of the jury found the defendant innocent.

38. $\frac{1}{4}\% = 0.25\%$

$6\frac{1}{4}\% = 6.25\% = 06.25\% = 0.0625$

$6\frac{1}{4}\%$ is 0.0625.

39. 20 min is what percent of 50 min?

$\downarrow\qquad\downarrow\qquad\downarrow\qquad\downarrow\;\downarrow$

$20\quad = \quad x\quad\cdot\;50$

$20 = 50x$

$x = \dfrac{20}{50} = \dfrac{2}{5} = 0.40 = 40\%$

20 min is 40% of 50 min.

40. $\dfrac{1}{10} = 0.10 = 10\%$

About 10% of Americans are left-handed.

41. $0.632 \approx 0.63 = 63\%$

The team's standing is 63%.

42. $6.3 million is what percent of $90 million?

       ↓   ↓   ↓   ↓   ↓

$6,300,000 = \quad x \quad \cdot \quad 90,000,000$

$6,300,000 = 90,000,000x$

$$x = \frac{6,300,000}{90,000,000} = 0.0\underline{7} = 7\%$$

$6.3 million is 7% of 90 million.

43. 360 million is what percent of 2 billion?

       ↓   ↓   ↓   ↓   ↓

$360,000,000 = \quad x \quad \cdot \quad 2,000,000,000$

$360,00,000 = 2,000,000,000x$

$$x = \frac{360,000,000}{2,000,000,000} = 0.1\underline{8} = 18\%$$

In that year, 18% of the wheat grown in the United States came from Kansas.

44. A reasonable estimate is to find 25% of what height is 20 in.

$25\% \cdot x = 20$

$$\frac{1}{4} \cdot x = 20$$

$x = 80$

The person's height is about 80 in.

45. What is $87\frac{1}{2}\%$ of 72?

   ↓ ↓ ↓   ↓ ↓

$x \quad = 0.875 \quad \cdot \quad 72$

$$x = (0.875)(72) = \frac{7}{8} \times 72 = 63$$

63 first serves went in.

46. You are 160 lb − 130 lb or 30 lb overweight.

20% of 130 lb is (0.2)(130 lb) or 26 lb, so you are more than 20% over your ideal weight, which is considered overweight.

47. 20% of what amount is $20,000?

   ↓ ↓   ↓   ↓   ↓

$0.20 \quad \cdot \quad x \quad = 20,000$

$0.2x = 20,000$

$$x = \frac{20,000}{0.2} = 100,000$$

You paid $100,000 for the house.

48. The increase in circulation was $60,000 - 50,000$ or 10,000.

10,000 is what percent of 50,000?

      ↓   ↓   ↓   ↓ ↓

$10,000 = \quad x \quad \cdot \quad 50,000$

$10,000 = 50,000x$

$$x = \frac{10,000}{50,000} = \frac{1}{5} = 0.\underline{20} = 20\%$$

The circulation increased by 20%.

49. 5% of $30,000 is (0.05)($30,000) or $1,500. You would have needed a raise of $1,500 to keep pace wit inflation, and you got only $1,000.

50. 109% of 53 million is (1.09)(53,000,000) or 57,770,000 cats.

51. You paid 110% of the $150 price. So you paid (1.10)($150) or $165.

52. 80 tons is 20% of what amount?

  ↓   ↓ ↓ ↓   ↓

$80 \quad = 0.20 \quad \cdot \quad x$

$80 = 0.2x$

$$x = \frac{80}{0.2} = 400$$

The total amount of food needed is 400 tons. Since you have 80 tons, you need 320 tons more.

53. 14,000 miles is 20% of how many miles?

   ↓   ↓ ↓ ↓   ↓

$14,000 \quad = 0.20 \quad \cdot \quad x$

$14,000 = 0.2x$

$$x = \frac{14,000}{0.2} = 70,000$$

The award requires 70,000 mi in all.

54. 10% of 8,600 hr is $\frac{1}{10} \times 8,600$ or 860 hr. Therefore brand Y's bulb lasts $8,600 + 860$ or 9,460 hr.

55. 20% of $5,000 is (0.2)($5,000) or $1,000, so the salesperson's commission is $1,000.

56. If 85% of receipts went for expenses, 15% were left for profit. 15% of $200,000 is (0.15)($200,000) or $30,000, so the store made a profit of $30,000.

57. $(1.065)^2 \times \$7,000 = \$7,939.575 \approx \$7,939.58$

The balance after two years will be $7,939.58.

58. $(1.02)^{10} = 1.218... \approx 1.\underline{22} = 122\%$

In ten years the economy will expand by 122%.

59.

Quarter	Income	Percent of Total Income
1	$375,129	27%
2	289,402	21%
3	318,225	23%
4	402,077	29%
Total	$1,384,833	100%

60.

Individual income taxes	$526,050,000,000
Social insurance taxes	$444,220,000,000
Corporate income taxes	$105,210,000,000
Excise taxes	$46,760,000,000
Other	$46,760,000,000

Posttest

1. $4\% = \dfrac{4}{100} = \dfrac{1}{25}$

2. $62\dfrac{1}{2}\% = \dfrac{125}{2}\% = \dfrac{\overset{5}{\cancel{125}}}{2} \times \dfrac{1}{\underset{4}{\cancel{100}}} = \dfrac{5}{8}$

3. $1\underset{\cdot}{5}0\% = 1.50$, or 1.5

4. $8\% = \underline{08}\% = .08$, or 0.08

5. $0.0\underset{\cdot}{09} = 0.9\%$

6. $3 = 3.\underline{00} = 300\%$

7. $\dfrac{5}{6} = 0.833... \approx 0.8\underset{\cdot\cdot}{3} = 83\%$

8. $2\dfrac{1}{5} = 2.\underset{\cdot\cdot}{20} = 220\%$

9. What is 25% of 30 mi?
$$\downarrow \quad \downarrow \quad \downarrow \quad \downarrow \quad \downarrow$$
$$x \quad = \quad 0.25 \quad \cdot \quad 30$$
$x = (0.25)(30) = 7.5$
25% of 30 mi is 7.5 mi.

10. 120% of 40 is (1.20)(40) or 48.

11. A possible estimate is 30% of $20, which is (0.3)($20) or $6.

12. 8% of what number is 16?
$$\downarrow \quad \downarrow \quad \quad \downarrow \quad \quad \downarrow\downarrow$$
$$0.08 \quad \cdot \quad \quad x \quad \quad = 16$$
$0.08x = 16$
$$x = \dfrac{16}{0.08} = 200$$
8% of 200 is 16.

13. What percent of 10 is 6?
$$\downarrow \quad \quad \downarrow \downarrow \downarrow$$
$$x \quad \quad \cdot \ 10 = 6$$
$10x = 6$
$$x = \dfrac{6}{10} = 0.6\underset{\cdot\cdot}{0} = 60\%$$
6 is 60% of 10.

14. What percent of 4 is 10?
$$\downarrow \quad \quad \downarrow \downarrow \downarrow$$
$$x \quad \quad \cdot \ 4 = 10$$
$4x = 10$
$$x = \dfrac{10}{4} = 2.5\underset{\cdot\cdot}{0} = 250\%$$
10 is 250% of 4.

15. $\$300 \times 0.05 \times 2 = \$30$
You make $30 in interest.

16. 6 is what percent of $1\dfrac{1}{2}$?
$$\downarrow\downarrow \quad \quad \downarrow \quad \quad \downarrow \ \downarrow$$
$$6 = \quad \quad x \quad \quad \cdot \ 1\dfrac{1}{2}$$
$$6 = 1\dfrac{1}{2} \cdot x$$
$$\dfrac{3}{2}x = 6$$
$$x = \dfrac{\overset{2}{\cancel{6}}}{1} \times \dfrac{2}{\underset{1}{\cancel{3}}} = 4.00 = 400\%$$
6 is 400% of $1\dfrac{1}{2}$.

17. $\dfrac{45}{50} = \dfrac{45}{\underset{1}{\cancel{50}}} \times \dfrac{\overset{2}{\cancel{100}}}{1}\% = 90\%$

18. 2 pints.is 50% of how many pints?

$\downarrow$ $\downarrow$ $\downarrow$ $\downarrow$ $\downarrow$

2   $= 0.50$ $\cdot$ x

$2 = 0.5x$

$x = \dfrac{2}{0.4} = 4$

4 pints of milk is needed to produce 2 pints of cream.

19. If your purchases cost $550, the amount by which they exceed $400 is $550 - $400 or $150. 10% of $150 is $(0.1)($150)$ or $15.

20. The increase was $3,100 - $3,000 or $100.

$100 is what percent of $3,000?

$\downarrow\downarrow$ $\downarrow$ $\downarrow$ $\downarrow$

100 $=$ x $\cdot$ 3,000

$100 = 3,000x$

$x = \dfrac{100}{3,000} = \dfrac{100}{3,000} \times \dfrac{100}{1}\%$

$x = \dfrac{10,000}{3,000}\% = \dfrac{10}{3}\% = 3\dfrac{1}{3}\%$

The percent increase was $3\dfrac{1}{3}\%$

Cumulative Review Exercises

1.

$$\begin{array}{r} 109 \\ 18\overline{)1{,}962} \\ \underline{18} \\ 16 \\ \underline{0} \\ 162 \\ \underline{162} \\ 0 \end{array}$$

2. $\dfrac{5}{6} = 0.833... \approx 0.83$

3.
   $3.5 \leftarrow$ one place
   $\times 0.2 \leftarrow$ one place
   $\overline{0.70} \leftarrow$ two places

4. $3\dfrac{4}{5} + 1\dfrac{9}{10} = 3\dfrac{8}{10} + 1\dfrac{9}{10} = 4\dfrac{17}{10} = 5\dfrac{7}{10}$

5.
$$\dfrac{x}{3} = 2.5$$
$$\left(\dfrac{x}{3}\right)(3) = (2.5)(3)$$
$$x = 7.5$$

6. 20% of what amount is $200?

$\downarrow$ $\downarrow$ $\downarrow$ $\downarrow$ $\downarrow$

0.20 $\cdot$ x $=$ 200

$0.2x = 200$

$x = \dfrac{200}{0.2} = 1,000$

20% of $1,000 is $200.

7. $\dfrac{\dfrac{1}{4}\text{ million}}{2\text{ million}} = \dfrac{\dfrac{1}{4}}{2} = \dfrac{1}{4} \cdot \dfrac{1}{2} = \dfrac{1}{8}$

The government withdrew $\dfrac{1}{8}$ of the troops.

8. $\dfrac{3\text{ lb}}{600\text{ ft}^2} = \dfrac{x}{800\text{ ft}^2}$

$600x = 2,400$

$x = 4$

You will need 4 lb of seed for a lawn with area 800 ft^2.

9.

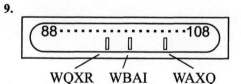

WQXR   WBAI   WAXQ

10. $(0.21)(760,000) = 159,600 \approx 160,000$

There were about 160 thousand female doctors.

Chapter 7

SIGNED NUMBERS

Pretest

1. +7 is to the right of –23 on the number line, so +7 is larger.

2. There are two numbers with an absolute value of 5, –5 and 5. The negative one is –5.

3. Find the absolute values and add them.

   $$|-8|=8 \text{ and } |-9|=9$$
   $$8+9=17$$

   –8 and –9 are both negative, so their sum is negative.

   $$-8+(-9)=-17$$

4. The numbers have the same absolute value but opposite signs, so their sum is 0.
   $$-20+20=0$$

5. Rewrite the subtraction as an addition.

   $$34-41=34+(-41)$$

   Subtract absolute values.

   $$41-34=7$$

   Since the absolute value of –41 is larger than the absolute value of 34, the answer to the addition problem is negative.

   $$34-41=-7$$

6. Rewrite the subtraction as an addition.

   $$-9-(-9)=-9+(+9)$$

   Since you are adding numbers with the same absolute value but opposite signs, the sum is 0.

   $$-9-(-9)=0$$

7. Multiply the absolute values and make the product negative since the numbers have different signs.
   $$-5\times15=-75$$

8. Multiply the absolute values and simplify the product.

   $$\frac{\cancel{3}^{1}}{\cancel{4}_{2}}\times\frac{\cancel{2}^{1}}{\cancel{3}_{1}}=\frac{1}{2}$$

Since the factors have different signs, the product is negative.

$$-\frac{3}{4}\times\frac{2}{3}=-\frac{1}{2}$$

9. The product of two negative factors is positive.
   $$(-8)^2=(-8)(-8)=64$$

10. The product of two negative factors is positive.

    $$\left(-\frac{1}{2}\right)^2=\left(-\frac{1}{2}\right)\left(-\frac{1}{2}\right)=\frac{1}{4}$$

b Divide the absolute values.

   $$18\div9=2$$

   Since the numbers have the same sign, the quotient is positive.

   $$-18\div(-9)=2$$

12. Divide the absolute values.

    $$\frac{1}{2}\div4=\frac{1}{2}\div\frac{4}{1}=\frac{1}{2}\times\frac{1}{4}=\frac{1}{8}$$

    Since the numbers have the different signs, the quotient is negative.

    $$\frac{1}{2}\div(-4)=-\frac{1}{8}$$

13.
$$-2+5+(-3)+8$$
$$=\underbrace{-2+(-3)}+\underbrace{5+8}$$
$$=\quad -5 \quad + \quad 13$$
$$=8$$

14.
$$\underbrace{10+(-3)}-(-1)$$
$$=\quad 7-(-1)$$
$$=7+(+1)$$
$$=8$$

15. Square, then multiply, then subtract.

    $$-9-3^2\times(-5)$$
    $$=-9-9\times(-5)$$
    $$=-9-(-45)$$
    $$=-9+(+45)$$
    $$=36$$

16. Multiply first, then add.
    $$8\cdot(-2)+3\cdot(-1)$$
    $$=-16+(-3)$$
    $$=-19$$

17. $-3 + (-4) = -7$
The temperature will be –7°F.

18. –1 is to the right of –3 on the number line, so a temperature of –1°F is warmer than –3°F.

19. The transaction can be represented by –$25,000 + $17,000 or –$8,000, a loss.

20. $\dfrac{-5 + 2 + (-6)}{3} = \dfrac{-3 + (-6)}{3} = \dfrac{-9}{3} = -3$

7.1   Introduction to Signed Numbers

Practice

1.
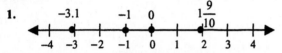

2.

Number	Opposite
a. 9	–9
b. $-4\frac{9}{10}$	$4\frac{9}{10}$
c. –2.9	2.9
d. 31	–31

3. a. $|9| = 9$ b. $\left|1\frac{3}{4}\right| = 1\frac{3}{4}$
c. $|-4.1| = 4.1$ d. $|-5| = 5$

4.

	Sign	Absolute value
a. –4	–	4
b. $6\frac{1}{2}$	+	$6\frac{1}{2}$

5. Because $\frac{1}{2}$ is to the right of 0, $\frac{1}{2}$ is larger.
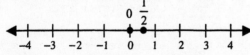

6. Because –5 is to the left of –2, –5 is smaller.
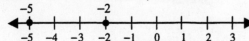

7. Because 2 is to the right of –4, 2 is larger.
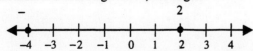

8. Since the number is a gain, we write it as a positive number: +2

9. Since –30°F is lower (colder) than –5°F and –20°F, you would plant the mums.

Exercises

1. The opposite of 8 is –8.

3. The opposite of 10.2 is –10.2.

5. The opposite of –5 is 5.

7. The opposite of $2\frac{1}{3}$ is $-2\frac{1}{3}$.

9. The opposite of –4.1 is 4.1.

11. The opposite of –1.2 is 1.2.

13.
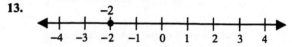

15.
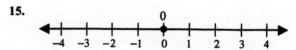

17. –$150   19. +14.5°C

21.
Number	Sign	Absolute Value
9	+	9

23.
Number	Sign	Absolute Value
–4.3	–	4.3

25.
Number	Sign	Absolute Value
–7	–	7

27.
Number	Sign	Absolute Value
$\frac{1}{5}$	+	$\frac{1}{5}$

29. $|-6| = 6$ 31. $\left|-\frac{4}{5}\right| = \frac{4}{5}$

33. $|2| = 2$ 35. $|-0.6| = 0.6$

37. Two, –5 and 5.   39. No; the absolute value is always positive or 0.

For Exercises 41 through 55, the larger number is boxed.

41. –4 and $\boxed{7}$ 43. $\boxed{12}$ and 0

45. –3 and $\boxed{2}$ 47. –4 and $\boxed{-2\frac{1}{3}}$

49. –29 and $\boxed{-2}$ 51. $\boxed{9}$ and –22

53. –8 and $\boxed{-2}$ 55. –7 and $\boxed{7\frac{1}{4}}$

57. –5 > –7 True   59. –1 < 3.4 True

61. $0 > -2\frac{3}{4}$ True   63. 2 > –2 True

65. $-3.5 > -3.4$ False

67. $-4\frac{1}{3} < 0$ True

69. $-3, 0, 3$

71. $-9, -4.5, 9$

73. Since $-100 > -1{,}000$, you are better off today than you were last week.

75. Since $1 > -5$, you will weigh more if you gain 1 lb than if you lose 5 lb.

77. Since $2 > -23$, the Trendsetters have a better record.

79. Putting the numbers $-2, -1$, and -3 in order, we get $-3, -2, -1$, so the temperature of $-1°F$ is the warmest of the three.

81. $-35 > -188$, so liquid chlorine boils at a higher temperature than liquid fluorine.

7.2 Adding Signed Numbers

Practice

1. $|-8| + |-17| = 8 + 17 = 25$

Both -8 and -17 are negative, so their sum is negative: $(-8) + (-17) = -25$

Visual check: Move 17 units *left*:

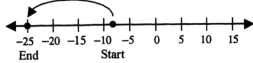

2. $|-3| = 3$ and $\left|-1\frac{1}{2}\right| = 1\frac{1}{2}$

$3 + 1\frac{1}{2} = 4\frac{1}{2}$

The sum of two negative numbers is negative, so

$-3 + \left(-1\frac{1}{2}\right) = -4\frac{1}{2}$

Visual check: Move $1\frac{1}{2}$ units *left*.

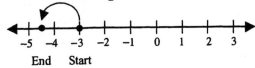

3. $|-2| = 2$ and $|9| = 9$ Subtract the smaller from the larger: $9 - 2 = 7$

Because 9 has the larger absolute value and its sign is positive, the sum is also positive: $-2 + 9 = 7$
Visual check: Move 9 units *right*.

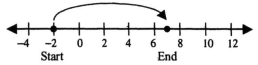

4. $|-35| = 35$ and $|35| = 35$

Subtract the absolute values: $35 - 35 = 0$

$-35 + 35 = 0$
Visual check: Move 35 units to the *right*.

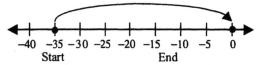

5. $\left|3\frac{4}{5}\right| = 3\frac{4}{5}$ and $\left|-1\frac{1}{5}\right| = 1\frac{1}{5}$

Subtract the absolute values. $3\frac{4}{5} - 1\frac{1}{5} = 2\frac{3}{5}$

Because $3\frac{4}{5}$ has the larger absolute value, the answer is positive.

$3\frac{4}{5} + \left(-1\frac{1}{5}\right) = 2\frac{3}{5}$

6. Rearrange the numbers by sign.
$\underbrace{1 + 8}_{\text{positives}} \underbrace{+ (-3) + (-6)}_{\text{negatives}}$

Add the positives: $1 + 8 = 9$

Add the negatives: $(-3) + (-6) = -9$

Combine the positive and negative subtotals: $9 + (-9) = 0$

Therefore, $-3 + 1 + 8 + (-6) = 0$

7. 100 B.C. can be represented by -100, so to find the year of Julius Caesar's death we need to compute $-100 + 56$.

$|-100| = 100$ and $|56| = 56$

Subtract the smaller from the larger.

$100 - 56 = 44$

-100 has the larger absolute value, so the answer is negative.

$-100 + 56 = -44$

The negative sign indicates a date B.C., so Julius Caesar died in 44 B.C.

Calculator Practice

p. 353. To enter the number -12, input 12 $\boxed{+/-}$.

To find the sum $(-1) + 7$, enter

1 $\boxed{+/-}$ + 7 = . The answer is 6.

To add $-6.002 + (-9.37) + (-0.22)$, input

6.002 $\boxed{+/-}$ + 9.37 $\boxed{+/-}$ + 0.22 $\boxed{+/-}$ =

The answer is -15.592.

Exercises

1. $|6| = 6$ and $|-5| = 5$ Subtract the smaller from the larger: $6 - 5 = 1$

Because 6 has the larger absolute value and its sign is positive, the sum is also positive: $6 + (-5) = 1$

Visual check: Move 5 units *left*.

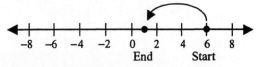

3. $|-2| = 2$ and $|5| = 5$

Subtract the smaller from the larger: $5 - 2 = 3$

Because 5 has the larger absolute value and its sign is positive, the sum is also positive: $-2 + 5 = 3$

Visual check: Move 5 units *right*.

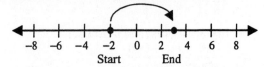

5. Any number plus 0 equals that number, so $7 + 0 = 7$.

Visual check: Adding 0 is equivalent to staying in the same place.

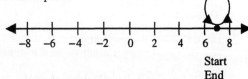

7. .A number added to its opposite always gives 0, so $7 + (-7) = 0$.

Visual check: You move 7 units right to get to $+7$. Adding -7 moves you 7 units left, back to the origin.

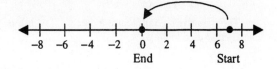

9. $|67| = 67$ and $|-67| = 67$

Subtract the absolute values: $67 - 67 = 0$

$67 + (-67) = 0$

11. $|-10| = 10$ and $|5| = 5$

Subtract the smaller from the larger: $10 - 5 = 5$

Because -10 has the larger absolute value and its sign is negative, the sum is also negative: $-10 + 5 = -5$

13. $|-100| = 100$ and $|300| = 300$

Subtract the smaller from the larger:

$300 - 100 = 200$

Because 300 has the larger absolute value and its sign is positive, the sum is also positive: $-100 + 300 = 200$

15. $|8| = 8$ and $|-2| = 2$

Subtract the smaller from the larger: $8 - 2 = 6$

Because 8 has the larger absolute value and its sign is positive, the sum is also positive: $8 + (-2) = 6$

17. $|60| = 60$ and $|-90| = 90$

Subtract the smaller from the larger: $90 - 60 = 30$

Because -90 has the larger absolute value and its sign is negative, the sum is also negative: $60 + (-90) = -30$

19. $|-7| = 7$ and $|2| = 2$

Subtract the smaller from the larger: $7 - 2 = 5$

Because -7 has the larger absolute value and its sign is negative, the sum is also negative: $-7 + 2 = -5$

21. Any number plus 0 equals that number, so $-7 + 0 = -7$.

23. A number added to its opposite always gives 0, so $-2 + 2 = 0$.

25. $|5.2| = 5.2$ and $|-0.3| = 0.3$

Subtract the smaller from the larger: $5.2 - 0.3 = 4.9$

Because 5.2 has the larger absolute value and its sign is positive, the sum is also positive: $5.2 + (-0.3) = 4.9$

27. $|-0.2| = 0.2$ and $|0.3| = 0.3$

Subtract the smaller from the larger: $0.3 - 0.2 = 0.1$

Because 5.2 has the larger absolute value and its sign is positive, the sum is also positive: $-0.2 + 0.3 = 0.1$

29. $|60| = 60$ and $|-0.5| = 0.5$

Subtract the smaller from the larger: $60 - 0.5 = 59.5$

Because 60 has the larger absolute value and its sign is positive, the sum is also positive:

$60 + (-0.5) = 59.5$

31. $|-9.8| = 9.8$ and $|3.9| = 3.9$

Subtract the smaller from the larger: $9.8 - 3.9 = 5.9$

Because -9.8 has the larger absolute value and its sign is negative, the sum is also negative:

$-9.8 + 3.9 = -5.9$

33. $|-5.6| = 5.6$ and $|-8.9| = 8.9$

Add the absolute values: $5.6 + 8.9 = 14.5$

Because both numbers are negative, their sum is negative: $(-5.6) + (-8.9) = -14.5$

35. $\left|-\dfrac{1}{2}\right| = \dfrac{1}{2}$ and $\left|-5\dfrac{1}{2}\right| = 5\dfrac{1}{2}$

Add the absolute values: $\dfrac{1}{2} + 5\dfrac{1}{2} = 6$

Because both numbers are negative, their sum is

negative: $\left(-\dfrac{1}{2}\right) + \left(-5\dfrac{1}{2}\right) = -6$

37. $\left|-1\dfrac{1}{5}\right| = 1\dfrac{1}{5}$ and $\left|\dfrac{3}{5}\right| = \dfrac{3}{5}$

Subtract the smaller from the larger: $1\dfrac{1}{5} - \dfrac{3}{5} = \dfrac{3}{5}$

Because $-1\dfrac{3}{5}$ has the larger absolute value and its

sign is negative, the sum is also negative:

$-1\dfrac{3}{5} + \dfrac{3}{5} = -\dfrac{3}{5}$

39. $\left|-\dfrac{2}{5}\right| = \dfrac{2}{5}$ and $|2| = 2$

Subtract the smaller from the larger: $2 - \dfrac{2}{5} = 1\dfrac{3}{5}$

Because 2 has the larger absolute value and its sign

is positive, the sum is also positive: $-\dfrac{2}{5} + 2 = 1\dfrac{3}{5}$

41. $\left|\dfrac{1}{2}\right| = \dfrac{1}{2}$ and $\left|-1\dfrac{3}{5}\right| = 1\dfrac{3}{5}$

Subtract the smaller from the larger: $1\dfrac{3}{5} - \dfrac{1}{2} = 1\dfrac{1}{10}$

Because $-1\dfrac{3}{5}$ has the larger absolute value and its

sign is negative, the sum is also negative:

$\dfrac{1}{2} + \left(-1\dfrac{3}{5}\right) = -1\dfrac{1}{10}$

43. $(-24) + 20 + (-98)$
$= 20 + (-24) + (-98)$
$= 20 + \quad (-122)$
$= -102$

45. $12 + (-7) + (-12) + 7$
$= 12 + 7 + (-7) + (-12)$
$= \quad 19 \quad + \quad (-19)$
$= 0$

47. $(-7) + 12 + 0 + (-7)$
$= 12 + 0 + (-7) + (-7)$
$= \quad 12 \quad + \quad -14$
$= -2$

49. $-0.3 + (-2.6) + (-4)$
$= \quad -2.9 \quad + (-4)$
$= -6.9$

51. $-12 + 7.58 + 12$
$= -12 + 12 + 7.58$ Pair the opposites.
$= \quad 0 \quad + 7.58$
$= 7.58$

53. $8.756 + (-9.08) + (-4.59)$
$= 8.756 + \quad (-13.67)$
$= -4.914$

55. $-3.001 + (-0.59) + 8$
$= \quad -3.591 \quad + 8$
$= 4.409$

57. $-3 + 10 = 7$
The temperature after the rise was $+7°$.

59. $197 + 50 + (-70)$
$= \quad 247 \quad + (-70)$
$= 177$
You had $177 left in your account.

61. $3 + (-4) = -1$
The total charge is -1.

63. $-10 + 4 = -6$
Your divorce was 6 years ago.

65. $5 + (-7) = -2$
The change in position was a loss of 2 yd.

67. $1,050.75 + (-1,000) + 2,177.85 + (-1,000)$
$= 1,228.60$
You will have $1,228.60 left, which is enough to buy the used car.

7.3   Subtracting Signed Numbers

Practice

1. Find the difference: $-4 - (-2)$
Change the subtraction to addition and change -2 to $+2$:
$$-4 - (-2)$$
$$\updownarrow \quad \updownarrow$$
$$= -4 + (+2)$$
$$= -4 + 2 = -2$$

2. Subtract: $9 - (-9)$

Negative 9   Positive 9
$$\downarrow \qquad\qquad \downarrow$$
$$9 - (-9) = 9 + (+9) = +18, \text{ or } 18$$
$$\uparrow \qquad\qquad \uparrow$$
Subtract   Add

3. Find the difference: $-9 - 12.1$
$$-9 - 12.1 = -9 + (-12.1) = -21.1$$

4. $\underbrace{-2 - 3} + (-5)$
$$= \underbrace{-5 \quad + (-5)}$$
$$= \quad -10$$

5. To find how much warmer the second temperature is, we need to find the difference between the second temperature and the first.
$$134 - (-80) = 134 + (+80) = 214$$
The California temperature is 214°F warmer than the Alaska temperature.

Exercises

1. $23 - 8 = 23 + (-8) = 15$

3. $-34 - 7 = -34 + (-7) = -41$

5. $-9 - 5 = -9 + (-5) = -14$

7. $42 - (-2) = 42 + (+2) = 44$

9. $50 - 75 = 50 + (-75) = -25$

11. $20 - (-1) = 20 + (+1) = 21$

13. $3 - (-3) = 3 + (+3) = 6$

15. $0 - 38 = 0 + (-38) = -38$

17. $-13 - 13 = -13 + (-13) = -26$

19. $13 - (-13) = 13 + (+13) = 26$

21. $0 - 1 = 0 + (-1) = -1$

23. $800 - (-200) = 800 + (+200) = 1,000$

25. $7 - 8.52 = 7 + (-8.52) = -1.52$

27. $9.2 - (-0.5) = 9.2 + (+0.5) = 9.7$

29. $-5.2 - (-5.2) = -5.2 + (+5.2) = 0$

31. $8.6 - (-1.9) = 8.6 + (+1.9) = 10.5$

33. $-10 - (-9.5) = -10 + (+9.5) = -0.5$

35. $4\frac{1}{2} - 9\frac{1}{2} = 4\frac{1}{2} + \left(-9\frac{1}{2}\right) = -5$

37. $10 - 2\frac{1}{4} = 10 + \left(-2\frac{1}{4}\right) = 7\frac{3}{4}$

39. $-7 - \frac{1}{4} = -7 + \left(-\frac{1}{4}\right) = -7\frac{1}{4}$

41. $5\frac{3}{4} - \left(-1\frac{1}{2}\right) = 5\frac{3}{4} + \left(+1\frac{1}{2}\right) = 7\frac{1}{4}$

43. $\underbrace{4 + (-6)} - (-9)$
$$= -2 \quad - (-9)$$
$$= -2 + (+9)$$
$$= 7$$

45. $7 - 7 + (-5)$
$$= \underbrace{7 + (-7)} + (-5)$$
$$= \quad 0 \quad + (-5)$$
$$= -5$$

47. $\underbrace{-8 + (-4)} - 9 + 7$
$$= -12 \quad - 9 + 7$$
$$= \underbrace{-12 + (-9)} + 7$$
$$= \quad -21 \quad + 7$$
$$= -14$$

49. $7.043 - 9.002 - 1.883$
$$= \underbrace{7.043 + (-9.002)} - 1.883$$
$$= \quad -1.959 \quad + (-1.883)$$
$$= -3.842$$

51. $\underbrace{-8.722 + (-3.913)} - 3.86$
$$= \quad -12.635 \quad + (-3.86)$$
$$= -16.495$$

53. $700 - (-300) = 700 + (+300) = 1,000$
The airplanes are 1,000 mi apart.

55. $-1,000 - 1,789 = -1,000 + (-1,789) = -2,789$
Ethiopia is 2,789 yr older than the United States.

57. $-7,301 - 367,120 = -7,301 + (+367,120) = 359,819$
The losses were reduced by $359,819.

59. $\frac{1}{8} - \frac{1}{2} = \frac{1}{8} + \left(-\frac{1}{2}\right) = -\frac{3}{8}$

The overall change in value was a drop of $\$\frac{3}{8}$.

7.4   **Multiplying Signed Numbers**

Practice

1. Compute: $-8(-4)$
   Find the absolute values.

   $|-8| = 8$ and $|-4| = 4$

   Multiply the absolute values.

   $8 \cdot 4 = 32$

   The factors have the same sign (negative) so the product is positive.

   $-8(-4) = 32$

2. Multiply: $(-5)(2)$
   Multiply from left to right:

   $|-5| = 5$ and $|2| = 2$

   The factors have different signs so the product is negative.

   $(-5)(2) = -10$

3. Evaluate $(-1)^2$.

   $(-1)^2$ is the same as $(-1)(-1)$. The product of two negative factors is positive, so $(-1)^2 = 1$.

4. Evaluate -1^2.

   Since there are no parentheses around the -1, compute the power first, then take the negative.

   $-1^2 = -(1)(1) = -1$.

5. Multiply: $-8(-2)(-3)$
   Multiply from left to right.

   $\underbrace{-8(-2)}(-3)$

   $= \underbrace{16 \cdot (-3)}$

   $= -48$

6. Multiply: $(-1.4)(-0.6)$
   Multiply the absolute values.

   $(1.4) \cdot (0.6) = 0.84$

   Since the numbers have different signs, the product is positive.

   $(-1.4)(-0.6) = 0.84$

7. Calculate: $-4 + (-2)^2 \cdot 3$
   First square, then multiply, then divide.

   $-4 + (-2)^2 \cdot 3$

   $= -4 + (4) \cdot 3$

   $= -4 + 12$

   $= 8$

8. To find the depth of the submarine after 4 min, compute $4(-50)$, which is -200. The submarine will sink 200 m in 4 min, so it will not reach the ocean floor which is 300 m below its starting point.

Exercises

1. $|2| = 2$ and $|-5| = 5$

   $2 \cdot 5 = 10$

   The factors have different signs so the product is negative.

   $(2)(-5) = -10$

3. $|-80| = 80$ and $|90| = 90$

   $80 \cdot 90 = 7,200$

   The factors have different signs so the product is negative.

   $-80 \cdot 90 = -7,200$

5. $|-5| = 5$

   $5 \cdot 5 = 25$

   The factors have the same sign so the product is positive.

   $-5 \cdot (-5) = 25$

7. $|34| = 34$ and $|-9| = 9$

   $34 \cdot 9 = 306$

   The factors have the same sign so the product is positive.

   $-34(-9) = 306$

9. $|2| = 2$ and $|-8| = 8$

   $2 \cdot 8 = 16$

   The factors have different signs so the product is negative.

   $2 \cdot (-8) = -16$

11. $|907| = 907$ and $|-9| = 9$

    $907 \cdot 9 = 8,163$

    The factors have different signs so the product is negative.

    $907 \cdot (-9) = -8,163$

13. $|5| = 5$ and $|-8| = 8$

    $5 \cdot 8 = 40$

    The factors have different signs so the product is negative.

    $5(-8) = -40$

15. $|-88| = 88$ and $|2| = 2$

$88 \cdot 2 = 176$

The factors have different signs so the product is negative.

$-88 \cdot 2 = -176$

17. $|-200| = 200$ and $|-4| = 4$

$200 \cdot 4 = 800$

The factors have the same sign so the product is positive.

$(-200)(-4) = 800$

19. $|4| = 4$ and $|3| = 3$

$4 \cdot 3 = 12$

The factors have the same sign so the product is positive.

$4 \cdot 3 = 12$

21. $|-2| = 2$ and $|5| = 5$

$2 \cdot 5 = 10$

The factors have different signs so the product is negative.

$-2 \cdot 5 = -10$

23. $|2.5| = 2.5$ and $|-2| = 2$

$(2.5)(2) = 5$

The factors have different signs so the product is negative.

$(2.5)(-2) = -5$

25. $|0.2| = 0.2$ and $|-50| = 50$

$(0.2)(50) = 10$

The factors have different signs so the product is negative.

$(0.2)(-50) = -10$

27. $|-1.2| = 1.2$ and $|-4.6| = 4.6$

$(1.2)(4.6) = 5.52$

The factors have the same sign so the product is positive.

$(-1.2)(-4.6) = 5.52$

29. $|5| = 5$ and $|-1.6| = 1.6$

$(5)(1.6) = 8$

The factors have different signs so the product is negative.

$(5)(-1.6) = -8$

31. $\left|-\dfrac{1}{3}\right| = \dfrac{1}{3}$ and $\left|\dfrac{5}{9}\right| = \dfrac{5}{9}$

$\dfrac{1}{3} \cdot \dfrac{5}{9} = \dfrac{5}{27}$

The factors have different signs so the product is negative.

$-\dfrac{1}{3} \cdot \dfrac{5}{9} = -\dfrac{5}{27}$

33. $\left|1\dfrac{1}{4}\right| = 1\dfrac{1}{4}$ and $\left|-\dfrac{2}{3}\right| = \dfrac{2}{3}$

$\left(1\dfrac{1}{4}\right)\left(\dfrac{2}{3}\right) = \left(\dfrac{5}{\cancel{4}_{2}}\right)\left(\dfrac{\cancel{2}^{1}}{3}\right) = \dfrac{5}{6}$

The factors have different signs so the product is negative.

$1\dfrac{1}{4}\left(-\dfrac{2}{3}\right) = -\dfrac{5}{6}$

35. $-5^2 = -(5)(5) = -25$

37. $(-100)^2 = (-100)(-100) = 10,000$

39. $(-0.5)^2 = (-0.5)(-0.5) = 0.25$

41. $\left(-\dfrac{3}{4}\right)^2 = \left(-\dfrac{3}{4}\right)\left(-\dfrac{3}{4}\right) = \dfrac{9}{16}$

43. $(-1)^3 = \underbrace{(-1)(-1)}(-1)$

$\qquad = \underbrace{1 \times (-1)}$

$\qquad = -1$

45. $\underbrace{(9)(12)}(-2)$

$= \underbrace{(108)(-2)}$

-216

47. Multiply from left to right.

$(5)(-2)(-1)(3)(-2)$

$= (-10)(-1)(3)(-2)$

$= (10)(3)(-2)$

$= (30)(-2)$

$= -60$

49. Any product with a 0 factor will be 0.

$(-5)(-3)(0) = 0$

51. $10 \cdot \left(-\dfrac{1}{2}\right) \cdot (-1)$

$= \underbrace{(-5)(-1)}$

$= 5$

53. $\dfrac{4}{5}\cdot\left(-\dfrac{8}{9}\right)\cdot\dfrac{1}{3}$

$=\left(-\dfrac{32}{45}\right)\cdot\dfrac{1}{3}$

$=-\dfrac{32}{135}$

55. $(-0.308)^2 = (-0.308)(-0.308) = 0.094864$

57. $\underbrace{(-2.64)(0.03)}(-1.85)$
$= (-0.0792)(-1.85)$
$= 0.14652$

59. $(-3)^2 + (-4) = 9 + (-4) = 5$

61. $-7 + 3(-3) - 10 = -7 + (-9) + (-10)$
$= -16 + (-10) = -26$

63. $-3(4) + (-6)(-2) = -12 + 12 = 0$

65. $2(-8) + 3(-4) = (-16) + (-12) = -28$

67. $(-0.5)^2 + 1^2 = 0.25 + 1 = 1.25$

69. $\dfrac{3}{5}(-10) - 6 = -6 - 6 = -12$

71. $-5\cdot(-3 + 1.2) = -5\cdot(-1.8) = 9$

73.

Input	Output
a. −2	$(-3)(-2) - 1 = 5$
b. −1	$(-3)(-1) - 1 = 2$
c. 0	$(-3)(0) - 1 = -1$
d. +1	$(-3)(+1) - 1 = -4$
e. +2	$(-3)(+2) - 1 = -7$

75. $6\left(-\dfrac{1}{4}\right) = -\dfrac{6}{4} = -\dfrac{3}{2}$ or $-1\dfrac{1}{2}$

The price fell $\$1\dfrac{1}{2}$.

77. $40 + 3(-3) = 40 + (-9) = 31$
The actual temperature was 31°F, one degree below freezing.

79. $\dfrac{1}{2}(-32)(2)^2 = \dfrac{1}{2}(-32)(4) = (-16)(4) = -64$
The object's height is 64 ft below the point of release.

81. $3(+2) + 2(+1) + 4(-1) + 1(0) = 6 + 2 - 4 + 0$
$= 8 - 4 + 0 = 4$
Your team scored 4 more points than its opponents.

7.5 Dividing Signed Numbers

Practice

1. Divide: $-24 \div (-2)$
Find the absolute values.
$|-24| = 24$ and $|-2| = 2$
Divide the absolute values.
$24 \div 2 = 12$
The numbers have the same sign (negative) so the quotient is positive.
$-12 \div (-2) = 12$

2. Simplify: $\dfrac{9}{-15}$
Find the absolute values.
$|9| = 9$ and $|-15| = 15$
Express the quotient of absolute values as a fraction.
$\dfrac{9}{15} = \dfrac{3}{5}$
Because the numbers have different signs, the answer is negative.
$\dfrac{9}{-15} = -\dfrac{3}{5}$

3. Divide: $-1.4 \div 5$
Find the absolute values.
$|-1.4| = 1.4$ and $|5| = 5$
Divide the absolute values.
$1.4 \div 5 = 0.28$
Because the numbers have different signs, the answer is negative.
$-1.4 \div 5 = -0.28$

4. Find the quotient: $-\dfrac{1}{2} \div 3$
Divide the absolute values of $-\dfrac{1}{2}$ and 3.
$\dfrac{1}{2} \div 3 = \dfrac{1}{2} \div \dfrac{3}{1} = \dfrac{1}{2} \times \dfrac{1}{3} = \dfrac{1}{6}$
Since the numbers have different signs, the quotient is negative.
$-\dfrac{1}{2} \div 3 = -\dfrac{1}{6}$

5. To find what each partner owes, compute $-16,480 \div 3$, which is $-5,493.33$. Each partner owes $\$5,493.33$.

6. To find the average daily change in temperature, we need to average the five numbers 2, 1, −1, 1, and −3.

$$\frac{2+1+(-1)+1+(-3)}{4} = \frac{4+(-4)}{4} = \frac{0}{4} = 0$$

The average daily change in temperature was 0°.

Exercises

1. $\left|-20\right| = 20$ and $\left|-4\right| = 4$

   $20 \div 4 = 5$

   The numbers have the same sign so
   the quotient is positive.

   $-20 \div (-4) = 5$

3. 0 divided by any nonzero number is 0.

   $0 \div (-5) = 0$

5. $\left|10\right| = 10$ and $\left|-2\right| = 2$

   $10 \div 2 = 5$

   The numbers have different signs so
   the quotient is negative.

   $10 \div (-2) = -5$

7. $\left|16\right| = 16$ and $\left|-8\right| = 8$

   $16 \div 8 = 2$

   The numbers have different signs so
   the quotient is negative.

   $16 \div (-8) = -2$

9. $\left|-250\right| = 250$ and $\left|-10\right| = 10$

   $250 \div 10 = 25$

   The numbers have the same sign so
   the quotient is positive.

   $-250 \div (-10) = 25$

11. $\left|-200\right| = 200$ and $\left|8\right| = 8$

    $200 \div 8 = 25$

    The numbers have different signs so
    the quotient is negative.

    $-200 \div 8 = -25$

13. $\left|-35\right| = 35$ and $\left|-5\right| = 5$

    $35 \div 5 = 7$

    The numbers have the same sign so
    the quotient is positive.

    $-35 \div (-5) = 7$

15. $\left|6\right| = 6$ and $\left|-3\right| = 3$

    $6 \div 3 = 2$

    The numbers have different signs so
    the quotient is negative.

    $6 \div (-3) = -2$

17. $\left|-17\right| = 17$ and $\left|-1\right| = 1$

    $17 \div 1 = 17$

    The numbers have the same sign so
    the quotient is positive.

    $-17 \div (-1) = 17$

19. $\left|30\right| = 30$ and $\left|-6\right| = 6$

    $30 \div 6 = 5$

    The numbers have different signs so
    the quotient is negative.

    $30 \div (-6) = -5$

21. $\left|-\dfrac{2}{3}\right| = \dfrac{2}{3}$ and $\left|\dfrac{4}{5}\right| = \dfrac{4}{5}$

    $$\frac{2}{3} \div \frac{4}{5} = \frac{\overset{1}{\cancel{2}}}{3} \times \frac{5}{\underset{2}{\cancel{4}}} = \frac{5}{6}$$

    The numbers have different signs so
    the quotient is negative.

    $$\left(-\frac{2}{3}\right) \div \frac{4}{5} = -\frac{5}{6}$$

23. $\left|7\right| = 7$ and $\left|-\dfrac{1}{3}\right| = \dfrac{1}{3}$

    $$7 \div \frac{1}{3} = \frac{7}{1} \times \frac{3}{1} = 21$$

    The numbers have different signs so
    the quotient is negative.

    $$7 \div \left(-\frac{1}{3}\right) = -21$$

25. $\left|-40\right| = 40$ and $\left|2\dfrac{1}{2}\right| = 2\dfrac{1}{2}$

    $$40 \div 2\frac{1}{2} = \frac{\overset{8}{\cancel{40}}}{1} \times \frac{2}{\underset{1}{\cancel{5}}} = 16$$

    The numbers have different signs so
    the quotient is negative.

    $$-40 \div 2\frac{1}{2} = -16$$

27. $\left|-1.5\right| = 1.5$ and $\left|5\right| = 5$

    $1.5 \div 5 = 0.3$

    The numbers have different signs so
    the quotient is negative.

    $-1.5 \div 5 = -0.3$

29. $|-4|=4$ and $|0.2|=0.2$

$4 \div 0.2 = 20$

The numbers have different signs so the quotient is negative.

$-4 \div 0.2 = -20$

31. $|-4.8|=4.8$ and $|0.3|=0.3$

$4.8 \div 0.3 = 16$

The numbers have different signs so the quotient is negative.

$-48 \div 0.3 = -16$

33. $|-15.1214|=15.1214$ and $|-2.45|=2.45$

$15.1214 \div 2.45 = 6.172$

The numbers have the same sign so the quotient is positive.

$(-15.1214) \div (-2.45) = 6.172$

35. $|-12.25|=12.25$ and $|3.5|=3.5$

$12.25 \div 3.5 = 3.5$

The numbers have different signs so the quotient is negative.

$-12.25 \div 3.5 = -3.5$

37. $|-1|=1$ and $|5|=5$

$\dfrac{1}{5}=\dfrac{1}{5}$

The numbers have different signs so the quotient is negative.

$\dfrac{-1}{5}=-\dfrac{1}{5}$

39. $|-11|=11$

$\dfrac{11}{11}=1$

The numbers have the same sign so the quotient is positive.

$\dfrac{-11}{-11}=1$

41. $|2|=2$ and $|-5|=5$

$\dfrac{2}{5}=\dfrac{2}{5}$

The numbers have different signs so the quotient is negative.

$\dfrac{2}{-5}=-\dfrac{2}{5}$

43. $|-11|=11$ and $|-2|=2$

$\dfrac{11}{2}=\dfrac{11}{2}$

The numbers have the same sign so the quotient is positive.

$\dfrac{-11}{-2}=\dfrac{11}{2}$ or $5\dfrac{1}{2}$

45. $|-17|=17$ and $|-4|=4$

$\dfrac{17}{4}=\dfrac{17}{4}$

The numbers have the same sign so the quotient is positive.

$\dfrac{-17}{-4}=\dfrac{17}{4}=4\dfrac{1}{4}$

47. $|-3|=3$ and $|-4|=4$

$\dfrac{3}{4}=\dfrac{3}{4}$

The numbers have the same sign so the quotient is positive.

$\dfrac{-3}{-4}=\dfrac{3}{4}$

49. $-8 \div (-2)(-2) = 4 \div (-2) = -2$

51. $(3-7)^2 \div (-4) = (-4)^2 \div (-4) = 16 \div (-4) = -4$

53. $\dfrac{2^2-(-6)}{2}=\dfrac{4-(-6)}{2}=\dfrac{10}{2}=5$

55. $\dfrac{2^2+(-6)}{-2}=\dfrac{4+(-6)}{-2}=\dfrac{-2}{-2}=1$

57. $\left(\dfrac{-8}{-2}\right)\left(\dfrac{8}{-2}\right)=(4)(-4)=-16$

59. $\dfrac{-9-(-3)}{2}=\dfrac{-6}{2}=-3$

61. $\dfrac{3(-0.2)^2}{-2}=\dfrac{3(0.04)}{-2}=\dfrac{0.12}{-2}=-0.06$

63. $(-15)+(-3)^2-2\cdot(-1)=-15+9-(-2)$

$=-15+9+(+2)=-6+2=-4$

65. $(-13-3)\div(-2-6)=(-16)\div(-8)=2$

67. $-49\div(-7)^2-4\cdot(-3)=-49\div49-(-12)$

$=-49\div49+(+12)=-1+12=11$

69. $-60,989\div10=-6,098.9$

The average annual change was a decrease of 6,098.9.

71. $-60,000 \div 12 = -5,000$
The average monthly expenses were $5,000.

73. $-7\frac{1}{2} \div 3 = -\frac{15}{2} \div 3 = -\frac{5}{2}$ or $-2\frac{1}{2}$

The average daily loss was $2\frac{1}{2}$ points.

75. $\frac{3+0-8-11+1}{5} = \frac{-15}{5} = -3$

The average high temperature was $-3°$, so your prediction was correct.

Review Exercises

1. The opposite of $+5$ is -5.

2. The opposite of -4 is 4.

3. The opposite of $-5\frac{1}{2}$ is $5\frac{1}{2}$.

4. The opposite of 10.1 is -10.1.

5. $|-8| = 8$ **6.** $|+2.5| = 2.5$

7. $\left|-1\frac{1}{5}\right| = 1\frac{1}{5}$ **8.** $|12| = 12$

For Exercises 9 through 12, the larger number is boxed.

9. -4 and $\boxed{-2\frac{1}{4}}$ **10.** $\boxed{9}$ and $-5\frac{1}{3}$

11. $\boxed{-8}$ and -22.5 **12.** -6.75 and $\boxed{2}$

13. $-8, -3.5, 8$ **14.** $-9.7, -6, 9$

15. $-2.9, -2\frac{1}{2}, 0$ **16.** $-4, -1\frac{1}{4}, 0$

17. $|-10| = 10$
Add the absolute values: $10 + 10 = 20$
The -10s are both negative so the sum is negative.
$-10 + (-10) = -20$

18. $|8| = 8$ and $|-10| = 10$
Subtract the absolute values. $10 - 8 = 2$
Because -10 has the larger absolute value, the sum is negative.
$8 + (-10) = -2$

19. $\left|-5\frac{1}{2}\right| = 5\frac{1}{2}$ and $|12| = 12$

Subtract the absolute values. $12 - 5\frac{1}{2} = 6\frac{1}{2}$

Because 12 has the larger absolute value, the sum is positive.
$-5\frac{1}{2} + 12 = 6\frac{1}{2}$

20. $\left|-\frac{1}{4}\right| = \frac{1}{4}$ and $\left|-\frac{3}{4}\right| = \frac{3}{4}$

Add the absolute values: $\frac{1}{4} + \frac{3}{4} = \frac{4}{4}$ or 1

Because the terms are both negative, the sum is negative.
$-\frac{1}{4} + \left(-\frac{3}{4}\right) = -1$

21. $|0.9| = 0.9$ and $|-5| = 5$
Subtract the absolute values. $15 - 0.9 = 4.1$
Because -5 has the larger absolute value, the sum is negative.
$0.9 + (-5) = -4.1$

22. $|-1.2| = 1.2$ and $|-0.8| = 0.8$
Add the absolute values: $1.2 + 0.8 = 2$
Because the terms are both negative, the sum is negative.
$-1.2 + (-0.8) = -2$

23. $-8 + 5\frac{1}{2} + (-4) = -8 + (-4) + 5\frac{1}{2}$
$= -12 + 5\frac{1}{2} = -6\frac{1}{2}$

24. $12 + (-12) + \left(-\frac{1}{4}\right) = 0 + \left(-\frac{1}{4}\right) = -\frac{1}{4}$

25. $-10 - (-10) = -10 + (+10) = 0$

26. $14 - (-14) = 14 + (+14) = 28$

27. $5 - 15 = 5 + (-15) = -10$

28. $-2 - 9 = -2 + (-9) = -11$

29. $2.5 - (-0.5) = 2.5 + (+0.5) = 3$

30. $-\frac{1}{8} - 4 = -\frac{1}{8} + (-4) = -4\frac{1}{8}$

31. $|-10| = 10$
$10 \cdot 10 = 100$
The factors have the same sign so the product is positive.
$-10 \times (-10) = 100$

32. $\left|-15\right|=15$ and $\left|3\right|=3$
$15\cdot 3=45$
The factors have different signs so
the product is negative.
$-15\times 3=-45$

33. $\dfrac{-2}{-3}\times\left(\dfrac{+10}{-11}\right)=\dfrac{2}{3}\times\left(-\dfrac{10}{11}\right)=-\dfrac{20}{33}$

34. $\left|3.5\right|=3.5$ and $\left|-2.1\right|=2.1$
$(3.5)(2.1)=7.35$
The factors have different signs so
the product is negative.
$(3.5)\times(-2.1)=-7.35$

35. $\left(\dfrac{1}{4}\right)^2=\left(\dfrac{1}{4}\right)\left(\dfrac{1}{4}\right)=\dfrac{1}{16}$

36. $(-3.1)^2=(-3.1)(-3.1)=9.61$

37. $\left|-14\right|=14$
$14\div 14=1$
The numbers have the same sign so
the quotient is positive.
$\dfrac{-14}{-14}=1$

38. $\left|20\right|=20$ and $\left|-4\right|=4$
$20\div 4=5$
The numbers have different signs so
the quotient is negative.
$20\div(-4)=-5$

39. $\left|-2\right|=2$ and $\left|8\right|=8$
$2\div 8=\dfrac{1}{4}$ or 0.25
The numbers have different signs so
the quotient is negative.
$-2\div 8=-\dfrac{1}{4}$ or -0.25

40. $\left|-5\right|=5$ and $\left|2\right|=2$
$5\div 2=\dfrac{5}{2}=2\dfrac{1}{2}$ or 2.5
The numbers have different
signs so the quotient is negative. $-5\div 2=-2.5$

41. $\left|-\dfrac{1}{8}\right|=\dfrac{1}{8}$ and $\left|-4\right|=14$
$\dfrac{1}{8}\div 4=\dfrac{1}{8}\cdot\dfrac{1}{4}=\dfrac{1}{32}$
The numbers have the same sign $-\dfrac{1}{8}\div(-4)=\dfrac{1}{32}$
so the quotient is positive.

42. $\left|15\right|=15$ and $\left|-0.3\right|=0.3$
$15\div 0.3=50$
The numbers have different signs so
the quotient is negative.
$15\div(-0.3)=-50$

43. $-8-(-3)+20=-8+(+3)+20=-5+20=15$

44. $12\cdot(-3)^2-(-6)=12\cdot 9-(-6)=108+(+6)=114$

45. $(-7+3)\cdot(-5)^2=(-4)\cdot(25)=-100$

46. $(20-30)\div(-10)=(-10)\div(-10)=1$

47. $\dfrac{(-9.1)(-0.6)}{2}=\dfrac{5.46}{2}=2.73$

48. $\dfrac{-8-5.1}{5}=\dfrac{-13.1}{5}=-2.62$

49. $10^2+\dfrac{-8-2}{2}=100+\dfrac{-10}{2}=100+(-5)=95$

50. $\dfrac{10}{2}-(5-9)^2=5-(-4)^2=5-16=-11$

51. $-1,027<-551$ and $-479<-256$, so the Chou
dynasty was in power throughout Confucius's
lifetime.

52. -500 is between -563 and -483, so Buddha was
alive in 500 B.C.

53. $200\cdot(-1.25)=-250$, so your total loss is $250.

54. $-4-3+1-1=-7$, so your total weight change was
a loss of 7 lb.

55. $83-(-2)=85$, so it was 85°F warmer in Honollulu.

56. $1000\div 5=200$, so each installment is $200.

57. $-650\div(-100)=6.5$, so the descent will take 6.5
min.

58. $1,687-(-323)=2,010$, so the books were written
2,010 years apart.

59. $\dfrac{2\cdot(20,000)+1\cdot(-10,000)}{3}=\dfrac{30,000}{3}=10,000$
The company had an average profit of $10,000 over
the three years.

60. $3\times(-30)=-90$, so you dove to a depth of 90 ft
below the surface.

61. $3\cdot(-1)+2\cdot(-2)+1\cdot(0)+2(+1)=-3-4+2=-5$
You are 5 strokes under par.

62. $-16\times 5^2+100\times 5=-16\times 25+500$
$=-400+500=100$
The object will be 100 ft above the point of release.

Posttest

1. -10 is to the left of -4 on the number line, so -10 is smaller.

2. $-\dfrac{1}{2}$

3. $-8 + 8 = 0$

4. $4.5 + (-5) = -0.5$

5. $42 - 91 = 42 + (-91) = -49$

6. $-12 - (-12) = -12 + (+12) = 0$

7. Different signs give a negative answer.
   $-23 \times 9 = -207$

8. Different signs give a negative answer.
   $-0.5 \times 0.2 = -0.1$

9. $(-12)^2 = (-12)(-12) = 144$

10. $\left(-\dfrac{1}{4}\right)^2 = \left(-\dfrac{1}{4}\right)\left(-\dfrac{1}{4}\right) = \dfrac{1}{16}$

11. Same signs give a positive answer.
    $-1.8 \div (-0.9) = 2$

12. Different signs give a negative answer.
    $-4 \div \dfrac{1}{2} = -\dfrac{4}{1} \times \dfrac{2}{1} = -8$

13. $-4 + 6 + (-7) + 9 = (-4) + (-7) + 6 + 9$
    $= -11 + 15 = 4$

14. $15 - (-7) + (-1) = 15 + (+7) + (-1)$
    $= 22 + (-1) = 21$

15. $-8 - 4^2 \times (-3) = -8 - 16 \times (-3) = -8 - (-48)$
    $= -8 + (+48) = 40$

16. $(2 - 8)^2 \div (-2) = (-6)^2 \div (-2) = 36 \div (-2) = -18$

17. -2 is less than 0, so a temperature of $-2°C$ is colder than $0°C$.

18. $-88\dfrac{1}{2} \div 15 = -\dfrac{\overset{59}{\cancel{177}}}{2} \times \dfrac{1}{\underset{5}{\cancel{15}}} = -\dfrac{59}{10} = -5\dfrac{9}{10}$

    Your weight change is $-5\dfrac{9}{10}$ lb/mo, or a loss of

    $5\dfrac{9}{10}$ lb per month.

19. $370 + 100 - 75 - 80 = 470 - 155 = 315$.
    Your new balance was +$315.

20. $-34.6 - (-100.98) = -34.6 + (+100.98) = 66.38$
    The boiling point is 66.38°C higher than the melting point.

Cumulative Review Exercises

1. $\underline{2},891 \approx 3,000$

2. A reasonable estimate is $90 \div 2$, or 45.

3. $(4)\left(2\dfrac{1}{2}\right) = \dfrac{\overset{2}{\cancel{4}}}{1} \times \dfrac{5}{\underset{1}{\cancel{2}}} = 10$

4. $8 + 2.1 + 3.9 = 10.1 + 3.9 = 14$

5. $16\dfrac{2}{3}\% = 16\dfrac{2}{3} \div 100 = \dfrac{\overset{1}{\cancel{50}}}{3} \times \dfrac{1}{\underset{2}{\cancel{100}}} = \dfrac{1}{6}$

6. What percent of 2.5 is 0.5?
   $$x \cdot 2.5 = 0.5$$
   $$2.5x = 0.5$$
   $$x = \dfrac{0.5}{2.5} = 0.2\underline{0} = 20\%$$

7. $\dfrac{1.4}{7} = \dfrac{13}{n}$
   $$7 \cdot 13 = 1.4 \cdot n$$
   $$91 = 1.4n$$
   $$\dfrac{91}{1.4} = n$$
   $$65 = n$$

8. $25 \cdot 11,000 = 275,000 \qquad 20 \cdot 15,000 = 300,000$
   $300,000 - 275,000 = 25,000$
   City University spent \$25,000 more.

9. $\dfrac{55}{5} = \dfrac{x}{15}$
   $$5x = 825$$
   $$x = 165$$
   $$165 \div 60 = 2\dfrac{45}{60} = 2\dfrac{3}{4} \text{ or } 2.75$$
   It will take you 2.75 hr.

10. $5,000 - 4,000 = 1,000$
    $$\dfrac{1,000}{4,000} = \dfrac{1}{4} = 0.2\underline{5} = 25\%$$

    This is a 25% increase in housing starts.

Chapter 8

BASIC STATISTICS

Pretest

1. Subtract the smallest number from the largest: $11 - 2 = 9$, so the range is 9.

2. The incomes listed in increasing order are
   $19,000 \quad $19,000 \quad $19,000 \quad $27,000 \quad $27,000 \quad $55,000
   Since the number of data values is even, the median is the average if the two middle values.
   $$\frac{$19,000 + $27,000}{2} = $23,000 \text{, so the median is}$$
   $23,000.

3. The sum of the absences for the 20 employees is 32.
   Their mean is $\frac{32}{20}$, which is equal to $\frac{8}{5}$, or 1.6.

4. In a non-leap year, 7 months have 31 days, 4 months have 30 days, and one month has 28 days, so the mode is 31.

5. Weight each grade by the number of credits and divide by the total number of credits.
   You got $3 + 2 + 4 + 1 = 10$ credits.

   For each subject, find grade $\times$ credits:

   $$\begin{aligned}
   \text{Spanish: } & 4 \times 3 = 12 \\
   \text{Music: } & 4 \times 2 = 8 \\
   \text{Social Science: } & 2 \times 4 = 8 \\
   \text{Phys. Ed.: } & 3 \times 1 = 3 \\
   \text{Total grade points: } & 31
   \end{aligned}$$

   $$GPA = \frac{31}{10} = 3.1$$

6. A female born in 1950 is expected to live 5.5 yr longer than a male born in 1950.

7. Car D needs about 173 ft to stop.

8. At age 50, there are more females (100) than males (approximately 97).

9. In September, Stock B was worth more than Stock A.

10. Earnings account for a larger percent of the respondents' income (30%) than does pensions (16%).

8.1 Introduction to Basic Statistics

Practice

1. The mean cost of the five textbooks was
   $$\frac{$25.70 + $31.70 + $12.50 + $42.20 + $31.75}{5} =$$
   $$\frac{$144.15}{5} = $28.83 \qquad $31.70 > $28.83$$
   The cost of the $31.70 book was $2.87 above the average.

2. Since the final counts as 2 quizzes, you need to multiply your score on the final by 2 and divide the sum of your scores by 2 + 3 or 5.
   $$\frac{2(90) + 3(80)}{5} = \frac{180 + 240}{5} = \frac{420}{5} = 84$$
   Your average was 84, just below the goal of 85.

3. a. Arrange the numbers in order from smallest to largest.

   Two middle numbers
   ↓
   2 2 5 5 6 |7 7| 8 8 9 10 10
   ↑
   $$\frac{7 + 7}{2} = 7$$
   The median is 7.

   b. Arrange the numbers in order from smallest to largest.

   The middle number
   ↓
   0 1 2 3 |4| 5 5 7 9
   The median is 4.

4. Arrange the prices in order.

   Two middle prices
   ↓
   $20.99 $35.98 |$57.49 $68.75| $125 $145.50
   ↑
   $$\frac{$57.49 + $68.75}{2} = $63.12$$

   a. The median is $63.12

   b. Since $69.95 > $63.12, the seventh book is priced above the median.

5. a. 2 occurs three times, 5 occurs twice, and 1 and 7 each occur once, so 2 is the mode.

   b. Both 9 and 4 occur three times and the other numbers occur fewer than 3 times, so there are two modes, 4 and 9.

6. Thirty states have a minimum age of 16, and the next most common minimum ages are 14 and 18, with five states each. The mode is 16.

7. The largest number on the list is 10, and the smallest is 3, so the range is $10 - 3$, or 7.

8. The range in the party described is $25 - 19$, or 6, so your previous party had a greater spread, with a range of 7.

Exercises

1.

Numbers	Mean	Median	Mode(s)	Range
a. 8, 2, 9, 4, 8	6.2	8	8	7
b. 3, 0, 0, 3, 10	3.2	3	0 and 3	10
c. 6.5, 9, 8.5, 6.5, 8.1	7.7	8.1	6.5	2.5
d. $3\frac{1}{2}, 3\frac{3}{4}, 4, 3\frac{1}{2}, 3\frac{1}{4}$	$3\frac{3}{5}$	$3\frac{1}{2}$	$3\frac{1}{2}$	$\frac{3}{4}$
e. 4, −2, −1, 0, −1	0	−1	−1	6

3. The sum of the six amounts is $73,600. Divide by 6 to find the mean, which is $12,266.67.

5. You got $2 + 4 + 2 + 3 + 1 = 12$ credits.

For each subject, find grade × credits:

College Skills: $4 \times 2 = 8$
World History: $3 \times 4 = 12$
Music: $2 \times 2 = 4$
History.: $4 \times 3 = 12$
Phys. Ed.: $3 \times 1 = 3$

Total grade points: 39

$$GPA = \frac{39}{12} = 3.25$$

7. The mean amount is $1,000,000 divided by 10, or $100,000. We can't compute the median without knowing the actual amounts given to each heir.

9. The average number of representatives per state is 435 divided by 50, or 8.7. A state with 10 representatives has above-average representation.

11. The number 7 appears 3 times, more than any other number in the list, so the mode is 7. To find the range, subtract the smallest number, 7, from the largest, 19. The range is 12.

13. a. $\dfrac{3+8+8+4+89+75+32+31+1}{9} = 27.8...$

                                ≈ 28.

   Since the diameters are given in thousands of miles, the mean diameter is approximately 28,000 mi.

   b. Arrange the diameters in order.

       The middle number
                      ↓
     1 3 4 8 [8] 31 32 75 89

   The median diameter is 8,000 mi.

   c. Only two planets have roughly the same diameter, Venus and Earth at 8,000 mi, so this is the mode.

   d. The difference in diameter between the largest planet (Jupiter) and the smallest (Pluto) is 89,000 mi − 1,000 mi, or 88,000 mi. This is the range.

15. a. Division, subtraction.

   b. $\dfrac{106 \text{ billion}}{226 \text{ million}} = 469.027$ $\dfrac{166 \text{ billion}}{248 \text{ million}} = 669.355$

      $669.355 - 469.027 = 200.328 \approx 200$

   c. A reasonable estimate for the first fraction would be $1,000 \div 2$, or 500, and for the second, $1,700 \div 2.5 = 680$. This gives 180 as an estimate for the increase.

8.2   Tables and Graphs

Practice

1. a. No, the weight room is not open at 3 P.M. on Fridays.

   b. Both the pool and weight room are open for less time on Fridays, but the gym is open for the same length of time on all days.

   c. The gym is open and the pool closed on Mondays from 2 to 4 P.M. and 7:45 to 8 P.M.

   d. Yes, the gym stays open without interruption.

2. a. The S&H charges are $4.95.

   b. You must pay $5.95.

   c. The S&H charges total $5.45.

3. a. The decade ending in 1990.

   b. 4 to 1

   c. One possible answer: The number of fatalities as a result of hurricanes in the United States declined by 7,975 from 1910 to 1990.

4. a. Each airplane represents 200,000 takeoffs and landings.

b. Dallas/Ft. Worth had about 700,000 takeoffs and landings, and Haneda had 200,000. Therefore Dallas/Ft. Worth had about 500,000 more takeoffs and landings than Haneda.

c. Los Angeles had 600,000 takeoffs and landings and Chicago had 800,000.

$$\frac{600,000}{800,000} = \frac{3}{4}$$

Therefore Los Angeles had about 75% as many takeoffs and landings as Chicago.

5. a. Approximately 2,000 more trucks and buses were sold in March than in February.

b. About 5,000 more passenger cars than trucks were sold in January.

6. a. On Wednesday a share was worth about $32.50.

b. Between Wednesday and Thursday the value of a share declined by about $1.50.

c. From Monday to Friday, the value of a share increased by about $1.50.

7. a. On May 12, about 30% of the public supported Cardoso.

b. The popularity difference between Cardoso and da Silva was greatest on September 1.

c. During the period from June 1 to July 1 support shifted from da Silva to Cardoso.

8. a. U.S. citizens invested $364,000,000,000 in Europe.

b. $283 billion − $197 billion = $86 billion

Investments in the Western Hemisphere exceeded investments in Other by $86,000,000,000.

c. The ratio of investments in Canada to investments in Japan was $\frac{132}{92}$, or $\frac{33}{23}$.

Exercises

1. a. Since the areas in the table are given in thousands of square miles, the area of Australia is 2,940,000 sq mi, which is more than 1 million sq mi.

b. $\frac{840}{290} \approx \frac{84}{30} = \frac{14}{5} = 2.8$

Greenland is about 2.8 times as large as Borneo.

3. a. In 1980, the average age of a groom was 24.7 years old.

b. $25.9 - 21.9 = 4$

In 1900 the difference between the average age of a groom and the average age of a bride was 4 yr.

c. $21.9 - 21.5 = 0.4$

The 1900 bride was 0.4 years older than the 1940 bride, on average.

d. In all three years, grooms were, on average, older than brides.

5. a. A price of $15.75 is in the $1–$20 row. Look in 300 shares column to find the commission, which is $60.

b. A price of $30 is in the >$20 row. The number in this row in the 500 column is $100.

c. Selling the shares in a single lot is cheaper. If you sell 400 at one time, you will pay either $70 or $90 in commission, whereas two deals of 200 shares will cost you either $100 or $120.

7. a. 8% of state governors were women.

b. 11% of members of the House were women; as a fraction this is $\frac{11}{100}$.

c. Since the Senate has 100 members and 7% were women, there were 7 women senators.

9. a. Two icons represent $2 \times 12,000$ or 24,000 households, so about 24,000 households had phones in 1950.

b. The pictograph for 1960 looks like about $2\frac{1}{2}$ telephones, which corresponds to $2\frac{1}{2} \times 12,000$ or 30,000 telephones.

c. There are four icons for the year 1980, so this is the year in which households had 48,000 telephones.

11. a. In January there was between 300,000 and 350,000 gallons in the reservoir, so there was less than 400,000 gallons for the whole month of January.

b. The lowest point on the graph is for the month of September, so this is the month in which the reservoir contained the least water.

c. The highest point on the graph is for May, so in May the reservoir came closest to overflowing, though it was still about 150,000 gallons from full capacity.

13. a. The child's vocabulary was larger than the chimp's for the first time at approximately 13 months.

b. At 15 months the child understood about 55 words and the chimp about 35, so the child knew approximately 20 more words.

15. a. According to the graph, 3¢ of each dollar went for environmental protection.

b. Education and higher education accounted for 23¢ of each dollar, or 23% of the city's expenses, which is nearly 25%.

Review Exercises

1.

Numbers	Mean	Median	Mode(s)	Range
a. 6, 7, 4, 10, 4, 5, 6, 8, 7, 4, 5	6	6	4	6
b. 1, 3, 4, 4, 2, 3, 1, 4, 5, 1	2.8	3	1 and 4	4

2. a. The median age for the presidents is 83 (Jefferson); for their wives the median age is 70 (Martha Washington). So using the median as the average, the husbands lived longer than the wives.
   b. The difference between the medians is 13 yr, so the husbands on average lived 13 yr longer.

3. a. Half of the people were younger than 32.9 and half were older.
   b. Answers will vary.

4. The range is 8.6 fl oz − 6.9 fl oz , or 1.7 fl oz.

5. The sum of the ten counts of paying customers is 10,000, so the average number of paying customers was 1,000, and the show made a profit.

6. a. To find games played, add games won and games lost. Milwaukee has played 128 games.
   b. Winning percentages are in the Pct. column. Detroit has the highest winning percentage for this season.
   c. Milwaukee has won 8 of its last 10 games, more than any other team, so its wining percentage of .800 is the highest for the last 10 games.
   d. Cleveland's total losses this season are given as 80, but if you add losses at home to losses away, you get 78.

7. a. Rounding to the nearest 10,000 tons, Baton Rouge handled 49,340,000 tons of domestic cargo.
   b. Valdez, Alaska, handled the least foreign cargo, with a total of 39,787 tons.
   c. Subtract and then round.
   $$100,252,774 - 83,082,893 = 17,169,881$$
   $$\approx 17,170,000$$
   The Port of South Louisiana handled about 17,170,000 more domestic tons than New York.
   d. All of the ports except Houston handled more domestic than foreign cargo.

8. a. In 1990 there were 21 theaters.
   b. Every 10 years the number of theaters has increased. Since 1970, the number has increased

by 3 theaters every ten years.
   c. Adding 3 to the total in 2000 gives a prediction of 27 for 2010.

9. a. Combining the pictures for Jan, Feb and Mar, we get six full missiles and about an additional half of a missile, which corresponds to about 65 launches.
   b. There were the most launches in February (30).
   c. The number of launches peaked in February and then declined.

10. a. The tick marks halfway between the numbered vertical grid lines mark the odd run numbers. On run number 3 the rat takes 10 min.
   b. On the tenth run the rat's time is about 3 min. With practice, the rat ran through the maze more quickly.

11. a. 10% of immigrants came from Europe.
   b. Yes; 37% of immigrants came from Asia, which is more than $\frac{1}{3}$, or $33\frac{1}{3}$%.
   c. Since about half of the immigrants came from the Americas and there were 7 million total immigrants, about 3.5 million immigrants came from the Americas.

12. a. In 1950, New York City had approximately 8 million people.
   b. In 1990 the rest of the state had about 10 million people and New York City had about 7 million, so the ratio was approximately $\frac{10}{7}$.
   c. Since 1940, the population of New York City stayed almost constant at 8 million until the period between 1970 and 1980 when it fell by approximately 1 million and then rebounded. Over the same time period (1940–1990), the population for the rest of the state increased from 6 million to 10 million.

13. a. At 40% of the total, paper is the largest type of trash.
   b. Glass is 7% or $\frac{7}{100}$ of trash.
   c. Plastic and metal together make up 17% of trash.

Posttest

1. There are three 5's and at most two of any other value, so the mode is 5.

2. The sum of the 10 sample values is 59, so the mean is 5.9 ppm. This is below the allowable maximum of 6 ppm, so the car passed the test.

3. The largest salary was \$25K and the smallest was \$9K, so the range was \$25K − \$9K or \$16,000.

4. When you arrange the unemployment numbers in order, there are two middle numbers, 4 million and 7 million. The median is their average, or 5,500,000.

5. You got $4 + 1 + 2 + 1 = 8$ credits.

   For each subject, find grade × credits:

   English Composition: $4 \times 4 = 16$
   Freshman Orientation: $4 \times 1 = 4$
   College Skills: $2 \times 2 = 4$
   Physical Education.: $3 \times 1 = 3$
   Total grade points: 27

   $$\text{GPA} = \frac{27}{8} = 3.375$$

6. $\$23.37 - \$15.33 = \$7.04$
   The L.I.R.R conductor's hourly wage is \$7.04 more than the hourly wage of the Metro-North bartender.

7. Approximately 3,000 students were enrolled during the summer quarter.

8. About 2 million 20-year-olds and about 250,000 30-year-olds lived with their parents. The difference is $2,000,000 - 250,000$, or 1,750,000.

9. Your total expenses were $\$550 + \$325 + \$125$ or \$1,000. The fraction that went to paying airfare was $\dfrac{550}{1,000}$, or $\dfrac{11}{20}$.

10. 1961–1975; during this period U.S. scientists received approximately 40 Nobel Prizes and U.K. scientists received approximately 20.

6. $x - 7\dfrac{1}{4} = 10$

   $x - 7\dfrac{1}{4} + 7\dfrac{1}{4} = 10 + 7\dfrac{1}{4}$

   $x = 17\dfrac{1}{4}$

7. $\dfrac{7}{10} = \dfrac{n}{30}$
   $10 \cdot n = 7 \cdot 30$
   $10n = 210$
   $n = 21$

8. If you're using this book, the current date, rounded to the nearest thousand, is 2000 A.D. The Great Pyramid of Khufu was built, to the nearest thousand years, in 3000 B.C.
   $2,000 - (-3,000) = 2,000 + (+3,000) = 5,000$
   The pyramid was built 5,000 yr ago.

9. $\dfrac{2\frac{1}{2} \text{ million}}{1 \text{ million}} = \dfrac{2.5}{1} = 2.5 = 250\%$

10. 31% preferred the airport and 17% preferred the chemical plant, a difference of 16%; 16% of 400 is

   $$\dfrac{16}{\cancel{100}_{1}} \times \dfrac{\cancel{400}^{4}}{1} = 64.$$ Therefore, 64 more scientists

   preferred living near the airport.

Cumulative Review Exercises

1. $\$3,\underline{3}84 \approx \$3,400$

2. $\dfrac{20}{25} = \dfrac{\cancel{5}^{1} \cdot 4}{\cancel{5}_{1} \cdot 5} = \dfrac{4}{5}$

3. The product is approximately equal to 8×5, or 40.

4. Move the decimal point 3 places to the right, adding a 0 placeholder.
   $(3.01)(1,000) = 3,010$

5. $12\dfrac{1}{2}\% \text{ of } 16 = \dfrac{1}{8} \times 16 = 2$

Chapter 9

MORE ON ALGEBRA

Pretest

1. $y + 8 = 2$ Check:
$y + 8 - 8 = 2 - 8$ $y + 8 = 2$
$y = -6$ $-6 + 8 \stackrel{?}{=} 2$
$2 \stackrel{\checkmark}{=} 2$

2. $x - 6 = -8$ Check:
$x - 6 + 6 = -8 + 6$ $x - 6 = -8$
$x = -2$ $-2 - 6 \stackrel{?}{=} -8$
$-8 \stackrel{\checkmark}{=} -8$

3. $-6x = 24$ Check:
$\dfrac{-6x}{-6} = \dfrac{24}{-6}$ $-6x = 24$
$x = -4$ $-6(-4) \stackrel{?}{=} 24$
$24 \stackrel{\checkmark}{=} 24$

4. $-1 = \dfrac{a}{5}$ Check:
$-1 \cdot 5 = \dfrac{a}{5} \cdot 5$ $-1 = \dfrac{a}{5}$
$-5 = a$ $-1 \stackrel{?}{=} \dfrac{-5}{5}$
$-1 \stackrel{\checkmark}{=} -1$

5. $3x + 1 = 10$ Check:
$3x + 1 - 1 = 10 - 1$ $3x + 1 = 10$
$3x = 9$ $3(3) + 1 \stackrel{?}{=} 10$
$x = 3$ $9 + 1 \stackrel{?}{=} 10$
$10 \stackrel{\checkmark}{=} 10$

6. $4 = 5y - 1$ Check:
$4 + 1 = 5y - 1 + 1$ $4 = 5y - 1$
$5 = 5y$ $4 \stackrel{?}{=} 5(1) - 1$
$1 = y$ $4 \stackrel{\checkmark}{=} 4$

7. $-2c + 3 = 7$ Check:
$-2c + 3 - 3 = 7 - 3$ $-2c + 3 = 7$
$-2c = 4$ $-2(-2) + 3 \stackrel{?}{=} 7$
$\dfrac{-2c}{-2} = \dfrac{4}{-2}$ $4 + 3 \stackrel{?}{=} 7$
$c = -2$ $7 \stackrel{\checkmark}{=} 7$

8. $\dfrac{a}{2} - 7 = -12$ Check:
$\dfrac{a}{2} - 7 + 7 = -12 + 7$ $\dfrac{a}{2} - 7 = -12$
$\dfrac{a}{2} = -5$ $\dfrac{-10}{2} - 7 \stackrel{?}{=} -12$
$\dfrac{a}{2} \cdot 2 = -5 \cdot 2$ $-5 - 7 \stackrel{?}{=} -12$
$a = -10$ $-12 \stackrel{\checkmark}{=} -12$

9. $\dfrac{w}{3} + 1 = -4$ Check:
$\dfrac{w}{3} + 1 - 1 = -4 - 1$ $\dfrac{w}{3} + 1 = -4$
$\dfrac{w}{3} = -5$ $\dfrac{-15}{3} + 1 \stackrel{?}{=} -4$
$\dfrac{w}{3} \cdot 3 = -5 \cdot 3$ $-5 + 1 \stackrel{?}{=} -4$
$w = -15$ $-4 \stackrel{\checkmark}{=} -4$

10. $2x + 3x = 10$ Check:
$(2 + 3)x = 10$ $2x + 3x = 10$
$5x = 10$ $2(2) + 3(2) \stackrel{?}{=} 10$
$x = 2$ $4 + 6 \stackrel{?}{=} 10$
$10 \stackrel{\checkmark}{=} 10$

11. $2x - 4 = x - 5$ Check:
$2x - x - 4 = x - x - 5$ $2x - 4 = x - 5$
$(2 - 1)x - 4 = x - 5$ $2(-1) - 4 \stackrel{?}{=} -1 - 5$
$x - 4 = -5$ $-2 - 4 \stackrel{?}{=} -6$
$x - 4 + 4 = -5 + 4$ $-6 \stackrel{\checkmark}{=} -6$
$x = -1$

12.
$$4x = 2(x-4)$$
$$4x = 2x - 8$$
$$4x - 2x = 2x - 2x - 8$$
$$2x = -8$$
$$\frac{2x}{2} = \frac{-8}{2}$$
$$x = -4$$

Check:
$$4x = 2(x-4)$$
$$4(-4) \stackrel{?}{=} 2(-4-4)$$
$$-16 \stackrel{?}{=} 2(-8)$$
$$-8 \stackrel{\checkmark}{=} -8$$

13. $l = \frac{1}{7}h$

14. $S = \dfrac{n(n+1)}{2}$

$$S = \frac{13(13+1)}{2}$$

$$S = \frac{13 \cdot \overset{7}{\cancel{14}}}{\underset{1}{\cancel{2}}}$$

$$S = 91$$

15. If x is your hourly rate, the equation is $4x + 5 = 45$.
$$4x + 5 = 45$$
$$4x = 40$$
$$x = 10$$

Check:
$$4x + 5 = 45$$
$$4(10) + 5 \stackrel{?}{=} 45$$
$$40 + 5 \stackrel{?}{=} 45$$
$$45 \stackrel{\checkmark}{=} 45$$

Your hourly rate was $10/hr.

16. If you let x be the number of *additional* hours he worked, the equation is $250 + 75x = 475$.
$$250 + 75x = 475$$
$$75x = 225$$
$$x = 3$$

Check:
$$250 + 75x = 475$$
$$250 + 75(3) \stackrel{?}{=} 475$$
$$250 + 225 \stackrel{?}{=} 475$$
$$475 \stackrel{\checkmark}{=} 475$$

He worked 3 additional hours, so he worked a total of 6 hr.

17. Let x be the cost of one book. The equation is $14x + 5 = 19$.
$$14x + 5 = 19$$
$$14x = 14$$
$$x = 1$$

Check:
$$14x + 5 = 19$$
$$14(1) + 5 \stackrel{?}{=} 19$$
$$19 \stackrel{\checkmark}{=} 19$$

Each book cost $1.

18. Let n be the number. The equation is $3(n+7) = 30$.
$$3(n+7) = 30$$
$$\frac{3(n+7)}{3} = \frac{30}{3}$$
$$n + 7 = 10$$
$$n = 3$$

Check:
$$3(n+7) = 30$$
$$3(3+7) \stackrel{?}{=} 30$$
$$3(10) \stackrel{?}{=} 30$$
$$30 \stackrel{\checkmark}{=} 30$$

The number is 3.

19. a. $B = \dfrac{1}{12}twl$

b. Substitute for t, w, and l.
$$B = \frac{1}{12}twl$$
$$B = \frac{1}{\underset{3}{\cancel{12}}} \times 2 \times \overset{1}{\cancel{4}} \times 20$$
$$B = \frac{40}{3}, \text{ or } 13\frac{1}{3}$$

The piece of lumber would contain $13\frac{1}{3}$ board ft.

20. a. $s = r - d$

b. Substitute for r and d.
$$s = r - d$$
$$s = \$400 - \$99$$
$$s = \$301$$
The sale price is $301.

9.1   Solving Two-Step Equations

Practice

1.
$$x + 7 = 4$$
$$x + 7 - 7 = 4 - 7$$
$$x + 0 = -3$$
$$x = -3$$

Check:
$$x + 7 = 4$$
$$-3 + 7 \stackrel{?}{=} 4$$
$$4 \stackrel{\checkmark}{=} 4$$

2.
$$m - 7 = -19$$
$$m - 7 + 7 = -19 + 7$$
$$m + 0 = -12$$
$$m = -12$$

Check:
$$m - 7 = -19$$
$$-12 - 7 \stackrel{?}{=} -19$$
$$-19 \stackrel{\checkmark}{=} -19$$

3.
$$9y = -18$$
$$\frac{9y}{9} = \frac{-18}{9}$$
$$y = -2$$

Check:
$$9y = -18$$
$$9(-2) \stackrel{?}{=} -18$$
$$-18 \stackrel{\checkmark}{=} -18$$

4. $\dfrac{y}{-3} = -2$ Check:

$\dfrac{y}{-3} \cdot (-3) = -2 \cdot (-3)$ $\dfrac{y}{-3} = -2$

$y = 6$ $\dfrac{6}{-3} \overset{?}{=} -2$

$-2 \overset{\checkmark}{=} -2$

5. -2% of what amount is $-\$50,000$?

$\downarrow$ $\downarrow$ $\downarrow$ $\downarrow$ $\downarrow$

-0.02 $\cdot$ x $= -50,000$

$-0.02x = -50,000$

$\dfrac{0.02x}{-0.02} = \dfrac{-50,000}{-0.02}$

$x = 2,500,000$

Check:

$-0.02x = -50,000$

$-0.02(2,500,000) \overset{?}{=} -50,000$

$-50,000 \overset{\checkmark}{=} -50,000$

The company's income was $\$2,500,000$.

6. $2x + 8 = -6$ Check:

$2x + 8 - 8 = -6 - 8$ $2x + 8 = -6$

$2x = -14$ $2(-7) + 8 \overset{?}{=} -6$

$\dfrac{2x}{2} = \dfrac{-14}{2}$ $-14 + 8 \overset{?}{=} -6$

$x = -7$ $-6 \overset{\checkmark}{=} -6$

7. $\dfrac{k}{5} - 5 = -3$ Check:

$\dfrac{k}{5} - 5 + 5 = -3 + 5$ $\dfrac{k}{5} - 5 = -3$

$\dfrac{k}{5} = 2$ $\dfrac{10}{5} - 5 \overset{?}{=} -3$

$\dfrac{k}{5} \cdot 5 = 2 \cdot 5$ $2 - 5 \overset{?}{=} -3$

$k = 10$ $-3 \overset{\checkmark}{=} -3$

8. $8 - 3d = -4$ Check:

$8 - 8 - 3d = -4 - 8$ $8 - 3d = -4$

$-3d = -12$ $8 - 3 \cdot 4 \overset{?}{=} -4$

$\dfrac{-3d}{-3} = \dfrac{-12}{-3}$ $8 - 12 \overset{?}{=} -4$

$d = 4$ $-4 \overset{\checkmark}{=} -4$

9. $\dfrac{x}{8} + 7 = -9$ Check:

$\dfrac{x}{8} + 7 - 7 = -9 - 7$ $\dfrac{x}{8} + 7 = -9$

$\dfrac{x}{8} = -16$ $\dfrac{-128}{8} + 7 \overset{?}{=} -9$

$x = 8 \cdot (-16)$ $-16 + 7 \overset{?}{=} -9$

$x = -128$ $-9 \overset{\checkmark}{=} -9$

10. Let x be the number of oranges in the box.

Weight of box	Weight of oranges	Total weight
$\downarrow$	$\downarrow$	$\downarrow$
2	$+$ 0.2x $=$	10

$2 + 0.2x = 10$ Check:

$2 - 2 + 0.2x = 10 - 2$ $2 + 0.2x = 10$

$0.2x = 8$ $2 + 0.2(40) \overset{?}{=} 10$

$\dfrac{0.2x}{0.2} = \dfrac{8}{0.2}$ $2 + 8 \overset{?}{=} 10$

$x = 40$ $10 \overset{\checkmark}{=} 10$

The box contains 40 oranges.

Exercises

1. $a - 7 = -21$ Check:

$a - 7 + 7 = -21 + 7$ $a - 7 = -21$

$a = -14$ $-14 - 7 \overset{?}{=} -21$

$-21 \overset{\checkmark}{=} -21$

3. $b + 4 = -7$ Check:

$b + 4 - 4 = -7 - 4$ $b + 4 = -7$

$b = -11$ $-11 + 4 \overset{?}{=} -7$

$-7 \overset{\checkmark}{=} -7$

5. $-11 = z - 4$ Check:

$-11 + 4 = z - 4 + 4$ $-11 = z - 4$

$-7 = z$ $-11 \overset{?}{=} -7 - 4$

$-11 \overset{\checkmark}{=} -11$

7. $x + 21 = 19$ Check:

$x + 21 - 21 = 19 - 21$ $x + 21 = 19$

$x = -2$ $-2 + 21 \overset{?}{=} 19$

$19 \overset{\checkmark}{=} 19$

9. $c + 33 = 14$ Check:

$c + 33 - 33 = 14 - 33$ $c + 33 = 14$

$c = -19$ $-19 + 33 \overset{?}{=} 14$

$14 \overset{\checkmark}{=} 14$

11.　$z + 2.4 = -5.3$　　　Check:

$z + 2.4 - 2.4 = -5.3 - 2.4$　　$z + 2.4 = -5.3$

$z = -7.7$　　$-7.7 + 2.4 \overset{?}{=} -5.3$

$-5.3 \overset{\checkmark}{=} -5.3$

13.　$2.3 = x + 5.9$　　　Check:

$2.3 - 5.9 = x + 5.9 - 5.9$　　$2.3 = x + 5.9$

$-3.6 = x$　　$2.3 \overset{?}{=} -3.6 + 5.9$

$2.3 \overset{\checkmark}{=} 2.3$

15.　$y - 2\frac{1}{3} = -3$　　　Check:

$y - 2\frac{1}{3} + 2\frac{1}{3} = -3 + 2\frac{1}{3}$　　$y - 2\frac{1}{3} = -3$

$y = -\frac{2}{3}$　　$-\frac{2}{3} - 2\frac{1}{3} \overset{?}{=} -3$

$-3 \overset{\checkmark}{=} -3$

17.　$-5 = t + 1\frac{1}{4}$　　　Check:

$-5 - 1\frac{1}{4} = t + 1\frac{1}{4} - 1\frac{1}{4}$　　$-5 = t + 1\frac{1}{4}$

$-6\frac{1}{4} = t$　　$-5 \overset{?}{=} -6\frac{1}{4} + 1\frac{1}{4}$

$-5 \overset{\checkmark}{=} -5$

19.　$39 = z + 51$　　　Check:

$39 - 51 = z + 51 - 51$　　$39 = z + 51$

$-12 = z$　　$39 \overset{?}{=} -12 + 51$

$39 \overset{\checkmark}{=} 39$

21.　$-5x = 30$　　　Check:

$\dfrac{-5x}{-5} = \dfrac{30}{-5}$　　$-5x = 30$

$x = -6$　　$-5(-6) \overset{?}{=} 30$

$30 \overset{\checkmark}{=} 30$

23.　$-36 = -9n$　　　Check:

$\dfrac{-36}{-9} = \dfrac{-9n}{-9}$　　$-36 = -9n$

$4 = n$　　$-36 \overset{?}{=} -9(4)$

$-36 \overset{\checkmark}{=} -36$

25.　$\dfrac{m}{-15} = 1$　　　Check:

$\dfrac{m}{-15} \cdot (-15) = 1 \cdot (-15)$　　$\dfrac{m}{-15} = 1$

$m = -15$　　$\dfrac{-15}{-15} \overset{?}{=} 1$

$1 \overset{\checkmark}{=} 1$

27.　$\dfrac{w}{10} = -24$　　　Check:

$\dfrac{w}{10} \cdot 10 = -24 \cdot 10$　　$\dfrac{w}{10} = -24$

$w = -240$　　$\dfrac{-240}{10} \overset{?}{=} -24$

$-24 \overset{\checkmark}{=} -24$

29.　$-6 = \dfrac{x}{-2}$　　　Check:

$-6 \cdot (-2) = \dfrac{x}{-2} \cdot (-2)$　　$-6 = \dfrac{x}{-2}$

$12 = x$　　$-6 \overset{?}{=} \dfrac{12}{-2}$

$-6 \overset{\checkmark}{=} -6$

31.　$1.7t = -51$　　　Check:

$\dfrac{1.7t}{1.7} = \dfrac{-51}{1.7}$　　$1.7t = -51$

$t = -30$　　$1.7 \cdot (-30) \overset{?}{=} -51$

$-51 \overset{\checkmark}{=} -51$

33.　$\dfrac{y}{9} = -\dfrac{5}{3}$　　　Check:

$\dfrac{y}{9} = \dfrac{-5}{3}$　　$\dfrac{y}{9} = -\dfrac{5}{3}$

$9 \cdot (-5) = 3 \cdot y$　　$\dfrac{\overset{-5}{\cancel{-15}}}{\cancel{9}}_{3} \overset{?}{=} -\dfrac{5}{3}$

$\dfrac{\overset{3}{\cancel{9}} \cdot (-5)}{\cancel{3}_{1}} = y$　　$-\dfrac{5}{3} \overset{\checkmark}{=} -\dfrac{5}{3}$

$-15 = y$

35.　$-10y = 4$　　　Check:

$\dfrac{-10y}{-10} = \dfrac{4}{-10}$　　$-10y = 4$

$y = -\dfrac{4}{10}$　　$-10 \cdot \left(-\dfrac{2}{5}\right) \overset{?}{=} 4$

$y = -\dfrac{2}{5}$　　$\dfrac{20}{5} \overset{?}{=} 4$

$4 \overset{\checkmark}{=} 4$

37.　$895 = -624n$

$\dfrac{895}{-624} = \dfrac{-624n}{-624}$

$-1.43... = n$

$n \approx -1.4$

Check:

$895 = -624n$

$-624(-1.4) = 873.6$

The product is reasonably close to 895.

39.

$$-2.5 = \frac{x}{5.91}$$

$$(-2.5)(5.91) = x$$

$$x = -14.775$$

$$x \approx -14.8$$

Check:

If $x \approx -14.8$, is $\dfrac{x}{5.91} \approx -2.5$?

Round -14.8 to -15 and 5.91 to 6.

$$\frac{-15}{6} = -2.5$$

41. $4n - 20 = 36$ Check:

$$4n = 56 \qquad 4n - 20 = 36$$

$$n = 14 \qquad 4(14) - 20 \overset{?}{=} 36$$

$$56 - 20 \overset{?}{=} 36$$

$$36 \overset{\checkmark}{=} 36$$

43. $3x + 1 = 7$ Check:

$$3x = 6 \qquad 3x + 1 = 7$$

$$x = 2 \qquad 3(2) + 1 \overset{?}{=} 7$$

$$6 + 1 \overset{?}{=} 7$$

$$7 \overset{\checkmark}{=} 7$$

45. $6k + 23 = 5$ Check:

$$6k = -18 \qquad 6k + 23 = 5$$

$$k = -3 \qquad 6(-3) + 23 \overset{?}{=} 5$$

$$-18 + 23 \overset{?}{=} 5$$

$$5 \overset{\checkmark}{=} 5$$

47. $3x + 20 = 20$ Check:

$$3x = 0 \qquad 3x + 20 = 20$$

$$x = 0 \qquad 3(0) + 20 \overset{?}{=} 20$$

$$0 + 20 \overset{?}{=} 20$$

$$20 \overset{\checkmark}{=} 20$$

49. $31 = 3 - 4h$ Check:

$$28 = -4h \qquad 31 = 3 - 4h$$

$$-7 = h \qquad 31 \overset{?}{=} 3 - 4(-7)$$

$$31 \overset{?}{=} 3 + 28$$

$$31 \overset{\checkmark}{=} 31$$

51. $34 = 13 - 4p$ Check:

$$21 = -4p \qquad 34 = 13 - 4p$$

$$\frac{21}{-4} = p \qquad 34 \overset{?}{=} 13 - 4\left(-5\frac{1}{4}\right)$$

$$-5\frac{1}{4} = p \qquad 34 \overset{?}{=} 13 + 4 \cdot \frac{21}{4}$$

$$34 \overset{?}{=} 13 + 21$$

$$34 \overset{\checkmark}{=} 34$$

53. $-7b + 8 = -6$ Check:

$$-7b = -14 \qquad -7b + 8 = -6$$

$$b = 2 \qquad -7(2) + 8 \overset{?}{=} -6$$

$$-14 + 8 \overset{?}{=} -6$$

$$-6 \overset{\checkmark}{=} -6$$

55. $21 + \dfrac{a}{3} = 10$ Check:

$$\frac{a}{3} = -11 \qquad 21 + \frac{a}{3} = 10$$

$$a = -33 \qquad 21 + \frac{-33}{3} \overset{?}{=} 10$$

$$21 - 11 \overset{?}{=} 10$$

$$10 \overset{\checkmark}{=} 10$$

57. $\dfrac{1}{2}y + 5 = -13$ Check:

$$\frac{1}{2}y = -18 \qquad \frac{1}{2}y + 5 = -13$$

$$y = -36 \qquad \frac{1}{2} \cdot (-36) + 5 \overset{?}{=} -13$$

$$-18 + 5 \overset{?}{=} -13$$

$$-13 \overset{\checkmark}{=} -13$$

59.

$$5 - \frac{x}{12} = 1$$ Check:

$$-\frac{x}{12} = -4 \qquad 5 - \frac{x}{12} = 1$$

$$-\frac{x}{12} \cdot (-12) = -4 \cdot (-12) \qquad 5 - \frac{48}{12} \overset{?}{=} 1$$

$$x = 48 \qquad 5 - 4 \overset{?}{=} 1$$

$$1 \overset{\checkmark}{=} 1$$

61. $\dfrac{c}{3}+3=-4$ Check:

$$\dfrac{c}{3}=-7$$
$$c=-21$$

$$\dfrac{c}{3}+3=-4$$
$$\dfrac{-21}{3}+3\overset{?}{=}-4$$
$$-7+3\overset{?}{=}-4$$
$$-4\overset{\checkmark}{=}-4$$

63. $\dfrac{4}{9}x-13=-5$ Check:

$$\dfrac{4}{9}x=8$$
$$\dfrac{9}{4}\cdot\dfrac{4}{9}x=\dfrac{9}{\overset{}{4}}\cdot\dfrac{\overset{2}{8}}{1}$$
$$x=18$$

$$\dfrac{4}{9}x-13=-5$$
$$\dfrac{4}{9}\cdot18-13\overset{?}{=}-5$$
$$\dfrac{4}{9}\cdot\dfrac{\overset{2}{18}}{1}-13\overset{?}{=}-5$$
$$8-13\overset{?}{=}-5$$
$$-5\overset{\checkmark}{=}-5$$

65. $-8-x=11$ Check:

$$-x=19$$
$$\dfrac{-x}{-1}=\dfrac{19}{-1}$$
$$x=-19$$

$$-8-x=11$$
$$-8-(-19)\overset{?}{=}11$$
$$-8+19\overset{?}{=}11$$
$$11\overset{\checkmark}{=}11$$

67. $58.3r+23.58=2.79$

$$58.3r=-20.79$$
$$r=-0.35660...$$
$$r\approx-0.4$$

Check: A version of the equation rounded for convenient arithmetic is $60r+23=3$, which has the solution $-\dfrac{1}{3}$, reasonably close both to the exact solution and the rounded solution.

69. $\dfrac{x}{0.24}-0.03=-0.14$

$$\dfrac{x}{0.24}=-0.11$$
$$x=(0.24)(-0.11)$$
$$x=-0.0264$$

Here rounding to the nearest tenth gives an answer of 0.0, which won't check very closely. Rounding to the nearest hundredth gives –0.03, which is a more useful approximation. Check: Treating the denominator on the left as 0.25 or $\dfrac{1}{4}$, and rounding

–0.11 to –0.12, the final equation becomes $4x=-0.12$ which has the solution $x=-0.03$, in agreement with the solution rounded to the nearest hundredth.

71. If x stands for the number of months it will take to lose 2 lb, the equation is $-3x=-21$.

$-3x=-21$ Check:

$$\dfrac{-3x}{-3}=\dfrac{-21}{-3}$$
$$x=7$$

$$-3x=-21$$
$$-3(7)\overset{?}{=}-21$$
$$-21\overset{\checkmark}{=}-21$$

It will take you 7 mo to lose 21 lb.

73. If x stands for the amount each partner owes, the equation is $3x=-6,000$.

$3x=-6,000$ Check:

$$x=-2,000$$

$$3x=-6,000$$
$$3(-2,000)\overset{?}{=}-6,000$$
$$-6,000\overset{\checkmark}{=}-6,000$$

Each partner owes $2,000.

75. If x stands for the original price of each ticket, the equation is $15x-25=155$.

$15x-25=155$ Check:

$$15x=180$$
$$x=12$$

$$15x-25=155$$
$$15(12)-25\overset{?}{=}155$$
$$180-25\overset{?}{=}155$$
$$155\overset{\checkmark}{=}155$$

The original ticket price was $12.

77. If x is the number of guests at each of the large tables, the equation is $8x+3=43$.

$8x+3=43$ Check:

$$8x=40$$
$$x=5$$

$$8x+3=43$$
$$8(5)+3\overset{?}{=}43$$
$$40+3\overset{?}{=}43$$
$$43\overset{\checkmark}{=}43$$

There were 5 people at each of the large tables.

79. Let x be the number of hours the client used the service.

a. The equation is $251.20=8.95+4.75x$.

b. $251.20=8.95+4.75x$
$$242.25=4.75x$$
$$51=x$$

She used the service for 51 hr.

c. Rounding the monthly charge to $10, the total charges to $250, and the hourly charge to $5 gives and estimate of $\dfrac{250-10}{5}$ or 48 hr.

9.2   Solving Multistep Equations

Practice

1. In each expression, combine like terms using the distributive property in reverse.

   a. $5x + 7x = (5+7)x$
   $\qquad\quad = 12x$

   b. $7y - y = 7y - 1y$
   $\qquad\quad = (7-1)y$
   $\qquad\quad = 6y$

   c. $4z - 5z + 6 = (4-5)z + 6$
   $\qquad\qquad\quad = -1z + 6$
   $\qquad\qquad\quad = -z + 6$

2. $2y - 3y = 8$

   $(-1)y = 8$ Combine like terms.

   $\dfrac{(-1)y}{-1} = \dfrac{8}{-1}$

   $y = -8$

   Check:
   $2y - 3y = 8$
   $2(-8) - 3(-8) \overset{?}{=} 8$
   $-16 + 24 \overset{?}{=} 8$
   $8 \overset{\checkmark}{=} 8$

3. $10x - 1 = 2x + 3$

   $10x - 2x - 1 = 2x - 2x + 3$

   $8x - 1 = 3$ Combine like terms.

   $8x - 1 + 1 = 3 + 1$

   $8x = 4$

   $x = \dfrac{1}{2}$

   Check:
   $10x - 1 = 2x + 3$
   $10 \cdot \dfrac{1}{2} - 1 \overset{?}{=} 2 \cdot \dfrac{1}{2} + 3$
   $5 - 1 \overset{?}{=} 1 + 3$
   $4 \overset{\checkmark}{=} 4$

4. $4(x + 2) = 3x$

   $4x + 8 = 3x$ Use the distributive property.

   $4x - 3x + 8 = 3x - 3x$

   $x + 8 = 0$ Combine like terms.

   $x + 8 - 8 = 0 - 8$

   $x = -8$

   Check:
   $4(x + 2) = 3x$
   $4(-8 + 2) \overset{?}{=} 3(-8)$
   $4(-6) \overset{?}{=} -24$
   $-24 \overset{\checkmark}{=} -24$

5. **a.** If the number is x, three times the number is $3x$ and 9 more than the number is $x + 9$. The equation is $x + 3x = x + 9$.

   b. $x + 3x = x + 9$
   $x - x + 3x = x - x + 9$
   $3x = 9$
   $x = 3$

   Check:
   $x + 3x = x + 9$
   $3 + 3(3) \overset{?}{=} 3 + 9$
   $3 + 9 \overset{?}{=} 12$
   $12 \overset{\checkmark}{=} 12$

   The number is 3.

6. Let y be the number of miles you traveled.

Cost of first mile		Miles *after* the first mile		Cost per additonal mile		Total cost
↓		↓		↓		↓
\$1.25	+	$(y - 1)$	×	\$1.25	=	\$4.25

   The equation is $1.50 + 1.25(y - 1) = 4.25$.

   $1.50 + 1.25(y - 1) = 4.25$
   $1.50 + 1.25y - 1.25 = 4.25$
   $0.25 + 1.25y = 4.25$
   $1.25y = 4$
   $y = \dfrac{4}{1.25}$
   $y = 3.2$

   Check:
   $1.50 + 1.25(y - 1) = 4.25$
   $1.50 + 1.25(3.2 - 1) \overset{?}{=} 4.25$
   $1.50 + 1.25(2.2) \overset{?}{=} 4.25$
   $1.50 + 2.75 \overset{?}{=} 4.25$
   $4.25 \overset{\checkmark}{=} 4.25$

   You traveled a total of 3.2 mi.

Exercises

1. $4x + 3x = (4+3)x = 7x$

3. $4a - a = 4a - 1a = (4-1)a = 3a$

5. $6y - 9y = (6-9)y = -3y$

7. $2n - 3n = (2-3)n = -1n = -n$

9. $2c + c + 12 = 2c + 1c + 12 = (2+1)c + 12 = 3c + 12$

11. $8 + x - 7x = 8 + 1x - 7x = 8 + (1-7)x = 8 - 6x$

13. $-y + 5 + 3y = -1y + 3y + 5 = (-1+3)y + 5 = 2y + 5$

15. $5m + 4m = 36$

    $9m = 36$

    $m = 4$

    Check:
    $5m + 4m = 36$
    $5 \cdot 4 + 4 \cdot 4 \overset{?}{=} 36$
    $20 + 16 \overset{?}{=} 36$
    $36 \overset{\checkmark}{=} 36$

17. $18 = 4y - 2y$ Check:
$18 = 2y$ 　　$18 = 4y - 2y$
$9 = y$ 　　$18 \overset{?}{=} 4 \cdot 9 - 2 \cdot 9$
　　　　$18 \overset{?}{=} 36 - 18$
　　　　$18 \overset{\checkmark}{=} 18$

19. $2a - 3a = 7$ Check:
$-a = 7$ 　　$2a - 3a = 7$
$\dfrac{-a}{-1} = \dfrac{7}{-1}$ 　$2(-7) - 3(-7) \overset{?}{=} 7$
$a = -7$ 　　$-14 + 21 \overset{?}{=} 7$
　　　　$7 \overset{\checkmark}{=} 7$

21. 　$7 = -5b + b$ Check:
$7 = -4b$ 　　$7 = -5b + b$
$\dfrac{7}{-4} = b$ 　$7 \overset{?}{=} -5\left(-1\dfrac{3}{4}\right) + \left(-1\dfrac{3}{4}\right)$
$-1\dfrac{3}{4} = b$ 　$7 \overset{?}{=} \dfrac{5}{1} \cdot \dfrac{7}{4} - \dfrac{7}{4}$
　　　　$7 \overset{?}{=} \dfrac{28}{4}$
　　　　$7 \overset{\checkmark}{=} 7$

23. $n + n - 13 = 13$ Check:
$2n = 26$ 　　$n + n - 13 = 13$
$n = 13$ 　$13 + 13 - 13 \overset{?}{=} 13$
　　　　$13 \overset{\checkmark}{=} 13$

25. 　$6 = 7x - 3x - 6$ Check:
$12 = 4x$ 　　$6 = 7x - 3x - 6$
$3 = x$ 　　$6 \overset{?}{=} 7 \cdot 3 - 3 \cdot 3 - 6$
　　　　$6 \overset{?}{=} 21 - 9 - 6$
　　　　$6 \overset{\checkmark}{=} 6$

27. $n + 3n - 7 = 29$ Check:
$4n = 36$ 　　$n + 3n - 7 = 29$
$n = 9$ 　$9 + 3 \cdot 9 - 7 \overset{?}{=} 29$
　　　　$9 + 27 - 7 \overset{?}{=} 29$
　　　　$29 \overset{\checkmark}{=} 29$

29. $2 + 3y - y = -8$ Check:
$2y = -10$ 　　$2 + 3y - y = -8$
$y = -5$ 　$2 + 3 \cdot (-5) - (-5) \overset{?}{=} -8$
　　　　$2 - 15 + 5 \overset{?}{=} -8$
　　　　$-8 \overset{\checkmark}{=} -8$

31. $60r - 17r + 23.58 = 2.79$
　　　$43r = -20.79$
　　　$r = -0.4834...$
　　　$r \approx -0.5$
Check: Using the rounded answer, the left side of the equation is $60(-0.5) - 17(-0.5) + 23.58$, which is equal to 2, reasonably close to 2.79.

33. $1.02m + 3.007m = 50.1$
　　　$4.027m = 50.1$
　　　$m = 12.4410...$
　　　$m \approx 12.4$
Check: A rounded version of the equation is $m + 3m = 50$ which has the solution $m = 12.5$.

35. 　$5x = 2x + 12$ Check:
$5x - 2x = 12$ 　　$5x = 2x + 12$
$3x = 12$ 　　$5 \cdot 4 \overset{?}{=} 2 \cdot 4 + 12$
$x = 4$ 　　$20 \overset{?}{=} 8 + 12$
　　　　$20 \overset{\checkmark}{=} 20$

37. 　$4p + 1 = 3p - 1$ Check:
$4p - 3p = -1 - 1$ 　　$4p + 1 = 3p - 1$
$p = -2$ 　　$4(-2) + 1 \overset{?}{=} 3(-2) - 1$
　　　　$-8 + 1 \overset{?}{=} -6 - 1$
　　　　$-7 \overset{\checkmark}{=} -7$

39. $8x + 1 = x - 6$ Check:
$8x - x = -6 - 1$ 　　$8x + 1 = x - 6$
$7x = -7$ 　$8(-1) + 1 \overset{?}{=} -1 - 6$
$x = -1$ 　　$-8 + 1 \overset{?}{=} -7$
　　　　$-7 \overset{\checkmark}{=} -7$

41. $3p - 2 = -p + 4$ Check:
$3p + p = 4 + 2$ 　　$3p - 2 = -p + 4$
$4p = 6$ 　$3\left(1\dfrac{1}{2}\right) - 2 \overset{?}{=} -1\dfrac{1}{2} + 4$
$p = \dfrac{6}{4}$, or $1\dfrac{1}{2}$ 　$\dfrac{9}{2} - \dfrac{4}{2} \overset{?}{=} -\dfrac{3}{2} + \dfrac{8}{2}$
　　　　$\dfrac{5}{2} \overset{\checkmark}{=} \dfrac{5}{2}$

43. 　$4n - 6 = 3n + 6$ Check:
$4n - 3n = 6 + 6$ 　　$4n - 6 = 3n + 6$
$n = 12$ 　$4 \cdot 12 - 6 \overset{?}{=} 3 \cdot 12 + 6$
　　　　$48 - 6 \overset{?}{=} 36 + 6$
　　　　$42 \overset{\checkmark}{=} 42$

45. $3 - 6t = 5t - 19$ Check:

$3 + 19 = 5t + 6t$ $3 - 6t = 5t - 19$

$22 = 11t$ $3 - 6 \cdot 2 \stackrel{?}{=} 5 \cdot 2 - 19$

$2 = t$ $3 - 12 \stackrel{?}{=} 10 - 19$

$-9 \stackrel{\checkmark}{=} -9$

47. $-7y + 2 = 3y - 8$ Check:

$-7y - 3y = -8 - 2$ $-7y + 2 = 3y - 8$

$-10y = -10$ $-7 \cdot 1 + 2 \stackrel{?}{=} 3 \cdot 1 - 8$

$y = 1$ $-7 + 2 \stackrel{?}{=} 3 - 8$

$-5 \stackrel{\checkmark}{=} -5$

49. $3x - 2 = 8 - 5x$ Check:

$3x + 5x = 8 + 2$ $3x - 2 = 8 - 5x$

$8x = 10$ $3\left(1\frac{1}{4}\right) - 2 \stackrel{?}{=} 8 - 5\left(1\frac{1}{4}\right)$

$x = \frac{10}{8}$, or $1\frac{1}{4}$ $\frac{3}{1} \cdot \frac{5}{4} - \frac{8}{4} \stackrel{?}{=} \frac{32}{4} - \frac{5}{1}\left(\frac{5}{4}\right)$

$\frac{15}{4} - \frac{8}{4} \stackrel{?}{=} \frac{32}{4} - \frac{25}{4}$

$\frac{7}{4} \stackrel{\checkmark}{=} \frac{7}{4}$

51. $0.0125x + 0.07x = 3,625$

$0.0825x = 3,625$

$x = 43,939.39...$

$x \approx 43,939.4$

Check the division by estimating: Round 0.0825 to 0.1 and 3,625 to 4,000. The division then gives 40,000, which is close to our exact and rounded answers.

53. $5.31y + 2.83 = -6.91 - 3.77y$

$5.31y + 3.77y = -6.91 - 2.83$

$9.08y = -9.74$

$y = -1.0726...$

$y \approx -1.1$

Check by solving the rounded equation

$5y + 3 = -7 - 4y$. This has the solution $y = -\dfrac{10}{9}$ or

$y = 1.111...$, which is close to the exact and rounded answers.

55. $2(n - 3) = 12$

$n - 3 = 6$ Since 2 goes evenly into 12, first divide both sides by 2.

$n = 9$

Check:

$2(n - 3) = 12$

$2(9 - 3) \stackrel{?}{=} 12$

$2 \cdot 6 \stackrel{?}{=} 12$

$12 \stackrel{\checkmark}{=} 12$

57. $8(x - 1) = -24$

$x - 1 = -3$ Since 8 goes evenly into -24, first divide both sides by 8.

$x = -2$

Check:

$8(x - 1) = -24$

$8(-2 - 1) \stackrel{?}{=} -24$

$8(-3) \stackrel{?}{=} -24$

$-24 \stackrel{\checkmark}{=} -24$

59. $6n = 5(n + 7)$ Check:

$6n = 5n + 35$ $6n = 5(n + 7)$

$6n - 5n = 35$ $6(35) \stackrel{?}{=} 5(35 + 7)$

$n = 35$ $210 \stackrel{?}{=} 5(42)$

$210 \stackrel{\checkmark}{=} 210$

61. $3(y - 5) = 2y$ Check:

$3y - 15 = 2y$ $3(y - 5) = 2y$

$3y - 2y = 15$ $3(15 - 5) \stackrel{?}{=} 2(15)$

$y = 15$ $3 \cdot 10 \stackrel{?}{=} 30$

$30 \stackrel{\checkmark}{=} 30$

63. $5y = 3(y + 1)$ Check:

$5y = 3y + 3$ $5y = 3(y + 1)$

$2y = 3$ $5\left(1\frac{1}{2}\right) \stackrel{?}{=} 3\left(1\frac{1}{2} + 1\right)$

$y = \frac{3}{2}$, or $1\frac{1}{2}$ $\frac{5}{1} \cdot \frac{3}{2} \stackrel{?}{=} \frac{3}{1} \cdot \left(\frac{3}{2} + \frac{2}{2}\right)$

$\frac{15}{2} \stackrel{?}{=} \frac{3}{1} \cdot \frac{5}{2}$

$\frac{15}{2} \stackrel{\checkmark}{=} \frac{15}{2}$

65. $4n = 7(n-9)$ Check:
$$4n = 7n - 63 \qquad 4n = 7(n-9)$$
$$-3n = -63 \qquad 4(21) \overset{?}{=} 7(21-9)$$
$$n = 21 \qquad\qquad 84 \overset{?}{=} 7(12)$$
$$84 \overset{\checkmark}{=} 84$$

67. $6r + 2(r-1) = 14$ Check:
$$6r + 2r - 2 = 14 \qquad 6r + 2(r-1) = 14$$
$$8r = 16 \qquad 6(2) + 2(2-1) \overset{?}{=} 14$$
$$r = 2 \qquad\qquad 12 + 2 \overset{?}{=} 14$$
$$14 \overset{\checkmark}{=} 14$$

69. $x + 3(2-x) = 12$ Check:
$$x + 6 - 3x = 12 \qquad x + 3(2-x) = 12$$
$$x - 3x = 12 - 6 \qquad -3 + 3(2-(-3)) \overset{?}{=} 12$$
$$-2x = 6 \qquad\qquad -3 + 3(5) \overset{?}{=} 12$$
$$x = -3 \qquad\qquad -3 + 15 \overset{?}{=} 12$$
$$12 \overset{\checkmark}{=} 12$$

71. $0.06 + 0.10(10{,}000 - x) = 900$
$$0.06 + 1{,}000 - 0.10x = 900$$
$$-0.04x = -100$$
$$x = \frac{-100}{-0.04}$$
$$x = 2{,}500$$

Check:
$$0.06x + 0.01(10{,}000 - x) = 900$$
$$0.06(2{,}500) + 0.110(10{,}000 - 2{,}500) \overset{?}{=} 900$$
$$150 + 0.10(7{,}500) \overset{?}{=} 900$$
$$150 + 750 \overset{?}{=} 900$$
$$900 \overset{\checkmark}{=} 900$$

73. $1.72y = 3.16(y - 8.72)$
$$1.72y = 3.16y - 27.5552$$
$$-1.44y = -27.5552$$
$$y = 19.1355\ldots$$
$$y \approx 19.1$$

Check by solving the rounded equation
$1.7y = 3.2(y-9)$.
$$1.7y = 3.2(y-9)$$
$$1.7y = 3.2y - 28.8$$
$$-1.5y = -28.8$$
$$y = 19.2$$

75. If x is your hourly rate, the equation is
$4x + 3x = 73$.
$$4x + 3x = 63$$
$$7x = 63$$
$$x = 9$$
You earned \$9/hr.
Check: You worked 7 hours at \$9/hr, so you made
$7 \times \$9$ or \$63.

77. The perimeter is twice the length plus twice the
width w, so the equation is $140 + 2w = 200$.
$$140 + 2w = 200$$
$$2w = 60$$
$$w = 30$$
The width is 30 ft.
Check: Twice the width is 60 ft, twice the length is
140 ft, so the perimeter is 60 ft + 140 ft, or 200 ft.

79. If x is your total time studying, in hours, the equation
is $\frac{1}{5}x + \frac{1}{2}x = 1\frac{3}{4}$.
$$\frac{1}{5}x + \frac{1}{2}x = 1\frac{3}{4}$$
$$\frac{1}{5}x + \frac{1}{2}x = \frac{7}{4}$$
$$20 \cdot \frac{1}{5}x + 20 \cdot \frac{1}{2}x = 20 \cdot \frac{7}{4} \quad \text{Multiply both sides by the LCM of the denominators}$$
$$4x + 10x = 35$$
$$14x = 35$$
$$x = \frac{35}{14}$$
$$x = \frac{5}{2}, \text{ or } 2\frac{1}{2}$$

You spend $2\frac{1}{2}$ hr studying.

To check, turn this answer into minutes; $2\frac{1}{2}$ hr is
150 min. Your times for mathematics and English
are then 30 min and 75 min, totaling 105 min. This
is 60 min + 45 min or $1\frac{3}{4}$ hr, as required.

81. The equation sets cost equal to income:
$15n + 3{,}000 = 20n$, where n is the number of books
produced and sold.
$$15n + 3{,}000 = 20n$$
$$3{,}000 = 5n$$
$$600 = n$$
The publisher must produce 600 books.
To check, find the cost and income, assuming the

figures are in dollars:
Cost = $15 × 600 + $3,000 = $12,000
Income = $20 × 600 = $12,000

83. If n is the number of sides the equation is
$180(n-2) = 540$.

$$180(n-2) = 540$$
$$n-2 = 3 \quad \text{Divide both sides by 180.}$$
$$n = 5$$

The polygon has 5 sides.
Check: If the polygon has 5 sides, the sum of the
measures of the interior angles should be
$180°(5-2) = 180°(3) = 540°$.

9.3   Using Formulas

Practice

1. The temperature t at altitude a is the ground
temperature g minus $\dfrac{1}{200}$ of the altitude. The
formula is $t = g - \dfrac{1}{200}a$.

2. Replace P with $3,000, r with 0.06 and t with 2.
$I = Prt$
$I = (\$3,000)(0.06)(2)$
$I = \$360$
The value of I is $360.

3. Use the formula $p = i - c$.
$p = i - c$
$p = \$800 - \$498$
$p = \$302$
The net profit was $302.

4. Substitute the given values, including units, into the
formula.
$$s = \frac{1}{2}gt^2$$
$$s = \frac{1}{2}\left(32\frac{\text{ft}}{\text{sec}^2}\right)(2\text{ sec})^2$$
$$s = \frac{1}{2} \cdot 32\frac{\text{ft}}{\text{sec}^2} \cdot 4 \text{ sec}^2$$
$$s = 64 \text{ ft}$$

Exercises

1. $d = \dfrac{t}{3}$

3. $A = \dfrac{a+b}{2}$

5. $A = 6e^2$

7.

Formula	Given	Find
$F = \dfrac{9}{5}C + 32$	$C = -5°$	$F = \dfrac{9}{5}(-5) + 32 = -9 + 32$
		$F = 23°$

9.

Formula	Given	Find
$i = prt$	$p = \$1,000$ $r = 7.5\%$ $t = 3$ yr	$i = (\$1,000)(0.075)(3)$ $i = \$225$

11.

Formula	Given	Find
$C = \dfrac{5}{9}(F - 32)$	$F = 32°$	$C = \dfrac{5}{9}(32 - 32) = \dfrac{5}{9}(0)$ $C = 0°$

13.

Formula	Given	Find
$s = \dfrac{1}{2}gt^2$	$g = 32\dfrac{\text{ft}}{\text{sec}^2}$ $t = 10$ sec	$s = \dfrac{1}{2}\left(32\dfrac{\text{ft}}{\text{sec}^2}\right)(100\text{sec}^2)$ $s = 160$ ft

15. Substitute for the variables c, r and t.
$v = c - crt$
$v = \$27,000 - \$27,000 \times 0.1 \times 5$
$v = \$27,000 - \$13,500$
$v = \$13,500$
The present value of the car is $13,500.

17. Substitute for the variables a and A.
$$C = \frac{a}{a+12} \cdot A$$
$$C = \frac{6}{6+12} \cdot 180$$
$$C = \frac{6}{\cancel{18}} \cdot \cancel{180}^{10}_{1}$$
$$C = 60$$
The prescribed dosage for a 6-year-old is 60 mg.

19. Let T be the total number of calves born.
a. $T = 0.48A + 0.42A$
b. $T = 0.48A + 0.42A$
$T = 0.9A$
$T = 0.9(328) = 295.2$

To the nearest 10 calves, 300 calves will be born.
c. Since $0.48 + 0.42 = 0.9$, we'd expect the number
of calves born to be a bit smaller than the number
of females. Rounding 328 up to 330 and taking
90% of 330 gives an estimate of 9×33, or 297.

Review Exercises

1. $x + 2 = -4$ Check:
$$x + 2 - 2 = -4 - 2$$ $x + 2 = -4$
$$x = -6$$ $-6 + 2 \overset{?}{=} -4$
$$-4 \overset{\checkmark}{=} -4$$

2. $y + 3 = -6$ Check:
$$y = 3 - 3 = -6 - 3$$ $y + 3 = -6$
$$y = -9$$ $-9 + 3 \overset{?}{=} -6$
$$-6 \overset{\checkmark}{=} -6$$

3. $a + 19 = 19$ Check:
$$a + 19 - 19 = 19 - 19$$ $a + 19 = 19$
$$a = 0$$ $0 + 19 \overset{?}{=} 19$
$$19 \overset{\checkmark}{=} 19$$

4. $c + 25 = -25$ Check:
$$c + 25 - 25 = -25 - 25$$ $c + 25 = -25$
$$c = -50$$ $-50 + 25 \overset{?}{=} -25$
$$-25 \overset{\checkmark}{=} -25$$

5. $d + 9 = 0$ Check:
$$d + 9 - 9 = 0 - 9$$ $d + 9 = 0$
$$d = -9$$ $-9 + 9 \overset{?}{=} 0$
$$0 \overset{\checkmark}{=} 0$$

6. $w + 11 = 0$ Check:
$$w + 11 - 11 = 0 - 11$$ $w + 11 = 0$
$$w = -11$$ $-11 + 11 \overset{?}{=} 0$
$$0 \overset{\checkmark}{=} 0$$

7. $8 = x + 17$ Check:
$$8 - 17 = x + 17 - 17$$ $8 = x + 17$
$$-9 = x$$ $8 \overset{?}{=} -9 + 17$
$$8 \overset{\checkmark}{=} 8$$

8. $4 = y + 20$ Check:
$$4 - 20 = y + 20 - 20$$ $4 = y + 20$
$$-16 = y$$ $4 \overset{?}{=} -16 + 20$
$$4 \overset{\checkmark}{=} 4$$

9. $c + 9 = -9$ Check:
$$c + 9 - 9 = -9 - 9$$ $c + 9 = -9$
$$c = -18$$ $-18 + 9 \overset{?}{=} -9$
$$-9 \overset{\checkmark}{=} -9$$

10. $p + 11 = 11$ Check:
$$p + 11 - 11 = 11 - 11$$ $p + 11 = 11$
$$p = 0$$ $0 + 11 \overset{?}{=} 11$
$$11 \overset{\checkmark}{=} 11$$

11. $a - 7 = -9$ Check:
$$a - 7 + 7 = -9 + 7$$ $a - 7 = -2$
$$a = -2$$ $-2 - 7 \overset{?}{=} -9$
$$-9 \overset{\checkmark}{=} -9$$

12. $b - 9 = -11$ Check:
$$b - 9 + 9 = -11 + 9$$ $b - 9 = -11$
$$b = -2$$ $-2 - 9 \overset{?}{=} -11$
$$-11 \overset{\checkmark}{=} -11$$

13. $-10 = y - 4$ Check:
$$-10 + 4 = y - 4 + 4$$ $-10 = y - 4$
$$-6 = y$$ $-10 \overset{?}{=} -6 - 4$
$$-10 \overset{\checkmark}{=} -10$$

14. $-12 = d - 5$ Check:
$$-12 + 5 = d - 5 + 5$$ $-12 = d - 5$
$$-7 = d$$ $-12 \overset{?}{=} -7 - 5$
$$-12 \overset{\checkmark}{=} -12$$

15. $x - 9 = -9$ Check:
$$x - 9 + 9 = -9 + 9$$ $x - 9 = -9$
$$x = 0$$ $0 - 9 \overset{?}{=} -9$
$$-9 \overset{\checkmark}{=} -9$$

16. $w - 14 = -4$ Check:
$$w - 14 + 14 = -4 + 14$$ $w - 14 = -4$
$$w = 10$$ $10 - 14 \overset{?}{=} -4$
$$-4 \overset{\checkmark}{=} -4$$

17. $c - 4 = -12$ Check:
$$c - 4 + 4 = -12 + 4$$ $c - 4 = -12$
$$c = -8$$ $-8 - 4 \overset{?}{=} -12$
$$-12 \overset{\checkmark}{=} -12$$

18.

$$p - 11 = -3$$
$$p - 11 + 11 = -3 + 11$$
$$p = 8$$

Check:
$$p - 11 = -3$$
$$8 - 11 \overset{?}{=} -3$$
$$-3 \overset{\checkmark}{=} -3$$

19. $3x + 1 = 13$

$$3x = 12$$
$$x = 4$$

Check:
$$3x + 1 = 13$$
$$3(4) + 1 \overset{?}{=} 13$$
$$12 + 1 \overset{?}{=} 13$$
$$13 \overset{\checkmark}{=} 13$$

20. $2a + 3 = 7$

$$2a = 4$$
$$a = 2$$

Check:
$$2a + 3 = 7$$
$$2(2) + 3 \overset{?}{=} 7$$
$$4 + 3 \overset{?}{=} 7$$
$$7 \overset{\checkmark}{=} 7$$

21. $4y - 3 = 17$

$$4y = 20$$
$$y = 5$$

Check:
$$4y - 3 = 17$$
$$4(5) - 3 \overset{?}{=} 17$$
$$20 - 3 \overset{?}{=} 17$$
$$17 \overset{\checkmark}{=} 17$$

22. $5w - 1 = 9$

$$5w = 10$$
$$w = 2$$

Check:
$$5w - 1 = 9$$
$$5(2) - 1 \overset{?}{=} 9$$
$$10 - 1 \overset{?}{=} 9$$
$$9 \overset{\checkmark}{=} 9$$

23. $2y - 1 = 6$

$$2y = 7$$
$$y = \frac{7}{2}, \text{ or } 3\frac{1}{2}$$

Check:
$$2y - 1 = 6$$
$$2\left(3\frac{1}{2}\right) - 1 \overset{?}{=} 6$$
$$\frac{\overset{1}{\cancel{2}}}{1} \cdot \frac{7}{\underset{1}{\cancel{2}}} - 1 \overset{?}{=} 6$$
$$7 - 1 \overset{?}{=} 6$$
$$6 \overset{\checkmark}{=} 6$$

24. $3y - 5 = 3$

$$3y = 8$$
$$y = \frac{8}{3}, \text{ or } 2\frac{2}{3}$$

Check:
$$3y - 5 = 3$$
$$3\left(2\frac{2}{3}\right) - 5 \overset{?}{=} 3$$
$$\frac{\overset{1}{\cancel{3}}}{1} \cdot \frac{8}{\underset{1}{\cancel{3}}} - 5 \overset{?}{=} 3$$
$$8 - 5 \overset{?}{=} 3$$
$$3 \overset{\checkmark}{=} 3$$

25. $-x + 9 = 4$

$$-x = -5$$
$$x = 5$$

Check:
$$-x + 9 = 4$$
$$-5 + 9 \overset{?}{=} 4$$
$$4 \overset{\checkmark}{=} 4$$

26. $-a + 7 = -6$

$$-a = -1$$
$$a = 1$$

Check:
$$-a + 7 = 6$$
$$-1 + 7 \overset{?}{=} 6$$
$$6 \overset{\checkmark}{=} 6$$

27. $1 - y = 6$

$$-y = 5$$
$$y = -5$$

Check:
$$1 - y = 6$$
$$1 - (-5) \overset{?}{=} 6$$
$$1 + 5 \overset{?}{=} 6$$
$$6 \overset{\checkmark}{=} 6$$

28. $2 - w = 4$

$$2 - 2 - w = 4 - 2$$
$$-w = 2$$
$$w = -2$$

Check:
$$2 - w = 4$$
$$2 - (-2) \overset{?}{=} 4$$
$$2 + 2 \overset{?}{=} 4$$
$$4 \overset{\checkmark}{=} 4$$

29. $-c - 6 = 6$

$$-c = 12$$
$$c = -12$$

Check:
$$-c - 6 = 6$$
$$-(-12) - 6 \overset{?}{=} 6$$
$$12 - 6 \overset{?}{=} 6$$
$$6 \overset{\checkmark}{=} 6$$

30. $-a - 9 = 9$

$$-a = 18$$
$$a = -18$$

Check:
$$-a - 9 = 9$$
$$-(-18) - 9 \overset{?}{=} 9$$
$$18 - 9 \overset{?}{=} 9$$
$$9 \overset{\checkmark}{=} 9$$

31. $\dfrac{a}{3}+1=9$ Check:

$\dfrac{a}{3}=8$ $\qquad \dfrac{a}{3}+1=9$

$a=24$ $\qquad \dfrac{24}{3}+1\overset{?}{=}9$

$\qquad\qquad\qquad 8+1\overset{?}{=}9$

$\qquad\qquad\qquad\quad 9\overset{\checkmark}{=}9$

32. $\dfrac{w}{4}+3=7$ Check:

$\dfrac{w}{4}=4$ $\qquad \dfrac{w}{4}+3=7$

$w=16$ $\qquad \dfrac{16}{4}+3\overset{?}{=}7$

$\qquad\qquad\qquad 4+3\overset{?}{=}7$

$\qquad\qquad\qquad\quad 7\overset{\checkmark}{=}7$

33. $\dfrac{x}{5}+4=-1$ Check:

$\dfrac{x}{5}=-5$ $\qquad \dfrac{x}{5}+4=-1$

$x=-25$ $\qquad \dfrac{-25}{5}+4\overset{?}{=}-1$

$\qquad\qquad\qquad -5+4\overset{?}{=}-1$

$\qquad\qquad\qquad\quad -1\overset{\checkmark}{=}-1$

34. $\dfrac{b}{2}+2=-3$ Check:

$\dfrac{b}{2}=-5$ $\qquad \dfrac{b}{2}+2=-3$

$b=-10$ $\qquad \dfrac{-10}{2}+3\overset{?}{=}-3$

$\qquad\qquad\qquad -5+3\overset{?}{=}-3$

$\qquad\qquad\qquad\quad -3\overset{\checkmark}{=}3$

35. $\dfrac{c}{7}-1=-1$ Check:

$\dfrac{c}{7}=0$ $\qquad \dfrac{c}{7}-1=-1$

$c=0$ $\qquad \dfrac{0}{7}-1\overset{?}{=}-1$

$\qquad\qquad\qquad 0-1\overset{?}{=}-1$

$\qquad\qquad\qquad\quad -1\overset{\checkmark}{=}-1$

36. $\dfrac{d}{8}-2=-2$ Check:

$\dfrac{d}{8}=0$ $\qquad \dfrac{d}{8}-2=-2$

$d=0$ $\qquad \dfrac{0}{8}-2\overset{?}{=}-2$

$\qquad\qquad\qquad 0-2\overset{?}{=}-2$

$\qquad\qquad\qquad\quad -2\overset{\checkmark}{=}-2$

37. $4y-2y=18$ Check:

$2y=18$ $\qquad 4y-2y=18$

$y=9$ $\qquad 4\cdot 9-2\cdot 9\overset{?}{=}18$

$\qquad\qquad\qquad 26-18\overset{?}{=}18$

$\qquad\qquad\qquad\quad 18\overset{\checkmark}{=}18$

38. $-2b+7b=30$ Check:

$5b=30$ $\qquad -2b+7b=30$

$b=6$ $\qquad -2\cdot 6+7\cdot 6\overset{?}{=}30$

$\qquad\qquad\qquad -12+42\overset{?}{=}30$

$\qquad\qquad\qquad\quad 30\overset{\checkmark}{=}30$

39. $2c+c=-6$ Check:

$3c=6$ $\qquad 2c+c=-6$

$c=-2$ $\qquad 2\cdot(-2)+(-2)\overset{?}{=}-6$

$\qquad\qquad\qquad -4-2\overset{?}{=}-6$

$\qquad\qquad\qquad\quad -6\overset{\checkmark}{=}-6$

40. $-8x+3x=-11$ Check:

$-5x=-11$ $\qquad\qquad -8x+3x=-11$

$x=\dfrac{11}{5}$, or $2\dfrac{1}{5}$ $\quad -8\cdot\left(2\dfrac{1}{5}\right)+3\cdot\left(2\dfrac{1}{5}\right)\overset{?}{=}-11$

$\qquad\qquad\qquad -\dfrac{8}{1}\cdot\dfrac{11}{5}+\dfrac{3}{1}\cdot\dfrac{11}{5}\overset{?}{=}-11$

$\qquad\qquad\qquad\qquad -\dfrac{88}{5}+\dfrac{33}{5}\overset{?}{=}-11$

$\qquad\qquad\qquad\qquad\qquad -\dfrac{55}{5}\overset{?}{=}-11$

$\qquad\qquad\qquad\qquad\qquad\quad -11\overset{\checkmark}{=}-11$

41. $y+y+2=18$ Check:

$2y=16$ $\qquad y+y+2=18$

$y=8$ $\qquad 8+8+2\overset{?}{=}18$

$\qquad\qquad\qquad 18\overset{\checkmark}{=}18$

42. $5-t-t=-1$ Check:

$\quad\quad 5-2t=-1$ $\quad\quad 5-t-t=-1$

$\quad\quad -2t=-6$ $\quad\quad 5-3-3\overset{?}{=}-1$

$\quad\quad\quad t=3$ $\quad\quad\quad\quad -1\overset{\checkmark}{=}-1$

43. $3x-4x+6=-2$ Check:

$\quad\quad\quad -x=-8$ $\quad\quad 3x-4x+6=-2$

$\quad\quad\quad\quad x=8$ $\quad\quad 3\cdot 8-4\cdot 8+6\overset{?}{=}-2$

$\quad\quad\quad\quad\quad\quad 24-32+6\overset{?}{=}-2$

$\quad\quad\quad\quad\quad\quad\quad\quad -2\overset{\checkmark}{=}-2$

44. $7=4m-2m+1$ Check:

$\quad\quad 6=2m$ $\quad\quad 7=4m-2m+1$

$\quad\quad 3=m$ $\quad\quad 7\overset{?}{=}4\cdot 3-2\cdot 3+1$

$\quad\quad\quad\quad 7\overset{?}{=}12-6+1$

$\quad\quad\quad\quad 7\overset{\checkmark}{=}7$

45. $0=-7n+4-5n$ Check:

$\quad\quad -4=-12n$ $\quad\quad 0=-7n+4-5n$

$\quad\quad \dfrac{1}{3}=n$ $\quad\quad 0\overset{?}{=}-7\cdot\dfrac{1}{3}+4-5\cdot\dfrac{1}{3}$

$\quad\quad\quad\quad 0\overset{?}{=}-\dfrac{7}{1}\cdot\dfrac{1}{3}+4-\dfrac{5}{1}\cdot\dfrac{1}{3}$

$\quad\quad\quad\quad 0\overset{?}{=}-\dfrac{12}{3}+4$

$\quad\quad\quad\quad 0\overset{?}{=}-4+4$

$\quad\quad\quad\quad 0\overset{\checkmark}{=}0$

46. $a-5a-6=30$ Check:

$\quad\quad\quad -4a=36$ $\quad\quad a-5a-6=30$

$\quad\quad\quad\quad a=-9$ $\quad\quad -9-5\cdot(-9)-6\overset{?}{=}30$

$\quad\quad\quad\quad\quad\quad -9+45-6\overset{?}{=}30$

$\quad\quad\quad\quad\quad\quad\quad 30\overset{\checkmark}{=}30$

47. $4r+2=3r-6$ Check:

$\quad\quad 4r-3r=-6-2$ $\quad\quad 4r+2=3r-6$

$\quad\quad\quad r=-8$ $\quad\quad 4\cdot(-8)+2\overset{?}{=}3\cdot(-8)-6$

$\quad\quad\quad\quad\quad -32+2\overset{?}{=}-24-6$

$\quad\quad\quad\quad\quad\quad -30\overset{\checkmark}{=}-30$

48. $-5y+8=-3y+10$ Check:

$\quad\quad -5y+3y=10-8$ $\quad\quad -5y+8=-3y+10$

$\quad\quad\quad -2y=2$ $\quad\quad -5\cdot(-1)+8\overset{?}{=}-3\cdot(-1)+10$

$\quad\quad\quad\quad y=-1$ $\quad\quad\quad\quad 5+8\overset{?}{=}3+10$

$\quad\quad\quad\quad\quad\quad 13\overset{\checkmark}{=}13$

49. $2x-8=x+1$ Check:

$\quad\quad 2x-x=1+8$ $\quad\quad 2x-8=x+1$

$\quad\quad\quad x=9$ $\quad\quad 2\cdot 9-8\overset{?}{=}9+1$

$\quad\quad\quad\quad 18-8\overset{?}{=}10$

$\quad\quad\quad\quad 10\overset{\checkmark}{=}10$

50. $4y-1=2y-3$ Check:

$\quad\quad 4y-2y=-3+1$ $\quad\quad 4y-1=2y-3$

$\quad\quad\quad 2y=-2$ $\quad\quad 4\cdot(-1)-1\overset{?}{=}2\cdot(-1)-3$

$\quad\quad\quad y=-1$ $\quad\quad\quad -4-1\overset{?}{=}-2-3$

$\quad\quad\quad\quad -5\overset{\checkmark}{=}-5$

51. $7s+4=5s+8$ Check:

$\quad\quad 7s-5s=8-4$ $\quad\quad 7s+4=5s+8$

$\quad\quad\quad 2s=4$ $\quad\quad 7\cdot 2+4\overset{?}{=}5\cdot 2+8$

$\quad\quad\quad s=2$ $\quad\quad 14+4\overset{?}{=}10+8$

$\quad\quad\quad\quad 18\overset{\checkmark}{=}18$

52. $2+8x=3x-8$ Check:

$\quad\quad\quad 5x=-10$ $\quad\quad 2+8x=3x-8$

$\quad\quad\quad x=-2$ $\quad\quad 2+8\cdot(-2)\overset{?}{=}3\cdot(-2)-8$

$\quad\quad\quad\quad 2-16\overset{?}{=}-6-8$

$\quad\quad\quad\quad -14\overset{\checkmark}{=}-14$

53. $5m-9=9-4m$ Check:

$\quad\quad 9m=18$ $\quad\quad 5m-9=9-4m$

$\quad\quad m=2$ $\quad\quad 5\cdot 2-9\overset{?}{=}9-4\cdot 2$

$\quad\quad\quad\quad 10-9\overset{?}{=}9-8$

$\quad\quad\quad\quad 1\overset{\checkmark}{=}1$

54. $x=-x+12$ Check:

$\quad\quad 2x=12$ $\quad\quad x=-x+12$

$\quad\quad x=6$ $\quad\quad 6\overset{?}{=}-6+12$

$\quad\quad\quad\quad 6\overset{\checkmark}{=}6$

55. $s+s-6\frac{2}{3}=4\frac{1}{3}+s$ Check:

$$s=4\frac{1}{3}+6\frac{2}{3} \qquad s+s-6\frac{2}{3}=4\frac{1}{3}+s$$

$$s=11 \qquad 11+11-\frac{20}{3}\overset{?}{=}\frac{13}{3}+11$$

$$\frac{66}{3}-\frac{20}{3}\overset{?}{=}\frac{13}{3}+\frac{33}{3}$$

$$\frac{46}{3}\overset{\checkmark}{=}\frac{46}{3}$$

56. $5z-6\frac{1}{2}=z-4z+\frac{1}{2}$ Check:

$$8z=7 \qquad 5z-6\frac{1}{2}=z-4z+\frac{1}{2}$$

$$z=\frac{7}{8} \qquad 5\cdot\frac{7}{8}-\frac{13}{2}\overset{?}{=}\frac{7}{8}-4\cdot\frac{7}{8}+\frac{1}{2}$$

$$\frac{35}{8}-\frac{52}{8}\overset{?}{=}\frac{7}{8}-\frac{28}{8}+\frac{4}{8}$$

$$-\frac{17}{8}\overset{\checkmark}{=}-\frac{17}{8}$$

57. $2(8+w)=22$ Check:

$$8+w=11 \qquad 2(8+w)=22$$

$$w=3$$

$$2(8+3)\overset{?}{=}22$$

$$2(11)\overset{?}{=}22$$

$$22\overset{\checkmark}{=}22$$

58. $-3(z+5)=-15$ Check:

$$z+5=5 \qquad -3(z+5)=-15$$

$$z=0$$

$$-3(0+5)\overset{?}{=}-15$$

$$-3(5)\overset{?}{=}-15$$

$$-15\overset{\checkmark}{=}-15$$

59. $6x+12(10-x)=84$ Check:

$$6x+120-12x=84 \qquad 6x+12(10-x)=84$$

$$-6x=-36$$

$$x=6 \qquad 6\cdot 6+12(10-6)\overset{?}{=}84$$

$$36+12\cdot 4\overset{?}{=}84$$

$$36+48\overset{?}{=}84$$

$$84\overset{\checkmark}{=}84$$

60. $3(y-1)+y=37$ Check:

$$3y-3+y=37 \qquad 3(y-1)+y=37$$

$$4y=40$$

$$y=10 \qquad 3(10-1)+10\overset{?}{=}37$$

$$3(9)+10\overset{?}{=}37$$

$$27+10\overset{?}{=}37$$

$$37\overset{\checkmark}{=}37$$

61. $6(y+4)=2y-8$ Check:

$$6y+24=2y-8 \qquad 6(y+4)=2y-8$$

$$4y=-32$$

$$y=-8 \qquad 6(-8+4)\overset{?}{=}2(-8)-8$$

$$6(-4)\overset{?}{=}-16-8$$

$$-24\overset{\checkmark}{=}-24$$

62. $5(m-1)=11-m$ Check:

$$5m-5=11-m \qquad 5(m-1)=11-m$$

$$6m=16$$

$$m=\frac{16}{6}, \text{ or } 2\frac{2}{3} \qquad 5\left(2\frac{2}{3}-1\right)\overset{?}{=}11-2\frac{2}{3}$$

$$5\left(1\frac{2}{3}\right)\overset{?}{=}8\frac{1}{3}$$

$$\frac{5}{1}\cdot\frac{5}{3}\overset{?}{=}\frac{25}{3}$$

$$\frac{25}{3}\overset{\checkmark}{=}\frac{25}{3}$$

63. $0=\frac{1}{3}(6b+9)+b$ Check:

$$0=2b+3+b \qquad 0=\frac{1}{3}(6b+9)+b$$

$$-3=3b$$

$$-1=b \qquad 0\overset{?}{=}\frac{1}{3}(6(-1)+9)+(-1)$$

$$0\overset{?}{=}\frac{1}{3}(3)-1$$

$$0\overset{\checkmark}{=}0$$

64. $-\frac{1}{5}(10d-5)=9$ Check:

$$-2d+1=9 \qquad -\frac{1}{5}(10d-5)=9$$

$$-2d=8$$

$$d=-4 \qquad -\frac{1}{5}(10(-4)-5)\overset{?}{=}9$$

$$-\frac{1}{5}(-40-5)\overset{?}{=}9$$

$$-\frac{1}{5}(-45)\overset{?}{=}9$$

$$9\overset{\checkmark}{=}9$$

65. $R = F + 460$

66. $C = \dfrac{W}{150} \cdot A$

67. $A = \dfrac{a+b+c+d+e}{5}$

68. $m = \dfrac{1}{2}(s+l)$

69.

Formula	Given	Find
$F = ma$	$m = 3.6$ $a = 14$	$F = (3.6)(14)$ $F = 50.4$

70.

Formula	Given	Find
$d = 16t^2$	$t = 3$	$d = 16\left(3^2\right) = 16(9)$ $d = 144$

71.

Formula	Given	Find
$P = n(p-c)$	$n = 8$ $p = 350$ $c = 240$	$P = 8(350-240) = 8(110)$ $P = 880$

72.

Formula	Given	Find
$C = \dfrac{5}{9}(F-32)$	$F = -4$	$C = \dfrac{5}{9}(-4-32) = \dfrac{5}{9}(-36)$ $C = -20$

73. $c = p \cdot n$

$\$269 = p \cdot 50$

$p = \dfrac{\$269}{50}$

$p = \$5.38$

The price per unit is $5.38/unit.

74. Let w be the number of weeks it takes you to pay for the camcorder.

$45 + w \cdot 50 = 895$

$50w = 850$

$w = 17$

It will take you 17 weeks.

75. Let w stand for the width of the rug.

$2 \cdot 12 + 2 \cdot w = 42$

$24 + 2w = 42$

$2w = 18$

$w = 9$

The width of the rug is 9 ft.

76. $s = r - d$

$s = 325 - 53.95$

$s = 271.05$

The sale price is $271.05.

77. $D = \dfrac{m}{V}$

$D = \dfrac{10\text{ g}}{10.9\text{ ml}}$

$D = 0.917...\text{ g/ml}$

$D \approx 0.9\text{ g/ml}$

The density is approximately 0.9 g/ml.

78. $h = 2.38t + 61.41$

$150 = 2.38t + 61.41$

$81.59 = 2.38t$

$t = 37.22...$

$t \approx 37.2$

The thigh-bone length that predicts a height of 150 cm is 37.2 cm, rounded to the nearest cm.

Posttest

1. $x + 5 = 0$

$x + 5 - 5 = 0 - 5$

$x = -5$

Check:

$x + 5 = 0$

$-5 + 5 \overset{?}{=} 0$

$0 \overset{\checkmark}{=} 0$

2. $y - 6 = -6$

$y - 6 + 6 = -6 + 6$

$y = 0$

Check:

$y - 6 = -6$

$0 - 6 \overset{?}{=} -6$

$-6 \overset{\checkmark}{=} -6$

3. $27 = -9a$

$\dfrac{27}{-9} = \dfrac{-9a}{-9}$

$-3 = a$

Check:

$27 = -9a$

$27 \overset{?}{=} -9(-3)$

$27 \overset{\checkmark}{=} 27$

4. $-2 = \dfrac{b}{5}$

$-2 \cdot 5 = \dfrac{b}{5} \cdot 5$

$-10 = b$

Check:

$-2 = \dfrac{b}{5}$

$-2 \overset{?}{=} \dfrac{-10}{5}$

$-2 \overset{\checkmark}{=} -2$

5. $2x + 3 = 4$

$2x = 1$

$x = \dfrac{1}{2}$

Check:

$2x + 3 = 4$

$2 \cdot \dfrac{1}{2} + 3 \overset{?}{=} 4$

$1 + 3 \overset{?}{=} 4$

$4 \overset{\checkmark}{=} 4$

6. $4y + 1 = -9$

$4y = -10$

$y = -\dfrac{10}{4}$

$y = -\dfrac{5}{2}, \text{ or } -2\dfrac{1}{2}$

Check:

$4y + 1 = -9$

$4\left(-2\dfrac{1}{2}\right) + 1 \overset{?}{=} -9$

$\dfrac{\cancel{4}}{1} \cdot \left(-\dfrac{5}{\cancel{2}}\right) + 1 \overset{?}{=} -9$

$-10 + 1 \overset{?}{=} -9$

$-9 \overset{\checkmark}{=} -9$

7. $-10 = 7w - 1$

$-9 = 7w$

$w = -\dfrac{9}{7}, \text{ or } -1\dfrac{2}{7}$

Check:

$-10 = 7w - 1$

$-10 \overset{?}{=} 7\left(-1\dfrac{2}{7}\right) - 1$

$-10 \overset{?}{=} \dfrac{\cancel{7}}{1}\left(-\dfrac{9}{\cancel{7}}\right) - 1$

$-10 \overset{?}{=} -9 - 1$

$-10 \overset{\checkmark}{=} -10$

8. $-y + 2 = 11$

$-y = 9$

$y = -9$

Check:

$-y + 2 = 11$

$-(-9) + 2 \overset{?}{=} 11$

$9 + 2 \overset{?}{=} 11$

$11 \overset{\checkmark}{=} 11$

9. $\dfrac{a}{5} + 6 = 6$

$\dfrac{a}{5} = 0$

$a = 0$

Check:

$\dfrac{a}{5} + 6 = 6$

$\dfrac{0}{5} + 6 \overset{?}{=} 6$

$0 + 6 \overset{?}{=} 6$

$6 \overset{\checkmark}{=} 6$

10. $3x - 5x = 12$

$-2x = 12$

$x = -6$

Check:

$3x - 5x = 12$

$3(-6) - 5(-6) \overset{?}{=} 12$

$-18 + 30 \overset{?}{=} 12$

$12 \overset{\checkmark}{=} 12$

11. $-4c + 3 = 7 - 2c$

$-4c + 2c = 7 - 3$

$-2c = 4$

$c = -2$

Check:

$-4c + 3 = 7 - 2c$

$-4(-2) + 3 \overset{?}{=} 7 - 2(-2)$

$8 + 3 \overset{?}{=} 7 + 4$

$11 \overset{\checkmark}{=} 11$

12. $-2x = 4(x - 3)$

$-2x = 4x - 12$

$-6x = -12$

$x = 2$

Check:

$-2x = 4(x - 3)$

$-2(2) \overset{?}{=} 4(2 - 3)$

$-4 \overset{?}{=} 4(-1)$

$-4 \overset{\checkmark}{=} -4$

13. $D = 4.9t^2$

14. $y = mx + b$

$y = \left(-\dfrac{1}{2}\right)(-3) + (-4)$

$y = \dfrac{3}{2} - 4$

$y = -2\dfrac{1}{2}$

15. If x represents the number of additional minutes, the equation is $0.35 + 0.16x = 2.75$.

$0.35 + 0.16x = 2.75$

$0.16x = 2.40$

$x = 15$

There were 15 additional minutes after the first, so the total length of the call was 16 min.

16. If P is the suggested retail price, the equation is $100 + \dfrac{8}{9}P = 12{,}906$.

$100 + \dfrac{8}{9}P = 12{,}906$

$\dfrac{8}{9}P = 12{,}806$

$P = 12{,}806 \cdot \dfrac{9}{8}$

$P = 14{,}406.75$

The suggested retail price is \$14,406.75.

17. If x is the cost of the keyboard, the equation is $(x + 300) + (x + 900) = 1{,}800$.

$$(x+300)+(x+900)=1,800$$
$$2x+1,200=1,800$$
$$2x=600$$
$$x=300$$
The cost of the keyboard is \$300.

18. Let n be the number. The equation is
$4(n+3)=5n$.
$$4(n+3)=5n$$
$$4n+12=5n$$
$$-n=-12$$
$$n=12$$
The number is 12. Check: $4(12+3)=60$ and
$5\cdot 12=60$.

19. a. $d=2.2r$
    b. $d=2.2r$
$$d=2.2(55)$$
$$d=121$$
The reaction distance is 121 ft.

20. a. $f=\dfrac{22}{15}m$
    b. $f=\dfrac{22}{15}m$
$$f=\dfrac{22}{\cancel{15}}\cdot\dfrac{\overset{3}{\cancel{45}}}{1}$$
$$\underset{1}{}$$
$$f=66$$
The object's speed is 66 fps.

6. $\dfrac{75}{1,275}=\dfrac{\overset{1}{\cancel{75}}\cdot 1}{\cancel{75}\cdot 17}=\dfrac{1}{17}$
$$\underset{1}{}$$

The ratio of officers to enlisted men is $\dfrac{1}{17}$.

7. $3x-5=13$
$$3x=18$$
$$x=6$$

8. The change represents an increase because 0.1 is larger than 0.075 (by 0.025).

9. The stock was least expensive on Monday.

10. $i=\dfrac{697.5w}{h^2}$
$$i=\dfrac{697.5(100)}{(60)^2}$$
$$i\approx\dfrac{700\times100}{60\times60}=\dfrac{70,000}{3,600}\approx\dfrac{70,000}{3,500}=20$$
A reasonable estimate for the body mass index is 20.

Cumulative Review Exercises

1. $3,\underline{8}17 \approx 3,800$

2. Three million, four hundred

3. $(0.1)^3 = (0.1)(0.1)(0.1) = 0.001$

4. $\dfrac{25}{30}=\dfrac{p}{100}$
$$30p=2,500$$
$$p=\dfrac{2,500}{30}$$
$$p=\dfrac{250}{3}, \text{ or } 83\dfrac{1}{3}$$
25 is $83\dfrac{1}{3}$% of 30.

5. $(-1)^2-3=1-3=-2$

Chapter 10

MEASUREMENT AND UNITS

Pretest

1. $8 \text{ qt} = 8 \, \cancel{\text{qt}} \times \dfrac{1 \text{ gal}}{4 \, \cancel{\text{qt}}} = 2 \text{ gal}$

2. $5 \text{ tons} = 5 \, \cancel{\text{tons}} \times \dfrac{2{,}000 \text{ lb}}{1 \, \cancel{\text{ton}}} = 10{,}000 \text{ lb}$

3.
$$
\begin{array}{r}
\overset{1 \text{ ft}}{7 \text{ ft } 11 \text{ in.}} \\
+4 \text{ ft } 7 \text{ in.} \\
\hline
\cancel{18 \text{ in.}} \\
6 \text{ in.}
\end{array}
$$
$$
\begin{array}{r}
\overset{1 \text{ ft}}{7 \text{ ft } 11 \text{ in.}} \\
+4 \text{ ft } 7 \text{ in.} \\
\hline
12 \text{ ft } 6 \text{ in.}
\end{array}
$$

4. b (a gram is a measure of length)

5. The width of a dime is about a centimeter (choice d).

6. $3.5 \text{ kg} = 3.5 \, \cancel{\text{kg}} \times \dfrac{1{,}000 \text{ g}}{1 \, \cancel{\text{kg}}} = 3{,}500 \text{ g}$

7. $2{,}100 \text{ mm} = 2{,}100 \, \cancel{\text{mm}} \times \dfrac{1 \text{ m}}{1{,}000 \, \cancel{\text{mm}}} = 2.1 \text{ m}$

8. To compare, convert 2.3 m into cm.

   $2.3 \text{ m} = 2.3 \, \cancel{\text{m}} \times \dfrac{100 \text{ cm}}{1 \, \cancel{\text{m}}} = 230 \text{ cm}$

   Since 230 is less than 700, 700 cm is larger.

9. $0.5 \text{ L} = 0.5 \, \cancel{\text{L}} \times \dfrac{1{,}000 \text{ ml}}{1 \, \cancel{\text{L}}} = 500 \text{ ml}$

10. $75 \text{ mg} = 75 \, \cancel{\text{mg}} \times \dfrac{1 \text{ g}}{1{,}000 \, \cancel{\text{mg}}} = 0.075 \text{ g}$

10.1 U.S. Customary Units

Practice

1. $5 \text{ pt} = 5 \, \cancel{\text{pt}} \times \dfrac{1 \text{ qt}}{2 \, \cancel{\text{pt}}} = \dfrac{5}{2} \text{ qt, or } 2\dfrac{1}{2} \text{ qt}$

2. $30 \text{ qt} = 30 \, \cancel{\text{qt}} \times \dfrac{1 \text{ gal}}{4 \, \cancel{\text{qt}}} = \dfrac{30}{4} \text{ gal} = 7.5 \text{ gal}$

   7.5 gal will be needed to fill the barrel.

3. $1 \text{ day} = 1 \text{ day} \times \dfrac{24 \, \cancel{\text{hr}}}{1 \, \cancel{\text{day}}} \times \dfrac{60 \, \cancel{\text{min}}}{1 \, \cancel{\text{hr}}} \times \dfrac{60 \text{ sec}}{1 \, \cancel{\text{min}}}$

   $= 86{,}400 \text{ sec}$

   There are 86,400 sec in 1 day.

4. $3 \text{ pt} = 3 \, \cancel{\text{pt}} \times \dfrac{1 \text{ qt}}{2 \, \cancel{\text{pt}}} = \dfrac{3}{2} \text{ qt, or } 1.5 \text{ qt}$

   You can't completely fill a 2-qt container since
   $3 \text{ pt} = 1.5 \text{ qt}$.

5.
$$
\begin{array}{r}
\overset{1 \text{ lb}}{3 \text{ lb } 10 \text{ oz}} \\
+1 \text{ lb } 14 \text{ oz} \\
\hline
\cancel{24 \text{ oz}} \\
8 \text{ oz}
\end{array}
$$
Because 24 oz = 1 lb 8 oz, replace 24 oz with 8 oz and carry 1 lb.
$$
\begin{array}{r}
\overset{1 \text{ lb}}{3 \text{ lb } 10 \text{ oz}} \\
+1 \text{ lb } 14 \text{ oz} \\
\hline
5 \text{ lb } \ 8 \text{ oz}
\end{array}
$$

6.
$$
\begin{array}{r}
\overset{1 \text{ yr}}{8 \text{ mo}} \\
11 \text{ mo} \\
+1 \text{ yr } \ 2 \text{ mo} \\
\hline
2 \text{ yr } \cancel{21 \text{ mo}} \\
9 \text{ mo}
\end{array}
$$
You worked 2 yr 9 mo in all.

7.
$$
\begin{array}{r}
6 \text{ gal} \\
-5 \text{ gal } 1 \text{ qt}
\end{array}
$$
Borrow 1 gal from 6 gal and replace it by 4 qt.
$$
\begin{array}{r}
\overset{5}{\cancel{6}} \text{ gal } 4 \text{ qt} \\
-5 \text{ gal } 1 \text{ qt} \\
\hline
3 \text{ qt}
\end{array}
$$
6 gal is 3 qt greater than 5 gal 1 qt.

8.
$$
\begin{array}{r}
\overset{1}{\cancel{2}} \text{ min } \overset{65}{\cancel{5}} \text{ sec} \\
-1 \text{ min } 59 \text{ sec} \\
\hline
6 \text{ sec}
\end{array}
$$
The difference between the two times was 6 sec.

Exercises

1. $48\text{ in.} = 48\ \cancel{\text{in.}} \times \dfrac{1\text{ ft}}{12\ \cancel{\text{in.}}} = 4\text{ ft}$

3. $9\text{ ft} = 9\ \cancel{\text{ft}} \times \dfrac{1\text{ yd}}{3\ \cancel{\text{ft}}} = 3\text{ yd}$

5. $6\text{ pt} = 6\ \cancel{\text{pt}} \times \dfrac{1\text{ qt}}{2\ \cancel{\text{pt}}} = 3\text{ qt}$

7. $32\text{ oz} = 32\ \cancel{\text{oz}} \times \dfrac{1\text{ lb}}{16\ \cancel{\text{oz}}} = 2\text{ lb}$

9. $36\text{ mo} = 36\ \cancel{\text{mo}} \times \dfrac{1\text{ yr}}{12\ \cancel{\text{mo}}} = 3\text{ yr}$

11. $7\text{ min} = 7\ \cancel{\text{min}} \times \dfrac{60\text{ sec}}{1\ \cancel{\text{min}}} = 420\text{ sec}$

13. $32\text{ pt} = 32\ \cancel{\text{pt}} \times \dfrac{16\text{ fl oz}}{1\ \cancel{\text{pt}}} = 512\text{ fl oz}$

15. $30\text{ min} = 30\ \cancel{\text{min}} \times \dfrac{1\text{ hr}}{60\ \cancel{\text{min}}} = \dfrac{1}{2}\text{ hr}$

17. $2\text{ mi} = 2\ \cancel{\text{mi}} \times \dfrac{5{,}280\ \cancel{\text{ft}}}{1\ \cancel{\text{mi}}} \times \dfrac{1\text{ yd}}{3\ \cancel{\text{ft}}}$

$= \dfrac{2 \times 5{,}280}{3}\text{ yd} = 3{,}520\text{ yd}$

19. $5\text{ wk} = 5\ \cancel{\text{wk}} \times \dfrac{7\text{ days}}{1\ \cancel{\text{wk}}} = 35\text{ days}$

21. $\dfrac{1}{2}\text{ hr} = \dfrac{1}{2}\ \cancel{\text{hr}} \times \dfrac{1\text{ day}}{24\ \cancel{\text{hr}}} = \dfrac{1}{48}\text{ day}$

23. $\dfrac{1}{2}\text{ gal} = \dfrac{1}{2}\ \cancel{\text{gal}} \times \dfrac{4\text{ qt}}{1\ \cancel{\text{gal}}} = 2\text{ qt}$

25. $7\text{ pt} = 7\ \cancel{\text{pt}} \times \dfrac{1\text{ qt}}{2\ \cancel{\text{pt}}} = 3.5\text{ qt}$

27. $1\dfrac{1}{2}\text{ tons} = \dfrac{3}{2}\ \cancel{\text{tons}} \times \dfrac{2{,}000\text{ lb}}{1\ \cancel{\text{ton}}} = 3{,}000\text{ lb}$

29. $5\text{ min } 10\text{ sec} = 5\ \cancel{\text{min}} \times \dfrac{60\text{ sec}}{1\ \cancel{\text{min}}} + 10\text{ sec}$

$= 300\text{ sec} + 10\text{ sec} = 310\text{ sec}$

31. $117\text{ mi} = 117\ \cancel{\text{mi}} \times \dfrac{5{,}280\text{ ft}}{1\ \cancel{\text{mi}}} = 617{,}760\text{ ft}$

33.
$$\begin{array}{r} \overset{3}{\cancel{4}}\text{ lb } \overset{23}{\cancel{7}}\text{ oz} \\ -2\text{ lb } 9\text{ oz} \\ \hline 1\text{ lb } 14\text{ oz} \end{array}$$

35.
$$\begin{array}{r} 20\text{ lb } 5\text{ oz} \\ +\ 9\text{ lb } 10\text{ oz} \\ \hline 29\text{ lb } 15\text{ oz} \end{array}$$

37.
$$\begin{array}{r} 1\text{ yr} \\ 5\text{ yr } 7\text{ mo} \\ +3\text{ yr } 11\text{ mo} \\ \hline \cancel{18\text{ mo}} \\ 6\text{ mo} \end{array} \qquad \begin{array}{r} 1\text{ yr} \\ 5\text{ yr } 7\text{ mo} \\ +3\text{ yr } 11\text{ mo} \\ \hline 9\text{ yr } 6\text{ mo} \end{array}$$

39.
$$\begin{array}{r} \overset{4}{\cancel{5}}\text{ gal } \overset{5}{\cancel{1}}\text{ qt} \\ -2\text{ gal } 2\text{ qt} \\ \hline 2\text{ gal } 3\text{ qt} \end{array}$$

41.
$$\begin{array}{r} 1\text{ qt} \\ 2\text{ qt } 1\text{ pt} \\ +1\text{ qt } 1\text{ pt} \\ \hline \cancel{2\text{ pt}} \\ 0\text{ pt} \end{array} \qquad \begin{array}{r} 1\text{ qt} \\ 2\text{ qt } 1\text{ pt} \\ +1\text{ qt } 1\text{ pt} \\ \hline 4\text{ qt } 0\text{ pt} = 4\text{ qt} \end{array}$$

43.
$$\begin{array}{r} 1\text{ min} \\ 6\text{ min } 2\text{ sec} \\ 70\text{ sec} \\ +1\text{ min } 3\text{ sec} \\ \hline \cancel{75\text{ sec}} \\ 15\text{ sec} \end{array} \qquad \begin{array}{r} 1\text{ min} \\ 6\text{ min } 2\text{ sec} \\ 70\text{ sec} \\ +1\text{ min } 3\text{ sec} \\ \hline 8\text{ min } 15\text{ sec} \end{array}$$

45. Convert the weight of the burger to ounces.

$\dfrac{1}{4}\text{ lb} = \dfrac{1}{4}\ \cancel{\text{lb}} \times \dfrac{16\text{ oz}}{1\ \cancel{\text{lb}}} = 4\text{ oz}$

The burger and the piece of cheese weigh the same.

47. Convert the width of the refrigerator to inches.

$3\text{ ft} = 3\ \cancel{\text{ft}} \times \dfrac{12\text{ in.}}{3\ \cancel{\text{ft}}} = 36\text{ in.}$

No, the refrigerator is 1 in. too wide.

49. $823\text{ sec} = 823\ \cancel{\text{sec}} \times \dfrac{1\text{ min}}{60\ \cancel{\text{sec}}} = \dfrac{823}{60}\text{ min}$

$= 13\dfrac{43}{60}\text{ min} = 13\text{ min} + \dfrac{43}{60}\ \cancel{\text{min}} \times \dfrac{60\text{ sec}}{1\ \cancel{\text{min}}}$

$= 13\text{ min } 43\text{ sec}$

823 sec is 13 min 43 sec.

51. $4\text{ score} = 4\ \cancel{\text{score}} \times \dfrac{20\text{ yr}}{1\ \cancel{\text{score}}} = 80\text{ yr}$

$80\text{ yr} + 7\text{ yr} = 87\ \cancel{\text{yr}} \times \dfrac{12\text{ mo}}{1\ \cancel{\text{yr}}} = 1{,}044\text{ mo}$

Four score and 7 years is 1,044 months.

53.
$$\begin{array}{r} {}^{2}\!\!\not{3}\,\text{lb}\ {}^{20}\!\!\not{4}\,\text{oz} \\ -1\ \text{lb}\ 15\ \text{oz} \\ \hline 1\ \text{lb}\ \ 5\ \text{oz} \end{array}$$

The difference between their weights was 1 lb 5 oz.

55.
$$\begin{array}{r} 3\ \text{yr} \\ -1\ \text{yr}\ \ 2\ \text{mo} \\ \hline \end{array}$$
Borrow 1 yr from 3 yr and replace it with 12 mo.

$$\begin{array}{r} {}^{2}\!\!\not{3}\,\text{yr}\ 12\ \text{mo} \\ -1\ \text{yr}\ \ 2\ \text{mo} \\ \hline 1\ \text{yr}\ 10\ \text{mo} \end{array}$$

You have 1 yr 10 mo left on the lease.

57. a. Division

b. $29,028\ \text{ft} = 29,028\ \not{ft} \times \dfrac{1\ \text{mi}}{5,280\ \not{ft}}$

$= 5.4977...\ \text{mi}$

$\approx 5.5\ \text{mi}$

Mt. Everest is approximately 5.5 mi high.

c. Rounding the height of Mt. Everest to 30,000 ft and the number of feet in a mile to 5,000 gives an estimate of 6 mi.

10.2 Metric Units and Metric/U.S. Customary Unit Conversions

Practice

1. $3,100\ \text{mg} = 3,100\ \not{mg} \times \dfrac{1\ \text{g}}{1,000\ \not{mg}} = 3.1\ \text{g}$

2. $2,500\ \text{cm} = 2,500\ \not{cm} \times \dfrac{1\ \text{m}}{100\ \not{cm}} = 25\ \text{m}$

3. $5,000,000\ \text{mm}$

$= 5,000,000\ \not{mm} \times \dfrac{1\ \not{m}}{1,000\ \not{mm}} \times \dfrac{1\ \text{km}}{1,000\ \not{m}}$

$= \dfrac{5,000,000}{1,000 \times 1,000}\ \text{km} = 5\ \text{km}$

4. $270\ \text{ml} = 270\ \text{ml} \times \dfrac{1\ \text{L}}{1,000\ \text{ml}} = 0.27\ \text{L}$

271 ml 0.27 L, which is less than a liter.

5. $10\ \text{gal} \approx 10\ \not{gal} \times \dfrac{3.8\ \text{L}}{1\ \not{gal}}$

$\approx 38\ \text{L}$

6. $973\ \text{km} \approx 973\ \not{km} \times \dfrac{1\ \text{mi}}{1.6\ \not{km}}$

$\approx \dfrac{973}{1.6}\ \text{mi}$

$\approx 608.1\ \text{mi}$

The distance from Washington, D.C., to Atlanta is approximately 608.1 mi.

Exercises

1. c (milliliter)   **3.** b (meter)

5. b (1 L)   **7.** b (170 m)

9. a (400 ml)

11. $1,000\ \text{mg} = 1,000\ \not{mg} \times \dfrac{1\ \text{g}}{1,000\ \not{mg}} = 1\ \text{g}$

13. $750\ \text{g} = 750\ \not{g} \times \dfrac{1\ \text{kg}}{1,000\ \not{g}} = 0.75\ \text{kg}$

15. $0.08\ \text{km} = 0.08\ \not{km} \times \dfrac{1,000\ \text{m}}{1\ \not{km}} = 80\ \text{m}$

17. $3.5\ \text{m} = 3.5\ \not{m} \times \dfrac{1,000\ \text{mm}}{1\ \not{m}} = 3,500\ \text{mm}$

19. $5\ \text{ml} = 5\ \not{ml} \times \dfrac{1\ \text{L}}{1,000\ \not{ml}} = 0.005\ \text{L}$

21. $4,000\ \text{mm} = 4,000\ \not{mm} \times \dfrac{1\ \text{m}}{1,000\ \not{mm}} = 4\ \text{m}$

23. $7,000\ \text{ml} = 7,000\ \not{ml} \times \dfrac{1\ \text{L}}{1,000\ \not{ml}} = 7\ \text{L}$

25. $413\ \text{cm} = 413\ \not{cm} \times \dfrac{1\ \text{m}}{100\ \not{cm}} = 4.13\ \text{m}$

27. $0.002\ \text{kg} = 0.002\ \not{kg} \times \dfrac{1,000\ \not{g}}{1\ \not{kg}} \times \dfrac{1,000\ \text{mg}}{1\ \not{g}}$

$= 2,000\ \text{mg}$

29. First convert 3 km to meters.

$3\ \text{km} = 3\ \not{km} \times \dfrac{1,000\ \text{m}}{1\ \not{km}} = 3,000\ \text{m}$

$3,000\ \text{m} + 250\ \text{m} = 3,250\ \text{m}$

31. First convert 98 kg to grams.

$98\ \text{kg} = 98\ \not{kg} \times \dfrac{1,000\ \text{g}}{1\ \not{kg}} = 98,000\ \text{g}$

$98,000\ \text{g} + 25.6\ \text{g} = 98,025.6\ \text{g}$

33. $30 \text{ oz} \approx 30 \cancel{oz} \times \dfrac{28 \text{ g}}{1 \cancel{oz}}$

$\approx 840 \text{ g}$

35. $10 \text{ cm} \approx 10 \cancel{cm} \times \dfrac{1 \text{ in.}}{2.5 \cancel{cm}}$

$\approx 4 \text{ in.}$

37. $48 \text{ in.} \approx 48 \cancel{in.} \times \dfrac{1 \text{ m}}{39 \cancel{in.}} = 1.2307... \text{ m}$

$\approx 1.2 \text{ m}$

39. $6{,}000 \text{ mg} = 6{,}000 \cancel{mg} \times \dfrac{1 \text{ g}}{1{,}000 \cancel{mg}} = 6 \text{ g}$

The average daily U.S. diet contains 6 g of sodium.

41. The dose needed for 120 days is $4 \text{ mg} \times 120$, or 480 ml. Since 1 L is 1,000 ml, 1 L will last your patient 120 days.

43. $7.5 \text{ cm} \approx 7.5 \cancel{cm} \times \dfrac{1 \text{ in.}}{2.5 \cancel{cm}}$

$\approx 3 \text{ in.}$

The pendulum string is approximately 3 in. long.

45. $312 \text{ g} = 312 \cancel{g} \times \dfrac{1 \text{ kg}}{1{,}000 \cancel{g}} = 0.312 \text{ kg}$

$\approx 0.3 \text{ kg}$

The can weighs approximately 0.3 kg.

47. $75 \text{ mm} \times 100 = 7{,}500 \text{ mm}$

$7{,}500 \text{ mm} = 7{,}500 \cancel{mm} \times \dfrac{1 \cancel{m}}{1{,}000 \cancel{mm}} \times \dfrac{100 \text{ cm}}{1 \cancel{m}}$

$= 750 \text{ cm}$

The total length of the tiles is 750 cm.

49. $700 \text{ ml} = 700 \cancel{ml} \times \dfrac{1 \text{ L}}{1{,}000 \cancel{ml}} = 0.7 \text{ L}$

$2.5 \text{ L} + 0.7 \text{ L} = 3.2 \text{ L}$

The combined amount is 3.2 L.

51. $10{,}000{,}000 \text{ gal} = 10{,}000{,}000 \cancel{gal} \times \dfrac{3.8 \text{ L}}{1 \cancel{gal}}$

$= 38{,}000{,}000 \text{ L}$

The spillage was 38,000,000 L.

53. $360 \text{ oz} = 360 \cancel{oz} \times \dfrac{28 \cancel{g}}{1 \cancel{oz}} \times \dfrac{1 \text{ kg}}{1{,}000 \cancel{g}} = 10.080 \text{ kg}$

$\approx 10.1 \text{ kg}$

The baby's weight was approximately 10.1 kg.

Review Exercises

1. $5 \text{ yd} = 5 \cancel{yd} \times \dfrac{3 \text{ ft}}{1 \cancel{yd}} = 15 \text{ ft}$

2. $20 \text{ mo} = 20 \cancel{mo} \times \dfrac{1 \text{ yr}}{12 \cancel{mo}} = \dfrac{20}{12} \text{ yr}$

$= \dfrac{5}{3} \text{ yr, or } 1\dfrac{2}{3} \text{ yr}$

3. $8 \text{ oz} = 8 \cancel{oz} \times \dfrac{1 \text{ lb}}{16 \cancel{oz}} = \dfrac{1}{2} \text{ lb}$

4. $10 \text{ ft} = 10 \cancel{ft} \times \dfrac{1 \text{ yd}}{3 \cancel{ft}} = \dfrac{10}{3} \text{ yd, or } 3\dfrac{1}{3} \text{ yd}$

5. $3\dfrac{1}{2} \text{ tons} = \dfrac{7}{2} \cancel{tons} \times \dfrac{2{,}000 \text{ lb}}{1 \cancel{ton}} = 7{,}000 \text{ lb}$

6. $8\dfrac{1}{2} \text{ lb} = \dfrac{17}{2} \cancel{lb} \times \dfrac{16 \text{ oz}}{1 \cancel{lb}} = 136 \text{ oz}$

7. $3\dfrac{1}{2} \text{ gal} = \dfrac{7}{2} \cancel{gal} \times \dfrac{4 \text{ qt}}{1 \cancel{gal}} = 14 \text{ qt}$

8. $2 \text{ pt} = 2 \cancel{pt} \times \dfrac{16 \text{ fl oz}}{1 \cancel{pt}} = 32 \text{ fl oz}$

9. $3 \text{ yd} = 3 \cancel{yd} \times \dfrac{3 \text{ ft}}{1 \cancel{yd}} = 9 \text{ ft}$

10. $150 \text{ sec} = 150 \cancel{sec} \times \dfrac{1 \text{ min}}{60 \cancel{sec}} = \dfrac{150}{60} \text{ min}$

$= \dfrac{5}{2} \text{ min, or } 2\dfrac{1}{2} \text{ min}$

11. $4 \text{ oz} \approx 4 \cancel{oz} \times \dfrac{28 \text{ g}}{1 \cancel{oz}}$

$\approx 112 \text{ g}$

12. $5 \text{ cm} \approx 5 \cancel{cm} \times \dfrac{1 \text{ in.}}{2.5 \cancel{cm}}$

$\approx 2 \text{ in.}$

13. $32 \text{ km} \approx 32 \cancel{km} \times \dfrac{1 \text{ mi}}{1.6 \cancel{km}}$

$\approx 20 \text{ mi}$

14. $4 \text{ gal} = 4 \cancel{gal} \times \dfrac{3.8 \text{ L}}{1 \cancel{gal}} = 15.2 \text{ L}$

$\approx 15 \text{ L}$

15. $10,000 \text{ ft} \approx 10,000 \text{ ft} \times \dfrac{1 \text{ mi}}{5,280 \text{ ft}} = 1.8939... \text{ mi}$

$\approx 2 \text{ mi}$

16. $2,000 \text{ oz} \approx 2,000 \text{ oz} \times \dfrac{1 \text{ lb}}{16 \text{ oz}}$

$\approx 125 \text{ lb}$

17.

1 hr	
4 hr 20 min	4 hr 20 min
+3 hr 50 min	+3 hr 50 min
~~70 min~~	8 hr 10 min
10 min	

18.   20 ft   Borrow 1 ft from 20 ft
      − 1 ft 3 in.   and replace it by 12 in.

```
       19
      20 ft 12 in.
    −  1 ft  3 in.
    ──────────────
      18 ft  9 in.
```

19.

```
   6    62
   7 min  2 sec
 −      53 sec
 ──────────────
   6 min  9 sec
```

20.

1 lb	1 lb
3 lb 6 oz	3 lb 6 oz
2 lb 9 oz	2 lb 9 oz
+1 lb 3 oz	+1 lb 3 oz
~~18 oz~~	7 lb 2 oz
2 oz	

21.

```
   2    6
   3 gal 2 qt
 −1 gal 3 qt
 ────────────
   1 gal 3 qt
```

22.   4 pt   Borrow 1 pt from 4 pt
      −2 pt 14 fl oz   and replace it by 16 fl oz.

```
    3
    4 pt 16 fl oz
  −2 pt 14 fl oz
  ───────────────
   1 pt  2 fl oz
```

23. c (kilograms)   **24.** a (millimeters)

25. b (liters)   **26.** c (kilometers)

27. b (16 cm)   **28.** a (100 ml)

29. a (200 mg)   **30.** c (6.72 m)

31. $72 \text{ min} = 72 \text{ min} \times \dfrac{1 \text{ hr}}{60 \text{ min}} = 1.2 \text{ hr}$

Your favorite disc plays for 1.2 hr.

32. $1,600 \text{ gal} = 1,600 \text{ gal} \times \dfrac{4 \text{ qt}}{1 \text{ gal}} \times \dfrac{2 \text{ pt}}{1 \text{ qt}} = 12,800 \text{ pt}$

The typical individual's water use for all purposes is 12,800 pt.

33. Convert the time for *Dracula* to minutes.
1 hr 50 min = 60 min + 50 min = 110 min

Since 130 min is longer than 110 min, *Frankenstein* is the longer film.

34. Since 1 L is 1,000 ml, rounding to the nearest liter is the same as rounding to the nearest thousand ml. Rounding 600 ml to the nearest thousand gives 1,000 ml, or 1 L.

35. $2,000 \text{ mg} = 2,000 \text{ mg} \times \dfrac{1 \text{ g}}{1,000 \text{ mg}} = 2 \text{ g}$

A teaspoon of common table salt contains about 2 g of sodium.

36. In 24 hr the process produced $3 \text{ mg} \times 24$, or 72 mg. Since 1 g is equal to 1,000 mg, rounding to the nearest tenth of a gram is the same as rounding to the nearest 100 mg. Rounding 72 mg to the nearest hundred gives 100 mg, or 0.1 g.

37. $\dfrac{160 \text{ mg}}{100 \text{ ml}} = \dfrac{160 \text{ mg} \times \dfrac{1 \text{ g}}{1,000 \text{ mg}}}{100 \text{ ml} \times \dfrac{1 \text{ L}}{1,000 \text{ ml}}} = \dfrac{0.16 \text{ g}}{0.1 \text{ L}} = \dfrac{1.6 \text{ g}}{1 \text{ L}}$

The average cholesterol level in U.S. children is 1.6 g/L.

38. $750 \text{ kg} = 750 \text{ kg} \times \dfrac{1,000 \text{ g}}{1 \text{ kg}} = 750,000 \text{ g}$

750,000 g of pesticide is sprayed on a typical U.S. golf course each year.

39. $\dfrac{1}{4} \text{ hr} = 15 \text{ min}$, so $5\dfrac{1}{4} \text{ hr} = 5 \text{ hr } 15 \text{ min}$

1 hr	1 hr
45 min	45 min
5 hr 15 min	5 hr 15 min
+ 30 min	+ 30 min
~~90 min~~	6 hr 30 min
30 min	

You returned home 6 hr 30 min after you left.

40.

```
   4  16
   5 ft 6 in.
 −4 ft 6 in.
 ───────────
       10 in.
```

The height difference is 10 in.

41. $60 \text{ cm} \approx 60 \text{ cm} \times \dfrac{1 \text{ in.}}{2.5 \text{ cm}}$

$\approx 24 \text{ in.}$

The dinosaur was approximately 24 in. long.

42. $6 \text{ qt} \approx 6 \text{ qt} \times \dfrac{1 \text{ L}}{1.1 \text{ qt}} = 5.4545... \text{ L}$

$\approx 5.5 \text{ L}$

There are about 5.5 L of blood in an average-sized man.

43. $\dfrac{1}{2} \text{ hr} = 30 \text{ min}$, so $3\dfrac{1}{2} \text{ hr} = 3 \text{ hr } 30 \text{ min}$.

Counting hours after 12:00, we get this sum:

$$\begin{array}{r} \overset{1\,\text{hr}}{} \quad 51 \text{ min} \\ + 3 \text{ hr } 30 \text{ min} \\ \hline 81 \text{ min} \\ 21 \text{ min} \end{array} \qquad \begin{array}{r} \overset{1\,\text{hr}}{} \quad 51 \text{ min} \\ + 3 \text{ hr } 30 \text{ min} \\ \hline 4 \text{ hr } 21 \text{ min} \end{array}$$

In $3\dfrac{1}{2}$ hr it will be 4:21 P.M.

44. $2.4 \text{ L} = 2.4 \text{ L} \times \dfrac{1,000 \text{ ml}}{1 \text{ L}} = 2,400 \text{ ml}$

$\dfrac{2,400 \text{ ml}}{200 \text{ ml}} = 12$

You can serve 12 portions.

Posttest

1. $120 \text{ sec} = 120 \text{ sec} \times \dfrac{1 \text{ min}}{60 \text{ sec}} = 2 \text{ min}$

2. $7 \text{ yd} = 7 \text{ yd} \times \dfrac{3 \text{ ft}}{1 \text{ yd}} = 21 \text{ ft}$

3. $1 \text{ hr} = 1 \text{ hr} \times \dfrac{60 \text{ min}}{1 \text{ hr}} \times \dfrac{60 \text{ sec}}{1 \text{ min}} = 3,600 \text{ sec}$

There are 3,600 sec in 1 hr.

4. b (gram)

5. c (kilograms)

6. $400 \text{ cm} = 400 \text{ cm} \times \dfrac{1 \text{ m}}{100 \text{ cm}} = 4 \text{ m}$

7. $500 \text{ ml} = 500 \text{ ml} \times \dfrac{1 \text{ L}}{1,000 \text{ ml}} = 0.5 \text{ L}$

8. Since 1 m is 1,000 mm, 4 mm is less than 1 m.
Since 1 km is 1,000 m, 2 km is greater than 1 m.
Therefore, 2 km is larger than 4 mm.

9. $6,052 \text{ km} = 6,052 \text{ km} \times \dfrac{1,000 \text{ m}}{1 \text{ km}} = 6,052,000 \text{ m}$

$\approx 6,000,000 \text{ m}$

The radius of Earth is 6,000,000 m, rounded to the nearest million meters.

10. $\begin{array}{r} \overset{1}{\cancel{2}} \text{ft } \overset{18}{\cancel{6}} \text{in.} \\ -1 \text{ ft } 9 \text{ in.} \\ \hline 9 \text{ in.} \end{array}$

The height is 9 in. more than the width.

Cumulative Review Exercises

1. $9^3 = 9 \cdot 9 \cdot 9 = 81 \cdot 9 = 729$

2. $\begin{array}{r} 5 \text{ R1} \\ 2\overline{)11} \\ 10 \\ \hline 1 \end{array} \qquad \dfrac{11}{2} = 5\dfrac{1}{2}$

3. $\dfrac{2.8}{0.2} = \begin{array}{r} 14 \\ 2\overline{)28} \\ 2 \\ \hline 8 \\ 8 \\ \hline 0 \end{array} \qquad \dfrac{2.8}{0.2} = 14$

4. 20% of $30 = 0.2 \times 30 = 6$
$30 + 6 = 36$
20% more than 30 is 36.

5. $(-3)^2 + 5 = (-3)(-3) + 5 = 9 + 5 = 14$

6. The smallest number is 1 and the largest is 9.
$9 - 1 = 8$, so the range is 8.

7. $7 \text{ ft} = 7 \text{ ft} \times \dfrac{12 \text{ in.}}{1 \text{ ft}} = 84 \text{ in.}$

8. $44 \text{ pt} = 44 \text{ pt} \times \dfrac{1 \text{ qt}}{2 \text{ pt}} = 22 \text{ qt}$

The average person in the United States ate 22 qt of ice cream.

9. $80\% = \dfrac{80}{100} = \dfrac{20 \cdot 4}{20 \cdot 5} = \dfrac{4}{5}$

10. Since a kilogram is 1,000 grams, 5 kg = 5,000 g.
According to an agricultural study, 5,000 g of grain are required to produce 1,000 g of steak.

Chapter 11

BASIC GEOMETRY

Pretest

1. a.

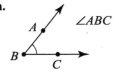

$\angle ABC$

b.

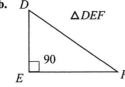

$\triangle DEF$

2. a. $\sqrt{36} = 6$
   b. $\sqrt{121} = 11$

3. If x is the supplement of 180°,
$$x + 100° = 180°$$
$$x + 100° - 100° = 180° - 100°$$
$$x = 80°$$

4. If y is the complement of 36°,
$$y + 36° = 90°$$
$$y + 36° - 36° = 90° - 36°$$
$$y = 54°$$

5. $P = 4s$
$$P = 4(3.5)$$
$$P = 14$$
The perimeter of the square is 14 in.

6. $P = 2l + 2w$
$$P = 2 \cdot 8 + 2 \cdot 2$$
$$P = 16 + 4$$
$$P = 20$$
The perimeter of the rectangle is 20 ft.

7. $C = \pi d$
$$C \approx (3.14)(4)$$
$$C \approx 12.56$$
The circumference is approximately 12.56 in.

8. $P = a + b + c$
$$P = 2.6 + 2.6 + 2.6$$
$$P = 7.8$$
The perimeter of the triangle is 7.8 m.

9. $A = \dfrac{1}{2}bh$
$$A = \dfrac{1}{2}(10)(6)$$
$$A = 30$$
The area of the triangle is 30 sq in.

10. If the diameter is 8 ft, the radius is 4 ft.
$$A = \pi r^2$$
$$A \approx (3.14) \cdot 4^2$$
$$A \approx (3.14) \cdot 16$$
$$A \approx 50.24$$
The area of the circle is approximately 50.24 sq ft.

11. $V = e^3$
$$V = 5^3$$
$$V = 125$$
The volume of the cube is $125\,\text{cm}^3$.

12. $V = \pi r^2 h$
$$V \approx (3.14) \cdot 3^2 \cdot 9$$
$$V \approx (3.14) \cdot 81$$
$$V \approx 254.34$$
The volume of the cylinder is approximately $254.34\,\text{m}^3$.

13.
$$a + 30° = 105°$$
$$a + 30° - 30° = 105° - 30°$$
$$a = 75°$$

14. $a^2 + b^2 = c^2$
$$3^2 + 5^2 = x^2$$
$$9 + 25 = x^2$$
$$34 = x^2$$
$$\sqrt{34} = x$$
The hypotenuse of the triangle is $\sqrt{34}$ m.

15. Assume that the figure is a parallelogram. Then since it has a 90° angle, it is a rectangle, so $a = b = 90°$. Opposite pairs of sides are equal. Therefore, $x = 7$ ft; $y = 5$ ft.

16. $a + 49° + 27° = 180°$
$$a + 76° = 180°$$
$$a + 76° - 76° = 180° - 76°$$
$$a = 104°$$

17. $\dfrac{6}{10} = \dfrac{9}{y} = \dfrac{12}{20}$
$$\dfrac{6}{10} = \dfrac{9}{y}$$
$$6y = 90$$
$$y = 15$$
$$y = 15 \text{ cm}$$

18. Find the area of a circle with radius 1 mi.
$$A = \pi r^2$$
$$A \approx (3.14) \cdot 1^2$$
$$A \approx 3.14$$
$$A \approx 3$$
The area of the search region is 3 mi^2.

19. $A = s^2$
$$A = 15^2$$
$$A = 225$$
The area of the square is 225 cm^2.

20. If the water is 1 ft below the top, the depth will be 5 ft – 1 ft, or 4 ft.
$$V = lwh$$
$$V = (60)(30)(4)$$
$$V = 7,200$$
It takes $7,200 \text{ ft}^3$ to fill the pool.

11.1 Introduction to Basic Geometry

Practice

1.
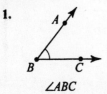
$\angle ABC$

2. Let $\angle A$ be the complementary angle.
$$\angle A + 37° = 90°$$
$$\angle A + 37° - 37° = 90° - 37°$$
$$\angle A = 53°$$

3. Let x be the measure of the angle that is supplementary to 15°.
$$x + 15° = 180°$$
$$x + 15° - 15° = 180° - 50°$$
$$x = 165°$$

4. $\qquad x + 27° = 109°$
$$x + 27° - 27° = 109° - 27°$$
$$x = 82°$$

5. $a + 27° = 180$
$$a + 27° - 27° = 180° - 27°$$
$$a = 153°$$
Since $a = b$, $b = 153°$, so $a = b = 153°$.

6.
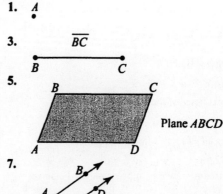

$\overline{PQ} \parallel \overline{SR} \quad \overline{PS} \parallel \overline{QR}$

7. $\angle R + \angle S + \angle T = 180°$
$$\angle R + 90° + 30° = 180°$$
$$\angle R + 120° = 180°$$
$$\angle R + 120° - 120° = 180° - 120°$$
$$\angle R = 60°$$

8. $\angle R + \angle S + \angle T + \angle U = 360°$
$$60° + 120° + 120° + \angle U = 360°$$
$$300° + \angle U = 360°$$
$$300° - 300° + \angle U = 360° - 300°$$
$$\angle U = 60°$$

9. The diameter is twice the radius of 0.67 ft, or 1.34 ft.

Exercises

1. A
 •

3. $\overline{BC}$
  •————————•
 B C

5.

Plane $ABCD$

7.
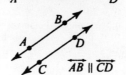
$\overleftrightarrow{AB} \parallel \overleftrightarrow{CD}$

9.

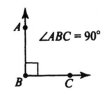

$\angle ABC = 90°$

11.

$AB = BC = AC$

13.

Circle with center O

15.

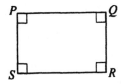

$\angle P = \angle Q = \angle R = \angle S = 90°$

17.

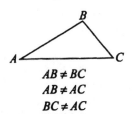

$AB \neq BC$
$AB \neq AC$
$BC \neq AC$

19.

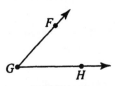

$\angle FGH$ is acute

21.
$$x + 33° = 66°$$
$$x + 33° - 33° = 66° - 33°$$
$$x = 33°$$

23.
$$\angle DEG + 37° = 90°$$
$$\angle DEG + 37° - 37° = 90° - 37°$$
$$\angle DEG = 53°$$

25. $\angle CPD$ is a straight angle, so $\angle CPD = 180°$.

27. Line $AB \perp$ Line CD , so $\angle BPD = 90°$.

29. $\angle APB$ is a straight angle, so $\angle APB = 180°$.

31. $\angle FPD$ and $\angle CPE$ are vertical angles, so
$\angle FPD = 35°$.

33.
$$c + 37° = 90°$$
$$c + 37° - 37° = 90° - 37°$$
$$c = 53°$$

35. Assume that the figure is a parallelogram. Then x is opposite the 90° angle, so $x = 90°$.

37. If x is the complement of 35°, then
$$x + 35° = 90°$$
$$x + 35° - 35° = 90° - 35°$$
$$x = 55°$$

39. If y is the supplement of 105°, then
$$y + 105° = 180°$$
$$y + 105° - 105° = 180° - 105°$$
$$y = 75°$$

41.
$$\angle A + \angle B + \angle C = 180°$$
$$35° + 75° + \angle C = 100°$$
$$110° + \angle C = 180°$$
$$110° - 110° + \angle C = 180° - 110°$$
$$\angle C = 70°$$

43. The sum of all four angles of the parallelogram is 360°. If x is the fourth angle, then
$$x + 275° = 360°$$
$$x + 275° - 275° = 360° - 275°$$
$$x = 85°$$

45. The radius of a circle is half the diameter. If the diameter of the rock circle is 26 ft, the radius is 26 ft ÷ 2, or 13 ft.

47.
$$x + 30° + 53° = 180°$$
$$x + 83° = 180°$$
$$x + 83° - 83° = 180° - 83°$$
$$x = 97°$$

11.2 Perimeter and Circumference

Practice

1. Add the lengths of the sides.
$$4 + 3 + 9 + 7 + 3 = 26$$
The perimeter is 26 in.

2. $P = 4s$
$$P = 4 \cdot \left(3\frac{1}{2} \, m \right)$$
$$P = 4 \cdot \frac{7}{2} \, m$$
$$P = 14 \, m$$
The perimeter of the square is 14 m.

3. $P = 4s$

$P = 4 \cdot (10 \text{ ft})$

$P = 40 \text{ ft}$

$40 \not{\text{ft}} \times \dfrac{\$1.75}{\not{\text{ft}}} = \$70$

The fence will cost $70.

4. $C = 2\pi r$

$C \approx 2 \cdot \dfrac{22}{\not{7}} \cdot \overset{3}{\not{21}}$

$C \approx 132 $

The circumference is approximately 132 in.

5. $C = 2\pi r$

$C \approx 2(3.14)(18) = 113.04$

$C \approx 113$

Approximately 113 ft of railing are needed.

6. The perimeter of the figure includes three of the 36-yd sides of the square and half the circumference of a circle with diameter 36 yd.

$P = 36 + 36 + 36 + \dfrac{1}{2}(\pi \cdot 36) = 108 + 18\pi$

$P = 108 + 18\pi \approx 108 + (18)(3.14) = 164.52$

$P \approx 164.5$

The perimeter is approximately 164.5 yd.

7. Subtract to find the missing lengths and make a diagram with all the lengths labeled.

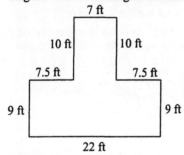

$P = 22 + 9 + 9 + 7\dfrac{1}{2} + 7\dfrac{1}{2} + 10 + 10 + 7$

$P = 82$

The decorator will need 82 ft of wallpaper border.

Exercises

1. $P = 5 + 1 + 6 + 2 + 3$

$P = 17$

The perimeter of the polygon is 17 in.

3. $P = 2l + 2w$

$P = 2 \cdot 25 + 2 \cdot 5$

$P = 50 + 10$

$P = 60$

The perimeter of the rectangle is 60 m.

5. $P = a + b + c$

$P = 3\dfrac{1}{2} + 3\dfrac{1}{2} + 3\dfrac{1}{2}$

$P = 9\dfrac{3}{2}$

$P = 10\dfrac{1}{2}$

The perimeter of the equilateral triangle is $10\dfrac{1}{2}$ yd.

7. $C = 2\pi r$

$C \approx (2)(3.14)(10)$

$C \approx 62.8$

The circumference of the circle is approximately 62.8 m.

9. $C = \pi d$

$C \approx (3.14)(7)$

$C \approx 21.98$

The circumference of the circle is approximately 21.98 ft.

11. The sides of the square are each 10 ft. To find the perimeter, add the lengths of three sides of the square and the two given legs of the triangle on top.

$P = 10 + 10 + 10 + 6 + 6$

$P = 42$

The perimeter of the figure is 42 ft.

13. The perimeter consists of four half-circles, each with diameter 4 in.

$P = 4\left(\dfrac{1}{2}\pi d\right)$

$P \approx 4(.5)(3.14)(4)$

$P \approx 25.12$

The perimeter of the figure is approximately 25.12 in.

15. The unlabeled side on top is 10 yd − 4 yd , or 6 yd, and the unlabeled side on the right is 10 yd − 2 yd , or 8 yd.

$P = 10 + 2 + 4 + 8 + 6 + 10$

$P = 40$

The perimeter of the figure is 40 yd.

17. $P = 4s$

$P = 4 \cdot 5\dfrac{1}{4}$

$P = 4 \cdot \dfrac{21}{4}$

$P = 21$

The perimeter of the square is 21 yd.

19. $P = 2l + 2w$

$P = 2 \cdot 5\frac{3}{4} + 2 \cdot 3\frac{1}{4}$

$P = 2 \cdot \frac{23}{4} + 2 \cdot \frac{13}{4}$

$P = \frac{23}{2} + \frac{13}{2} = \frac{36}{2}$

$P = 18$

The perimeter of the rectangle is 18 ft.

21. $C = 2\pi r$

$C \approx 2(3.14)(5)$

$C \approx 31.4$

The circumference of the circle is approximately 31.4 ft.

23. $P = a + b + c$

$P = 7\frac{1}{2} + 7\frac{1}{2} + 4$

$P = 15 + 4$

$P = 19$

The perimeter of the triangle is 19 cm.

25. $C = \pi d$

$C \approx (3.14)(3.54) = 11.1156$

$C \approx 11.12$

The circumference of the circle is approximately 11.12 m.

27. $P = 2l + 2w$

$P = 2 \cdot 78 + 2 \cdot 36$

$P = 156 + 72$

$P = 228$

The perimeter of the doubles court is 228 ft.

29. Call the larger diameter D and the smaller one d.
    difference $= \pi D - \pi d$

$\approx (3.14)(29) - (3.14)(27)$

$\approx (3.14)(29 - 27) = (3.14)(2) = 6.28$

≈ 6

The bike with the larger wheels goes approximately 6 in. farther in one wheel rotation.

31. $P = 2l + 2w$

$P = 2 \cdot 100 + 2 \cdot 50$

$P = 300$

If n is the number of posts, then $n = 300\text{ m} \div 10\text{ m}$, or 30; 30 posts are needed.

33. The belt includes two sections that are 24 in. long, and two half circles where it wraps around the pulleys with diameter 7 in. If L is the total length,

$L = 2 \cdot 24 + 2 \cdot \frac{1}{2} \cdot \pi \cdot 7$

$L \approx 48 + (3.14)(7)$

$L \approx 48 + 21.98$

$L \approx 69.98$

The length of the belt is approximately 69.98 ft.

35. a. Multiplication
    b. The radius of the satellite's orbit is
       $6,400\text{ km} + 400\text{ km},$ or 6,800 km.

$C = 2\pi r$

$C \approx (2)(3.14)(6,800)$

$C \approx 42,704$

$C \approx 42,700$

The satellite travels approximately 42,700 km in one orbit.

c. Rounding π to 3 and the radius of the satellite's orbit to 7,000 gives an estimate of 42,000 km.

11.3 Area

Practice

1. $A = lw$

$A = (6.3)(2.1)$

$A = 13.23$

The area of the rectangle 13.23 cm^2.

2. $A = s^2$

$A = (3.6)(3.6)$

$A = 12.96$

The area of the square is 12.96 cm^2.

3. $A = \frac{1}{2}bh$

$A = \frac{1}{2}(5)(3)$

$A = \frac{15}{2}$, or 7.5

The area of the triangle is 7.5 in^2.

4. $A = bh$

$A = (5)\left(2\frac{1}{2}\right)$

$A = 5 \cdot \frac{5}{2}$

$A = \frac{25}{2}$, or $12\frac{1}{2}$

The area of the parallelogram is $12\frac{1}{2}$ ft^2.

5. $A = \dfrac{1}{12}h(b + B)$

$A = \dfrac{1}{2}(2)\left(1\dfrac{1}{2} + 2\right)$

$A = 1 \cdot \left(\dfrac{3}{2} + \dfrac{4}{2}\right)$

$A = \dfrac{7}{2},$ or $3\dfrac{1}{2}$

The area of the trapezoid is $3\dfrac{1}{2}$ sq ft.

6. $A = \pi r^2$

$A = \pi(5)(5)$

$A \approx 3.14(5)(5)$

$A \approx 78.5$

The area of the circle is approximately 78.5 yd^2.

7. Find the area of a circle with radius 5 mi.

$A = \pi r^2$

$A = \pi(5)(5)$

$A \approx 3.14(5)(5)$

$A \approx 78.5$

$A \approx 79$

The region in which the light is visible has an area of approximately 79 mi^2.

8. Subtract the area of the small rectangle from the area of the large square.

Shaded area = $\dfrac{\text{Area of large}}{\text{square}} - \dfrac{\text{Area of small}}{\text{rectangle}}$

$= (3.5)(3.5) - (2.5)(1.4)$

$= 12.25 - 3.5$

$= 8.75$

The shaded area is 8.75 m^2.

9. Subtract the area of the central circle from the area of the whole floor. The radius of the circle is 5 ft.

Area to coat = Area of floor − Area of circle

$= (90)(50) - \pi(5)(5)$

$\approx 4,500 - 78.5$

$\approx 4,412.5$

The area that still needs coating is approximately $4,421.5$ sq ft.

Exercises

1. $A = lw$

$A = 25 \cdot 5$

$A = 125$

The area of the rectangle is 125 m^2.

3. $A = \dfrac{1}{2}bh$

$A = \dfrac{1}{2} \cdot 12 \cdot 5$

$A = 30$

The area of the right triangle is 30 ft^2.

5. $A = bh$

$A = 29 \cdot 10$

$A = 290$

The area of the parallelogram is 290 yd^2.

7. $A = \pi r^2$

$A \approx 3.14 \cdot 15^2$

$A \approx 3.14 \cdot 225$

$A \approx 706.5$

The area of the circle is approximately 706.5 cm^2.

9. $A = \dfrac{1}{2}h(b + B)$

$A = \dfrac{1}{2} \cdot 4 \cdot (7 + 9)$

$A = \dfrac{1}{2} \cdot 4 \cdot 16$

$A = 32$

The area of the trapezoid is 32 in^2.

11. $A = bh$

$A = 4 \cdot 3.9$

$A = 15.6$

The area of the parallelogram is 15.6 m^2.

13. $r = \dfrac{d}{2} = \dfrac{20}{2} = 10$

$A \approx \pi r^2$

$A \approx (3.14) \cdot 10^2$

$A \approx 3.14 \cdot 100$

$A \approx 314$

The area of the circle is approximately 314 m^2.

15. $A = \dfrac{1}{2}bh$

$A = (0.5)(5)(2.5)$

$A = 6.25$

The area of the triangle is 6.25 ft^2.

17. $A = \frac{1}{2}h(b + B)$

$A = \frac{1}{2}(4.2)(7 + 14)$

$A = (2.1)(21)$

$A = 44.1$

The area of the trapezoid is 44.1 yd^2.

19. $A = lw$

$A = (2.6)(1.4)$

$A = 3.64$

The area of the rectangle is 3.64 m^2.

21. $A = s^2$

$A = \left(\frac{1}{4}\right)^2$

$A = \frac{1}{16}$

The area of the square is $\frac{1}{16} \text{ yd}^2$.

23. The figure is a trapezoid with a height of 4 yd and bases of 10 yd (top) and 13 yd (bottom).

$A = \frac{1}{2}h(b + B)$

$A = \frac{1}{2} \cdot 4 \cdot (10 + 13)$

$A = 2 \cdot 23$

$A = 46$

The area of the figure is 46 yd^2.

25. The figure consists of a square with side 5 ft and four semicircles with diameter 5 ft, and radius $5 \div 2$ or 2.5 ft.

$A = s^2 + 4 \cdot \frac{1}{2} \cdot \pi r^2$

$A \approx 5^2 + 4 \cdot \frac{1}{2} \cdot (3.14) \cdot \left(2.5^2\right)$

$A \approx 25 + 2 \cdot (3.14) \cdot (6.25)$

$A \approx 64.25$

$A \approx 64.3$

The area of the figure is approximately 64.3 ft^2.

27. Find the shaded area by subtracting the area of the inner square from the area of the big rectangle.

$A = lw - s^2$

$A = 9 \cdot 6 - 1.5^2$

$A = 54 - 2.25$

$A = 51.75$

The area of the figure is 51.75 ft^2.

29. $A = lw$

$A = 12 \cdot 9$

$A = 108$

The area of the room is 108 ft^2. Since the tiles measure 1 ft^2 each, you will need 108 tiles.

$\$4.99 \times 108 = \$538.92$

The total cost will be $\$538.92$, which is more than $\$500$, so $\$500$ won't be enough.

31. $d = \frac{1}{2}r = \frac{1}{2} \cdot \frac{1}{100} = 0.005$

$A = \pi r^2$

$A \approx (3.14)\left(0.005^2\right)$

$A \approx (3.14)(0.000025)$

$A \approx 0.000079$

$A \approx 0.00008$

The area of the region you can see is approximately 0.00008 in^2.

33. Find the area of the yard by subtracting the area of the house from the area of the lot.

Area of lot:

$A = lw$

$A = 100 \cdot 70$

$A = 7,000$

The area of the lot is $7,000 \text{ ft}^2$.

Area of house:

The left side of the house has length $30 \text{ ft} + 25 \text{ ft}$, or 55 ft. The short unlabeled side has length $50 \text{ ft} - 20 \text{ ft}$, or 30 ft. Find the area of the house by adding the area of a tall rectangle on the left and a square on the right.

$A = lw + s^2$

$A = 55 \cdot 20 + 30^2$

$A = 1,100 + 900$

$A = 2,000$

The area of the house is $2,000 \text{ ft}^2$.

The area of the yard is

$7,000 \text{ ft}^2 - 2,000 \text{ ft}^2$, or $5,000 \text{ ft}^2$.

35. a. Multiplication and subtraction

b. Area of CD:

$$r = \frac{d}{2} = \frac{1}{2} \cdot 4\frac{3}{4} = \frac{1}{2} \cdot \frac{19}{4} = \frac{19}{8} = 2.375$$

$$A = \pi r^2$$

$$A \approx (3.14)\left(2.375^2\right) = 17.711562$$

$$A \approx 18$$

The area of the CD is approximately $18\ \text{in}^2$.

Area of LP:

$$r = \frac{d}{2} = \frac{12}{2} = 6$$

$$A = \pi r^2$$

$$A \approx (3.14)\left(6^2\right)$$

$$A \approx (3.14)(36)$$

$$A \approx 113.04$$

$$A \approx 113$$

The area of the LP is approximately $113\ \text{in}^2$.
The difference in areas is approximately
$113\ \text{in}^2 - 18\ \text{in}^2$ or $95\ \text{in}^2$. Rounded to the
nearest $10\ \text{in}^2$, this difference is $100\ \text{in}^2$.

c. Rounding π to 3 and the radius of the CD to 2 in.
gives an estimate of
$3 \cdot 6^2 - 3 \cdot 2^2 = 108 - 12$, or $98\ \text{in}^2$, which also
rounds to $100\ \text{in}^2$.

11.4 Volume

Practice

1. $V = lwh$
$V = 6 \cdot 3 \cdot 4$
$V = 72$

The volume of the box is $72\ \text{ft}^3$.

2. $V = e^3$
$V = (15)^3$
$V = 15 \cdot 15 \cdot 15$
$V = 3{,}375$

The volume of the cube is $3{,}375\ \text{cm}^3$.

3. The radius of the base is 1 in.

$V = \pi r^2 h$
$V \approx 3.14(1)(1)(3.5)$
$V \approx 10.99$

The volume of the can is approximately $10.99\ \text{in}^3$.

4. The radius is half the diameter, or 3 in.

$$V = \frac{4}{3}\pi r^3$$

$$V \approx \frac{4}{\cancel{3}} \cdot \frac{22}{7} \cdot \frac{\cancel{3}^{\,1}}{1} \cdot \frac{3}{1} \cdot \frac{3}{1}$$

$$V \approx \frac{729}{7},\ \text{or } 113\frac{1}{7}$$

The volume of the ball is approximately $113\frac{1}{7}\ \text{in}^3$.

5. When the diameter is 2 m, the radius is 1 m.

$$V = \frac{4}{3}\pi r^3$$

$$V \approx \frac{4}{3}(3.14)(1)^3$$

$$V \approx 4.186...$$

$$V \approx 4.19$$

The volume of the balloon is approximately
$4.19\ \text{m}^3$.

6. The box is a cube with all edges equal to 10 in. The
ball is a sphere with a radius of 5 in.

Volume of box $= 10^3 = 1{,}000$

Volume of ball $= \frac{4}{3}\pi(5)^3 \approx \frac{4}{3}(3.14)(125) = 523.33...$

≈ 523.3

The volume of the box is $1{,}000\ \text{in}^3$ and the volume
of the ball is approximately $523.3\ \text{in}^3$. Therefore
the ball occupies more than one half of the box's
volume.

Exercises

1. $V = e^3$
$V = 6^3$
$V = 216$

The volume of the cube is $216\ \text{in}^3$.

3. $V = lwh$
$V = 16 \cdot 10 \cdot 16$
$V = 2{,}560$

The volume of the box is $2{,}560\ \text{m}^3$.

5. $V = \pi r^2 h$

$$V \approx (3.14)\left(2^2\right)(5)$$

$$V \approx (3.14)(20)$$

$$V \approx 62.8$$

The volume of the cylinder is approximately
$62.8\ \text{ft}^3$.

7. $r = \dfrac{d}{2} = \dfrac{16}{2} = 8$

 $V = \dfrac{4}{3}\pi r^3$

 $V \approx \dfrac{4}{3} \cdot (3.14) \cdot \left(8^3\right)$

 $V \approx \dfrac{4}{3}(3.14)(512)$

 $V \approx 2{,}143.5733\ldots$

 $V \approx 2{,}143.6$

 The volume of the sphere is approximately 2,143.6 in^3, or, rounding to the nearest 10 in^3, 2,150 in^3.

9. $V = lwh$

 $V = (3.5)(5.5)(6.5)$

 $V = 125.125$

 The volume of the solid is 125.125 ft^3.

11. $V = e^3$

 $V = 1.25^3$

 $V = 1.953125$

 $V \approx 1.95$

 The volume of the cube is approximately 1.95 m^3.

13. The solid is a cylinder with radius 2 ft and height 6 ft topped by a half-sphere with radius 2 ft.

 $V = \pi r^2 h + \dfrac{1}{2} \cdot \dfrac{4}{3}\pi r^3$

 $V \approx (3.14)\left(2^2\right)(6) + \dfrac{1}{2} \cdot \dfrac{4}{3}(3.14)\left(2^3\right)$

 $V \approx 92.106667$

 $V \approx 92.1$

 The volume of the solid is approximately 92.1 ft^3.

15. **a.** Multiplication and division

 b. $V = lwh$

 $V = 7 \cdot 5 \cdot 3$

 $V = 105$

 The volume of the block is 105 cm^3.

 $\text{Density} = \dfrac{\text{Weight}}{\text{Volume}}$

 $= \dfrac{300\ \text{g}}{105\ \text{cm}^3}$

 $= 2.8571\ldots\ \text{g}/\text{cm}^3$

 $\approx 2.9\ \text{g}/\text{cm}^3$

 The density of the wood is approximately

2.9 g/cm^3.

 c. Rounding the volume to 100 cm^3 gives an estimate of 3 g/cm^3.

17. $V = lwh$

 $V = 20 \cdot 10 \cdot 6$

 $V = 1{,}200$

 $\text{Density} = \dfrac{13\ \text{kg}}{1{,}200\ \text{cm}^3} = 0.01083\ldots\ \text{kg}/\text{cm}^3$

 $\approx 0.01\ \text{kg}/\text{cm}^3$

 The weight per cubic centimeter is approximately 0.01 kg/cm^3.

19. Find the volume of a sphere with a radius of 1,000 mi.

 $V = \dfrac{4}{3}\pi r^3$

 $V \approx \dfrac{4}{3}(3.14)\left(1{,}000^3\right)$

 $V \approx \dfrac{4}{3}(3.14)(1{,}000{,}000{,}000)$

 $V \approx 4{,}186{,}666{,}666.6\ldots$

 $V \approx 4{,}186{,}667{,}000$

 The crew searched a volume of approximately 4,186,667,000 mi^3.

21. $r = \dfrac{d}{2} = \dfrac{3}{2} = 1.5$

 $V = \pi r^2 h$

 $V \approx (3.14)\left(1.5^2\right)(6.5)$

 $V \approx 45.9225$

 $V \approx 46$

 The displacement of the cylinder is approximately 46 in^3.

23. Subtract the volume of the box from the volume inside the truck.

 $V = lwh$

 Truck vol. $= (3.5)(2.5)(2)$ Box vol. $= (1.5)(1.4)(1.1)$
 $= 17.5$ $= 2.31$

 $17.5\ \text{m}^3 - 2.31\ \text{m}^3 = 15.19\ \text{m}^3$

 The volume of the remaining space is 15.19 m^3.

11.5 Similar Triangles

Practice

1. $\triangle ABC \sim \triangle GHI$

    Because $\angle C$ corresponds to $\angle I$,
    $\overline{AB}$ corresponds to $\overline{GH}$.

    Because $\angle B$ corresponds to $\angle H$,
    $\overline{AC}$ corresponds to $\overline{GI}$.

    Because $\angle A$ corresponds to $\angle G$,
    $\overline{BC}$ corresponds to $\overline{HI}$.

2. $\dfrac{DT}{PN} = \dfrac{DO}{PA} = \dfrac{OT}{AN}$

    $\dfrac{y}{18} = \dfrac{12}{9} = \dfrac{16}{12}$

    $\dfrac{y}{18} = \dfrac{12}{9}$

    $9y = 216$

    $y = 24$

3. Let h stand for the height of the tree.

    $\dfrac{6}{17} = \dfrac{h}{102}$

    $17h = 612$

    $h = 36$

    The height of the tree is 36 ft.

Exercises

1. $\dfrac{DE}{AB} = \dfrac{EF}{BC} = \dfrac{DF}{AC}$

    $\dfrac{DE}{AB} = \dfrac{EF}{x}$

    $\dfrac{15}{20} = \dfrac{8}{x}$

    $160 = 15x$

    $x = \dfrac{160}{15} = \dfrac{32}{3}$, or $10\dfrac{2}{3}$

    $x = 10\dfrac{2}{3}$ in.

3. $\dfrac{DO}{PA} = \dfrac{DT}{PN} = \dfrac{OT}{AN}$

    $\dfrac{DO}{PA} = \dfrac{x}{PN}$

    $\dfrac{12}{9} = \dfrac{x}{18}$

    $9x = 216$

    $x = 24$

    $x = 24$ m

5. $\dfrac{DE}{AB} = \dfrac{EF}{BC} = \dfrac{DF}{AC}$

    $\dfrac{6}{10} = \dfrac{9}{x} = \dfrac{12}{y}$

    $\dfrac{6}{10} = \dfrac{9}{x} \qquad \dfrac{6}{10} = \dfrac{12}{y}$

    $90 = 6x \qquad\quad 120 = 6y$

    $15 = x \qquad\qquad 20 = y$

    $x = 15$ ft; $y = 20$ ft

7. $\dfrac{TA}{RO} = \dfrac{TP}{RN} = \dfrac{AP}{ON}$

    $\dfrac{12}{9} = \dfrac{x}{18} = \dfrac{16}{y}$

    $\dfrac{12}{9} = \dfrac{x}{18} \qquad \dfrac{12}{9} = \dfrac{16}{y}$

    $9x = 216 \qquad\quad 144 = 12y$

    $x = 24 \qquad\qquad 12 = y$

    $x = 24$ yd; $y = 12$ yd

9. $\dfrac{AB}{DE} = \dfrac{BC}{EC} = \dfrac{AC}{DC}$

    $\dfrac{6.1}{2.4} = \dfrac{x}{1.5}$

    $2.4x = 9.15$

    $x = 3.8125$

    $x = 3.8125$ m

11. Let h stand for the height of the giraffe.

    $\dfrac{180}{100} = \dfrac{x}{320}$

    $100x = 57,600$

    $x = 576$

    The giraffe is 576 cm tall.

13. $\dfrac{1}{5} = \dfrac{40}{x}$

    $200 = x$

    The ship is 200 m from shore.

11.6 Square Roots and the Pythagorean Theorem

Practice

1. a. $\sqrt{49} = 7$

    b. $\sqrt{144} = 12$

    c. $\sqrt{225} = 15$

2. n $\sqrt{n}$
    36   6
    47   $\sqrt{47}$
    49   7

$\sqrt{47}$ lies between 6 and 7.

3. a. $\sqrt{56} = 7.4833... \approx 7.48$
    b. $\sqrt{12} = 3.4641... \approx 3.46$

4. $a^2 + b^2 = c^2$

    $6^2 + 8^2 = c^2$

    $36 + 64 = c^2$

    $100 = c^2$

    $\sqrt{100} = c$

    $10 = c$

    The missing side length is 10 in.

5. $a^2 + b^2 = c^2$

    $2^2 + b^2 = 4^2$

    $4 + b^2 = 16$

    $b^2 = 12$

    $b = \sqrt{12} = 3.46101...$

    $b \approx 3.5$

    The length of the other leg is approximately 3.5 ft.

6. $a^2 + b^2 = c^2$

    $3^2 + 4^2 = W^2$

    $9 + 16 = W^2$

    $25 = W^2$

    $\sqrt{25} = W$

    $5 = W$

    The length of the wire is 5 m.

Exercises

1. $\sqrt{9} = 3$ 3. $\sqrt{36} = 6$

5. $\sqrt{81} = 9$ 7. $\sqrt{144} = 12$

9. $\sqrt{169} = 13$ 11. $\sqrt{400} = 20$

13. n $\sqrt{n}$
     1   1
     2   $\sqrt{2}$
     4   4

$\sqrt{2}$ lies between 1 and 2.

15. n $\sqrt{n}$
     9   3
     14   $\sqrt{14}$
     16   4

$\sqrt{14}$ lies between 3 and 4.

17. n $\sqrt{n}$
    36   6
    39    $\sqrt{39}$
    49   7

$\sqrt{39}$ lies between 6 and 7.

19. n $\sqrt{n}$
    64   8
    80    $\sqrt{80}$
    81   9

$\sqrt{80}$ lies between 8 and 9.

21. $\sqrt{5} = 2.2361... \approx 2.2$

23. $\sqrt{37} = 6.0828... \approx 6.1$

25. $\sqrt{139} = 11.7898... \approx 11.8$

27. $\sqrt{9,801} = 99 = 99.0$

29. $a^2 + b^2 = c^2$

    $a^2 + 30^2 = 34^2$

    $a^2 + 900 = 1156$

    $a^2 = 256$

    $a = 16$

    The missing side length is 16 cm.

31. $a^2 + b^2 = c^2$

    $1^2 + 3^2 = c^2$

    $1 + 9 = c^2$

    $10 = c^2$

    $c = \sqrt{10} = 3.1623... \approx 3.2$

    The missing side length is approximately 3.2 m.

33. | a | b | c |
    |---|---|---|
    | 24 m | 7 m | 25 m |

35. | a | b | c |
    |---|---|---|
    | 6 ft | 8 ft | 10 ft |

37. | a | b | c |
    |---|---|---|
    | 12 m | 16 m | 20 m |

39. | a | b | c |
    |---|---|---|
    | 7 cm | 9 cm | 11.4 cm |

41. | a | b | c |
    |---|---|---|
    | 8.7 ft | 18 ft | 20 ft |

43. Let d be the girl's distance from the base of the tree.

$$d^2 + 15^2 = 25^2$$
$$d^2 + 225 = 625$$
$$d^2 = 400$$
$$d = \sqrt{400}$$
$$d = 20$$

The girl is 20 ft. from the bottom of the tree.

45. Let l be the length of the rectangular plot.

$$l^2 + 180^2 = 300^2$$
$$l^2 + 32,400 = 90,000$$
$$l^2 = 57,600$$
$$l = \sqrt{57,600} = 240$$

The length of the plot is 240 ft.

47. The bottom leg of the right triangle the includes the sloping beam is half the width of the building, that is, $72 \text{ ft} \div 2$, or 36 ft.

$$36^2 + 10^2 = l^2$$
$$1,296 + 100 = l^2$$
$$l^2 = 1,396$$
$$l = \sqrt{1,396} = 37.3631... \approx 37.4$$

The length of the sloping beam is approximately 37.4 ft.

Review Exercises

1.

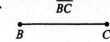

$$\overline{BC}$$

2.

$$\angle ABC$$

3.

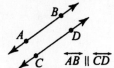

$$\overrightarrow{AB} \parallel \overrightarrow{CD}$$

4.

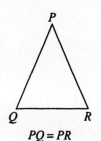

$$PQ = PR$$

5.
$$x + 65° = 140°$$
$$x + 65° - 65° = 140° - 65°$$
$$x = 75°$$

6.
$$x + 49° = 180°$$
$$x + 49° - 49° = 180° - 49°$$
$$x = 131°$$

7.
$$x + 39° = 90°$$
$$x + 39° - 39° = 90° - 39°$$
$$x = 51°$$

8. In the parallelogram, x is opposite the 80° angle, so $x = 80°$; y is opposite the 100° angle, so $y = 100°$.

9. $P = a + b + c$
$$P = 1.8 + 1.8 + 1.8$$
$$P = 5.4$$
The perimeter of the triangle is 5.4 m.

10. $C = 2\pi r$
$$C \approx 2(3.14)(10)$$
$$C \approx 62.8$$
The circumference of the circle is 62.8 in.

11. $P = 2l + 2w$
$$P = 2 \cdot 6 + 2 \cdot 3\frac{1}{2}$$
$$P = 12 + 7$$
$$P = 19$$
The perimeter of the rectangle is 19 cm.

12. $P = 4.5 + 9 + 7.5 + 3 + 3 + 6$
$$P = 33$$
The perimeter of the polygon is 33 ft.

13. $A = s^2$
$$A = 15^2$$
$$A = 225$$
The area of the square is 225 yd^2.

14. $A = \frac{1}{2}h(b + B)$
$$A = \frac{1}{2} \cdot 3 \cdot (4 + 6)$$
$$A = \frac{1}{2} \cdot 3 \cdot 10$$
$$A = 15$$
The area of the trapezoid is 15 m^2.

15. $A = \dfrac{1}{2}bh$

$A = \dfrac{1}{2} \cdot 16 \cdot 8$

$A = 64$

The area of the triangle is 64 in².

16. $A = \pi r^2$

$A \approx (3.14)\left(14^2\right)$

$A \approx 3.14 \cdot 196 = 615.44$

$A \approx 616$

The area of the circle is approximately 616 ft².

17. $V = \pi r^2 h$

$V \approx (3.14)\left(10^2\right)(4.2)$

$V \approx (3.14)(100)(4.2)$

$V \approx 1{,}318.8$

The volume of the cylinder is approximately 1,318.8 in³, or, rounded to the nearest 10 in., 1,320 in³.

18. $V = lwh$

$V = 16 \cdot 4\dfrac{1}{2} \cdot 3$

$V = \overset{8}{\cancel{16}} \cdot \dfrac{9}{\underset{1}{\cancel{2}}} \cdot 3$

$V = 216$

The volume of the rectangular solid is 216 ft³.

19. $V = e^3$

$V = 1.25^3 = 1.953125$

$V \approx 1.95$

The volume of the cube is approximately 1.95 m³.

20. $r = \dfrac{d}{2} = \dfrac{2.5}{2} = 1.25$

$V = \dfrac{4}{3}\pi r^3$

$V \approx \dfrac{4}{3}(3.14)\left(1.25^3\right)$

$V \approx \dfrac{4}{3}(3.14)(1.953125) = 8.177083\ldots$

$V \approx 8.18$

The volume of the sphere is approximately 8.18 cm³.

21. The perimeter includes the three lower sides of the trapezoid and a semicircle with diameter 26 ft.

$P = 20 + 42 + 20 + \dfrac{1}{2} \cdot \pi \cdot 26$

$P \approx 82 + 13 \cdot 3.14$

$P \approx 122.82$

The perimeter is approximately 122.82 ft, or, rounded to the nearest foot, 123 ft.

22. Subtract the area of the inner circle from the area of the outer circle.

$A = \pi \cdot 6^3 - \pi \cdot 3^2$

$A \approx (3.14)(36) - (3.14)(9) = (3.14)(36 - 9)$

$A \approx 84.78$

The area of the shaded region is approximately 84.78 ft².

23. Assume that line DE is parallel to line GH, which means that $\triangle DEF \sim \triangle HGF$.

$\dfrac{DE}{HG} = \dfrac{EF}{GF} = \dfrac{DF}{HF}$

$\dfrac{9}{y} = \dfrac{x}{7} = \dfrac{12}{10.5}$

$\dfrac{x}{7} = \dfrac{12}{10.5} \qquad \dfrac{9}{y} = \dfrac{12}{10.5}$

$84 = 10.5x \qquad 12y = 94.5$

$8 = x \qquad\qquad y = 7.875$

$x = 8$ ft; $y = 7.875$ ft

24. $\dfrac{AB}{DE} = \dfrac{BC}{EC}$

$\dfrac{6}{2} = \dfrac{x}{1.5}$

$2x = 9$

$x = 4.5$

$x = 4.5$ m

25. $\sqrt{9} = 3$

26. $\sqrt{64} = 8$

27. $\sqrt{121} = 11$

28. $\sqrt{900} = 30$

29.
n	$\sqrt{n}$
1	1
3	$\sqrt{3}$
4	2

$\sqrt{3}$ lies between 1 and 2.

30.
n	$\sqrt{n}$
9	3
10	$\sqrt{10}$
16	4

$\sqrt{10}$ lies between 3 and 4.

31.

n	$\sqrt{n}$
36	6
40	$\sqrt{40}$
49	7

$\sqrt{40}$ lies between 6 and 7.

32.

n	$\sqrt{n}$
81	9
84	$\sqrt{84}$
100	10

$\sqrt{84}$ lies between 9 and 10.

33. $\sqrt{8} = 2.8284... \approx 2.83$

34. $\sqrt{29} = 5.3852... \approx 5.39$

35. $\sqrt{195} = 13.9642... \approx 13.96$

36. $\sqrt{1,225} = 35 = 35.00$

37.

a	b	c
9 ft	12 ft	15 ft

38.

a	b	c
10 in.	24 in.	26 in.

39.

a	b	c
8 yd	5 yd	9.4 yd

40.

a	b	c
2 ft	2 ft	2.8 ft

41. $A = lw$

$A = (2,400)(12)$

$A = 28,800$

The area of the roll is $28,800 \text{ in}^2$.

42. Find the area of a circle with radius 2 mi.

$A = \pi r^2$

$A \approx (3.14)\left(2^2\right)$

$A \approx (3.14)(4)$

$A \approx 12.56$

$A \approx 13$

The affected area was approximately 13 mi^2.

43. First find the floor area. It is the area of a rectangle with dimensions $(8 \text{ ft} + 15 \text{ ft})$ by 5 ft added to the area of a rectangle with dimensions 15 ft by 10 ft.

$A = 5 \cdot (8 + 15) + 10 \cdot 15$

$A = 5 \cdot 23 + 150$

$A = 265$

$V = A \cdot h = A \cdot 10$

$V = 2,650$

The volume of your living room is $2,650 \text{ ft}^3$, so the air conditioner can cool the room.

44. First find the two areas.

Area of large screen	Area of small screen
$= (15)(20)$	$= (12)(16)$
$= 300$	$= 192$

The difference between the two areas is $300 \text{ in}^2 - 192 \text{ in}^2$, or 108 in^2. Now find what percent of 192 is 108.

$$\frac{108}{192} \times \frac{100}{1}\% = \frac{\cancel{4} \cdot 9 \cdot \cancel{3}}{\cancel{4} \cdot \cancel{4} \cdot 4 \cdot \cancel{3}} \times \frac{\cancel{4} \cdot 25}{1} = \frac{225}{4} = 56\frac{1}{4}$$

The area of the larger screen is $56\frac{1}{4}\%$ larger than the area of the smaller screen, so it is more than 50% larger.

45. The pilot's two trips form the legs of a right triangle, and the straight-line distance is the length of the hypotenuse.

$a^2 + b^2 = c^2$

$12^2 + 5^2 = c^2$

$144 + 25 = c^2$

$169 = c^2$

$\sqrt{169} = c$

$13 = c$

The straight-line distance from city A to city C is 13 mi.

46. The ladder is the hypotenuse of a right triangle, with the 6-ft distance as one of the legs and the height on the wall as the other leg.

$a^2 + b^2 = c^2$

$6^2 + b^2 = 12^2$

$36 + b^2 = 144$

$b^2 = 108$

$b = \sqrt{108} = 10.3923...$

$b \approx 10$

The ladder reaches approximately 10 ft up the wall.

47. $\dfrac{AB}{ED} = \dfrac{BC}{CD}$

$\dfrac{4}{3} = \dfrac{3}{CD}$

$9 = 4 \cdot CD$

$CD = \dfrac{9}{4}$, or $2\dfrac{1}{4}$

$CD = 2\dfrac{1}{4}$ ft

48. $\dfrac{DC}{CB} = \dfrac{ED}{BA}$

$\dfrac{100}{400} = \dfrac{75}{x}$

$30,000 = 100x$

$300 = x$

The lake is 300 m wide.

49. The unlabeled wall along the bottom is 25 ft + 15 ft, or 40 ft. The two unlabeled walls on the left add up to 40 ft, the same as the wall on the right.

$P = 40 + 40 + 15 + 25 + 40$

$P = 160$

The total length of the walls is 160 ft.

50. $P = 8 + 6\dfrac{3}{4} + 10\dfrac{1}{2}$

$P = 8 + 6\dfrac{3}{4} + 10\dfrac{2}{4}$

$P = 24\dfrac{5}{4}$, or $25\dfrac{1}{4}$

The perimeter of the work triangle is $25\dfrac{1}{4}$ ft, too large to be efficient.

51. First find the volume of the can.

$V = \pi r^2 h$

$V \approx (3.14)\left(2^2\right)\left(5\dfrac{1}{2}\right)$

$V \approx (3.14)(4)(5.5) = 69.08$

$V \approx 69.1$

The can contains approximately 69.1 in^3 of coffee, with a weight of 13 oz.

$\dfrac{13\ \text{oz}}{69.1\ \text{in}^3} = 0.1881...\ \text{oz}/\text{in}^3$

The weight of a cubic inch of coffee is approximately 0.19 oz.

52. If the container is filled to within 1 cm of the top, the height of the volume of soil is 15.25 cm − 1 cm, or 14.25 cm.

$V = lwh$

$V = (17.5)(5.4)(14.25)$

$V = 1,346.625$

$V \approx 1,347$

The amount of soil needed is 1,347 cm^3.

53. Subtract the area of the picture from the area inside the frame.

$A = (25)\left(20\dfrac{1}{2}\right) - \left(7\dfrac{1}{4}\right)(5)$

$A = 25 \cdot \dfrac{41}{2} - \dfrac{29}{4} \cdot 5$

$A = \dfrac{1025}{2} - \dfrac{145}{4}$

$A = \dfrac{2050}{4} - \dfrac{145}{4} = \dfrac{1905}{4}$, or $476\dfrac{1}{4}$

The area of the matting is $476\dfrac{1}{4}$ in^3.

54. Subtract the volume of the inner empty space from the total volume inside the surface of the ball. Let R stand for the radius of the ball, and r for the radius of the space inside.

$V = \dfrac{4}{3}\pi R^3 - \dfrac{4}{3}\pi r^3$

$V \approx \dfrac{4}{3}(3.14)\left(1.5^3 - 1.4^3\right)$

$V \approx \dfrac{4}{3}(3.14)(3.375 - 2.744)$

$V \approx \dfrac{4}{3}(3.14)(0.631) = 2.6417...$

$V \approx 2.6$

The volume of rubber in the ball is approximately 2.6 in^3.

Posttest

1. a.

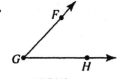

∠FGH is acute

b.

$\overrightarrow{AB}$

2. a. $\sqrt{49} = 7$

b. $\sqrt{225} = 15$

3. Let x stand for the complement of 25°.

$x + 25° = 90°$

$x + 25° - 25° = 90° - 25°$

$x = 65°$

The complement of 25° is 65°.

4. Let y stand for the measure of an angle that is supplementary to a 91° angle.
$$y + 91° = 180°$$
$$y + 91° - 91° = 180° - 91°$$
$$y = 89°$$
The measure of an angle that is supplementary to a 91° angle is 89°.

5. $P = 4s$
$$P = 4 \cdot 3\frac{1}{2}$$
$$P = 4 \cdot \frac{7}{2}$$
$$P = 14$$
The perimeter of the square is 14 ft.

6. $\qquad P = a + b + c$
$$P = 1.5 + 1.5 + 1.5$$
$$P = 4.5$$
The perimeter of the triangle is 4.5 m.

7. $C = \pi d$
$$C \approx (3.14)(8)$$
$$C \approx 25.12$$
The circumference of the circle is approximately 25.12 cm.

8. $P = 2l + 2w$
$$P = 2 \cdot 5\frac{1}{2} + 2 \cdot 2$$
$$P = 2 \cdot \frac{11}{2} + 4$$
$$P = 11 + 4$$
$$P = 15$$
The perimeter of the rectangle is 15 ft.

9. $A = lw$
$$A = 6 \cdot 9$$
$$A = 54$$
The area of the rectangle is 54 ft^2.

10. $A = \frac{1}{2}h(b + B)$
$$A = \frac{1}{2} \cdot 10 \cdot (8 + 14)$$
$$A = 5 \cdot 22$$
$$A = 110$$
The area of the trapezoid is 110 cm^3.

11. $V = lwh$
$$V = 9 \cdot 3 \cdot 7$$
$$V = 189$$
The volume of the box is 189 m^3.

12. $V = \frac{4}{3}\pi r^3$
$$V \approx \frac{4}{3}(3.14)\left(2^3\right)$$
$$V \approx \frac{4}{3}(3.14)(8) = 33.4933...$$
$$V \approx 33.5$$
The volume of the sphere is approximately 33.5 ft^3.

13. Assume that the figure is a parallelogram. Then b is opposite a 60° angle, so $b = 60°$; a is opposite a 120° angle, so $a = 120°$; x is opposite a side of length 10 m, so $x = 10$ m; y is opposite a side of length 5 m, so $y = 5$ m.

14. $\qquad a + 65° + 46° = 180°$
$$a + 111° = 180°$$
$$a + 111° - 111° = 180° - 111°$$
$$a = 69°$$

15. $\qquad x + 100° = 180°$
$$x + 100° - 100° = 180° - 100°$$
$$x = 80°$$

16. $a^2 + b^2 = c^2$
$$5^2 + 12^2 = y^2$$
$$25 + 144 = y^2$$
$$169 = y^2$$
$$\sqrt{169} = y$$
$$13 = y$$
$$y = 13 \text{ yd}$$

17. $\dfrac{AB}{DE} = \dfrac{BC}{EF} = \dfrac{AC}{DF}$
$$\frac{10}{x} = \frac{16}{y} = \frac{12}{18}$$
$$\frac{10}{x} = \frac{12}{18} \qquad \frac{16}{y} = \frac{12}{18}$$
$$12x = 180 \qquad 12y = 288$$
$$x = 15 \qquad\quad y = 24$$
$$x = 15; \, y = 24$$

18. $V = lwh$

$V = 54 \cdot 25 \cdot 6$

$V = 8,100$

$8,100 \text{ ft}^3$ of earth are removed.

19. The dog's run is a circle with radius 5 m.

$A = \pi r^2$

$A \approx (3.14)\left(5^2\right)$

$A \approx (3.14)(25) = 78.5$

$A \approx 79$

The area of the dog's run is approximately 79 m^2.

20. Let h stand for the height of the tree.

$\dfrac{9}{h} = \dfrac{12}{36}$

$12h = 324$

$h = 27$

The height of the tree is 27 m.

Cumulative Review Exercises

1. $23,802 \div 396 \approx 24,000 \div 400 = 60$

2. $\dfrac{24}{30} = \dfrac{\overset{1}{\cancel{6}} \cdot 4}{\underset{1}{\cancel{6}} \cdot 5} = \dfrac{4}{5}$

3. $3.\underline{0}61 \approx 3.1$

4. 40% of what number is 20?

$\downarrow\downarrow\downarrow\downarrow\downarrow$

$0.40\cdotx= 20$

$0.40x = 20$

$x = \dfrac{20}{0.4}$

$x = 50$

40% of 50 is 20.

5. $(-4)(-2) + 7 = 8 + 7 = 15$

6. $\dfrac{y}{12} = \dfrac{2}{3}$

$24 = 3y$

$8 = y$

7. There are two straightaways of 100 ft, and the two semicircles at the end form one circle with diameter 100 ft.

$P = 2 \cdot 100 + \pi \cdot 100$

$P \approx 200 + 314$

$P \approx 514$

The total length of the track is approximately 514 ft.

8. Let w stand for the width of the river.

$\dfrac{2}{1} = \dfrac{w}{0.5}$

$w = 1$

The river is 1 mi wide.

9. The full mixture contains 51 parts, of which 1 is insecticide. The fraction of insecticide in the mixture is $\dfrac{1}{51}$.

10. $-10 + 15 - 5 = 5 - 5 = 0$

The final temperature was 0°F.